W9-BTD-872

THROUGH THE EARTH DARKLY

Regis College Library
15 ST. MARY STREET
TORONTO, ONTARIO, CANADA
M4Y 2R5
WITHDRAWN

Through the Earth Darkly

BL
458
P36
1997

Female Spirituality
in Comparative Perspective

BY

JORDAN PAPER

with

Elizabeth and Paul Aijin-Tettey	*Marilyn Nefsky*
Louise Bäckman	*Li Chuang Paper*
Jacqui Lavalley	*Johanna Stuckey*

FOREWORD BY RITA GROSS
AFTERWORD BY CATHERINE KELLER

Regis College Library
15 ST. MARY STREET
TORONTO, ONTARIO, CANADA
M4Y 2R5

WITHDRAWN

CONTINUUM   NEW YORK

1997
The Continuum Publishing Company
370 Lexington Avenue, New York, NY 10017

Copyright © 1997 by Jordan Paper

All rights reserved.
No part of this book may be reproduced,
stored in a retrieval system, or transmitted,
in any form or by any means,
electronic, mechanical, photocopying,
recording, or otherwise,
without the written permission of
The Continuum Publishing Company.

Printed in the United States of America

Library of Congress Cataloging-in-Publication Data

Paper, Jordan.
    Through the earth darkly : female spirituality in comparative
perspective / by Jordan Paper ; with Elizabeth Aijin-Tettey . . . [et
al.] ; foreword by Rita Gross ; afterword by Catherine Keller.
        p.   cm.
    Includes bibliographical references and index.
    ISBN 0-8264-1050-2 (pbk.)
    1. Women and religion.   I. Aijin-Tettey, Elizabeth.   II. Title.
BL458.P36   1997
200'.82—dc21   97-23307
                                                          CIP

WHEN IN THE 1930s, Ruth Underhill was doing fieldwork among the Papago and was perturbed at the seemingly secondary role of the women in religious ceremonies, she received a very different interpretation of their situation from them:

"You see, we have power. Men have to dream to get power from the spirits and they think of everything they can—songs and speeches and marching around, hoping that the spirits will notice them and give them some power. But we have power." When I looked a little surprised, the answer was: "Children. Can any warrior make a child, no matter how brave and wonderful he is?"

"Warriors do take a little part in starting children."

They sniffed. "A very little part. It's nothing compared to the months that a woman goes through to make a child. Don't you see that without us, there would be no men? Why should we envy the men? We made the men."

—from Ruth Underhill, *Papago Woman*

For Henya-Golda and Sarah,
Hsü P'ei-chen and Shang Wen-chen,
grandmothers we did not know or barely knew;
for all the slighted Grandmothers;
and for our daughter, Leila Hsüan-li.

CONTENTS

FOREWORD

To some of us in religious studies, the androcentric inadequacies of some conventional methodologies still utilized by many scholars are so glaringly obvious that we are hard-pressed to understand their persistence. Thus, any book that forthrightly renounces androcentrism and tries to demonstrate what religious studies free of androcentrism might look like is a welcome addition to the literature. Clearly, such an agenda is Jordan Paper's avowed methodology in this book, which looks at the multi-faceted topic of women and religion in new ways. But his purpose is not only to add new data to the growing collection of materials on women and religion; he wishes to ask, over and over, why this material was suppressed in the first place, to explore the reasons for the androcentric presuppositions of most of the earlier religious studies scholarship about these societies. In answering this question, Paper links the androcentric methodologies so prevalent in Western scholarship with other aspects of the Western worldview, especially its male monotheism, correctly in my view. Thus the prevalence of androcentrism in Western scholarship has something to do with the erasure of female sacred beings from monotheist religion and the diminished female ritual roles that accompanied monotheism. Used to the near eclipse of femaleness in monotheistic religions, Western scholars assumed a similar practice elsewhere. If they did find strong female sacred beings or culturally valued religious roles for women, they either ignored them or actively suppressed them in the case of the earlier missionary-scholars.

Women's studies scholars are beginning to realize that female–male complementarity is more characteristic of many societies than either total male dominance or radical equality between men and women—the two possibilities most discussed by Western feminists reacting against Western androcentrism. This book contributes to that exploration of male–female religious complementarity by looking at female spirits, rituals for women, and women's roles in mixed

gender rituals in a number of quite diverse religious contexts. Clearly, androcentric methodologies are, by definition, ill-suited to notice or explore such
complementarity, and it is not surprising that complementarity could not be
seen by scholars wearing androcentric glasses. But since single-sex societies do
not exist, except for temporary stages of the life cycle or as sub-groups within
the larger society, some complementarity will be found in virtually all societies,
even when, as is frequent, it co-exists with a public ideal of male control and
male dominance. Thus, it is not surprising that Paper and his colleagues find so
much evidence of female–male complementarity in the societies they discuss; I
predict that male–female complementarity will be employed successfully to
analyze more and more religious settings as androcentrism, blind to the existence of women, is left behind.

However, it must also be clearly recognized that, while male–female complementarity is being suggested as a more adequate representation of the actual
facts found in many religions and societies, not every instance of complementarity necessarily constitutes a feminist recommendation for the human future.
Some situations of complementarity exhibit rather rigid gender roles, not usually regarded as an ideal by feminists. In other cases, the complementarity and
interdependence of women and men is clearly recognized by the culture in
question, but it is a male-dominant complementarity which would not be seen
as an ideal by feminists either. One of the most difficult questions in feminist
scholarship and commentary is disentangling the issue of finding adequate
scholarly methodologies to represent accurately the religions being studied
from the issue of what relevance, if any, such data about past or current config-
urations of male–female relationships may have for feminist visions of a just and
equitable human future. The exploration of complementarity is clearly a more
adequate method for studying religion than the obliteration of women mandated by androcentrism, but not all examples of complementarity would be
seen as exemplary models by feminists.

Androcentrism did not merely leave a small corner of our inherited picture
of the world's religions blank. The androcentric outlook so distorts our understanding of most religions that, as Paper is well aware, much more is at stake in
correcting androcentrism than simply "adding women and stirring." Usually the
whole picture has to be redone and in that process we often find androcentric
distortions in the most unsuspected places. One of the many strengths of this
book is Paper's frankness about that experience, particularly in connection with
his continuing explorations of one of his own specialties—Chinese religions.
Scholars of comparative religion are relatively aware, for example, of the
Chinese pairing of Heaven and Earth in cosmological thinking. But who would

notice that the Western tendency to capitalize "Heaven" but not "earth" in writings about Chinese cosmology is a hangover from androcentrism which viewed the male Heaven as worthy of divine status but could not envision the same status for the female earth? This illustration is only one small example of the corrective given us by Paper and his colleagues in this book.

Rita M. Gross
University of Wisconsin—Eau Claire

Prologue
A Personal Journey

I F IT WERE NOT FOR THE FEMINIST MOVEMENT, this book would not have come into being. As it is written by a male, however, there is no pretense that it is a feminist work. Rather, it is an inquiry blending comparative religion with women's studies, and it is hoped that it will be of assistance to feminists engaged in revalorizing their own religious traditions as well as exploring new, or rather old, relationships with the sacred.

One of the important lessons taught by feminist scholarship is the need to identify the writer's voice. In religious studies, this is looked upon askance. Scholars are supposed to be objective and report a truth that is beyond themselves. Perhaps the influence of Buddho-Daoist epistemology on my thinking coincides with feminist perspectives, but I do assume that there are only subjective truths. If we are to approach a truer understanding, it must come through the scholar, not around him or her, for reality is understood by humans only through human understanding. Hence, the reader has the right to know where the author is on her or his life journey, particularly in regard to the topic of this book, to be able to evaluate what is being read. If the reader is bothered by this approach or could not care less about the mind projecting a reality, then I encourage the reader to skip this brief part and move on to the Introduction.

The following is intended to answer two questions: What leads a male to spend a number of years studying female aspects of religion? And what advantages, if any, would follow from a male studying female spirituality from a comparative perspective, given the obvious disadvantages?

I was brought up in the most androcentric culture of which I am aware, and many of my teachers and other influential adults around me during my childhood, in hindsight, were misogynists. Most of my education until college was in all-male institutions. My mother, once a ballet dancer with the Metropolitan

Opera of New York, was of that generation of women who dropped their careers when they married, and my father further destroyed her sense of self-worth and identity. My sister was much younger than I. In other words, in my youth, I knew little about females, and what I knew, I learned from males.

In my early religious training, I learned to daily thank God, an indubitably male deity, that I was not born a female. Females were presented to me as a lesser breed living an inferior existence. They were not capable of studying Torah, and they were not worthy of praying to God in the synagogue. They were created from man to serve men and had no other purpose in life. Now this may be an unfair representation of Orthodox Judaism, but this is what I was taught in the 1940s.

My teachers were in the main survivors of the Holocaust, refugees from Europe. It is but recently that I realized that they were also refugees from a God too horrible to contemplate, whose punishment of His Chosen People was beyond comprehension. They sought surcease in a joyless following of detailed but empty rituals, of a tradition solely for its own sake, and I grew up in a spiritual vacuum.

By chance, while in high school, I happened upon an anthology of Buddhist sutras and was instantly hooked. In the mid-1950s, there were as yet no centers of Buddhist training in North America; my evolution was more parallel to that of the poets Gary Snyder and Philip Whalen than those who become oriented towards Buddhism today. Contrary to my previous religious orientation, theoretically in Buddhism sex is not only irrelevant but illusory, as is every other aspect of the individual.

As an undergraduate at the University of Chicago, I shifted from major to major, further and further away from the preparation for a profession expected of my background. Finally, as a graduate student, I began to study literary Chinese and, via Chinese philosophy and Buddhology, became a classical sinologist.

Chinese culture too is patriarchal, but, as will be explained later in this book, not to the degree it is described in Western presentations. Typical of traditional cultures, males and females lead separate lives. During my first residence in a Chinese cultural milieu, Taiwan in the mid-1960s, I had the good fortune to become close friends with two individuals of the last generation to be imbued with classical Chinese culture and became part of a circle of artists and connoisseurs. Opposite to my experiences of male environments in Western culture, road survey crews and merchant seamen as well as more educated milieus, females were not topics of discussion and never denigrated. A similar attitude was present among the male Chinese university students with whom I also associated.

Having become involved with *kendo* (Japanese swordsmanship) in Taiwan, I continued the study in Kyoto in the context of Zen Buddhism. Since most Japanese males begin the practice in childhoood, I was far behind adults in skill and ability. I was paired with a young woman novice for practice matches, although she was also well ahead of me in training. This was my first experience of a physical activity in which sex was of no consequence; one's opponent was virtually invisible behind mask, armor and sword. The sword, whether a male or a female wields it, equally kills.

I returned to the United States to work on my dissertation, the life, poetry, memorials, and philosophical writings of a third-century scholar-official.[1] Among his œuvre was a poem on the sad lot of females in Chinese society, a work which first drew my attention to culturally grounded sex/gender inequality.

Shortly afterwards, I began my first faculty position in a history department at a Midwestern university, a department which, on the whole, turned out to be quite prejudiced against non-whites, non-Christians, non-Anglo-Euroamerican culture, and non-males. I found myself gravitating towards a nearby Catholic women's college, some of whose students took my courses and whose president was a nun with a doctorate in Chinese literature. After five years there, I assumed my present position at York University to help found a religious studies program and finally be able to move towards my major intellectual and personal interest.

My first graduate year had been in the Divinity School of the University of Chicago, but in 1960, certain comprehensive examinations were graded as much on theological orientation as academic learning. This was equally true at other similar institutions; a bachelor of divinity degree or its equivalent was deemed essential background for research in history of religions. A non-Christian could not continue, and I shifted to the Oriental Institute. Hence, my engaging in religious studies a dozen years later was a re-entry from outside the field. By then, my approach was more from a Chinese viewpoint than from a normative Western monotheistic one. This provided my scholarship with new perspectives and led me to critique the Eurocentrist hold on religious studies long before it became acceptable to do so,[2] but it also made me a maverick in the field.

At York University, at least in the Division of Humanities in which I was engaged and the Department of Anthropology towards which I was also oriented, I found a very different situation with regard to gender from my first university teaching experience. A significant proportion of the faculty of these units were female. Unfortunately, the Religious Studies Program, incorporating a strong Jewish studies component, remained a bastion of unspoken androcentrism. My frequent pleas to invite female anthropologists of religion at the university, some with world-wide reputations, to join the program long fell on deaf ears, and my comparative religion course on female spirituality was for several years not credited in the Religious Studies Program but only in the Women's Studies Program.

Shortly after arriving at York University, I took a year off to return to Taiwan. There I taught at a university and engaged in explicit study of Chinese religion for the first time. I married a colleague at the university, a woman who came, we both later discovered, from a family with a history of a matrilineal orientation.[3] (My first marriage, which took place when I was twenty, failed, at least in part, because of my then highly androcentric orientation.)

A slowly developing interest in Native American traditions was furthered by the opportunity to participate in Anishnabe rituals. From my experience in studying Chinese culture, I knew that understanding came from internalization through participation in rituals. Through the kindness of a Native community, I was able to participate in seasonal and life-cycle rituals, as well as undertake a series of traditional fast-vision quests. After the last, when I was recounting my visions to the male elder who was guiding me, he pointed out to me that the theriomorphic spirit involved was female. This was a spirit that I had first encountered in my youth, twenty years before, but I had never thought of her in terms of sex or gender. The logic of her gender was instantly obvious. The realization was, to borrow a term from Christian theology, an epiphany. Since in the previous fast I had furthered a relationship with a male spirit with whom I had an equally long relationship, the interrelationship between the two spirits with regard to sex and gender for the purpose of curing, the subject of the major vision of the fast, became lucid. She set me to a new task of healing, to reintegrate the sexes; that was the beginning of this book, although, of course, I did not realize it at the time.

A number of years ago, I was asked to speak on the status of women in China for a lecture series that led to the formation of the Women's Studies Program at York, an undergraduate program that was the first in Canada and eventually expanded to offer graduate degrees. After the above fast experience, I was writing a paper on the theological effects of Euroamerican domination on Native American religions when I found myself quite unexpectedly, indeed subconsciously (writing in trance on a computer), concluding with an argument that called for a subtitle, "The Suppression of Female Spirituality." I showed the paper to my colleague, Johanna Stuckey, the founder of the Women's Studies Program at York, who subsequently included my course on Native American religions in the program. This brought me into contact with a number of bright, feminist students, an experience that was influential on my subsequent comparative religion analyses. Later I initiated a course on comparative female spirituality, which I now co-teach with Prof. Stuckey.

I had returned to Taiwan several times and had traveled in China, but on a subsequent trip to China after these experiences, I found myself reevaluating Chinese religion with regard to gender. By now familiar with female roles in Native American religions as well as female spirits, in spite of Western scholarship's denial of them, I came to realize, through a series of experiences, that the study of Chinese religion in the West was similarly biased and skewed. Following an article on this topic that was published in the *Journal of Feminist Studies in Religion*, an experience in and of itself, I wrote a related one on Native American traditions, as well as a critical review of the scholarship in this regard. Comparing the two cultures, I found considerable commonality that led to a comparison with Western religions and inspired the planning and research for this book.[4]

The study of female spirituality has become for me the foremost intellectual task in the comparison of religions. I have studied for a number of years two major cultural complexes, Chinese religion and specific Native American religious traditions, and studied for a shorter period of time early South Asian and Japanese religions. But until the research that led to this book, I had related only with males of the relevant cultures. I tell my students in my course on female spirituality, almost entirely females, usually to their astonishment if not incomprehension, that as a male, I have a closer rapport with males of any culture, no matter how different, than with females in my own. All males (whether heterosexual or homosexual) share many physical and a number of cultural experiences, but there are many experiences of females in my own culture that I can never share. To paraphrase Martin Buber, the I-Thou relationship to my comprehension is not one between myself and a monotheistic male (or androgynous) God, but between myself and females, both human and divine. When the male editor of the *Daode-jing* (*Laozi*), the early, important Daoist text, concludes one of a series of brief discourses on the femaleness of creation, physiologically symbolized, with the expression "darkness of darknesses, the gateway of all mysteries," it should resound in the mind of any thinking, mature male.

For a comparativist, the ultimate cultural other is the paramount subject for research. It is this aspect, I believe, that a male can contribute to women's studies: an entirely comparative perspective. Moreover, as should be evident from the following cultural studies, female spirits and spirituality affect not only females in cultures where they have a recognized role, but males are also affected.

The cultural relationship between females and males has long been broken in Western cultures. If, by showing the many sorts of sex/gender relationships that exist between females and males in a number of cultures, particularly in regard to that which is most meaningful within cultures and to individuals in those cultures, that is, religion, my colleagues and I can in some small way help heal the fission between males and females in Western culture, then the purpose of this book is accomplished.

ACKNOWLEDGMENTS

T HE RESEARCH FOR THIS BOOK was partially funded by a Social Sciences and Humanities Research Council of Canada Grant from 1992 to 1996 for which I am most appreciative. I am also grateful to the Senate of York University for a special sabbatical research fellowship for 1992–93 and to the Faculty of Arts of York University for a grant to support the preparation of this manuscript. Part of the research was also funded by a grant from the Ministry of Education of the Republic of China administered by the Canadian Association of University Teachers.

So many people have assisted this work that, unfortunately, it would not be practical to list them all. Those whose names appear in the Prologue or the Introduction I will not list here, although many of these colleagues assisted me far beyond the specific mention in those sections of the book. Other than these persons, certain individuals over many years have made me cognizant of aspects of female spirituality and encouraged me in this endeavor to the degree that this work would not have come into existence without my relationships with them. Marilyn Johnson, one of my first students in Canada and a Native healer, introduced me to the realities of Native religion. Edna Manitowabi illustrated in her person the best of Anishnabe female spirituality. Amanda Porterfield, of Syracuse University, early directed me to so much that is missing in the study of religion. My student through all academic levels, Sherry Rowley, never let me move too far from feminist approaches to religious studies. Also at my own university, Amila Buturovic, Saroj Chawla, Nancy Mandell, and Carol Yawney provided inspiration and support. My chair of the Division of Humanities while writing this book, Margo Gewurtz, and the Coordinator of Religious Studies, Jamie Scott, encouraged me, in many subtle ways, to continue this massive project. The late R. Clark Mallam brought me to the cave that I found so meaningful, and subsequently Harv Klevar and Lori Stanley, also of Luther College, were most hospitable in encouraging my studies of the area. Sung Zhaolin, Curator of the National Historical Museum (Beijing), with whom I have so many interests in common, shared his research with me and arranged for me to work with the two fine women scholars in China who assisted on this project. The faculty of the National Folklore Institute at Beijing Normal University gave me considerable moral support. Further encouragement and hospitality came from Yolotl Gonzalez-Torres of Mexico City. Theresa Smith of Indiana University of Pennsylvania, whom I met as I began this work, became not only a most supportive colleague, but a dear friend.

Three conferences have spun out of this project. The entire 1994 program of the annual meeting of the North American Society for the Study of Religion was on the theme, "Towards A New Comparativism: Degendering and Regendering Religion." Most of those on the program have already been mentioned or will be named in the Introduction, save Nancy Auer Falk, of Michigan State University, who delivered a superb, major survey of the study of Hinduism with regard to sex/gender. At the International Congress for the History of Religions in Mexico City in 1995, there were a substantial number of panels on women and religion on various aspects coordinated by Sylvia Marcos, who has continuously supported my work; they included one I organized involving thirteen scholars. Finally, the Centre for Feminist Research of my university sponsored, with the support of the Social Sciences and Humanities Research Council of Canada, a "Celebration of Female Spirituality" over a weekend in 1996 that brought together scholars and the general interested public. The mornings were devoted to scholarly presentations and the afternoons to community-led workshops, rituals, etc. It was most gratifying to find 250 members of the general community at an outlying location early on a Saturday morning, in spite of unpleasant weather, attending a scholarly session.

Bits and pieces of this work have appeared previously in preliminary or tangential studies. I have entirely rewritten most, but some sentences or paragraphs may have previously been published. The following chronological list covers all such works: "The Post-contact Origin of An American Indian High God: The Suppression of Feminine Spirituality," *American Indian Quarterly* 7/4 (Fall, 1983): 1–24; "The Forgotten Grandmothers: Amerindian Women and Religion in Colonized North America," *Canadian Woman Studies* 5 (1983): 48–51; "The Divine Principle, The Bible From a Korean Perspective," *Studies in Religion* 15 (1986): 450–460; *Offering Smoke: The Sacred Pipe and Native American Religion* (Moscow, Idaho: University of Idaho Press, 1988); "The Normative East Asian Understanding of Christian Scriptures," *Studies in Reli-*

gion 18 (1989): 451–65; "The Persistence of Female Spirits in Patriarchal China," *Journal of Feminist Studies in Religion* 6 (1990): 25–40; "Comparative Cosmology and the Concepts of Good and Evil, Male and Female," *Explorations* 8 (1990): 17–28; "'Sweat Lodge': A Northern Native American Ritual for Communal Shamanic Trance," *Temenos* 26 (1990): 85–94; "Through The Earth Darkly: The Female Deity in Native American Religions," Christopher Vecsey, ed., *Religion in Native North America* (Moscow, Idaho: University of Idaho Press, 1990): 3–19; "Slighted Grandmothers: The Need for Increased Research on Female Spirits and Spirituality in Native American Religions," *Annual Review of Women in World Religions*, A. Sharma & K. Young, eds. (Albany: State University of New York Press, 1994), III, 88–106; *The Spirits are Drunk: Comparative Approaches to Chinese Religion* (Albany: State University of New York Press, 1995); "Mediums and Modernity: The Institutionalization of Ecstatic Religious Functionaries in Taiwan," *Journal of Chinese Religions* 24 (1996): 105–129.

Finally, I would like to thank Theresa Smith and Johanna Stuckey for carefully reading the first draft of the entire manuscript (each chapter had been separately read by the specificaly involved scholars) and making many valuable suggestions. Of course, neither would share all of my opinions expressed in the Conclusions. Frank Oveis of Continuum Publishing provided much needed criticism, and this work is much better for it.

1
INTRODUCTION

The effort to express contemporary experience in a cultural and historical vacuum is both self-deluding and unsatisfying. It is self-deluding because to communicate at all to oneself and others, one makes use of patterns of thought, however transformed by new experience, that have a history. It is unsatisfying because, however much one discards large historical periods of dominant traditions, one still seeks to encompass this "fallen history" within a larger context of authentic and truthful life.[1]

ROSEMARY RADFORD RUETHER wrote the above in referring to the Judeo-Christian and earlier western Mediterranean traditions in the context of seeking to revalorize Christianity from a feminist perspective. For reasons discussed in the concluding chapter, this set of traditions led to a religious complex (Judaism-Christianity-Islam) that is the most androcentric, with significant elements of misogyny, in the human experience. Contemporary culture is rapidly becoming a global one; its cultural and historical background potentially includes all of human experience. Those seeking to fill the female vacuum in Western religions, as well as those seeking to create new or revitalize old non-Christian European religious traditions, need as well to know how a variety of religions outside of Europe and its Near East have responded to femaleness.

Most prior attempts to synthesize human experience in this regard have relied on questionable sources of data; some attempts are imaginative to the point of fiction. Data bases have been created from the writings of anthropologists and historians that are not only Eurocentric but androcentric, whether written by males or females. Until very recently, Western scholars only considered male aspects of culture meaningful and were blind to female religious roles, understanding, and symbolism. Their writings, of course, are highly skewed, ignoring half the populations of the described cultures. Our earliest reports of non-Western religions came from missionaries who did perceive

1

these elements but sought to destroy them out of duty to a misogynist theology, equating femaleness with evil, as well as savagery.

With regard to the latter, we find Jesuit missionaries in both China and "New France" (present-day Canada) from the late sixteenth century reflecting these attitudes. Le Jeune, who missionized among the Montagnais-Naskapi in the early seventeenth century, understood that female subservience to the male was part of God's plan and the mark of a civilized society. He regarded women having "great power" to be evidence of the Native Americans' savagery. He strove to civilize them by introducing into the egalitarian society means for enforcing male authority over women, "I told him that he was the master, and that in France women do not rule their husbands." These attitudes of the Jesuit male monastic order towards women continue into the present. Father Paul Steinmetz, S.J., has relatively recently expressed this theoretically archaic view using a mistaken historical "fact": "[That] it was not the general practice for women to smoke in pre-contact days . . . helps us to appreciate the sacramental nature of the Sacred Pipe by way of contrast." In other words, he assumes an inverse ratio between sacredness and female participation. This attitude in and of itself has blinded Western observers of Native American religions to the major and crucial participation of women in religious practice and ideology.[2]

One of the reasons that the Jesuits wrote glowing accounts of China as a model civilization apparently was their perception of China as totally patriarchal, in religion as well as social structure. Mateo Ricci, in a letter dated to 1609, wrote that the Chinese "worship only heaven and earth and the master of both." The Chinese, however, objected to the creation of a monotheistic male Master of the dualistic male Heaven and female Earth. In a work dated to 1639, a Chinese critic of Christianity and Ricci's interpretation wrote: "The mode of action [the *dao*] of Heaven and Earth can be summed up in a word. It is not double. How could it be controlled by the Master of Heaven, Yesu?" The same critic noted that the Jesuits particularly objected to the Chinese sacrificing to a female deity:

> Confucius and Zilu [Confucius's main disciple] always associate Heaven and Earth together . . . these Western monsters disrupt the ideas of our Confucianism [*rujia*] on the subject of Heaven and the Sovereign on High [*shangdi* = supreme power, not sexed]. That is why they are absolutely set against speaking of prayers to the spirits of the Earth. . . .[3]

Twentieth-century missionaries continued the late medieval attitude. W. E. Soothill, in the most influential English language work on Chinese religion of this century, seems to have accepted the concept of ur-monotheism, the universality of a single, male supreme deity in all early human cultures. He argued that the concept of Heaven was originally a monotheistic deity in China, "[But] as time passes, 'Heaven' underwent a change by the addition of the word Earth. . . . Here, then, is an apparent *descent* from the earlier supreme monotheism."[4]

Given these influences, it is understandable that there has been a tendency in Western writing to consider only Heaven, half of the paired Heaven-Earth, as a deity. Most translators of Chinese texts capitalize only the "H" in Heaven and not the "E" in Earth. Even contemporary works written by females from a feminist perspective have unintentionally continued this essentially misogynist practice.[5] For many Westerners, it is inconceivable that civilized people could consider a female deity worthy of the respect due to a male deity. Hence, data bases, as well as world religions textbooks, will state that China has a supreme male deity, a notion that is both incorrect and grossly misleading, for most major Chinese deities are female. Data bases are equally blatantly incorrect regarding female ritual roles in China.

Similar mistaken Western understandings of non-Western religions are routine. Among scholars of Native American religious traditions, as romanticized sympathy developed for primal cultures, the concept of ur-monotheism allowed a positive orientation towards assumed early religious patterns. If a male high god is the indicator of superior culture, then it was necessary to identify the concept among cultures that scholars admired. The development of evolutionary theories of religion limited the major female spirit, Earth, to the development of early agriculture, an understanding which is obviously incorrect to anyone who has experienced gathering-hunting religions.[6] Intellectual imperialism has led to the claim that the Native American understanding of the Earth as mother was derived, at least partially, from Euroamerican culture![7]

Until quite recently, anthropologists in the main have been equally as androcentric as Christian missionaries. The social sciences developed out of patriarchal cultural milieus. Scholars from a late nineteenth century middle-class German-Austrian Jewish background, which, as did Christianity, considered females inferior to males in virtually all regards, were among the major founders of both anthropology and psychology. Early ethnologists studying Native American religions, including females, excepting Ruth Underhill (see Chapter 9) and a few others, considered only male cultures of interest and were oblivious to female roles, particularly in religion. For example, in Gene Weltfish's otherwise excellent depiction of the Pawnee ritual year, one gains the impression from her writings that women had virtually no relationship to Pawnee religion.[8] Where information was gathered from female informants, it often did not see the light of publication.[9] As little as a decade ago, studies published by female ethnologists bemoaned their being ignored by male informants, yet in turn ignored the opportunity to be involved with women's rituals and understandings. Of many examples, Christine Hugh-Jones belatedly realized that during her field work of 1968–70 she "suffered from the conviction that everything important was going on in the men's world. . . ." Her presentation of menstrual myths is apparently those of the males, as she refers to the ones gathered by Stephen Hugh-Jones.[10] Even studies from the late 1980s of non-literate cultures in other parts of the world by some female ethnologists, who explicitly state that they are writing feminist anthropology and refer to the book by Diane Bell quoted below, interview males for an understanding of female power and apply a Eurocentric feminist interpretation to male myths to understand female perceptions.

Our understanding of the religions of non-literate cultures is based on a limited number of academic disciplines: primarily comparative religion, ethnohistory, anthropology, and sociology. In the last few decades, feminist analyses of the traditional academic disciplines has brought into question the reliability of virtually all previous studies of Native American religions. Among various revisionist analyses, the anthropologist Eleanor Leacock has challenged the normative understanding of female social and other roles in gathering-hunting societies in general and northeastern Algonkian-speaking cultures in particular, from the seventeenth century Jesuit Relations to the ethnology of Frank Speck;[11] the ethnohistorian Irene Silverblatt has provided a reinterpretation of Andean religion from contact through the colonial period;[12] the sociologist Marla Powers has provided a similar revised understanding of female roles in Lakota society;[13] and, as mentioned in the Prologue, I have written several works criticizing the ignoring of female spirits and female religious roles in northern North American indigenous cultures. The conclusion that follows from these and similar studies is that not only has our understanding of Native American religions studiously ignored a full half of the relevant populations, but this ignorance has seriously distorted much of our common wisdom as well as data bases regarding these cultures.

Although Native American traditions were the focus of American ethnology, it was ethnological studies of Native Australian cultures that most impressed European scholars, particularly those interested in religion. To the evolutionary mindset prevalent at the turn of the century, Australian aboriginal culture exemplified the most primitive culture known and was considered the most appropriate basis for understanding religion. From the limited, androcentric studies then available, Émile Durkheim based his analysis of the "elementary forms of religious life" on Australian aboriginal cultures, which he understood as essentially singular. His analysis, arising within a culture which understood church and state not only to be separate institutions but to involve separate realms of existence, determined a sacred/profane dichotomy to be the foundation of the evolution of society and culture. To this dichotomy sex and gender were crucial: the sacred domain was exclusively male, and females were linked and limited to the profane.[14]

From Durkheim to those who followed him, whether critically or not, the male-sacred realm came to be understood as the basis of religion, society, and all things cultural; the female-profane realm became understood as that of uncivilized nature, being both non-spiritual and asocial. The Christian theological distinction between spirit and flesh, found first in the letters of Paul and later linked to the "Original Sin" of Eve by the Church Fathers, became the foundation of both the history and sociology of religion. This dichotomy but reinforced androcentric methodology: now women were not simply ignored, but they were by definition external to religion and its study. Further Euro-centric analyses added Western notions of purity and pollution to the sexed/gendered sacred/profane dichotomy. Females, being unclean because of menstruation and childbirth, are capable of polluting the ritual cleanliness of males; hence, females are limited to the profane realm and consequently subordinated to males, only males having access to the superior sacred realm.[15]

Subsequent studies of Australian aboriginal religion could but reinforce this premise, as ethnologists talked only to males about male rituals and myths, interpreting any reference to females as secular and irrelevant to the sacred. Particularly influential in this regard were the writings of A.P. Elkin and Mircea Eliade. Neither Durkheim nor Eliade felt uncomfortable writing books on Australian aboriginal religions without any experience with the cultures themselves, the Aboriginals being for them theoretical intellectual constructs rather than real living persons.[16]

Around the time of the publication of Eliade's book and the second edition of Elkin's, female ethnologists and historians of religion were turning this accepted wisdom on its head, although their work was of little consequence until the feminist movement grew to incorporate studies of non-Western religions. In 1977, Rita Gross first published the work arising from her doctoral thesis (in microfiche—her research did not reach print until 1980).[17] In reanalyzing the ethnographic data, Gross demonstrated that it is not that the males are sacred and the females profane, but quite the reverse if such a dichotomy must be made. In at least some aboriginal cultures, men knew that they had stolen their rituals and understanding of the sacred from the women; they restricted women from aspects of their rituals to hide (symbolically not actually) this fact from them (an understanding and practice also found among many Amazonian cultures):

> But we really have been stealing what belongs to them [the women], for it is
> mostly all women's business; and since it concerns them, it belongs to them. Men

have nothing to do really, except copulate, it belongs to the women . . . Women can't see what men are doing, although it really is their own business, but we can see their side. This is because all the Dreaming business came out of women— everything. . . .[18]

Women were sacred by their very nature. In a men's myth, mythic sisters state:

We know everything. We have really lost nothing, for we remember it all, and we can let them [males] have that small part. For aren't we still sacred, even if we have lost the [sacred] bags [stolen by men]? Haven't we still our uteri?[19]

Moreover, Gross demonstrated that menstrual blood in the Aboriginal understanding was not polluting but the reverse: it was sacred and powerful. Hence, as in many traditions elsewhere, men avoided menstruating women so as not to be overpowered by this most potent of sacred substances, a holy fluid specific to females. Not only are menarche and subsequent menstruation the focus of major female rituals, but her own menstrual blood is rubbed on the shoulders of the young female initiate. More telling is that, in their rituals, males produce the equivalent of menstrual blood from their own bodies, either through subincision when males create a vagina-like opening in the undersides of their penises or through piercing the upper arm:

I was told during a ceremony: "that blood we put all over those men is all the same as the blood that came from that old woman's vagina. It isn't [ordinary male] blood any more because it has been sung over and made strong. The hole in the man's arm isn't that hole any more. It is all the same as the vagina of that old woman that has blood coming out of it. . . . [20]

A few years after Rita Gross's original publication, Catherine Berndt published a more wide-ranging reanalysis of the ethnographic material regarding Native Australian women, pointing to their importance in all aspects of life.[21] This was shortly followed by the most devastating critique of all with the publication of Diane Bell's *Daughters of the Dreaming* in 1983. With two children in tow and no husband, she carried out extensive field-work among women. As a mother of young children, she accorded with Native notions of femaleness and was integrated by the community into the female social and ritual life. From her subsequent analysis based on women's understanding, a picture arises of Native Australian women and spirituality utterly at odds with the accepted Western wisdom in these regards:

New understandings emerge when women are allowed to speak. Without a knowledge of the complexities and richness of women's ritual world, our ethnographic understanding of desert society is impoverished. Too often we have taken male ritual activity to be the totality of the religious experience in Aboriginal society. The vital and complementary role of women in maintaining the *jukurrpa* [Dreaming/Dreamtime] heritage is thus obscured. It is through the cooperative endeavors of both women and men that the *jukurrpa* is maintained across space and through time; it is women who keep the land alive and nurture the relationship of the living to the *jukurrpa;* it is through the links established by women that knowledge is transmitted and ritual reciprocity established; and it is through women's interactions with the country that the *jukurrpa* is reaffirmed and activated. That desert society is a living, vibrant, dynamic culture is apparent when woman's ritual contribution to her society is explored.[22]

Given the work of Bell, Berndt, Gross, and others, it must be apparent that the foundations of the study of religion, based as they are in large part on Native Australian as well as Native American religions, whether humanistic or social scientific, are fundamentally flawed. If there is to be a sexed/gendered sacred/profane dichotomy, and this is hardly suggested here, then we must reverse the accepted premises; it is women who are sacred and males profane. But as the above and the more detailed analyses to follow will indicate, the notion of a sacred/profane dichotomy in itself is limited to Christianity and a male/female dichotomy with regard to the sacred is limited to the Western religious traditions: Judaism, Christianity and Islam. The reasons for this will be analyzed in the concluding chapter. Particularly with regard to sex and gender, we must free ourselves as much as possible from cultural biases, let the traditions of other cultures speak to us from their perspectives, and then carry out a genuine comparison of religious traditions.

Methodology

The above analyses should be sufficient to indicate that if we are to understand female spirituality in non-Western cultures we cannot use extant cultural databases which are in the main based on androcentric scholarship, often quite incorrect, in regard to religion. Moreover, if we rely on interpreting cultures that have long since disappeared, we have no actual knowledge of how people of those cultures actually understood life and the world around them; we run the danger of imagining cultures that actually never existed. Some feminist encyclopedias of religion, as well as reconstructions of late paleolithic and early neolithic southern European religions, describe female monotheistic and exclusively female-centered cultures that have no correspondence whatsoever with any extant or recently extant tradition, no matter how isolated these cultures might have been from patriarchal cultures.

In response to these problems, this work is intended to fill the void in comparative studies of female religion and female aspects of religion. Ideally, if religious studies did not have a history of androcentrism, a work such as this would not be needed. Preferable would be a study of sex/gender and religion. Unfortunately, until the overwhelming imbalance between our knowledge of male aspects of religion and our knowledge of female aspects is rectified, such a study is not possible.

In the following chapters, a number of cultures around this planet, illustrating different types of religio-ecological circumstances, will be analyzed with regard to the culture's understanding of female spirits and female spirituality. The latter will be approached through delineating female rituals and female roles in mixed-gender rituals. As a result, we should gain a degree of understanding of what it means to females to be female in the respective culture. In focusing on the meaning, the hermeneutics, of femaleness, this work utilizes the method of ethnohermeneutics.

Ethnohermeneutics is a new religious studies methodology to interpret that which is significant to specific cultures and to culture in and of itself. The subject of the methodology is that which engenders meaning to other cultures and the individuals within it. The word "ethnohermeneutics" avoids the pitfalls inherent in the use of the term "religion," but the word religion is too well-known simply to be dropped.[23]

"Religion" is a Western term that has no close correspondence in non-European languages and carries with it a host of theological assumptions and, outside of the West, a relationship with Western imperialism via pre-contemporary Christian missionaries. Most definitions of "religion" impose Western criteria on cultures that may have none of the normative expectations of the word: a concept of a supernatural, a transcendent meaning to life, a separation of secular and religious aspects of culture, a focus on belief rather than behavior, etc. The term "religion" is problematic because it is derived from androcentric cultures and androcentric studies of culture.

To ensure that these cultural analyses are not exercises in imaginative thinking, as so many are, the cultures chosen, excepting Israelite religion, are those that are extant, albeit they may have a very long history, or those of the recent past, for which aspects are still extant, especially the spoken language. To lessen the possibility of the imposition of androcentric presuppositions and to gain entrée to the realm of the female in the respective cultures, all chapters are based on the knowledge or research of either women of the culture or female scholars with a long familiarity with the culture and its people and who speak the language of the respective culture.

The Structure of This Book

Originally, the plan was to cover selected cultures around the planet, but the task would have taken far longer than the five years this more limited approach required. Such a massive project would also have led to a cumbersome and impractical volume. For example, we will not cover the Nāyar culture of southern India, which continues a matrilineal social structure in spite of several thousand years of contact with and then dominance by a variety of patrilineal and patriarchal traditions, as well as devotion to the Earth Mother. Similarly, this study will not deal with those European folk traditions which maintain a pre-Christian orientation towards female spirits disguised as Christian saints. Other traditions, which this book should cover, but have been well studied from feminist perspectives, such as Australian indigenous religions mentioned above and Hinduism, have to be omitted.

The cultures that are covered fall into four parts. The first part brackets European culture in two directions. This is important for providing an inkling of the pre-Christian situation in Europe, given that the primary comparative analysis will be between non-Western cultures and the Western monotheistic traditions. The Saami tradition of northern Scandinavia, Finland, and northwestern Russia represents the extreme north of Europe. The chapter on this religion was written with the eminent historian of religion and Saami herself, Louise Bäckman, the Professor of Comparative Religion at Stockholm University, as well as a vice-president of the International Association for the History of Religion (IAHR), at the time. The basis of Israelite religion, itself the basis, in part, of the monotheistic religions, developed just beyond Europe's southeastern frontier. The chapter analyzing these traditions was written with my colleague at York University, Johanna Stuckey, the founder of Women's Studies in Canada, who has been critically reflecting on religion and archeology in the eastern Mediterranean area for many years. The first chapter in this part focuses on a gathering-hunting culture that shifted to herding; the second, on cultures in the early stage of agriculture.

The second part will center on China, the major focus of my own studies for several decades. Given the immensity of the subject, I have divided the topic into two: the traditional and contemporary periods. The latter was written with my wife, Chuang Li (Zhuang Li), a specialist in comparative culture and language, with important input, their doctoral dissertation research, from two excellent young Chinese scholars, the first female scholars to focus on contemporary Chinese religion, Wang Xiaoli, of the National Institute for the Study of Minorities, and Yang Lihui, of Bejing Normal University. These chapters provide the only analysis in this book of a large agricultural civilization, covering a quarter of the human population, now becoming an industrial civilization (and Taiwan, which is in a post-industrial phase of development). A third chapter briefly looks at the effects of Chinese religion with regard to sex and gender on the religions of Japan and Korea. Marilyn Nefsky, a specialist on East Asian religions at the University of Lethbridge, collaborated on the first part, and the second is highly dependent on the work of Laurel Kendall, of the American Museum of Natural History.

The third part covers Native North America; it provides the opportunity for study of cultures ranging from gathering-hunting ones that shifted, first, to a fur-trading economy and then to modern culture, to horticultural societies, to those in an early phase of agriculture. The first chapter in this part, to balance the following three chapters, provides four small sections that cover corollary aspects of other areas or peoples: a South American civilization and a South American horticultural people, the circum-polar Inuit, and symbols which bridge Eurasia and the Americas. The major tradition covered, the Anishnabe, is the one with which I am most familiar, and was written with an articulate elder. Jacqui Lavalley, who grew up with and continues to live the tradition, is a Midéwiwin initiate and the Native-way teacher at the First Nations School in Toronto. Research on the chapter was assisted by a former student of mine, Cory Silverstein, now completing a doctorate in anthropology at McMaster University. A third chapter, on the Hopi, I could not have written without the help and guidance of Alice Schlegel, an eminent anthropologist at the University of Arizona, and Armin Geertz, the Professor of Comparative Religion at Aarhus University in Denmark and the Secretary-General of the IAHR. The final chapter in this part concerns the fusion of gathering-hunting traditions and agricultural ones leading to one of the most impressive menarche rituals to be found anywhere. The conversations I had with two Chiricahua and Mescalero scholars, respectively D.C. Cole of Moorhead College and Inés Talamantez of the University of California at Santa Barbara, were influential in my conceiving this chapter; the material on northern Athapaskan cultures was informed by conversations with Marie-Françoise Guédon of the University of Ottawa.

The final part is important given that the subject cultures of Parts II and III were probably connected in the far distant past. Some might argue that any shared religious features are due to a common ur-structure. This could hardly be said about Africa, a vast continent with many different cultures and, prior to the impact of European imperialism, the home of many kingdoms. The selected cultures include those most influential, as a result of the horrendous slave trade, on the cultures of the Americas. The section on Yoruba culture was written with the advice of Rosalynd J. Hackett, a professor of religious studies at the University of Tennessee and Deputy Secretary-General of the IAHR, who has done much to promote the study of African religions, and the second section was written as a result of the kind collaboration of a scholarly couple from Ghana, Elizabeth and Paul Aijin-Tettey, the former a doctoral candidate at York University and the latter a recent Ph.D. in religious studies at McMaster University. A final chapter discusses aspects of these traditions as they manifest themselves in the Americas, a subject with which I am more familiar.

A concluding chapter presents several analyses. It begins with a summary of commonalities of non-Western religion with regard to sex and gender. I then compare these commonalities to the Western traditions (Judaism, Christianity and Islam). Finally, an analysis explores the bearing of these inquiries on the study of religion.

Two scholars have kindly bracketed this work with important essays that I am not capable of writing. Rita Gross, a professor of religious studies at the University of Wisconsin—Eau Clair, mentioned at the beginning of this introduction, who has written major revisionist studies of South Asian religions, in a Foreword has contextualized this study in the context of feminist studies of religion. Catherine Keller, a professor of theology at Drew University and a leading liberal, feminist theologian, has written an Afterword, expressing the potential significance of this work to contemporary Christians.

Limitations of This Study

This work is exclusively concerned with female aspects of religion examined cross-culturally from a religious studies perspective. It does not deal with most of the important concerns of feminist scholarship; there is a considerable body of excellent studies that readers can refer to for these topics. Also, although there will be a number of references to anthropological, historical and sociological studies, the analyses here will not be from these disciplinary perspectives. Again, there is a much larger feminist-oriented literature in these disciplines than there is in religious studies.[24]

The primary concern of this work is the ethnohermeneutics of femaleness: the meaning and significance to females of being female in a number of different cultures. This is a new topic in religious studies and there are few prior models; hence, it should be clear that this work is experimental. Moreover, the focus of this study requires input from females; male understanding from within the selected cultures can at best be of tangential usefulness. For this reason, the range of cultures that this study could explore was limited. Most cultural studies, even many by feminist female scholars, have focused on male knowledge and understandings of femaleness from the subject culture, severely limiting their usefulness for this study. In spite of this difficulty, it has been possible to gain a very modest understanding of the hermeneutics of femaleness in a number of cultures. Finally, I must reiterate that this work is a study of female spirituality, the hermeneutics of femaleness, not feminist spirituality, spirituality arising out of the feminist movement in the West; for the latter, readers might consult Cynthia Eller's excellent study.[25] It is hoped that what follows will be of interest and perhaps stimulate other scholars towards further, improved studies on this topic.

A Note on Terminology

It is common in feminist studies to distinguish "gender" from "sex"; the former relating to cultural construction and the latter to biological differences. This has led to a minor problem in terminology for this study, for the strict separation of culture and biology, arising from the early Christian distinction of spirit and flesh, as well as sacred and profane, is not found in many of the cultures analyzed in this volume. Where possible, the distinction between "gender" and "sex" will be maintained, but in those cultures where the distinction would impose a Eurocentric meaning on the subject culture, the term "gender" will be used as an inclusive term that encompasses aspects of our concept of physical sexual distinctions along with its reference to culture.

Chronology

Where possible, the various studies focus on the present. But this was not always possible or desirable. Some cultures dealt with are archaic; others are in the process of major change and the analysis was based on the culture just prior to the impact of modernity; other religious traditions disappeared in the last couple of hundred years due to forced Christianization. In all cases, the various time periods of the analyses are specified, but they will vary and so should not accordingly be confused.

Part I
Framing Europe

When Saul saw the camp of the Philistines, he was afraid and his heart trembled greatly. When Saul inquired of the Lord, the Lord did not answer him, either by dreams or by Urim or by prophets. Then Saul said to his servants, "Seek for me a woman who is a medium, that I may go to her and inquire of her." And his servants said to him, "Behold, there is a woman who is a medium at En-dor."

—1 Samuel 28:5-7
(New American Standard Bible [NASB])

2
PRE-CHRISTIAN SAAMI RELIGION

with Louise Bäckman

BACKGROUND

THE SAAMI (called Lapps in the literature by non-Saami), a Finno-Ugric speaking people, have for thousands of years inhabited the northern to central parts of Scandinavia, Finland, and the bordering Kola peninsula of Russia. Their language divides into Eastern Saami, spoken on the Kola peninsula and nearby parts of Finland; Northern or Central Saami, spoken in the western parts of northern Finland and northern Sweden and Norway; and Southern Saami, spoken in the southern Saami districts of Sweden and Norway. Until several hundred years ago, their life-style was part of a Northeurasian macro-culture, being based on the gathering of wild plants, the hunting of animals with a focus on reindeer, and fishing. Their religion accorded with the circum-Polar cultural complex, including shamanism and the bear sacrifice.

As the agricultural and cattle and sheep herding Scandinavian, Finnish, and Russian populations expanded and pressed northward, previous tenuous trading relationships shifted to a domination-subordination pattern. Taxes of furs and reindeer hides imposed by the Scandinavian kingdoms, as well as a growing fur trade, led to the decimation of the wild reindeer and a reliance for subsistence on flour from trade. Some of the Saami, who had long tamed reindeer to carry packs, pull sleds, and serve as decoys for wild reindeer, domesticated the remaining reindeer in the seventeenth century. This led to a differentiation of life-styles based on dependence on reindeer herding: fully nomadic life-style in the mountains, partially nomadic lifestyle in the lowland forests, and a partially maritime lifestyle for those living on the coast, where fishing and the hunting of sea mammals continued in importance.

The shift from gathering-hunting to herding led to major changes in the Saami cultural ecology, including the above described residence patterns that

15

varied regionally in the degree of nomadism according to the dependence on herding; a shift in diet among the herding Saami with the development of reindeer milking and the manufacture of cheese and other milk products; and notions of clan ownership of herds and pasturage. These shifting socioeconomic patterns resulted in changing religio-ecological patterns. Most important was the transformed relationship with the reindeer: from hunting, in which humans depended on the voluntary gift by the reindeer of their bodies, to herding, in which the reindeer was subordinated to humans. The latter situation involved the concept of a mistress of the reindeer comparable in function, but superior, to that of the herder and an emphasis on reindeer sacrifice. Shamanism may have become more of a specialty in the switch from hunting to the herding of domesticated animals. No longer did each individual require personal relationships with theriomorphic spirits (spirits in animal form) to survive; instead, there were inherited family and clan guardian spirits. The major concern became the welfare of the reindeer herd.

More important with regard to religion is the forced Christianization of the Saami, first by Roman Catholics, followed by Lutherans in the west and Eastern Orthodox in the east. From the standpoint of Saami religion as discerned from ethnography, this led to a division between eastern and western traditions. Typical of the pattern throughout the long Christianization of Europe, indigenous religions were ruthlessly suppressed, forcing those aspects which continued into secrecy, resulting in a loss of communal aspects.

Different from the rest of Europe, this Christianization took place later in time. Hence, more of traditional Saami religion survived into the period of written records than the other cultures further south. Equally important in this regard, the Saami language is still spoken in areas where the Saami remain in the majority. Reindeer herding persists among a minority of the Saami population. As among other oppressed cultures, there were in the first half of the twentieth century, attempts by the dominant cultures to suppress the use of native languages as well as religion. As elsewhere, there is a contemporary renewed interest among many Saami in their language and traditional culture.[1] For these reasons, Saami religion is the best understood of the pre-Christian, non-Mediterranean European traditions.

The earliest descriptions of Saami religion are from seventeenth- and eighteenth-century missionaries' accounts and court records. In these we find the inevitable ethnocentric misinterpretations, lapses in observations and biased values. Many of the descriptions are based on confessions, often forced, from Saami converts. In other words, we must always be aware that these descriptions are partial at best and prone to misunderstandings. Later descriptions by ethnologists and analyses by ethnohistorians may be skewed by the earlier data and more contemporary ethnocentrism. For example, even some recent scholarly publications maintain the premise that religion is a function of the male sphere; accordingly, they consider a prohibition on female participation a mark of genuine sacredness. Our understanding is further handicapped by an imbalance in the records. While early missionaries described aspects of western Saami religion, the material on the eastern Saami, recorded more recently by linguists and ethnologists, is further removed in time from the traditional practices.[2]

Under these circumstances, the following depictions of the female aspects of traditional Saami religion are to be understood as partial and tentative. Particularly unclear are the interrelationships between female and male components with regard to both spirits and ritual practices.

FEMALE SPIRITS

Cosmic Spirits

In various Saami myths, the sun may be characterized as male or female. The latter is of interest, as it correlates with the far northern pattern as, for example, among the Inuit, so different from the normative cultural perception of Sun as male. *Bieve*, the sun, was understood in some of the Saami sub-cultures to be the mother of all living creatures, particularly the reindeer, who are a gift from her to the Saami. Cereals, brass rings, and young animals, preferably female, were ritually offered to her.

Associated with Sun, whether conceived as male or female, are the *Bieve Neide* or *Sala Neide* (Sun Maidens), the latter term possibly deriving from the Nordic word for the sun, *sol*. Following contact with Christianity, in some areas *Bieve* was associated with Anna, the mother of Mary, and called *Marian Edni* (Maria's Mother).

The other major heavenly spirit, *Aske*, the moon in old Saami, was connected with a negative male spirit, *Staallo*. *Aske* was also understood to help the wolf find the reindeer, of concern when the economy shifted to herding, and wolf depredations became a serious threat.

This cosmic understanding correlates with the human perception of the sun and the moon in the Arctic. After the period of continual darkness surrounding the winter solstice, the sun first appears as a golden glow on the mountains. Day by day, the glow becomes more intense and beautiful. The appearance of the sun, at first low on the horizon, creates a joyous feeling among the Saami. During the winter dark period, the moon remains high in the sky, shining with a

bright, cold light, felt to be malevolent. The moon engenders a feeling of discomfort and dread. Throughout much of the year, the sun, when it is visible,
remains low on the horizon, close to the earth; it is the moon alone that appears
high in the sky. During the brief, warm summer, the moon can hardly be seen
because of the sun's continual brightness.

The Arctic appearance of these cosmic forces is replicated on the earliest
Saami drumhead designs recorded, drawn in the 17th century. Of the fourteen
recorded designs, nearly half have cosmic imagery. On all of these, the moon
and stars are depicted at the top of the drumhead, while the sun is found on the
lower portion.[3] On one of these drawings, the sun is placed just above the symbol that may represent the earth, and on two others, the sun is placed over an
image of a snake, a common chthonic image. (The snake is one of the helping
spirits of Saami shamans and is related to the world below.) On a fourth drum,
a snake is twined about a vertical line that joins the horizontal lines, seemingly
representing the sky and earth realms, where the image of the moon and sun
are respectively found, above and below the vertically drawn serpent. The symbol of the snake emerging from the earth or water and writhing upwards to the
sky is a common cultural symbol for varying connections between earth and sky
and is found in both northern and eastern Asia and North America.

In summary, in the Arctic regions, the understanding of the sun as female
may be due to the respective appearance of the sun and the moon, the sun
being equated with the earth. Hence, *Bieve*, close to the earth, is associated
with life and warmth; *Aske*, high above, signifies cold and darkness.

Creation Spirits

Among the Saami residing in present-day Norway, the creation spirit is *Madder-
Akka* (basis/foundation/root/origin-Grandmother/Old Woman). She may be
connected to the Nordic *Jord-Gumma* (Earth-Grandmother/Old Woman:
meaning, in part, spirit mid-wife, because the newborn baby is placed on the
earth before being placed in the hands of the father). *Madder-Akka* has three
daughters: in order, *Sar-Akka* (*saaret*: Splitting-Grandmother; i.e., Birth
Grandmother), *Juks-Akka* (*jukse*: Bow-Grandmother), and *Uks-Akka* (*ukse*:
Door-Grandmother). These divinities give life to all creatures, including
humans.

In one myth relating to human origins, *Sar-Akka* creates the fetal body of the
human after she receives the new fetus's soul from her mother, *Madder-Akka*.
The body is then placed in the child-to-be's mother. In another version of the
myth, *Madder-Akka* gives the child-to-be to *Sar-Akka* if it is to be female or

Juks-Akka if it is to be male. These respective daughters assign the fetus sex and place it in the human mother. The third daughter, *Uks-Akka*, protects the infant when it begins to walk.

A preliminary mythic aspect has been added to this understanding of the creation of life in some versions, probably due to contact with the Nordic patriarchal and hierarchal society. *Radien-Pardne*, who receives his power from his father, *Radien* (the Ruler), creates a soul and delivers it to *Madder-Ajja* (Origin-Grandfather), who takes it into his belly, journeys around the sun, and then delivers it to *Madder-Akka*. This overlay adds not only notions of an aristocracy among the spirits but a male assumption of female physiology as well.

These interrelated female deities are individually connected to specific aspects of the *kåta*, the traditional round Saami dwelling. *Madder-Akka* dwells under the floor of the dwelling, which suggests that, as the "root" deity, she is an earth mother. In some Saami dialects, the floor area along the inside walls of the *kåta* is called *maddere*. *Sar-Akka* lives in the hearth, the central fire, the heart of the home. Hence, she is connected to the home fire, and, as fire, she may be symbolically related to *Bieve*, the sun who is the mother of all living creatures. *Uks-Akka* is, of course, the door deity. One further deity of importance in this regard is *Bassjo-Akka* (*Boassjde*-Grandmother). The *boassjde* is the male sacred area of the home opposite the door, to which we will return when discussing Saami rituals, opposite the female sacred area near the door.

Madder-Akka and her daughters have parallels with both the former contiguous Nordic religion, particularly in the area now called Norway, and other parts of the Northeurasian culture area of which Saami culture is a part. With regard to the former, *Madder-Akka*'s daughters share common traits with the *Norns* (*Urd*, *Verdandi*, and *Skuld*), the three Nordic female spirits who decided an individual's fate. The Saami birth ritual to be discussed below is similar to the *nornagreytur* (Norn's porridge) in which divination pegs are placed, which is shared by the Scandinavian mother and her female friends. As well, *Uks-Akka* is paralleled by *Dörrkäringen*, the door-woman of Scandinavian myths. The ritual offerings to *Sar-Akka* placed on the hearth may be likened to Nordic drink offerings for *Eldborg*, a household spirit, also poured on the hearth.

Equal parallels are to be found, however, in other Northeurasiatic cultures to the east of the Saami. The creation of life involved both Sky (Samoyed: *Num*; Mansi: *Numi-Torem*) and Earth, sometimes the wife of Sky. But it was the female creation deity that determined a person's fate, and she was the protector of human females and the progenitor spirit of animals. Rituals directed towards her—the daily offering of food and drink and occasional offerings of animals—were the responsibility of women. This female deity assisted women in childbirth, and after delivery, the mother, her female friends, and the deity shared a meal. The same divinatory rite as the among the Saami with a bow and arrow placed in the food (see below) was performed among the Yakut and other northern peoples. Among the Selkup, this mother deity had daughters with functions similar to those of *Madder-Akka*.

With respect to the Northeurasian pairing of Sky and Earth, the ethno-historical sources which provided the above depiction of *Madder-Akka* and her daughters in the role of creation may be incomplete. In some Saami myths, we find both *Madder-Akka* and *Madder-Ajja* (Origin-Grandfather). Perhaps it is their pairing which is ultimately responsible for the creation of life.

Spirits of the Game and the Herd

Among the Kola Saami, in present-day Russia, two female spirits were associated with the reindeer, the primary source of subsistence: *Pots-Husjik* and *Luot-Hosjik*, the terms being a fusion of Russian and Saami words. *Hosjik* (alternatively: *Hosjin*) is Russian for "Mistress," while *pots* is Saami for the reindeer herd, that is, domesticated reindeer, and *luot*, Saami for the wild reindeer. Rituals were directed towards *Pots-Hosjik* in the spring as the reindeer were turned free to browse, so that she would lead them to good pasture and protect them from wolves and other carnivores. In the autumn, when the reindeer were again herded, there were ritual offerings to express appreciation for her protection. *Lout-Hosjik* was the object of rituals during the reindeer hunt, but the two deities seem to have been similar in some Saami areas.

The need to utilize a Russian word to indicate a ruler of the reindeer seems to indicate influence from hierarchical cultures. The original term for the spirit of the hunted wild reindeer was probably *Mintis*, understood to be female. She correlates with the virtually ubiquitous human understanding that the spiritual essences of those animals and plants on which our lives depend are female, the sex which provides life and nurture.

Another important source for subsistence, migratory birds, was also protected by a Mother. Among the western Saami, she was called *Barbmo-Akka*, while, in the eastern area, she was known as *Loddisjäd'ne*. Among the coastal Saami, there were also tutelary spirits for fish, as well as for sea mammals.

Spirit for the Dead

The realm of the dead was under the surface of the earth, where the dead were buried—a place called Jabmiaimo. This was the location of *Jabmi-Akka* (Death

Grandmother). *Jabmi-Akka* is a counterpart of *Madder-Akka*, as death is an essential aspect of life. Both are female earth spirits.

Certain of the dead reside in another locale, the *aurora borealis* (Northern Lights). These are women who die in childbirth and men who die in battle. The equation of the two signifies the original Saami understanding of both the equality of males and females and those gender-specific activities most honored by the culture.

Guardian Spirits

Typical of gathering-hunting cultures, the Saami had close relations with supportive theriomorphic spirits. These could be clan or individual and were important to both females and males. The term for these spirits is *kaddz*, which has somewhat different meanings in different areas (although this may simply indicate the limitations of the ethnohistorical sources). Among the northern Saami, *kaddz* referred to the shaman's helping spirits. Among the eastern Saami, the term referred to individual and clan protecting spirits. In the latter regard, the meaning of *kaddz* is similar to that of the Nordic *fulgia* (follower), the supportive spirit which accompanies one.

Although a late source from the Kola peninsula indicates that males inherited *kaddz* patrilineally and females matrilineally, the actual situation seems to have been bilateral inheritance. When a Saami woman married, she brought guardian spirits from her family to her new patrilocal residence. This was necessary as the spirits of her husband's family could not be expected to protect her. In some Siberian cultures, these spirits were expressed in images made by the woman's mother or grandmother and were placed in the female sacred space of the home by the door, opposite the male sacred space housing her husband's family images.

Sar-Akka, as the deity of the hearth-fire, the protector of home and family, is also a guardian spirit. She is offered food and drink daily on the hearth. She seems to have been the deity to whom the Saami felt closest and her name survives in use to the present. It is recorded that, when Saami were forced to go to church, they offered her drink for her support in not losing the Saami traditions. When compelled to take communion, they drank a toast to her, asking her forgiveness. It also seems that *Madder-Akka* and *Sar-Akka* eventually merged and became linked to the Virgin Mary, allowing their worship to continue under the guise of Christianity.

FEMALE RITUALS AND RITUAL ROLES

Female Participation in "Male" Rituals

The literature on Saami religion abounds with statements that women were forbidden to enter sacred sites or be in the vicinity of religious implements, especially the shaman's drum. For some male authors, this is an indication of true spirituality, as they understand females to be either incapable of appreciating, or, by their very nature, polluting the sacred. This attitude is characteristic of Western religions, and its application to Saami traditions is unsupported by the available evidence.

What seems not to be understood in these androcentric analyses is that the studies have focused on hunting rituals, as well as herding rituals derived from hunting rituals. As discussed in other chapters, the women's avoidance of men's hunting implements and often men, particularly during menstruation or childbirth, seems to be universal and is undoubtedly a functional necessity. The hormones and other pheromones produced by women at this time can be smelled by hunted animals for considerable distances. It was essential for the survival of the community, females and males, that hunters not be handicapped by having their presence announced to the hunted in such a manner. Hence, menstruating females or even fertile females avoided any potential contact with the hunters prior to hunting as well as with any item the hunters would be touching or bringing with them while hunting. From the standpoint of religion, this is understood as the potentiality of female spiritual power to overwhelm male power. This understanding does not determine women as polluting or unspiritual but rather the opposite.

It is for this reason that women were normally not in the vicinity of *seite*, shrines with a sacred stone or wooden figure, which were sites for sacrifices of reindeer and other animals, and they did not come near a male shaman's drums. These drums were once crucial for locating the migrating wild reindeer prior to domestication, as they still are among the Algonkian-speaking peoples of Labrador and eastern Quebec in Canada for locating the similar caribou. A woman did not enter the *boassjde*, the male sacred area of the *kåta*, although she sat next to it with her husband. When menstruating, however, she sat in the area opposite, sacred to women. In this regard, there is clear indication of gender equality with regard to spirituality, as males equally did not sit in the female area of the home, nor did they participate in the women's rituals (unfortunately, little information has survived as to the nature of these rituals).

With regard to the important bear ritual, statements that women did not take part are contradicted by other descriptive material. The bear was to be pierced by the gaze of *Bassjo-Akka*, a female deity discussed above. When the hunters carried the dead bear back to the community, they were conveying a potent spiritual force that could harm both the hunters and the community, the bear being the most powerful theriomorphic spirit. To neutralize this danger, the bear was to be viewed by the women through brass rings or rings were drawn around their eyes with charcoal. The women also attached brass rings to the skin of the bear. The women chewed alder bark and spit the resultant red fluid on the men as they entered the *kåta*, on the *kåta* itself, and on the food. (In some Siberian cultures, women spit snow melted in their mouths on the sacrificed bear.)

Both the brass rings and the alder bark are of interest. The Saami early came upon brass when they visited northern medieval market towns which would have had churches. In the churches, which the Saami were invited to enter, were brass candelabra and chandeliers. The Saami may have identified the shining metal with the sacred power of the Christians. It is also possible, although there is no direct evidence for the interpretation, that the Saami used the brass primarily in rings specifically to represent *Bieve*, the sun goddess, given the color of brass and the ring shape. Brass rings were energized by having a ray of the sun shine through them. Viewing potent Bear, in Saami culture a male spirit, through the equally potent symbol of female Sun would create a balance of male-female energies as well as sky-earth forces. There is a direct connection between Bear and Sun in an eastern Saami myth in which Bear drew up Sun each morning. (The Northeurasian brown bear is as large as the North American grizzly, also primarily understood as male in Native American cultures, which understand the smaller and gentler black bear as essentially female.)

In one region, the alder tree (*leipe*) is related to *Leib-Olmai* (Alder Man), who had influence on the bear hunt. Indeed, it is possible that *Leib-Olmai* is Bear. When alder bark is mixed with saliva through mastication, it turns blood red. Moreover, this red juice is identified with menstrual blood; in Southern Saami, menstrual blood is called *leipe*. The sanctity of chewed alder bark is further indicated by its use for painting designs on the sacred drums, similar to the use in many cultures of red ocher, a symbol for the energy of life. Again, we seem to have an impressive balancing of sacred energies: symbolic menstrual blood from the spirit of Bear spit by women on those in contact with male Bear, the liquid neutralizing the potential harmful energy from the sacrificed deity. Obviously, the significance of menstrual blood is not that it is polluting; on the contrary, it is imbued with considerable female spiritual potency.

Childbirth Rituals

Because *Madder-Akka* and her daughter *Sar-Akka* stay by the woman's side to assist her during childbirth, as they protect women during menstruation and pregnancy, animals are sacrificed to them. Immediately after the birth, a dish called *Sar-Akka* porridge is shared by the new mother and her female friends. The porridge has divinatory functions, the details apparently varying from area to area. In one version, three pegs are placed in the porridge, one white, one black, and one with three rings carved on it. When the meal is finished, the pegs are placed under the threshold for three nights. If the black one disappears, the child is not expected to live; if the white one is gone, both mother and child will be fine.

In another version, a dismantled bow and arrow is placed in the porridge, if the child is male. Whatever archery piece turns up in the mother's spoon has divinatory significance. The bow was afterwards hung over the infant's cradle to ensure the child's becoming a good marksman. There is no record of the equivalent ritual for female children. Since parallel rituals can be found in many premodern cultures around the world, with different divinatory items for females and males, it is most likely that there was a corollary divinatory ritual for female infants as well.

Female Religious Functionaries

The question of whether or not females functioned as shamans (Saami: *noaide*) is controversial. A number of texts assume the *noaide* to be a male role. If the *noaide*'s functions were limited to shamanizing with regard to hunting and herding, then this is a logical assumption. However, if the *noaide*'s functions are broader, then one might expect that, as in some other Northeurasian cultures, women, at least those who had reached menopause, also functioned as shamans. In Eastern Saami, there are terms which indicate that both men and women were shamans: Old Noaide Man (*noitkalles*) and Old Noaide Woman (*noidtahkk*).

A second possibility is that, in most Saami dialects, *noaide* stood for male religious functionaries and *quaps* for female religious specialists. In the records from the early Christian missionaries, *quaps* forms the suffix of compound terms relating, in the Christian mind, to witches, female magic, trolls, sorceresses, etc. The word *quaps* itself means "eyes that have turned inwards or upwards," a condition indicative of a trance state. The ethnographic record confirms that women were involved in healing, and there is no reason to assume that they would not have utilized ecstatic aspects of the healing arts.

Folktales are told of women who performed male *noaide* roles, for example, Rijkuo-Maja and Silbo-Gåmmoe. The former is said to have sacrificed at *seite*, which women normally avoided. Both women, as well as several others, had shaman's drums, which women were supposed never to go near, and were described as going into states that could refer only to deep shamanic trances with the drum. While these stories were recorded long after the women were said to have lived and, therefore, may be apocryphal, comparison with other cultures provides an alternative explanation.

In Anishnabe cultures of the North American Great Lakes region (see Chapter 8), the literature also points out that only males touched drums. While this is true of the Dream-dance Drum, a ritual inspired by a woman's dream, it is not true of other types of drums, particularly those used for shamanizing. Some women do have drums, understood as drums belonging to women, as drums belonging to men are men's drums. A traditional woman who has a drum would not touch a man's drum. Hence, it is possible that the statements regarding Saami drums are correct in the main, but certain women did have their own drums.

Given that, by the time the cultural traditions were being recorded, drums had long since been confiscated and burned when found and those possessing them were beaten, if not burned at the stake, those who continued to shamanize went underground and hid their drums. Furthermore, given the tremendous antagonism towards women religious specialists by Christians in Europe and the Americas in the 17th and 18th centuries, such women, when discovered, were certain to be deemed witches and burned at the stake. Hence, it is hardly surprising that the Saami made no mention of such women while they were still alive.

FEMALE SELF-UNDERSTANDING

The Saami today have been nominally Christian for over two hundred years, although increasing contacts with previously colonized indigenous peoples elsewhere has led to a renewed interest in Saami traditions. Thus, the current Saami understanding does not necessarily reflect that of several hundred years ago. The above accounts of the female aspects of Saami religion are based on primarily androcentric, fragmentary, ethnographic and ethnohistorical recordings from different dialects, regions, and chronological periods. We have far from a complete picture of the religion of the herding period, let alone the underlying gathering-hunting foundation. Missing are many of the traditions relating to the spiritual qualities of fish and plants. Also missing are menarche and menstrual rituals. Yet despite these gaps in the records, as well as anti-Saami, anti-female biases in the earlier records, there are sufficient hints to outline the basis of women's spiritual lives in relation to those of men.

Women's vocation, from late adolescence to menopause, was as elsewhere based on reproduction and nurturing (including foraging); hence, their lives centered on home and hearth. In the Saami tradition, both were female realms (with the interesting exception that Saami men cooked meat and fish, the food for which they were responsible). The deities of and under the home were female, as was the deity of the hearth. These deities of home and hearth were also the deities of female protection, pregnancy, childbirth, and childrearing. Both men and women had their exclusive, special spaces within the home where resided their respective guardian spirits, inherited bilaterally.

The spiritual essences of the primary animals hunted for subsistence were female as was the guardian of the domesticated reindeer herds. Probably this was also true of the fish and the gathered plant foods. As among other far northern peoples, the sun, the most powerful spirit in the sky, was understood to be female.

Saami women in the traditional culture, accordingly, were surrounded by powerful, elemental female divinities. This would have influenced their understanding of female worth, and the theology undoubtedly reflected the female role in the cultural ecology. This interpretation is supported by a backhanded observation from the ethnohistorical records where a missionary critiques Saami culture for the "dominion and tyranny of the women over their husbands." This assessment should not be construed as indicating a matriarchal situation but rather to reflect the typical pre-contemporary Christian critique of the non-subordination of females by males, found in missionary records elsewhere; for example, the seventeenth-century Jesuit Relations from northern North America. The equation of women who die during childbirth with fallen warriors, both receiving a honored status, confirms sex and gender equality in both the conceptual and social realms.

Women not only had their own rituals but carried out vital duties in communal rituals as well. In the major bear ritual, women played important roles when the men brought the slain bear to the community. Other communal rituals, let alone female roles, are most unclear. Women seem to have played no role in rituals oriented towards hunting and fishing, but this is to be expected, given that these activities were of the male realm. Similarly, males did not take part in those rituals exclusively of the female realm, such as childbirth. These generalizations, however, must be understood as exactly that and necessarily simplistic. Clearly, the role of women in the return of the men with the hunted bear indicates participation in aspects of hunting rituals, as well there may have been other female rituals oriented towards hunting that have been lost, as for example, the distant religious role of women in male hunting as related by an Inuit in Chapter 7.

Although, with some possible exceptions, the hunting-herding shaman was a male role; nevertheless, it is certain that women did serve as religious functionaries. Unfortunately, the records by Christian missionaries who considered such women to be witches do not provide us with an adequate understanding of their communal roles and activities.

No knowledge of those rituals central to the lives of females, except aspects of childbirth rituals, have come down to us. But it is to be noted that the most powerful symbol of female power and spirituality in many cultures, menstrual blood, was symbolically sprayed by women on the men upon their returning with a ritually slain bear, a powerful spiritual entity, to counteract any potential negative energy. This single factor alone informs us of the enormous regard Saami culture held for not only female spirits, but the spiritual essence of human females, that is, women themselves. Surely women were aware of this regard and so understood themselves.

3
ISRAELITE RELIGION AND ITS PRECURSORS

with Johanna Stuckey

BACKGROUND[1]

THE RELIGION OF SEMITIC-SPEAKING PEOPLES of the area now known as Israel and somewhat earlier as Palestine, including parts of present-day Jordan, Lebanon, and Syria, led to the creation of a text that has come down to us as the Hebrew Bible. This text records a temple-centered religion and hints at its roots prior to the formation of the Israelite kingdom. The destruction of the temple over nineteen hundred years ago shifted the religion away from the temple-priestly-sacrificial complex to a community-centered religion focusing on studying and interpreting the text in and of itself: Judaism.

As Judaism was developing, so was a modified form of Judaism, Christianity, that shifted from Israelite roots to Hellenistic ones, especially in adopting many of the rituals and concepts of Mithraism, a Hellenized Persian religion. Christianity, in its Roman and Byzantine (Eastern Orthodox) forms, as well as a much later offshoot of the Roman mode, Protestantism, over time became the dominant religion of Europe, ruthlessly suppressing the indigenous European religions.

A second major religion developed in Arabia, Islam, also greatly influenced by the Hebrew Bible, that similarly came to dominate all of North Africa, West Asia, and much of Central Asia. Christianity and Islam clashed at the western (Spain) and eastern (the Balkans) parts of Europe, the conflict continuing to the present in Bosnia. The two traditions were also in conflict during Europe's period of imperialism, and these conflicts as well continue in the present in southwestern Asia. As the Saami religion provides hints about the religion of far northern Europe prior to Christianity, so too an analysis of Israelite religion with regard to the theme of this book assists us in understanding female spirituality at the southeastern edge of Europe prior to Christianity.

28

Of the sixteen cultures or cultural complexes discussed to varying degrees in this book, only the cultures dealt with in this chapter did not continue to the present. For example, although the Inca empire and its state religion (see Chapter 7) ended with the Spanish conquest of the Andes, the religion of the non-elite at that time continues to this day in the Andes. Judaism, Christianity, and Islam are sufficiently different from Israelite religion that they cannot be said to be continuations, although all or parts of their sacred texts are from the Israelite period. Also different from all the other traditions discussed in this book, the Hebrew Bible, at least as interpreted in normative Judaism and Christianity, is antagonistic to female spirituality.

The area that now includes Israel and parts of Jordan, Lebanon, and Syria, did not exist in a cultural vacuum. Influences came from the area of the Tigris and Euphrates Rivers, now primarily in Iraq. Hence, we will begin our analysis with the early Mesopotamian kingdoms. These kingdoms, at their earliest phase, were connected, at least by trade, to the Indus Valley civilization in present-day Pakistan, but we know too little to bring this culture into our discussion.

Agriculture, as distinct from horticulture and in connection with urbanization, first begins in Mesopotamia about six thousand years ago and develops somewhat later in the Indus Valley of South Asia (important for an understanding of sex/gender issues in Hinduism and Buddhism). Over four thousand years ago, we find similar developments in East Asia, Mesoamerica, and the Andes. In Chapter 9, we will discuss the earliest stages of agriculture, what might be called incipient agriculture. Agriculture differs from horticulture, among other ways, in a shift from female gardening to male larger-scale farming. With use of irrigation or other forms of intensive agriculture and the plow, a surplus of produce allows the formation of class distinctions; that is, there is sufficient produce to permit a small number of people to become non-producers. If this becomes an hereditary situation, we have the beginning of castes (hereditary socio-economic classes).

In some areas, urbanization developed prior to agriculture, based on horticulture and the gathering of wild grains. These societies maintained egalitarianism in interesting ways. For example, the Mississippian kingdoms had hereditary castes that were temporary: the highest ranking males and females, the royalty, married persons of the lowest caste. Their children were of intermediate status. Those of intermediate status had customs insuring the mixing of the castes.

There are two impetuses leading to the development of castes. On the one hand, especially after the development of writing, ritual leaders become specialists, also incorporating into their occupation the recording of cultural memories and the direction of labor to enhance the surplus productivity to be used for ritual-oriented activities and constructions. On the other hand, the surplus productivity would have encouraged raids by others to obtain the agricultural surplus, to monopolize water resources for increased agricultural output, etc. This would lead to elaborate defensive structures, walls, and a professional warrior class, impossible without the surplus productivity. The professional warriors would not wish to limit themselves to defense but aggrandize their situation through offense, leading to kingdoms and eventually empires.

In early China, as we shall see in the next chapter, these two professions, priests and warriors, were never separated. The professional warriors were at one and the same time ritual specialists, as well as the literate members of the society. In the early Mesopotamian kingdoms too, there may not have been separation of the elite castes; for example, as discussed below, the daughter of Sargon, the king of Semitic-speaking Akkad, who unified southern Mesopotamia, became the chief priest of the city of Ur. Certainly, by the time of the Israelite kingdom, much later, kings and priests were two distinctly different castes.

One possible scenario for Mesopotamia is that the first elite groups developed from male and female ritualists who took on their occupation as full-time jobs. Since the deities were understood to own the land, their priests, female and male, became the overseers of production who controlled both the economy and society. As the growing urban areas competed for the scarce water resources and rights to fertile land, warfare developed along with professional warriors. Over time, the chief of the warriors became an hereditary king, who, in conjunction with priests, ordered and controlled society. Since warfare is usually a male activity, it led to the ascendancy of males in a society already stratified by occupation. Where we find social classes, that is, a non-egalitarian situation, we also find sex stratification. In these warrior-dominated societies, females tended to become relegated to the lower strata of each caste.

It is instructive to compare the incipient agricultural situation discussed in Chapter 9, which is egalitarian, matrilineal, matrilocal, and matrifocal—both males and females agree that women are more important—with the developments of male-dominated kingdoms. Here we find patrilineal, patrilocal, and patrifocal cultures. This, of course, required many centuries, if not millennia, to develop. For example, writing first developed about five thousand years ago in Mesopotamia. Because the scribe of the deities and the deified inventor of writing was a female, it is quite possible that the inventor of writing was a woman, one of many female priests. Women but slowly lost their status and importance in Mesopotamia and elsewhere in the ancient eastern Mediterranean. Nonetheless, by the time the received version of the Hebrew Bible was put together, women were clearly considered inferior to males, at least by those who compiled the text over two thousand years ago.

There are direct linkages between the development of agriculture and cities in Mesopotamia and later similar developments in the eastern Mediterranean. Not only is it likely that Mesopotamian culture provided some of the impetus and models for the cities and towns of Canaan and Israel, but, as we shall see, there were close connections between concepts of deities as well as religious roles. Moreover, Abraham, the patriarch of the Hebrew tribes, according to the foundation myth of Israelite religion, was brought by God from Ur, a city in Mesopotamia, to Canaan. Approximately 3500 years ago, Canaan consisted of many agriculturally based city-states ruled by kings and aristocratic families. Fortunately, we have other Syro-Palestinian material than the disparaging accounts in the Hebrew Bible. Since 1929, archaeologists excavating Ugarit, an ancient Semitic-speaking city in Syria, have recovered well over the original 15,000 clay tablets, written in the earliest example we have of alphabetic writing and dating from ca. 1550–1200 BCE, that contain mythic poems, deity and offering lists, and lists of religious functionaries. This material suggests that Ugaritic religion was essentially similar to Canaanite religion and, given the closeness of the Ugarit language to Hebrew, probably related to Israelite religion.

The Canaanite cities were successfully attacked by a coalition of invaders that the Egyptians called "the Sea Peoples." After conquering the Hittite Empire and the city-states of Ugarit and its neighbors, the Sea Peoples succeeded in appropriating the coastal area of Canaan and seem to have become the people called the "Philistines" in the Bible. The people who came to be called the Israelites settled the hill country of Canaan, where they eventually formed a kingdom that warred against the Philistines.

FEMALE SPIRITS

Ancient Mesopotamia

It is difficult to examine the nature of female deities in Mesopotamia as they would have been understood by females, because the writings that have been excavated are often later revised versions of earlier myths by androcentric males. For example, the great deity Ninhursag, the Earth Mother of ancient Mesopotamia, is primarily depicted as supporting a divine male hierarchy though she is, in her own right, very powerful. In an important origin myth, the male deity Enki impregnates Ninhursag who gives birth to the female deity

Ninsar. Ninsar, in turn, is impregnated by Enki and bears the female deity Ninkur, who is also impregnated by Enki. The result of this rather involved process is the birth of the female deity Uttu, who is the deity of plants. When, in her turn, she is impregnated by Enki and gives birth to eight different plants, Enki immediately eats them all. Consequently, Ninhursag curses Enki—"Until you are dead, I shall not look upon you with the 'eye of life'"—and disappears. The assembled gods can do nothing to help the ailing Enki. Eventually, when he is close to death, Ninhursag returns and cures him by bringing to birth a special deity to remedy each of his eight ailments, one for each of the plants he devoured.

The most important deity seems to have been the venerated and awesome Inanna, termed in the literature "Queen of Heaven" (*Nin-an-na*, "Lady of Sky"—probably referring to the Evening Star), protector deity of the city of Uruk. She probably was originally a fertility deity. In one hymn, seeking a mate, Inanna asks, "Who will plough my vagina?", indicating a linkage between herself and the earth. She is termed a "maiden," for, although she is presented in some texts as a bride, she is never described as a wife and rarely, if ever, as a mother. A "young woman who loves to laugh," she is, it seems, always in late adolescence and not fulfilling a typical, socially accepted role. So she is both extremely attractive and extremely dangerous.

One poem that has survived describes Inanna's descent to and return from the underworld, the "Great Below." Descending through seven great gates, she arrives naked to the realm of her sister, Erishkigal, Ruler of the Underworld. After three days in the world of the dead, she returns to the surface of the earth, with the help of the male deity, Enki. That Inanna and Erishkigal were sisters suggests that originally they were a single deity, and the world of the dead was one of the many realms of the Evening Star (the Lady of Sky). As we shall see in subsequent chapters, in many cultures, the major female deity is the evening star, who is also earth. Evening Star is seen low in the west at the time of the setting sun, where the dead are often thought to reside. Also, as found in Greek and other myths, Earth dies (or sleeps) in the winter, to be resurrected in the spring. So plants, central in the conceptions of the agricultural societies, go through the yearly round of birth, death, and birth again. Inanna descends to the realm of the dead and rises again on the third day.

Inanna's "bridegroom," the god Dumuzi, the prototype of king, reigns at her will. Indeed, when Inanna descends into the underworld, she leaves Dumuzi in charge of Uruk; on her return she finds him dressed in all his finery and lording it over her city, instead of mourning her departure. As a condition of her release from the underworld, she was obliged to send down a substitute.

Dumuzi's disrespect and lack of feeling anger her, and so she surrenders him to the demons of the underworld: "Inanna fastened on Dumuzi the eye of death./She spoke against him the word of wrath./She uttered against him the cry of guilt./ 'Take him! Take Dumuzi away!'" However, as a result of the self-sacrifice of Dumuzi's sister, Geshtinanna, who takes his place there for part of the year, Dumuzi comes back to earth yearly to live for five or six months with Inanna.

In Sumer, the power of the male kingship appears to have been entirely dependent on Inanna. In what is termed in the scholarly literature the "Sacred Marriage Rite," the man who was to become the king, or who sought to renew his kingship, was understood to incarnate Dumuzi: "The king embraces his beloved bride,/Dumuzi embraces Inanna." The king had to achieve Innana's support by sexually pleasing her in the ritual mating: "After he enters her holy vulva, causing Inanna to rejoice,/Inanna holds him to her and murmurs:/'O Dumuzi, you are truly my love.'" Only then could he ascend the throne she provided and sustained. The justification for kingship was the king's satisfying Inanna so that she would continue to assure the fertility and safety of the land. The mythic early material of Mesopotamia repeatedly insists that no king could reign without Innana's approval.

The mythic(-actual?) ritual, as depicted in the odes, seems to have begun with a procession of the king-elect and his retinue to the inner sanctum of Inanna's temple, her house on earth. Inanna greets the king-elect at the gate of her chambers, while the attendants sang love songs, may of which have been found. Accepting the gifts brought by the king-elect, the couple proceed to the bed constructed for the occasion and covered with herbs, spices and rich cloths. They lay on the bed and made love. Pleased with her lover, now king, Inanna grants him long life on the throne. There appears to be a connection between the marriage bed and the throne. In a poem, Inanna seeks to have both a bed and a throne manufactured.

Kingship and fertility are conjoined in this ritual. In one of the "Sacred Marriage" hymns, Inanna sings of her vulva as "my untilled plot" seeking a ploughman. The reply to her quest is "Young lady, may the king plough them for you!/May the king, Dumuzi, plough them for you!" Inanna responds: "The man of my heart! The ploughman is the man of my heart!"

Hence, Inanna is central to Sumerian religion in many respects. One hymn to Inanna lauds her: "The gods of the land, wishing to hear their fate, come before you./The gods of heaven and earth kneel before you./The living creatures and the people of Sumer come before you./The people of Sumer who parade before you/ Are caught in your gaze,/And held in your holy yoke."

With the passing of time, Inanna became identified with the Semitic Ishtar. As male dominance tightened its hold on Mesopotamian society, Inanna/Ishtar's sphere slowly shrank until she became specialized as a deity of love and war. Still, her grip on the religious understanding was so strong that even later kings considered it necessary to present themselves as the "beloved of Ishtar."

Syro-Palestine

The religious texts from ancient Ugarit describe female deities similar to those attacked in the Hebrew Bible. These deities seem to have been subordinate to male deities in a pantheon presided over by El ("God") from his distant palace. Elat ("Goddess"), Lady Asherah of the Sea, who was perhaps El's consort, was mother to many of the other deities, on whose behalf she often interceded with ancient El. The name Asherah appears about forty times in the Hebrew Bible, usually in the masculine plural form *asherim*.

In the Ugarit texts, the female deity Anat is powerful and blood-thirsty; her normal epithet, "Maiden," indicates that, like Inanna/Ishtar, she was beholden to no husband and was understood to be in a state of permanent late adolescence. In the Ugarit poems, of her own free will she supports the male deity Baal and his cause. Fiercely protective of him, she fights his battles and works to increase his position in the hierarchy. Deity of rain and thunderstorm, Baal, possibly Anat's sibling, seems to have been in charge of fertility at Ugarit. When Anat functions alone, the texts show her as warlike, lusting for blood, arrogant, and very frightening. For instance, in one myth Anat takes part in a battle, wades up to her thighs in gore, and strings human heads and hands around her back and waist. On her return to her temple, she still feels the need of blood; so she turns her furniture into soldiers and fights the battle all over again: "Anat's soul was exuberant,/as she plunged knee-deep into the soldiers' blood,/up to her thighs in the warriors' gore,/until she was satisfied with her battling in the house. . . ." She has no hesitation in threatening the "King, the Father of Time" El when she is trying to get concessions for Baal: "I'll smash your head,/I'll make your gray hair run with blood,/your gray beard with gore." When Baal is devoured by Mot, the male deity of sterility and death, Anat searches for him and eventually, in order to get Baal back, does not hesitate to take on Mot: "She seized El's son Death:/with a sword she split him;/with a sieve she winnowed him;/with a fire she burned him;/with a hand mill she ground him;/in the fields she sowed him." In the Hebrew Bible, Anat is mentioned only in personal and place names.

Astarte, a female deity who, in later times, was widely worshiped in the eastern Mediterranean, appears rarely in the Ugarit texts, but always in close association with Baal. As *ashtoreth*, she is roundly attacked in the Hebrew Bible, in which she occurs nine times, either in the singular or plural form, but always firmly tied to Baal.

For a long time, it seems, Asherah was revered, both officially and unofficially, as an Israelite deity, perhaps even as consort of the Israelite deity, Yahweh. Some scholars support the view that Asherah was an official Israelite deity for most of the Israelite period, at least until the temple of Solomon was destroyed in the sixth century BCE. Most of the Hebrew Bible, however, considers Asherah, in company with Baal and Astarte, as an abominated and alien deity. Nevertheless, the fact that the Hebrew Bible reports repeated attacks on the Baals and the Ashtoreths all through the period of the kings suggests that these deities were important to many, if not the majority, of Israelites. Archaeologists have unearthed numerous female figurines throughout the area, especially in what they interpret as shrines and private houses, and they have therefore concluded worship of female deities was not only common, but also very popular.

FEMALE RITUALS AND RITUAL ROLES

Ancient Mesopotamia

Ancient Mesopotamian texts have yielded a number of Semitic and some Sumerian names for different types of female priests, including *entu*, *naditu*, *ishtaritu*, and *qadishtu*. Since these terms and other information about Mesopotamian priests come from various places and periods, the following generalizations are to be understood as speculative. Given the antagonism towards most female religious functionaries found in the Hebrew Bible, the interpretational literature tends to posit that all ancient eastern Mediterranean female religious functionaries were not priests but rather temple or sacred prostitutes. There is no evidence, however, to support this long tradition of scholarly misogyny.

Of the temple personnel, the Sumerian "Lady Deity" (*nin-dinger*) was probably the female high priest. She was of high social status, but according to the written law, was subject to a strict code of ethics. Should the "Sacred Marriage Rite" have involved human participants, the "Lady Deity" (Semitic *entu*) would probably have incarnated the deity Inanna (in later periods, Ishtar), who had ritual intercourse with her divine consort Dumuzi (later Tammuz). Although we do not know what actually happened when the female high priest and the king retired into the decorated ritual bedchamber in the temple, it is likely, at least in the early period, that the king, incarnating Dumuzi, and the female priest (*entu*), the female deity on Earth, had sexual intercourse.

The "Sacred Marriage Rite" was crucial to early Mesopotamian kingship. As the evidence suggests that originally a high priest (*enu*) incarnated Dumuzi in the ritual, it may be that Sumerian kings took over a ritual that once had other functions, such as inaugurating a new female high priest (*entu*). In this way they would have been able to associate themselves with Inanna/Ishtar's fertility, her undeniable power, and, to a large extent, her divine status.

By the historical period, the "Sacred Marriage Rite" functioned as the validation of Mesopotamian kingship. In cities aside from Inanna's Uruk, the woman participating in the ritual was usually incarnating the female protector deity of the city or the consort of the city's male protector deity. Most commonly, she was identified with Inanna/Ishtar in order to associate the city's ruler with the powerful female deity. Well after the "Sacred Marriage Rite" and the high priesthood (*en*-ship) had ceased to be important in Mesopotamia, rulers still found it necessary to style themselves "beloved of Inanna" or "beloved of Ishtar."

The office of high priest (*en*-ship) in Mesopotamia was so important that the conqueror of a city usually appointed a family member as the female high priest (*entu*) (or a male relative as *enu*) of that city's protector deity. In this way Enheduanna, perhaps the best known Mesopotamian priest, became *entu* of Ur, high priest of Ur's protector divinity, the Moon deity Nanna-Sin. Living about 4300 years ago, Enheduanna was a daughter of Sargon, the earliest empire-building Semitic king. As author of many hymns to Inanna/Ishtar, she has the distinction of being the very first named poet in history.

Archaeologists digging in what turned out to have been the residence of the *naditu* female priests inside the temple-complex of Nanna-Sin at Ur found a damaged disk. On one side, there is a relief showing a ritual in progress, and, on the other, an inscription. The ritual is being supervised by a female priest who is taller and, hence, more important than the other figures. She wears a flounced dress such as those that female deities normally wear; moreover, her hat seems to be one that indicated female priests. The fact that she is supervising a naked male priest in his ritual watering of a sacred tree also suggests high rank. The inscription describes "Enheduanna" as the consort of Nanna-Sin, as well as Sargon's daughter. Together the inscription and the image suggest that the large figure in the relief is Enheduanna, *entu* of Ur.

It is significant that the disk came from the temple's residential area, for it is possible that the *entu* was the senior *naditu*, a kind of female abbot. At Sippar between about 1880 and 1550 BCE, royal and elite women were listed as among the *naditum*. The word *"naditu"* may derive from a root that means "fallow, uncultivated." In some places, *naditu* could marry, but they were not allowed to have children. It may be, then, that every *naditu* was potentially an *entu*; *entu* priests were also prohibited from having children, except, perhaps, as a result of the "Sacred Marriage Rite."

The daily task of *naditu* priests was to pray and make offerings to the divine couple of their temple. At Sippar, they made offerings twice a day, as well as a special one monthly. Furthermore, *naditu* priests were present yearly at the initiation ceremonies of new *naditu* priests, as well as attending at least six festivals.

Though there are many references to another type of female priest, the *ishtaritu*, "devotee of Ishtar," they provide scant information. This priest appears to have been "a dedicated woman" who seemingly also could not bear children, even though she could marry.

Very little is known about the *qadishtu* priest, the "holy" or "set-apart woman," but, according to legal documents, *qadishtu* priests could become mothers. As temple personnel, they chanted at rituals, held aloft the deity's image, and joined in other religious ceremonies.

The expectation that Mesopotamian society had of its female ritual functionaries was that they be chaste; hence, as far as can be ascertained from the evidence available, no female priest had a sexual role in ritual, excepting possibly the *entu*. Female priests were probably necessary at most, if not all rituals, for female-male complementarity in priests, as in deities, seems to have been the Mesopotamian norm.

Ancient Syro-Palestine and the Bible

Until recently, most scholars considered Canaanite religion to have been orgiastic and to have involved sexual promiscuity for both priests and worshipers. The scholars came to this conclusion from their interpretation of the Hebrew Bible's pronouncements on Canaanite religion and, to a lesser extent, from information gleaned from later sources, such as the Greek historian Herodotus (ca. 480–ca. 425 BCE), the Greek travel writer Strabo (ca. 64 BCE–19 CE), and some Christian writers. However, the late writers were describing Mesopotamian customs, not Canaanite ones; furthermore, they were writing well over a millennium after the period they were describing. Yet, many modern scholars have used these sources to bolster their view that female religious functionaries must *ipso facto* be prostitutes. In addition, one kind of Mesopotamian female priests, the *qadishtu*, was understood, on no evidence, to be a "sacred prostitute." This allowed these scholars to interpret the term *qedeshah* in the Hebrew Bible as "sacred prostitute."

The Greek satirical writer Lucian (ca. 115–ca. 200 CE) also had a great influence on these scholars. It was Lucian who portrayed similar religious functionaries in Syro-Palestine. According to him, during rituals of mourning for Adonis, women normally shaved their heads. Those refusing to do so had to put themselves up for sale in a "foreigners-only market" for one day. Whatever fee they received they then offered to the female deity Astarte. Of course, this "evidence" is not only considerably later than the time in question, but these modern scholars seem to have forgotten that Lucian was a skilful satirist, who almost certainly did not expect everything he wrote to be taken seriously.

Qdsh, the root of the Mesopotamian Semitic word *qadishtu*, means "holy, sacred"; the same root is found in the word *qedeshah* in the Hebrew Bible. Thus, both words should mean "holy" or "sacred woman" and not "sacred prostitute," as much modern scholarly literature maintains.

In some of the Ugaritic tablets, there are listed titles of a few religious functionaries, although none is grammatically in the feminine gender. Probably, the masculine gender form, at Ugarit as elsewhere, was understood to encompass both male and female. The *qdshm*, "holy persons," seem to have formed a significant priestly group, for in lists they occur second after the *khnm*, "priests." The group possibly included women. The *qdshm* were of high status; they could marry and hold other positions.

A category of female priest, the *qedeshah*, seems to have been important in Canaan. If not, it makes little sense for the writers of the Hebrew Bible to trouble themselves with attacking them. What their part was in Canaanite religion is at present unknown, but it is very likely that they were religious functionaries, as their Mesopotamian equivalents.

The Hebrew Bible makes explicit reference to female religious functionaries within the Israelite tradition. Two are cast in negative terms. *Ob* or mediums, as well as *yiddeoni*, those who work with a familiar spirit, perhaps shamans, are to be stoned to death. Why this should be so is far from clear. Nevertheless, Saul, the first Israelite king, seeks out a female medium, the so-called "Witch of Endor," in order to obtain advice from a dead prophet, Samuel. A third type of female religious functionary is the *nebiah* (female prophet). A number are mentioned in the Hebrew Bible, from Miriam, the sister of Aaron, to Deborah, who was also a *shaphat* (judge or governor), and there is mention of them in the New Testament as well. In the Gospel of Luke, there is reference to an Anna, a *prophetis* (in Greek), who lived in the Temple when Jesus as a child was understood to have been brought to Jerusalem. Apparently, women, although infrequently mentioned in the Bible, had religious roles throughout the Israelite period, including in the Temple.

FEMALE SELF-UNDERSTANDING

Because the literary records we have were almost certainly written by males and male oriented and because none of these cultures have continued to the present, even in an attenuated form, it is virtually impossible to capture more than a glimpse of female hermeneutics from the ancient Mesopotamian and Syro-Palestinian cultures. Nonetheless, a few small points can be made.

Whether or not the Biblical *qedeshah* had a sexual function in ritual, it is relatively certain that, in ancient Mesopotamia in early times, at least one category of female religious functionary, the *entu* priest, did engage in sexual intercourse as the central act of the major fertility rite. This female priest almost certainly incarnated a female deity on earth. In the temple-complex she was surrounded by other female priests with varied roles and functions, most of whom were also not expected to become mothers. They served as priests in a religious institution that practiced complementarity in female and male roles; the "Sacred Marriage Rite" is a major example.

As far as is known at present, female and male deities in Canaanite religion were also complementary, a complementarity necessary to the maintenance of world order. Ugarit provides an example of complementarity on the human level: both the king and the queen took part in central state rituals, normally not together, but both understood as equally essential to the proper ordering of human affairs (as was the case in the Chinese, African, and Incan empires discussed in this book). It is likely that a similar complementarity was practiced in the Canaanite religion so vilified by the Hebrew Bible. For example, the Hebrew Bible presents the male deity Baal as having a close relationship with the female deity Ashtoreth (Astarte); they are usually mentioned together in the same phrase.

There were clearly female religious functionaries in Israelite religion. Some, particularly mediums and possibly shamans, were abhorred by the male authors and editors of the Hebrew Bible. Others, female prophets, were looked upon with favor. Given the ubiquity of female figurines in association with religious sites both within and without the home, there seems to be a hidden stream of female spirituality throughout Israelite religion, for which we have but tantalizing glimpses.

Finally, female spirituality continued well into the time when the Hebrew Bible was being created; for example, Susan Ackerman has pointed to a major mode of women's religion, suggesting

> that the women of Judah and Israel had a rich religious tradition. The women of early sixth-century Judah, for example, devoted themselves to the worship of a goddess called the Queen of Heaven. Indeed, although the prophet Jeremiah makes the women of Judah and Jerusalem the object of his special scorn due to their devotion to the Queen of Heaven, the women are steadfast in their worship of the goddess: baking cakes "in her image" as offerings and pouring out libations and burning incense to her.[2]

Part II
East Asia

The celestial movements provide teachings . . . [At the sacrifices,] the ruler is at [the top] of the steps [of the eastern hall]; the principal wife is at the [most western] chamber. The Great Brightness (Sun) comes up in the east; the Moon comes up in the west. This is the differentiation of Yin and Yang and the principle of husband and wife. The ruler [facing west] offers wine in a vessel decorated with an elephant (a symbol of male fecundity: thunderstorm), the wife [facing] east offers wine in a vessel [decorated with clouds and mountains] (female symbol: earth). The rituals proceed with mutuality above [the stairs] and the musicians respond to each other below [the sacrificial hall]. Thus, harmony is achieved.

—from the archaic Chinese *Record of Rituals*
translation by J. Paper

4
TRADITIONAL CHINESE RELIGION

INTRODUCTION

C HINESE CULTURE IS THE LONGEST CONTINUOUS CULTURE for which we have a literary record. Archaeology has provided us with a growing body of oracular texts from approximately 3500 years ago, and we have limited extant texts from 3000 years ago, plus a voluminous body of literature of divers sorts from 2000 years ago to the present. Because of the separation of the written and spoken languages, China not developing an alphabetic script, the extant texts could be read by all the educated until very recent times. Indeed, the earliest of these texts formed the basis of education for the elite into the twentieth century. China is also the largest single human culture today, being the culture of nearly a quarter of all living people. Hence, the analysis of Chinese religion not only affords us with the best recorded model for the development of religion with regard to sex/gender but also provides understanding of a significant portion of humanity. Furthermore, Chinese culture had a notable effect on the surrounding cultures, and both Korean and Japanese religion will be later discussed in regard to the theme of this work.

At the time of the earliest surviving oracular writings, Chinese culture was a fully developed civilization in the technical use of the term, with a stratified, hierarchical society; intensive agriculture; walled administrative and manufacturing centers; and political hegemony of one of these centers over others. By the time of the production of a large body of writings, China had become an empire, with a large portion of the planet's readily inhabitable land under the control of a single, bureaucratic government, with an increasingly unified culture, and outlying regions subject to the center's military sway due to superior military technology. Two thousand years ago, there were three empires controlling much of the temperate areas of Eurasia, from west to east: China, Parthia, and Rome.

All of these empires were patriarchal, but patriarchy is not, as commonly misunderstood, a monolithic cultural trait. There are many kinds of patriarchy, and few include what is usually considered normative to patriarchy in Western cultures: Christian misogyny. Chinese culture provides us with a major example of a non-western patriarchal situation and its effects, or lack of effect, on the culture's religion. And these are effects which we can trace over a longer period of time than for any other extant culture.

From the beginning of Chinese civilization, we have a sociopolitical pattern of an aristocracy composed of hereditary professional warriors organized into patrilineal clans. The clan chieftain of the politically superior clan took the title *wang*, normally translated as "king," and later, with the first empire, the title *di*, usually translated as "emperor." The Chinese term for the clan name, the surname, is a composite of two glyphs, one meaning female and one meaning birth. Under the influence of the seminal nineteenth century anthropologist, Morgan, and his theory of an early matriarchy in the development of human culture, which was adopted by Engels, the primary formulator of Marxist social theory, this glyph was understood to indicate a primordial Chinese matriarchy. While theories of early matriarchal cultures have long been discredited, the glyph for surname possibly indicates that Chinese clans were matrilineal prior to the shift from horticulture to agriculture, as is the norm for horticultural societies.

Unfortunately, we have no data for the nature of the shift from matrilineal clans to patrilineal clans, assuming such a shift actually occurred. By the time we are aware of early Chinese socio-economic patterns, in theory at least, males did the farming and women the spinning and weaving of cloth. In actuality, as was certainly the case later, among the peasantry, while males did much of the farming, everyone helped out as needed.

More important with regard to religion is that, until about two thousand years ago, only the aristocracy was organized into clans. In early China, warfare had become professionalized; that is, martial technology had reached the point of development that required years of training, leading to specialization. It seems that the control of flooding through damming large rivers and the use of widescale irrigation led to sufficient surplus agricultural production to support a non-producing class to both protect and organize the population. It is to be noted that the tools of this class included not only the war-chariot (which diffused from Indo-European speaking peoples to China's west), and the compound-recurve bow with thumbring, but brush and ink as well, all but the first indigenous inventions. These developments may be responsible for a shift from small-scale horticultural societies organized into matrilineal clans to a larger, differentiated society divided into a producing population (farmers, miners, craftspersons, etc.), of whose social organization we are not aware, and a non-producing population of warrior-officials, organized into patrilineal clans. Either the concept that males farmed, providing the necessities of life, or that the clans were oriented towards professional warriors, predominantly males in all human societies could have led to a patrilineal social order; the combination ensured that development.

The early Chinese clans were not simply a sociopolitical structure, they formed the basis of religion as well. From the distant past to the present, Chinese religion is indistinguishable from family *per se* to the degree that some authors have termed the religion "familism." In distinction from Indo-European and Semitic language cultures in the main, Chinese religion did not develop a separate class of priests, although there were some religious specialists (diviners, non-family mediums, etc.) of moderate social status.

From the standpoint of ideology, the clans had origin myths, the few surviving from the early period involving the impregnation of a human woman by a male bird or bird-headed spirit. The result of this union was the male clan founder, often a culture-hero. Rituals focused on the feeding of the dead members of the clan, both males and females married into the clan, by the living members of the clan so that the dead members of the clan would insure the prosperity of the clan, with regard to harvest, military success, and children, for the continuance of the clan. Hence, those that carried out the rituals were the clansmembers themselves, including females married into the patrilocal clans. We will return to this theme in the section on rituals.

How this religion related to the non-aristocracy in the early period is unclear, but there are hints in the very early sacrificial odes that the non-aristocracy was attached to the aristocratic clans and received benefits from their rituals. Approximately two thousand years ago, the entire population of China took on surnames, the relatively few of the aristocratic clans of that time, and the religion of familism become the major religion and the unifying factor of Chinese culture.

Beginning about twenty-five hundred years ago, the grounds for entering government service slowly shifted from an hereditary basis to one based on ability and merit; preparation involved learning a set body of texts. After a failed *coup d'etat* twelve hundred years ago, military roles became subordinate to civil offices, and, about a thousand years ago, the civil-service examination system for choosing government officials, who were also subsidiary priests to the emperor and his spouse as chief priests of humankind, reached its fully developed form. Nonetheless, the ancient term for an hereditary, professional, aristocratic warrior, *shi*, continued as the term for scholar and the non-hereditary class of government officials and never lost its martial characteristics—a sword was an essential furnishing in a scholar-official's study. This, in large part, accounts for government offices remaining a male prerogative. Again, we shall return to these points in the concluding part of this chapter.

The above thumbnail depiction of Chinese religion is considerably at odds with typical Western depictions of Chinese religion. These depictions emphasize a trinity of Chinese religions rather than a single one, although no other unitary culture in the world is understood to have multiple religions. Indeed, given that Chinese culture is the most homogeneous for a very large population, it is inexplicable how there could not be a single underlying religion. These so-called "Three Religions of China" exclude 99% of Chinese religious practices. The concept was invented because sixteenth and seventeenth century Jesuit missionaries in China accepted government offices, which, in part, entailed participation in Chinese state rituals, and they converted officials and members of the imperial family who continued to carry on normative Chinese religion. The solution was to interpret the term *sanjiao*, "Three Teachings," as "Three Religions" and ignore Chinese religion *per se*, hence, avoiding being charged with heresy by the Church (at least for a time).

This understanding continued in the West as it accorded with Western assumptions about religion: that religions have founders, that these founders are male, that religions have a body of sacred texts, and that they focus on transcendence. Buddhism is understood to be founded by Gautama Buddha and has a body of texts attributed to the Buddha, and Daoism was incorrectly understood to be founded by a Laozi ("Old Master"), whose white-bearded image harmonized nicely with Renaissance images of Yahweh; Daoism also has a set of (ever-changing) scriptures. Confucianism was made up on the spot and understood to have a founder, Confucius, and scriptures, the Classics. Actually, the Jesuits conflated two terms: *rujia*, the evolving ideology of the civil-service system, with the Classics as the basis of education for the civil-service examinations, and *kungjiao*, temples in major administrative centers dedicated to Confucius and other predominant figures in the development of *rujia* ideology, that countered Buddhist and Daoist temples with those directly connected with the state. All of these religious modes functioned as optional adjuncts to the central aspect of Chinese religion discussed in this and the following chapter.

Given the immense period of time and the enormous size of the population involved, a continuous and thorough analysis of these developments would be a major study in itself. Accordingly, we will sample the subject of this study. There will be some reference to archaeological finds and the earliest texts for the period preceding the first empire, the Han (202 BCE–220 CE); some focus on the Han dynasty, the formative period of Chinese culture; and discussion of the Song dynasty (960–1279), where general aspects of the pattern for the next thousand years of traditional culture solidified (it should *not* be understood that Chinese culture was thereafter static). The period of the last hundred years, for which we have ethnographic studies and a religion that is readily observable, will be treated in the following chapter.[1]

FEMALE SPIRITS

The Western Invention of a Chinese High God

A reading of world religions textbooks, let alone the majority of Western general texts on Chinese religion, would leave the impression that Chinese religion adheres to what in the West is understood to be normative to all civilized religions, an anthropomorphic, male, singular, supreme deity. This deity was understood to be named *di* or *shangdi* (usually translated as "God") to about three thousand years ago and *tien* (translated as "Heaven") thereafter.

Given the textual contexts of the terms, *di* more likely means nonanthropomorphic "Power" and *shangdi* means "Supreme Power" or "Power Above." One scholar has presented a plausible argument that these terms referred to the combined and abstracted spiritual power of the clan ancestors (which would include female as well as male ancestors). As the *shen* souls (see below for explanation) rose above and became the "bright spirits" which descended to possess the Incorporator of the Dead at the time of sacrifice (or the sacrifice was understand to ascend to the sky to the *shen* in an earlier period), it would make sense that *shangdi* was a generic term for the ancestral spirits above. Hence, the same term later utilized to replace *wang* (king) for the ruler of the first empire, usually translated as "emperor," would be the equivalent of *tienzi* (see below), "Son of Sky," meaning king or emperor.

Tien was extracted from the binomial expression *tiendi*, "Sky (Heaven) and Earth." As early as the beginning of the seventeenth century, Chinese scholars objected to Jesuits ignoring the female Earth in the pair and further noted that the Jesuits objected to Chinese sacrificing to Earth but did not object to their sacrificing to Sky ("Heaven"). Since that time, translations of the term *tiendi*, even by feminist scholars, tend to capitalize the "H" in Heaven but not the "E" in Earth. Clearly, to most Western scholars, only a male cosmic power is worthy of respect.

The meaning of *di*, "Power," is still not definite, but it can be at least pointed out that there is no evidence in the Chinese context for the Western interpretive translation. With regard to *di-*"Earth" (an entirely different Chinese word), we can be more definite, since the spirit is still of major importance in the Chinese understanding.

The concept of Sky and Earth as sexed major cosmic powers is mentioned in China's oldest literary text, the early strata of the *Yi*, "Changes," which is nearly three thousand years old. In this text, the first hexagram refers to Sky and the second to Earth. In this regard, some scholars have noted that, given the ordering, Earth is subsidiary to Sky. Certainly the order of reference is fixed, but the import is far from clear. After the full development of the Yin-Yang concept, about twenty-three hundred years ago, Chinese cosmogony, as a continual process, has been understood in this wise as follows: Humans (and all things) receive their form from Sky and Earth and their life-force from Yin and Yang. Hence, the order of male-female in Sky-Earth is balanced by the reversed order of female-male in Yin-Yang.

Since the Han dynasty, sacrifice to Sky and Earth has been the prerogative of the Emperor and Empress, as they are the chief sacrificers for all of humankind (the traditional Chinese understanding being that China is the center of the world and the only civilization). Lesser rulers could sacrifice at altars dedicated to Soil and Grain, but for anyone other than the Emperor-Empress to sacrifice to Sky and Earth was considered treason. Nevertheless, Sky and Earth are not the most important traditional Chinese spirits.

Ancestors

According to the *Liji* (Record of Rituals), the Han dynasty manual of elite rituals that became part of the Classics, humans developed cooking and clothing in order to better serve the *gueishen shangdi*. China, typical of shamanistic cultures, as very early China was, understood humans to have two souls. In shamanism, two souls explains how one can travel in spirit leaving the body without the body dying: one soul travels and one remains giving life to the body. These souls are the *guei*, which on death resides with the corpse in the earth, and the *shen*, which ascends to join the collective of ancestors, to which *shangdi* probably refers. (*Guei* alone does not refer to ancestral spirits but the spirits of non-family, while *shen* alone can refer to the compound *gueishen*.) Sacrifices are offered to bring down the dead spirits of the family, including the first ancestor, but specific parts of the meal are dedicated to *shen* and to *guei*. In the clan temple (and in the homes of non-aristocrats), name tablets of the dead are placed on an altar, before which sacrifices are offered.

Ancestral spirits include both males and females, and, accordingly, *shangdi* includes males and females. The *Liji* provides explicit instructions on the place-ment of the tablets of all the members of the family, including the primary wife, secondary wives and concubines. All became ancestral spirits, and to all sacri-fices were offered. Although this is crystal clear in the ritual text, Western writ-ings on Chinese religion, when they mention sacrifice at all, tend to imply that the ancestral spirits are all male; i.e., Western notions of absolute patriarchy are read into Chinese patriarchy, which, as discussed in the concluding part of this chapter, is quite different.

Rituals that transform the living into ancestors, that is, burial rites, similarly are the same for males and females. During the centuries surrounding the com-pilation of the *Liji*, tombs of the aristocratic females and males are equal in size and sumptuousness. Even earlier, a very early Chinese tomb for a female was found with sufficient martial furnishings to suggest to scholars that she was a general.

The understanding expressed in the *Liji* is far from archaic. It will be found in Zhu Xi's *Jiali* (Family Rituals). Compiled by the foremost *rujia* theorist of the Song dynasty, it became the standard manual for ancestral sacrificial rituals into the twentieth century. Male and female ancestral tablets continued to be paired to today in all Chinese homes where the culture continues. Hence, the family dead are the object of the vast majority of Chinese ritual practices, the sacrifi-cial meals offered to the ancestral spirits, both male and female. These are the most important spirits in Chinese religion.

Earth

As mentioned above, sacrifice to *tiendi* was the prerogative of the ruler. Usually the sacrifice was at a single altar, but at times it was split into two. In present-day Beijing, following the ritual prescriptions, the Altar to Sky (termed "Heaven" in the literature) is south of the Inner City and the Altar to Earth to the north (balanced by an Altar to Sun to the east and an altar to Moon to the west). This pattern was created in the late Ming dynasty (sixteenth century) and continued in the last dynasty, the Qing. Both are open platforms, the Altar to Sky being round and surfaced with stone, and the Altar to Earth square and made of earth. In the compound of the Altar to Sky is a beautiful round temple often misidentified in guide books as the Altar to Sky. But this building is the Temple for Good Harvests and possesses a superb intertwining of round and square (sky and earth symbols) structural elements throughout.

The entrance to the former imperial palace is flanked by the imperial clan temple to the east and the Altar to Soil and Grain to the west (both now public parks), again following ancient ritual prescriptions. This balance further exemplifies the continual and conscious sex balancing in Chinese religion. For the clan temple is for rituals to the patrilineal clan ancestors, although they equally contain the tablets of females married into the clan, and the Altar to Soil and Grain, with its square, open earthen altar, focuses on a female spirit. Subsidiary rulers were allowed this altar during China's semi-feudal period.

Ordinary people, particularly farmers, had shrines in their farm fields to Earth. On the altars in their homes, there was an image of Earth, as well as the ancestral tablets. While we do not know how Earth in this mode was conceptualized in early China, for the last several hundred years at least, Earth in farm fields and farmhouses is portrayed as a couple: *tudipo-tudigung*, Grandmother and Grandfather Earth, an elderly married couple. This symbolism reinforces the Chinese understanding that fertility requires the conjoining of male and female essences and energies.

It is in another guise that Earth is portrayed as male, and this has led many Westerners to assume that Earth in China is a male deity, as these same observers assume that every aspect of Chinese religion is male or male oriented. As Chinese government became increasingly bureaucratic, so the world of spirits, particularly the realm of the dead, became understood in bureaucratic terms. With the assimilation of aspects of Buddhism was adopted the notion of heavens and hells (as way-stations not permanent abodes); these became understood on the model of the Chinese governmental apparatus. Folktales tell of a woman who died and was sent back to the world of the living because she did not have the correct stamp in her passport.

Because Chinese bureaucrats, as discussed above, were males, so the deity of earth, as an official governing the realm of the corpse and the *guei* soul, was portrayed as male. Throughout the southern part of China, alongside the graves will be found a shrine to *houtu*, the Lord of Ground. When portrayed by an image rather than the written title, it is of a male with a long, white beard. This image is easy to spot and led foreigners to understand that the Chinese view Earth as male. But Earth is male only in regard to Earth being the repository of the corpse, and this was most likely a development following the reinterpretation of the abode of the corpse as being in the control of a male bureaucracy.

Houtu was considered male at least by the Song dynasty, but earlier, during the Han dynasty, the deity was female, for the emperor sacrificed to *houtu* in a parallel ceremony to the sacrifice to Sky. At that time, she was also called *houtu fuao*, Sovereign Earth-Mother of Happiness. In the popular mind to today, the deity is known as *houtu niangniang*, Sovereign Earth Mother. (*Niangniang* is difficult to translate; it is formally used for an older woman who is a mother, but, informally within the family and in many but not all regions of China, the term means "mama.")

Creator and Other Fertility Deities

In the chapter on Native American religions, I will be discussing a particular female image that may represent Earth; it is found throughout the Americas, from the southern Andes to Alaska. Two small pottery images seemingly related to this image were excavated in 1979 at Dongshanzui in Liaoning Province (Manchuria). These images have been interpreted by Chinese scholars as pregnant; however, this interpretation is certain for but one of the two. The excavated images were found on a circular platform, 2.5 m. in diameter, probably an outdoor altar, of stamped earth framed by worked stones. Nearby is a rectangular platform, 11.8 by 9.5 m., similarly constructed, with carved jade images found in the foundation.

Elsewhere in Liaoning Province, at Niuheliang, during the excavation of what was probably a temple complex, a life-sized, pottery head, typically northern Chinese, was found in the central hall. It was associated with other body parts including a breast, indicating that this was part of a complete, life-sized female body. The back of the head is flat, and a wooden support was attached to it, suggesting the statue stood against a wall. Parts of six images of varying sizes, some smaller and some larger, were also found. Some or all of these were females kneeling or sitting cross-legged. In one of the upper-arm pieces, a human bone was found. Burial mounds and underground tombs were found in conjunction with the structures; but the archaeological work is far from complete. Both Liaoning sites are associated with the Hongshan culture of 6000–4500 years ago, which is related to the Yangshao culture, one of the precursors of Chinese civilization.

Since then, female images have been excavated in Hebei and Shanxi Provinces in northern China. The latter image was found in a pit with male figurines and was wrapped in woven material with pig bones, jade rings, carved bones, a pearl necklace, and other jade pieces. Chinese scholars have variously interpreted these images as (1) female ancestors, particularly Nüwa, to be discussed below, (2) a fertility deity, (3) the Earth Mother, (4) agricultural deities, etc. All are possible, and many are interrelated. What can be noted for certain is that female images, as elsewhere in the world, have been found at a number of early sites in China (some seven to eight thousand years old) and undoubtedly connote female fertility spirits of divers sorts. Also, as in other parts of the world (see chapter on Anishnabe religion), petroglyphs of vulva have been found, particularly in caves, in many parts of China.

Nüwa is an ancient Chinese goddess, who is still a major fertility deity today; pilgrimages to her main temple will be discussed in the next chapter. Literally, her name means "female melon" (*wa = gua*); the melon/gourd is a fertility symbol worldwide. In a fourth-century text, the *Baopuzi*, it is said that Nüwa comes out of Earth (*Nüwa di chu*); in other words, she is an Earth deity. And from earth, the yellow earth of the north China plain, she created humans. But in myths, she also repaired the sky-vault with five-colored stones (five being the sacred Chinese number since the Han dynasty) and controls the earth. She is primarily worshiped today, as are most fertility deities, by women who desire male children to perpetuate the patrilineal family line. Her cosmic role continues, because she is understood to be the grand ancestor of all humans, either alone or in an incestuous relationship with her brother, Fuxi. When portrayed together, they are depicted as humans with lower torsos of snakes, their tails intertwined.

During the Han dynasty and for centuries thereafter, although she is mentioned in the literature much earlier, the most important deity is the King Mother of the West (*xi wang mu*). The usual Western translation, "Queen Mother of the West," is misleading, for *wang* is a title for a male ruler. Certainly, the title makes clear her supreme power. As for the "West" in her name, from the perspective of comparative religion, the meaning is quite obvious. In many cultures, the West, as the place where the sun sets, is the realm of female power, the beginning of night, while the East, where the sun rises, is a place of male power. In Pawnee religion, as one of many examples, Morning Star is a male spirit and Evening Star is female. Other examples are mentioned in this book. Many images pair her with the King Father of the East as a couple. Her title, as well as the images themselves, signify that they are of equal status. In the earliest Chinese history (*Shiji*—1st century BCE), the well-known story of King Mu travelling on a tour of inspection, meeting her, and becoming so ecstatic that he forgot his kingdom, also indicates her equality with, if not superiority to, earthly kings.

She is also Earth, as, in many versions of her myth, she resides in a cave. Again, this accords with the ubiquitous mythic pattern of Sun rising in the east, travelling across the day sky to enter Earth in the west, where Sun abides with Earth until Sun again rises in the east at dawn (see the chapter on Hopi religion for another example). The King Mother of the West is also associated with Mt. Kunlun, a mythic mountain variously identified in different parts of western China, which in myth functions as the pivot of the world.

When she is described or depicted in images, an important symbol is her special headdress, the *sheng*, which seems to be two spools used in weaving joined by a horizontal rod, with threads attached to the spools. When she is depicted with the King Father of the East, both are wearing this headdress. This has multiple implications. First, weaving and web-spinning as creation are paired in many cultures. In a number of African and Native American traditions, Spider is a female creator who is also connected to human weaving. Secondly, as far back as our records go for Chinese culture, male labor was plowing and female labor spinning. As in imperial rituals, the Emperor plows the first furrow of spring at the altar to the First Agriculturist, so the Empress spins silk at the altar to the First Sericulturist. Finally, two constellations of the Chinese heavenscape, the Weaving Maid and the Oxherd Boy, a mythic complex referred to in the *Shi*, one of the oldest extant Chinese texts, is also linked to the King Mother of the West. In some stories, she is the grandmother of the Weaving Maid. This mythic and ritual complex is very rich, and the reader is recommended to Michael Loewe's penetrating analysis of the relationship of the King Mother of the West to the cycling of the seasons.[2]

In the year 3 BCE, a movement directed towards the King Mother of the West swept through China. Perhaps instigated by the passing of a massive meteor or a comet, large crowds of people gathered at the capital and in administrative centers to hold rituals to her. Written talismans promising immortality from the King Mother for people who wore it were widespread. Both she and the King Father of the East are in some instances portrayed with symbols that indicate their control over the search for longevity, an important religious goal among the elite at that time. Until about eleven hundred years ago, she seems to have been the most important deity to assist women in achieving this aim; a number of stories of women who became "immortals" have survived.

The King Mother of the West is mentioned in many poems and other writings and features in many different myths. The preceding is but a sampling of the many roles she has in Chinese religion: Earth deity, creatrix, weaving deity, controller of the world and its seasons, etc.

Euhemeristic Goddesses

Particularly from the Song dynasty on, most Chinese deities, other than the ancestral spirits, are the *shen* soul of deceased humans. These deities have biographies of their lives while living, either mythic or from historical records, and their specific spiritual powers relate to their past life. As examples, protecting and martial deities were famous generals, famous magistrates become judicial spirits, famous scholars become patrons of education and success in the civil-service examinations, famous physicians become healing spirits, etc. But others have lives not to be found in the historical records or biographies of noted Daoist adepts, Buddhist monks, exorcists, etc.

Because becoming an ancestor is dependent upon the living carrying out the proper transitional rites (mortuary rituals) and continued nurture (sacrificial rituals), there are those dead who become *guei*, "ghosts" (not to be confused with the compound expression *shenguei*, "ancestral spirits"). By the Song Dynasty, this notion had become amalgamated with the Buddhist concept of "wandering ghosts."

Ghosts included those who died a violent death yet to be avenged and suicides, as well as those uncared for by family. Most suicides, as will be discussed below, were female. Although unmarried female dead were cared for by their natal families in the early period, by the Song dynasty, unmarried females were cared for by no one. By that time, females were not understood to belong to their natal families; hence, there developed the practice of spirit marriages, where a living male married a dead unmarried female so that her souls could be cared for by his family.

Chinese religion is mediumistic; communication with the spirit realm, particularly ancestral spirits and effective deities, takes place with the assistance of spirit mediums who allow themselves to be possessed by required spirits. Ghosts seem to have a propensity to possess people against their will; exorcists conduct rituals to rid persons of these evil emanations. But sometimes ghosts on possessing individuals prove themselves beneficial to the individual, the person's family, or the community. The community elevates these ghosts to the status of deities. A small temple may be built. If others find themselves benefitted by this deity, they will show their gratitude by contributing to a larger, more magnificent temple. People in other communities may be possessed by this spirit, and the deity's fame will spread. A few reach national recognition, and then the imperial court will grant royal titles to the deity.

Given that the majority of ghosts are probably unmarried females, it is not surprising that the most popular non-family Chinese deities were unmarried females while alive. Today, the two most important of these deities are Guanyin and Mazu. Although each goes back to the Song dynasty, because of their contemporary importance, they will be discussed in some detail in the next chapter on contemporary Chinese religion.

Discussion

In the differing types of early Chinese deities, sex varies in consequence. The ancestral spirits are equally male and female but not of equal importance. Since the clans are patrilineal, there is more of a focus on the male founder of the line. Secondly, because of the different sex social roles of the aristocracy to be discussed later—males being warriors converted to government officials, and females being in charge of the household—males bring far more prestige to the clan—both living and dead—than do females; the male ancestors are more important to the fame and fortune of the clan. Hence, while sacrifices are equally presented to males and females among the immediate dead (one to five generations, depending on the social status of the living); there is far more mention of the male ancestors among the dead of the distant past.

For example, for the clan which ruled during the Zhou dynasty, from three thousand to nearly two thousand years ago, the most revered ancestors of the distant past were Houji (Lord of Millet—the northern Chinese grain staple), the male clan founder, and King Wu and King Wen, responsible for conquering the preceding ruling dynasty and instituting the Zhou dynastic kingdom. Female ancestors of the distant past were honored as progenitors; male ancestors were honored as mythic culture-heroes and as conquerors or for other accomplishments that brought power, prestige and wealth to the clan. Nevertheless, for the continued prosperity of the clan, it is the more immediate dead that are of utmost importance; both male and female ancestors affect the fortunes of the living.

Cosmic deities are understood in equal, sexed pairs; it is from the interaction of female and male cosmic forces that humans are conceived and continue to have life. It is not Chinese but Western patriarchal understanding that desacralized Earth from the pair Sky-Earth, and this fact, as will be discussed at the conclusion to this book, tells us much about the nature of Western patriarchy. Earth, in and of itself or abstractly as soil, is female, but Earth as agricultural land is perceived as a generating couple that can ensure the fertility of the fields.

Creator deities, rather than cosmic forces, seem to have been originally female, to whom a male is later added to form a creating couple. It is generally agreed by Chinese scholars that the understanding of the King Mother of the West is older than the King Father of the East and that Nüwa at first was a single deity before the appearance of her brother, Fuxi. The patriarchalizing tendencies of the elite culture tended to place more emphasis on the males of these pairs, but, as will be discussed in the next chapter, this was resisted by the popular culture, and all such attempts failed. As mothers give birth to humans, so the female deities are seen to have more power over birth and life than male ones; it is Nüwa alone who is more commonly understood as the ancestor of humanity.

While euhemeristic deities are of both sexes, with males predominating as protecting city, martial, judicial, etc., deities, those deities that provide the necessities of life and continue life by enhancing human fertility are invariably female, and these deities are the most important in the popular mind. Guanyin is ubiquitous over much of China as the one deity who appears along with the ancestral tablets on family, but not clan, altars; and an image of her, if not a separate shrine, will be found in virtually all temples—popular, Buddhist, and Daoist. Mazu is the major deity of southeastern China, including Taiwan; there are more temples dedicated to her than to any other deity. In homes and urban neighborhood or village temples, after the ancestral spirits, it is the female deities that receive the most attention, similar to Mary in Catholic cultures. This is not only because they are mother figures—ironic in that they were unmarried women when alive—but because it is women who carry out the rituals in the homes and far outnumber men in worshiping in these temples, as we will see in the following chapter.

In summary, males in the elite clans are usually oriented towards the famous male ancestors of the clan, while females, as will be discussed in the next section, are usually oriented towards the female ancestors of the clans into which they marry. But for the population as a whole, it is female deities that predominate in thought and ritual.

FEMALE RITUALS AND RITUAL ROLES

Three ritual texts were edited into their extant form during the Han dynasty, approximately two thousand years ago, and became part of the Five, later Thirteen, Classics, the basis of elite education for the civil-service examinations. These texts are the *Liji*, which focuses on the rituals of royalty; the *Yili*, which provides the rituals of the ordinary aristocrats; and the *Zhouli*, which is a descriptive list, probably idealistic, of all the offices of the preceding historical period. As we shall see in the concluding section, there was strict separation of the sexes in elite culture, including education. Males were to teach males, females to teach females. Hence, these texts were written by males for males and only tangentially refer to exclusively female rituals, but have a more complete account of those rituals in which males and females took part. We have no extant records of female teachings in these regards.

While these texts include elements that were already anachronistic at the time they were finally edited and romanticize an ideal past, they undoubtedly include much of the practices of the day. These ritual practices continued with little change in regard to those aspects that will be discussed in this section, for but minor changes can be found in Zuxi's *Family Rituals* of the Song dynasty, a thousand years later.

Female Rituals

Hairpinning Ceremony

Aside from childbirth rituals, which are not discussed in the ritual texts as they were not carried out by males, the only sex-specific rituals were those that denoted the transition from childhood to adulthood. Much has been made in Western writings on Chinese religion of an assumption that only elite males had such a ritual: the Capping Ceremony. Yet the *Liji*, in several places, mentions the parallel female Hairpinning Ceremony that seems to have slipped unnoticed by these scholars (including myself, until I did this research). Clearly, a particular hairpin, which the text mentions need not be worn with informal dress, was the female equivalent of the adult male formal cap. For both males and females, this ritual of status transition took place at the age of twenty (Chinese count). However, in one place the text gives the age of fifteen for females, and the ceremony is to take place whenever a young woman is betrothed if she has not reached the age of twenty. The ritual was conducted by the principal wife of the household, but no details are provided as they are for the equivalent male ritual.

Mixed Gender Rituals

Sacrifices

Chinese religion focuses on sacrificial rituals, sacrifices primarily directed towards the dead of the family, including mortuary rites. The Chinese focus on balance, particularly sex balance, requires equal participation of males and females in these sacrifices. This was so important that it was the theoretical purpose of marriage, at least from the standpoint of religion. In the *Liji*, we find the following passage:

Confucius said [in a discussion of funerals]: "The head of the clan [the eldest son on the death of the clan head], even if seventy years of age, must not be without a principal wife [to carry out the rituals]."

A prince, on asking for a consort from another prince, is to make the request as follows:

I request the ruler's elegant daughter to share my poor state, to serve in the ancestral temple and at the Altar to Soil and Grain.

The passage goes on to elucidate the sacrificial duties of husband and wife, constantly alternating their respective preparation for and activity in the sacrificial rites.

According to the *Liji*, the essential sex balance of the sacrificial celebrants models cosmic patterns:

The celestial movements provide teachings . . . [At the sacrifices,] the ruler is at [the top] of the steps [of the eastern hall]; the principal wife is at the [most western] chamber. The Great Brightness (Sun) comes up in the east; the Moon comes up in the west. This is the differentiation of Yin and Yang and the principle of husband and wife. The ruler [facing west] offers wine in a vessel decorated with an elephant (a symbol of male fecundity: thunderstorm), the wife [facing] east offers wine in a vessel [decorated with clouds and mountains] (female symbol: earth). The rituals proceed with mutuality above [the stairs] and the musicians respond to each other below [the sacrificial hall]. Thus, harmony is achieved.

Throughout the descriptions of the details of the sacrificial rituals, male and female activities are balanced and reciprocal. For some rituals, the ruler and his consort, together with clan members and their wives and the higher officials and their wives, carry out the various procedures in the sacrificial hall or at various altars. For other rituals, the ruler, etc., is in the clan ancestral temple, which is just outside the palace, while his consort is carrying out similar rituals in the inner chamber, modeling the practice and theory that males concern themselves with outer affairs, that is, matters outside of the household, while females concern themselves with inner, household, affairs.

The *Yili* text, which is written in more mundane prose and concerned with the details of the practices of the ordinary elite, confirms that the above were not just theoretical ideals. In describing the different sacrifices, in every case, there are parallel offerings by the wife of each celebrant with the same ritual. And when the wife pours wine for the celebrant to drink, the husband then pours wine for his wife to drink.

This text also clarifies the banquet that follows the ancestral sacrifices, where the living of the family eat the sacrificial food and drink the wine after the spirits have taken their fill. Western scholars have read the sacrificial odes of the earlier *Shi* (Odes) to the effect that only the men took part in the feasting and drinking. The *Yili* makes clear that, while the clansmen and their guests feasted in the outer hall, their wives were feasting in the inner, female, chambers.

In examining Zhu Xi's *Family Rituals* of a thousand years later, we find little change in the overall understanding of sex roles in sacrificial rituals. Both in the offering hall and at the grave site, males and females place themselves respectively to the east and the west. Rituals are presided over by the appropriate male and his wife, who each perform virtually the same rituals. One interesting change is due to the influence of Buddhism, aspects of which by this time were amalgamated into Chinese religion. As Buddhists avoided alcoholic beverages, tea became a popular drink. In the Song dynasty sacrifices, we find men offering wine and women offering tea. Spirit tablets continue for both female and male ancestors to five generations, and women handle the spirit tablets of females as men do those of males.

Ritual Roles

There were two important roles in the sacrificial rituals. First was the Descendant, the person who offered the sacrifice. Second was the Incorporator of the Dead, the person who was possessed by the ancestral spirit to whom the sacrifice was offered, who drank the wine and ate the food, and who was, for all intents and purposes at the time of the sacrifice, the honored dead. Since these ritual texts were written by and for males, the Descendant and the Incorporator of the Dead, when sex is mentioned, are almost always referred to as male. Fortunately, there is one passage in the *Liji*, which, in describing how a female is to receive a gift from a ruler, also provides the behavior she is to use when serving as an Incorporator of the Dead, as well as the circumstances in which she would be in this ritual role.

The strict separation of the sexes required that an elite individual of one sex would not be possessed by an ancestor of the opposite sex, nor would a male be the chief celebrant in the sacrifice to a female ancestor. When an ancestral sacrifice was to be held, the son of the deceased male or the daughter-in-law of the deceased female, with a specialist in divination, divined the appropriate day for the fast. During the preparations leading up to the sacrifice, including extended fasting and meditation, the Descendant, with other members of the family, divined which grandson or granddaughter-in-law should become the Incorporator of the Dead. We can but assume that during the sacrifice, as the wife supported the husband in his role of Descendant, so the husband supported his wife when she took on the role of Descendant.

There are other situations, mentioned in the *Liji*, in which a female would preside at sacrificial rituals. If there were no son, an unmarried female would preside at the funeral and subsequent sacrifices of her mother or father. Also, as mentioned earlier in this chapter, it must be noted that the ritual of the ruler ploughing the first furrow in the spring at the altar to the First Agriculturist was paralleled by the ruler's wife carrying out a spinning ritual at the altar to the First Sericulturist. Again, as this is a female ritual, no details are provided.

The *Zhouli*, in listing the duties of the many officials, also mentions female offices. In this regard, it must be understood that the king, and later the emperor, had multiple wives. In Chinese culture, because of the ideology of sex balance, there can be only one wife who is the equal of her husband, who is termed in this chapter, the principal wife. Multiple wives were essential to a ruler for two reasons: to insure a son for the patrilineal succession and to cement various political alliances that arose during a reign. Based on their natal families' status, these wives are termed wives of the second rank, of the third rank, and concubines. The latter were also members of the family into which they entered and had their tablets on death placed with the female ancestors of the family. (The one female emperor during the Tang dynasty—eighth century—had a harem of male concubines.)

All of these wives had official and ritual roles, and the following descriptions directly follow the *Zhouli* text. Wives of the second rank were to oversee the concubines with regard to their education, etc. They assisted in the sacrifices, with details provided in the text. When visitors were received, they accompanied the Queen or Empress (the wife of the first rank, the principal wife). During grand funeral ceremonies, they again accompanied and assisted the Empress.

Wives of the third rank were in charge of the preparation for sacrifices, funerals, and receiving visitors. They were in charge of the palace's female staff and the visitations required by the funerals of ministers and other high officials. The royal concubines aided the wives of the third rank in the preparations for sacrifices.

The palace staff included female ritual specialists to assist the above in carrying out their duties. These women seem to have been shamans and/or mediums, as they also functioned as exorcists to rid the inner chambers of any evil emanations and to drive away calamities, and they were to be able spiritually to create a felicitous atmosphere.

Government officials included female mediums. They were in charge of removing negative influences. In times of drought, they called down rain with special ritual dances. When the Queen made a visit of condolence, they walked in front of her with a male ritual specialist. When there was a great calamity, they chanted, cried, and supplicated the spirits. From other texts, we know that mediums were predominantly female and had important government roles which continued to the end of the first millennium of the common era.

FEMALE SELF-UNDERSTANDING

With a few exceptions, the texts that have come down to us are written by males and male oriented. Therefore, we will begin this section on the hermeneutics of femaleness in traditional Chinese culture not with the female understanding of females, but with the male theoretical understanding of femaleness. Of course, females, utilizing the same texts when educated and immersed in the same religion, probably shared this understanding. It is to be noted, however, that in later periods women far more than men tended also to be oriented towards Buddhism, suggesting that females were less satisfied with normative Chinese religion alone than were males.

In theory, males and females were completely equal; the human rulers were a pair modeling cosmic pairs. According to the *Liji*, "The Son of Sky (Emperor) manages the way (*dao*) of *yang* (male cosmic energy); the Empress governs the potency (*de*) of *yin* (female cosmic energy)." The ruler and his consort were equally important in the affairs of the world. Were he to neglect his duties in guiding males, there would be a solar eclipse; if she were to neglect her duties in guiding females, there would be a lunar eclipse: "Therefore, the Son of Sky is to the Empress as Sun is to Moon, as *yin* is to *yang*. When they are interdependent, all is complete." The Son of Sky and the Empress teach appropriate virtues to men and women respectively: "Therefore, it is said, 'The Son of Sky with the Empress are as the father and mother [of the people].'"

The female's status was not dependent on that of her natal family, but on that of her husband; she acquired the status of his family. In the *Liji*, we find the passage, "[Bridegroom and bride] eat together from the same [sacrificial] animal, [indicating] they have the same status. Therefore, the wife is without [her own] rank; she follows the rank of her husband." This is the most equality to be expected in this patrilineal, patrilocal social environment.

Males and females are theoretically equal but also to be strictly separated. Even fathers and daughters were not to sit together, and brothers-in-law and sisters-in-law cannot ask about each other. According to the *Liji*, "Matters spoken of on the outside should not enter the inner [female] part of the home; matters spoken of on the inside should not leave the inner part of the home." This sentiment was perhaps honored in theory, but, given the frequent role of women as political advisors to their husbands at that time, not likely to have been carried out in practice. When walking on the roads, a man was to pass on the right side and the woman on the left, with carriages taking up the middle of the road.

Was this theoretical separate but equal status, excluding the political realm, understood to go beyond ritual? The *Liji* indicates that, during the Han dynasty, women had far more freedom and individual status than they did later on in Chinese history. For example, if a woman died before the completion of the marriage ritual, she was sent back to her natal family to be buried among her relatives. Hence, at that time, an unmarried dead female was cared for by her natal relatives; this would not be the case later on, as pointed out in the above section on euhemeristic female deities. Moreover, a woman could divorce a man, as a man could a woman. In both cases, the situation had to be handled with great circumspection and without resistance among the powerful families, which were not to be angered. In the *Liji*, what a man says in this regard and the response of a woman's family are paralleled by a following passage which reverses the situation. Later in Chinese history, women would not have this freedom.

What about this supposed equality? What was the actual status of women? As discussed in the introduction to this chapter, Chinese culture, as far back as we can trace it, encompassed a hierarchal, stratified sociopolitical system. By the Han dynasty, this had become codified in several ways. At the top of the social classes was the imperial clan, so powerful that they were actually above the social structure. This class was followed by the noble families, followed by the bureaucratic/landholding aristocracy, followed by everyone else. Struggling for political power were also wealthy merchants, the families of imperial consorts, and powerful eunuchs employed in the inner quarters of the palace. This sociopolitical hierarchy did not stop at families; it also covered sex.

The creation of a stratified society based on martial training led to the formation of patrilineal clans that were the basis not only of political power but of religious power as well; it determined that females were subsidiary to males. First, with rare exceptions—women who took on male roles and titles—military and political power was in the hands of males. The segregation of elite males and females to the outer and inner parts of the residential compound, respectively, meant that all public expressions of power were male roles, although at times powerful females controlled the throne from inside the palace. Secondly, patrilineality meant that clan power went from male to male, and males of the clan alone were responsible for the continued prestige of the clan. Thirdly, patrilocality meant that young women left their natal families for the inner compounds of their husband's families where they began as strangers with no power base. (From the very early period of Chinese civilization, there are hints that when an aristocratic male married, he married the eldest daughter of a family, and she brought all her sisters with her as co-wives; that is, she brought her own power base with her.)

Finally, social stratification in the Chinese context included age. The oldest male in direct line of descent ruled the clan, as the eldest female ruled the inner part of the clan dwelling and its domestic operations, including the clan treasury. In the stated ethical norms from before the Han dynasty, sons are subservient to parents, younger brothers are subservient to elder brothers, and wives are subservient to husbands as ministers are subservient to the ruler. All should obey, yet remonstrate with their superior when they consider their superior to be wrong or taking an incorrect action. Hence, females were burdened with a double yoke; although equal in status to their husbands, they were to be subservient both to him and to the older females of his family. It is not surprising that the most common suicide was that of a young wife. A young elite male, browbeaten by overdomineering parents, paternal uncles, or older brothers, could at times escape to the exterior of the household or lose himself in governmental affairs; a female had no escape. Nor is it surprising that longevity became a major religious goal by the Han dynasty. Freedom, for both females and males, came only with becoming the eldest female and male of the family.

A male scholar-official, Fu Xuan, of the century following the Han, poignantly captured this disparity between the lives of elite men and women in the following poem:

> How sad it is to be a woman!
> Nothing on earth is held so cheap.
> Boys stand leaning at the door
> Like gods fallen from the sky.
> Their hearts brave the Four Seas,
> The wind and dust of a thousand miles.
> No one is glad when a girl is born:
> By her the family sets no store.
> When mature, she is confined to inner rooms,
> Ashamed that a man see her face.
> Tears shed for her when she goes to her husband's home
> Are brief as a sudden shower.
> She bows her head and composes her face
> Her teeth are pressed against her red lips:
> She bows and kneels countless times.
> She must humble herself even to the servants.
> . . . . [3]

Fortunately, we do have writings by a female of the Han dynasty.[4] Ban Zhao, the sister of the second major historian of China and daughter of a famous scholar, was herself so renowned as a scholar that the Emperor passed on to her the task of completing the history her brother was writing on his death (and which was begun by their father). She served as an instructor to the Empress, and several of her memorials to the Empress have survived, as have some of her poems. Most important, we have the brief manual she wrote for her daughters and other female members of her family towards the end of her life.

From this text, it is clear that her own upbringing, being trained in literature by her mother and female teachers, was not the normal one, for she pleads for the literary education of girls, not just boys. Nor, however, was she unique, for there were other famous female scholars in those days. As in the ideological texts, Ban Zhao understands *yin* and *yang* to exemplify the nature and appropriate behavior of females and males. The male mode of acting is to be forceful and unyielding; the female mode is to be gentle and yielding. This should not be understood as weakness. The *Daode-jing* (Classic of Dao-De/Laozi), compiled during the century preceding the Han, is a political manual teaching a ruler to control the world through the female principle: by being an unflagging void, by being underneath, by yielding. For Ban Zhao, by following the way (*dao*) of *yin*, a female fosters her natural power (*te*).

A woman's life is as a wife:

> The Way of husband and wife is intimately connected with *Yin* and *Yang*, and relates the individual to gods and ancestors. Truly it is the great principle of Heaven and Earth, and the great basis of human relationships. Therefore the "Rites" honor union of man and woman; and in the "Book of Poetry" the "First Ode" manifests the principle of marriage. For these reasons the relationship cannot but be an important one.

Yet it must also be a proper one; Ban Zhao considered a husband striking his wife grounds for divorce.

Ban Zhao taught that there were three primary aspects to a woman's life: she should practice humility, particularly before her in-laws; she should be industrious, particularly in the female tasks in her in-laws' household; and she is responsible for the maintenance of the sacrificial rituals, in her in-laws' home. Hence, while she understood the theoretical equality of males and females, particularly within marriage, she well comprehended that any happiness a female can have is in humble and obedient service to her husband's family.

Still, her own life provides exception to this teaching. Certainly, while married she was familiar with her brother's scholarship, and she accepted the commission from the emperor; of course, her husband's family could hardly contradict the emperor's edict. Undoubtedly, she understood just how exceptional her life was, for she taught her daughters to accept and take pride in a female's normal fate.

Another text compiled during the Han dynasty, the *Lienü-juan* (Biographies of Exemplary Women), although written by a male, also demonstrates that, throughout history to that time, there had been many women who had affected history. These brief accounts of legendary and mythic figures, mothers of the mythic founders of the ruling dynasties of the past, etc., as well as historical biographies, recount stories of mothers, wives, and daughters who through their advice and actions had considerable impact on the world around them.[5]

Elite women continued a somewhat independent life for over another millennium—two rose to the position of Emperor—maintaining links with their natal families as well as the family into which they married. In the supplementary religious traditions as well, women played important and relatively equal roles to males. Chinese Buddhist nuns had equal roles to monks, different from the southern Buddhist traditions, and many, certainly the majority of those for whom we have biographies, were literate and educated in the *sutra* tradition during the time frame under discussion (later monks and nuns were often illiterate).

Women served as Daoist priests, and some became noted adepts. Prior to the last few centuries, Daoist rituals required an equal number of male and female officiants; husbands and wives who were Daoist priests held the same ranks; and the transmission of office could be patrilineal or matrilineal. Initiation into the exalted rank of Master was for a married couple, not an individual, and consisted of an elaborate ritual involving the relationships between the female and male on an equal basis.[6] Hence, the Daoist rituals and rituals roles, with regard to sex, were similar to the imperial ones, and accord with Chinese ideological principles.

It is in the later dynasties, particularly the Ming (fourteenth to seventeenth centuries), with the adoption of rigidity in the civil-service education and the slow stultification of intellectual developments, that we also find increasing suppression of female independence. While widows in the earlier periods could, and often did, remarry, remarriage among elite women was no longer tolerated. A woman could no longer divorce her husband, although a man could divorce a woman if there were no children. The practice of footbinding, which had begun during the early Song dynasty as a fashion statement in imitation of the practice of dancers (the equivalent of the Western ballet shoe for dancers and spike-heeled shoes for others), became entrenched among elite females and, in effect, physically hobbled them to the inner chambers of the household. A late Ming dynasty manual for magistrates notes with concern that women are visiting temples and monasteries and recommends a number of measures:

> The magistrate should post notices to the effect that no woman is permitted to visit temples on the pretext of burning incense . . . Buddhist and Taoist [Daoist]

nuns should remain in their monasteries performing their religious services, and are not permitted to visit any household . . . Procuresses (marriage brokers) and sorceresses (*wu*, mediums) are parasites on the community; they should be banned and driven away. . . .[7]

Yet women still retained power within the inner quarters. The well-known 18th century semi-autobiographical Chinese novel, *Hungloumeng* (Dream of the Red Chamber, also entitled "Story of a Stone"),[8] was written by a male who preferred the inner female realm to that of males, to the disgust of his father. The novel provides us with a window into the inner chambers and gardens of a powerful and wealthy Chinese family. We find that the oldest female and her female assistants control the lives of the males, because they control the family treasury. It is they who decide what rituals the males can perform and what political alliances they can make. Females had not lost their *yin* power to balance the *yang* power of the males.

From the above synopsis, we can make only an intelligent guess as to the hermeneutics of femaleness in the traditional Chinese religion of the past; for the contemporary situation discussed in the next chapter, we have but to ask. There are many examples of female numinous power for women: half the cosmos is female, the majority of affective spirits are female, and they themselves will become ancestral spirits, crucial to the well-being of their families. Their children, particularly their sons, will revere them on their death as powerful spirits. During their lives, they are constantly involved in religious rituals and are responsible for the well-being of the family through their care of the ancestral shrine. At least through the Han dynasty, girls had a ritual to transform them into adults exactly parallel to that for boys. Prior to the Song dynasty, women experienced being the center of the rituals when sacrifices were made to their husband's mother and grandmother, and women took on the role of the Incorporator of the Dead and were possessed by the spirit to whom the sacrifice was offered. In the earlier periods, women had major governmental roles as mediums and continue to serve in this capacity on the popular level. Women had and have important roles in the Buddhist and Daoist churches. If they lived long enough, they would become family matriarchs, controlling from within the lives of their family members.

Most women probably were satisfied with their lives, expecting no other, if they were not made to suffer by the females of their husband's family upon marriage. Particularly if they had sons, their lives were full of respect and growing authority, authority that continued to grow after death as they were transformed from living humans into ancestors. But, as we know from other texts, particularly *Fusheng liuji* (Six Chapters from a Floating Life),[9] part autobiography and part biography of the author's wife, intelligent women oriented towards self-development could also be quite frustrated by their constrained life and reduced opportunities, particularly after the Song dynasty. Certainly, these women did not feel that their *yin* power matched *yang* opportunity.

The immense body of Chinese writings by males evidence all the possibilities of male-female interrelationships. Some ideologues were afraid of their own sexuality and avoided females. Indeed, after the influence of Buddhism, some blamed females for social ills. But others expressed concern about the increasing inequalities of females' lives and sought to change the culture in this regard.

Among ordinary people, life was hard, sometimes extremely so, for males and females alike. Some women became prostitutes and courtesans. The latter, if talented in music and literature, could achieve independence, fame, and wealth. For they offered a female companionship to aristocratic and wealthy merchant males which they could not find at home, where they were separated from females, who, over the course of history, tended to receive less and less education.

Relatively recently, it came to light that in a small area of south-central China, village women used a unique form of writing that had been kept secret from men.[10] Rather than the logographic nature of the Chinese writing system, this special writing used signs for syllables; it may have been invented in the Song period, about nine hundred years ago. Few examples have survived, the bulk apparently having been burned at the death of the women who wrote the various pieces to accompany them to the afterworld. The extant pieces are recent, being from the nineteenth and twentieth centuries.

The religious understanding found in these writings is little different from the general religious understanding of Chinese culture as a whole, with, of course, regional variations. One difference is the large number of references to Buddhist concepts, but this is not exceptional. As mentioned above, women tend to have been more oriented to the Buddhist aspect of Chinese religion than men. One reason is that women are but partially within the families of their husbands; they are always to a degree outsiders. Buddhism offers a non-family mode of religiosity. Another reason is that upper-class women had been confined to the family compound since the Song period, and Buddhist nuns were the only outsiders, other than servants, admitted to the inner quarters of the women, bringing not only religious teachings but news of the outside world.

These texts also refer to the many festivals, including those in which women would gather together away from men. At these times, the women would read from the secret texts. We also have explicit references to those times of the year when it was customary for women to return to their natal homes to make offerings to the departed of their natal families. Pilgrimages by groups of women to sacred sites, as will be detailed for other regions in the next chapter, are also described. The purposes and activities during these pilgrimages are again similar to the contemporary ones. Of interest is that in addition to the usual offerings, pieces of this special writing were also sacrificed. (The offering of writing in and of itself is common and as old as writing in China.) In essence, these writings confirm that non-elite women had as rich a religious life as elite women.

In summary, what we find in traditional Chinese culture and religion is that patriarchy was limited to the sociopolitical realm: all governmental offices, for reasons discussed above, were male roles, and women were increasingly confined to the inner world of family. Patriarchy did not affect religion, which, repeatedly and explicitly, posits an essential equality of male and female spirituality, both in the realm of the numinous and in ritual practices. For example, contrary to the wording of world religions textbooks, until the end of the imperial regime in the early twentieth century, both emperor and empress had to carry out the sacrificial rituals together. It is rather patrilineality which formed the pattern of Chinese "familism," so that females became ancestral spirits in their husband's families, and patrilocality which determined where females would carry out the bulk of their ritual roles. This is not to suggest that males and females had equal opportunities in their lives, but that females were spiritually equal to males, the opposite of the situation in the monotheistic traditions, as well as quite different from the attitudes of Buddhism and northern (Indo-European language) Hinduism. Except for a few odd, later *rujia* theorists, no loathing of women will be found in the enormous body of androcentric Chinese texts. The few writings of women that have survived reinforce the viewpoint that the texts written by males are not that different from the religious understanding of females.

5
CONTEMPORARY CHINESE RELIGION

with Li Chuang Paper
assisted by Wang Xiaoli and Yang Lihui[1]

INTRODUCTION[2]

THE PREVIOUS CHAPTER OUTLINED FEMALE SPIRITUALITY in traditional elite Chinese religion focusing on the period from the first major dynasty, the Han, approximately 2000 years ago, through the Song, approximately 1000 years ago, when traditional elite culture achieved the shape that continued into this century. Beginning with the Song dynasty, we also have some description of non-elite traditions, and some developments in this regard of the last few centuries were discussed. By the Song dynasty, elite status had become based on a series of civil-service examinations; hence, many families over time would shift in and out of the aristocracy. This led to a homogenization of religious practices between social classes, the differences tending to be quantitative rather than qualitative. That is, the differences between elite and non-elite religion was in the matter of the elaboration of sacrificial rituals, not with the rituals in and of themselves, excepting state rituals, which were limited to the imperial family and government officials, retired officials, and those qualified for officialdom who did not take up office.

Cultural homogenization was also taking place throughout China. During the Song dynasty, the political boundaries were similar to the cultural ones. In the previous dynasty, the Tang, and in the last, the Qing, as well as the present, the political boundaries are those of an empire and include regions that are only partially sinified. By the end of the Song dynasty, the thirteenth century, all of the area now considered Han (of Chinese culture) had assimilated a generalized Chinese culture, including religion. Although there are obvious regional differences in language and specific cultural practices, the use of a single written language and an essentially similar basic religion led to a degree of cultural uniformity unparalleled elsewhere with regard to both geographic size and historical depth. One of the government policies which enhanced this development, as we shall see, was the adoption of major local cults into the state rituals.

By the Song dynasty, although the process began considerably earlier, Buddhism had become totally sinified. Only two forms were of major importance: Chan and Pure Land Buddhism. The first appealed primarily to the intelligentsia and was seen as little different from those aspects of Daoism that appealed to the elite. The latter form of Buddhism affected the majority of Chinese, many aspects so amalgamated with normative Chinese religion that it was no longer Buddhist (in the sense that the use of mistletoe in British Christmas celebrations is no longer Druidic). Although the roots of Pure Land lie in India, its fusion with the ancestral focus of Chinese religion is entirely indigenous. Hence, Buddhism for most Chinese became an adjunct set of practices for the well-being of the family dead. Similarly, Daoism continued to evolve, developing both monastic orders modeled on Buddhism and a tradition of part-time, semi-literate priests who performed rituals again closely connected with the ancestral focus of normative Chinese religion. Chinese families who engage Daoist priests and Buddhist monks or nuns to carry out various specific rituals with regard to funerals or memorial services, respectively, would not consider themselves adherents to either Buddhism or Daoism for that reason alone.

Chinese religious practices are primarily carried out in front of the altar in the main room of a traditional house where the ancestral tablets are placed on the left, of those facing the altar, and deities specific to the particular family, for example, the earth deities for farming families, are placed in the middle. On the wall above the altar is usually a large picture of Guanyin, to be discussed below. In urban homes, where the ground floor is often a store, the altar is in the main room on an upper floor. In modern dwellings as well, the television set has shifted to the central location, with the altar above or in some other location in conjunction with the now, virtually universal contemporary family focus. In recent upper-middle class multi-story homes, the highest room has became an elaborate family temple. Other than at burials or reburials, the family repairs once a year at a spring festival (*Qingming*) to offer food directly at the grave site. Many but not all families will also make offerings at a clan temple. Of course, families are also involved with village or urban neighborhood temples.

In many areas, because the family itself is the basic social structure, the neighborhood temple, whose care rotates among the affected families, is the only public area. Hence, the temple is multifunctional. Aside from being a temple for housing local deities and making offerings to them, it is where local mediums may carry out their calling, the place for neighborhood meetings, a communal threshing and grain-drying ground, and an area where retired persons congregate, where neighbors can get together to play ensemble music, where traditional athletics can be practiced, and where operas and puppet-theater are put on, in theory, to entertain the deities of the temple.

People may also avail themselves of major temples, famed for the efficacy of their deities, or city, guild, and other temples. Except for those Buddhist monasteries, which also functioned as temples, or a limited number of Daoist temples, there are no clergy associated with these temples. If large enough to justify the expense, there will be a caretaker, usually a retired worker, and perhaps a person selling necessities for worship—incense, spirit money, etc.—but each individual knows the simple procedure and acts accordingly.

Offerings are also multifunctional. During special days for sacrifices, a common pattern is to bring the uncooked food to the local temple to be offered to the deities there. The food is then brought home and cooked. From there it may be carried to a clan temple to be offered to all the clan ancestral spirits, then brought back home to be offered to the immediate family dead (a maximum of five generations), and then eaten by the living members of the family as an enjoyable, nutritious banquet.

Modernity has had some effects on Chinese traditional religion as discussed above. In the first half of the twentieth century, modern education was in the hands of Christian missionaries who taught that Chinese religion was superstition and incompatible with science, etc. Until the mid-1980s the governments on both the Mainland and in Taiwan sought to suppress traditional Chinese religious practices. In keeping with Marxist atheism, the Chinese Communist Party considered traditional religion to be superstition. They also sought to eradicate it because as the traditional religion is not institutionalized, it could not be controlled by the government. In Taiwan, the Guomindang (Nationalist Party) to a degree suppressed traditional practices, in part, to garner American support as a Christian oriented (Methodist) government opposed to "godless" communism. On the Mainland, the suppression reached the point of persecution, particularly during the Cultural Revolution, when virtually all temples, including those famed for their history and architecture, were destroyed, as were all structures and artifacts of the past, whether or not connected with religion.

Since the early 1920s, Chinese Buddhism has undergone a renaissance. Long moribund, Buddhism modeled itself on liberal Christian institutions, such as the YMCA, and increasingly came to be seen as an indigenous parallel to Christianity. Buddhism offered enhancements to family religion, except for those who became nuns or monks, quite different from Christianity, which until the effects of Vatican II, did not allow converts to care for their ancestors, in other words, to be Chinese. More recently, with the expansion of the economies of Hong Kong, Singapore, and Taiwan—particularly among those families which fled the Mainland in the late 1940s and have since been cut off from the family cult—much wealth and interest have poured into Buddhist institutions. Universities, large monasteries and temples, and hospitals are increasing in number and size. Chinese Buddhist temples, funded from Taiwan, can now be found in Canada and the United States.

Traditionally, as mentioned in the previous chapter, Buddhism appealed more to women than men. Buddhism offers a religion of salvation outside of the normative patrilineal family-oriented religion, and this can be as important to Chinese women today as in the past. Also, many aspects of Buddhism have become universally Chinese, such as worship of Guanyin. As but one example, in the early 1990s, it has become a popular fad for many women and a smaller number of men, Buddhist and non-Buddhist, to wear the smaller Buddhist rosary as a bracelet symbolizing spirituality in general or simply for good luck.

On the Mainland, only institutional religion that could be controlled by the government was allowed until the relaxation of the last decade. The government recognized the Western determined "Three Religions" (Buddhism, Daoism and "Confucianism," although, of course, the latter did not actually exist as understood in the West) plus Islam (of considerable importance in the western autonomous regions) and Christianity (under Chinese government control). Non-Buddhist temples that have been reconstructed following the devastation of the Cultural Revolution are declared Daoist, regardless of previous affiliation or lack of it, and put in the hands of government-paid Daoist clergy. Buddhist temples may be served by "monks" and "nuns" who go home to spouse and family at the close of their working day.

In spite of all of these changes, it is remarkable how traditional family-oriented Chinese religion is flourishing in Hong Kong and Singapore and among those who resided in Taiwan before the 1940s in cultures that are now, by any standard of measurement, as modern as anywhere else in the world. On the Mainland, after over a decade of increasing relaxation towards what is still officially deemed superstition, evidence of traditional practices, even in Beijing, abounds. By the early 1990s, the newest major deity was Mao Zedong who, following his death and the change in ideology, became a very popular God of Wealth.

FEMALE SPIRITS

The Family Dead

The orientation of normative Chinese religion to the dead of the family, as discussed in the previous chapter, does not merely mean that the living ritually serve the dead, so that the dead will support the living. The religion also means that the living will, in the normal course of events, become worshiped spirits upon death. Given the patrilineal and patrilocal orientation of the religion, this means that women become spirits only in the families of their husbands. The possibilities of becoming spirits of their natal families that existed during the Han dynasty had disappeared by the Song. Females have name-tablets on the family altar after death as do their husbands, if they have a son, and also in the clan temple, if their husbands or sons contributed to the clan's well-being.

This is one of the reasons why it is as important for women as for men to have sons. The ritual offerings of their daughters are primarily directed towards the dead of their husband's family; it is sons (and their daughters-in-laws) who maintain sacrifices to their natal family. Also, sons financially support their mothers, while daughters work for the material benefit of their husband's family (contemporary changes will be discussed below). Traditionally, among the elite, a woman could receive honorific titles only as a result of her son's fame. Hence, as will be discussed below with regard to pilgrimages, women who worship fertility deities in order to have sons are doing so at least as much for their own good as for their husband's.

Nevertheless, women also make offerings to the spirits of their natal family. It was and remains traditional for married women, when it was geographically and financially possible, to travel to their natal homes once a year during the Spring (New Year's) Festival, where they made offerings at the family altar.

There is also a long-standing exception to the above. If a family has a daughter(s) but no son, it may seek for their daughter a husband who is willing to be adopted into the family. Either he, or at least one of the couple's sons, will take the surname of his wife's family and worship them as his paternal grandparents after their death.

In contemporary Chinese culture, however, differences from the above can be observed. Often it is difficult to tell whether some of these changes are recent or of long standing. Married women may have ancestral-tablets of their immediate natal-family dead on the altar of their home, particularly if it is a one-generation home. A few years ago, while I was meeting with a group of female mediums in a small town in central Taiwan, the women noticed that the medium in whose home we were meeting lacked her family tablets on the altar. The altar was a highly Buddhist one, as the home was dominated by her widowed mother-in-law. The medium responded that her natal family lived nearby, and she preferred to go to her natal home to make offerings to her natal ancestors. In a previous study, we described a family with a three-generation history of matrilineal sacrificial orientation, contrary to the norm.[3]

Daughters now may also materially support their own parents. With the development of women working outside of the home, in factories and offices and in the professions, women have become, to a degree, financially independent. While a son's salary belongs to his family, his wife's is generally considered her own. She may use part of her earnings to support her natal family should she so wish.

The one-child family program on the Mainland, promulgated to control China's extremely serious over-population problem, can only be successful in the long term if the patrilineal orientation of Chinese religion changes to one based on bilateral worshipping of ancestors, as well as other types of support. This was the explanation given by one of the husbands for the matrilineal sacrifices of his wife of the family mentioned above. It is not yet known just how widespread this understanding is.

Household Deities[4]

The second most important altar in every traditional home is that of the Stove Deity, who reports on the family's good or bad qualities to the celestial authorities during the Spring (New Year's) Festival. This deity, now most commonly called the King or Lord of the Stove, in many areas with his wife, is enshrined in the kitchen. His report greatly affects the fate of the family for the coming year.

This deity is probably a conflation of many different regional traditions. Very early texts mention a Stove Ghost, of uncertain sex. There was also a deity of the alchemical furnace. There were fire deities associated with stoves. Some myths describe the stove deity as a beautiful woman; others as a male spirit-official, a descendant of the Celestial Goddess; and others yet, that she has six daughters who assist in observing the behavior of the family members. Sometimes, the stove deity is an old woman called the First Cook, the inventor of cooking, or the Old Spirit Mother of Cooking.

It seems that the deity is a conflation of a cooking deity in the guise of a nurturing mother, a male fire deity associated with stoves, and a functionary of the celestial bureaucracy, who modeled on the traditional civil-service system, is necessarily male. The typical Chinese solution is to envision the deity as a marital pair and so resolve the issue of sexual identification.

Other household deities would include the Bed Mother (or the couple Sir Bed—Mother Bed). She protects young children.

Earth and Other Cosmic Deities

The imperial worship of Sky-Earth disappeared with the end of the last dynasty in the early twentieth century. Shrines to Earth in farm-fields and temples to

Earth in farming communities continue unchanged, and images of the Earth-deity as a couple are common on the shrines of farming families. Even on the Mainland, shrines to Earth are reappearing in the fields. In Taiwan, at least, the deity is known as the couple, Tudipo-Tudigung (Grandmother Earth—Grand-father Earth), as discussed in the last chapter. Elsewhere in China, she may appear singly as Timu (Earth Mother), the couple Tugung-Tumu (Sir Earth—Mother Earth), etc. Of course, as a bureaucrat of the traditional civil-service system, the deity will be portrayed as male; for example, at shrines by the sides of graves.

Related deities would include Qingshen (Well-spirit), portrayed as a female riding a dragon. All aspects of the earth, including mountains and rivers, are understood as female numinous beings; the *lung* ("dragon"—the horned, legged serpent also found in Native North America) is a male spirit that resides in waters to rise to the sky during spring thunderstorms. Many female river deities are mentioned in Chinese literature over the last two millennia.

Bixia Yuanjun

Among the many deities who are particularly potent regarding human fertility and who have a China-wide distribution is The First Lord of Purple and Azure Clouds (Bixia Yuanjun). She is found as far afield as Taiwan, where she is best known under the title, Zhusheng Niangniang (Mother of Generations), but her primary locus is as the deity of Mount Tai (the Great Mountain). Mount Tai, although not high from the standpoint of the Alps or the Rockies, is the tallest mountain in northeastern China and the site of sacrifices by rulers as far back as can be traced in recorded history, and even earlier by mythic culture-heroes. It remains the foremost sacred mountain in China. Its spiritual qualities have not diminished in the present; the embalmed body of Mao Zedong lies on a block of granite from Mount Tai.

Mount Tai remained throughout history to the present the major Chinese pilgrimage site. According to the local press, on May Day, the Communist hol-iday, in 1986, more than 60,000 ascended the mountain, the day before I had the opportunity to ascend the mountain myself amid crowds. It seemed to me that at least half of those making the ascent did so as pilgrims publicly making offerings at the many temples along the route; and this occurred at the begin-ning of the relaxation of the prohibition against public demonstrations of tradi-tional Chinese religion.

The main temple to the God of Mount Tai, one of the three largest in China (the other two being the temple to Confucius in his nearby birthplace and the main temple in the Imperial Palace in Beijing), is in the town at the foot of the mountain. In this temple, the image of the Deity of Mount Tai, with a long beard, is clearly male. Of the many temples along the route to the summit, there are temples to the Grandmother and to the Mother of the God of Mount Tai, as well as to Guanyin.

On the summit, however, the largest and most popular temple complex is to The First Lord of Purple and Azure Clouds. In some myths, she is the daughter of the Mountain, and his granddaughter in others. But she is also called the Mount Tai Mother (Taishan niangniang) and the Jade Maiden (Yünü). The latter name refers to an alternate myth, in which she was sent down to the mountain as a fairy by the Yellow Emperor, the mythic first emperor.

Next to her temple was a smaller one to the God of Mount Tai, already beginning to collapse in the early twentieth century, while the temple to the First Lord was being kept in good repair. According to photographs taken in 1942, the remains had already been cleared away; today, there is just a clear space where the temple to the God of Mount Tai once stood.

The last temple constructed on the summit, surrounding the highest rock, is comparatively recent, having been built only several hundred years ago. It is dedicated to the Jade Emperor, the supreme celestial deity in the Daoist pantheon, who is associated with the sacred mountain to the west; Mount Tai is the sacred mountain of the east. Many of the pilgrims do not visit this temple. Those I asked expressed to me an intuitive feeling that it did not belong there.

The history of the temples on Mount Tai illustrate both the attempts by the state to patriarchalize traditional worship centers following a patriarchal ideology, as well as the failure of these attempts to change the sex of female deities. Readers of Western texts on Chinese religion that follow textual sources will often find male gods named, who, in the popular mind, are female.

The sex variation of the Deity of Mount Tai also illustrates the functional differences that sacred sites can have. Imperial sacrifices were made in thankfulness to the powers of the earth for the empire, a masculine enterprise; the masses of pilgrims beseech the female deity for male progeny. It is hardly surprising that far more than half the pilgrims are female, but it is not uncommon to see the elders of clans and villages, males and females, together making the trek. Again, without being aware of the fertility aspects of the female deity, it would be difficult to understand why Mount Tai is a popular honeymoon destination.

Star and Moon Deities

The seventh day of the seventh lunar month is devoted to several deities; it included a celebration for the annual meeting of the Spinning Girl and Oxherd

Boy (in Western terminology, the constellations Lyra and Aquila) mentioned in the preceding chapter, patrons of courtship and marital fidelity. On this evening, unmarried young women make offerings of incense, flowers, fruit, and cosmetics to Moon and the Spinning Girl, seeking their assistance in finding a suitable husband.

The Mid-Autumn Festival, on the fifteenth day of the eight lunar month, is also devoted to Moon, that day being the birthday of the Moon Mother (Taiyin Niangniang—Great Yin Mother). Included with the offerings are flat, circular sweet pastries called "mooncakes," which are given as gifts to those important to one's life on the preceding day. This offering is particularly felicitous for curing illness and having children, but it is also a festive evening when the family gathers together to enjoy the autumn moon and the sweet cakes. The Moon Mother is the wife the archer Hoyi, associated with Sun.

Creator and Other Fertility Deities

Nüwa

Near the beginning of the lunar year, in celebration of Fuxi's birthday, there is a month-long Renzu (Ancestors of Humans) Festival at the Taihao (Fuxi) Mausoleum in Huaiyang, Honan Province. The county contains the archaeological remnants of China's oldest city, contiguous with the mythic past. This ancient city is understood to be the capital of Fuxi's mythic kingdom. The "Ancestors of Humans" refers to the paired deities, the male Fuxi and the female Nüwa, briefly introduced in the previous chapter. Prior to the destruction of the Cultural Revolution, among the many temples at the Taihao complex, there were several to Fuxi and one to Nüwa. As of 1993, the three temples to Fuxi, but not the one to Nüwa, had been reconstructed.

Before the Han period, the two deities had independent myths. Among her achievements, Nüwa brought the yellow earth (the color of the north China plain's loess soil) together and created humans, and she patched the vault of the heavens by melting and melding five-colored stones. As the Supreme Matchmaker, she presides over marriages. Fuxi is one of the three Sage Emperors or culture-heroes, inventing, among other cultural developments, the fishing-net and creating the Eight Trigrams. Brother and sister in Han myths, after a deluge they married to continue the human species. They are portrayed with human upper bodies and serpent lower bodies, their lower parts intertwined. Among the Chinese, there is still some discomfort with their incestuous relationship.

The Festival draws tens of thousands of pilgrims daily from provinces near and far. Others may come to worship on the first or fifteenth of any lunar month. Most are women, and many stay for the full month of the celebration. They are there to reverence their ultimate ancestors and to pray for children. Many of the pilgrims travel together in Xianghui (Pilgrim Societies) led by a woman; the members are considered sisters and brothers to each other. Women are usually supported by their husbands and their families in making these trips, for the benefit is to the family as a whole. Images of Nüwa, as well as Guanyin (see below), are likely to be on the pilgrims' family altars along with the ancestral tablets.

Among the many customs specific to the festivals are songs to Nüwa that women learn in dreams and fertility dances that are passed on matrilineally. These dances elicit ecstasy and lead to possession by the deity.

A major industry of the area is the manufacture of clay figures called Ninigou ("mud dogs") of divers shapes relating to relevant myths, including one of a simian-figure with a human face and a large vulva painted on its abdomen. The clay figures are reminiscent of Nüwa's creating humans from earth. Among many rituals associated with these images is soaking them in water and drinking the liquid as a medicine. Clay children, after a monetary donation, are displayed before Nüwa's statue. A red string is then tied around their necks, and the images are then hidden in the worshipers' clothes. The worshipers will talk to the image on the journey home but to no one else. On reaching home, the images are placed under the mattress. If a child is born within three years, it is attributed to Nüwa, and thanksgiving offerings are accordingly made.

Although the temple to Nüwa had yet to be rebuilt as of 1993, its former site was crowded with people praying for children, and the wall remnants have been blackened by the smoke of burning incense. In a cornerstone to one of the rebuilt temples, there is a round hole four centimeters in diameter. Called the Zisui Yao (Pit for Descendants), it undoubtedly represents Nüwa's vagina. The hole is black from the tens of thousands of women who have touched it to gain children.

Hence, although Fuxi is the apparently dominant deity of the Renzu Festival, the most important customs all relate to Nüwa and are oriented towards worship of the pudenda and reproductive power. And this is far from a modern phenomenon, for the Renzu Festival accords in timing with the Shangsi Festival of the distant past. In the *Liji* and *Zhouli* (see previous chapter), a Gathering in the Second Month of Spring is described, when offerings were made to the Supreme Matchmaker and otherwise illicit erotic behavior between males and females was tolerated, a ritual certain to increase fertility.

As at Taishan, the patriarchal aspect of Chinese culture over time may have merged Nüwa with Fuxi and made the male deity officially dominant, but the people know to whom offerings are due. Women, especially, understand who really birthed humans and to whom they should pray for children.

Euhemeristic Goddesses[5]

During the Song dynasty, the tendency to understand affective spirits as formerly historical or legendary persons became entrenched. Except for nature and cosmic deities, spirits, in the main, shifted from a mythic to a mythohistorical background. One influence on this development may have been the Mahayana Buddhist understanding of the Boddhisattva, a concept similar to that of the Christian saint, the two influencing each other during their respective developments. Boddhisattvas are human beings who, through the course of many lifetimes, reached the spiritual development that would have allowed them to become enlightened, Buddhas, but turned away from the Buddhist goal to help other beings achieve the same stage of development. Boddhisattvas are understood to accumulate merit for which they have no need but which they can use for the benefit of others, materially as well as spiritually.

At the same time, mediums lost their official status with the government. There are suggestions of non-governmental mediums long before the Song period, but the lack of their services as government officials may have meant their increased importance outside of officialdom. As was suggested in the previous chapter, mediumistic experience is the basis for understanding affective spirits as ghosts become benevolent, and there are probably far more female ghosts than male. This numerical disparity also presumably developed during the Song dynasty as unmarried female spirits were no longer cared for by their natal families as in the past. Two of the most important Chinese deities, Guanyin and Mazu, both unmarried females, originated during the Song dynasty.

Guanyin

It is well known that the Indian male Boddhisattva, Avalokiteśvara, retranslated into Chinese as Guanyin in the Tang period, shifted sex in the Song period. There are many biographies of her, but the best known version is the life of Miaoshan, who, according to most of the various biographical myths, lived during the Song dynasty. Guanyin appears to have gained widespread popularity in the same general time period as The First Lord of Purple and Azure Clouds and Mazu.

In outline, Miaoshan was a princess who defied her family and convention and refused to marry. Living a life of Buddhist meditation, according to some versions, her father, in response to her disobedient behavior in refusing to marry, had her killed. In the Buddhist hell, she freed the souls of the damned, thus making known her actual identity as Guanyin. She returned to earth and cured her father of a deathly illness by offering her eyes and arms. Miraculously restored to a complete body, she achieved the state of spiritual perfection.[6]

Most likely, Guanyin was a popular deity acquired by Buddhism to balance the important female deities accepted by Daoism, particularly, the King Mother of the West. In this regard, it is worth noting that Guanyin took on the responsibility for souls in the Western Paradise. Guanyin in turn was probably the stimulus for the supreme deity, the Eternal Mother of the late Ming sectarian movements, although the two may originally have been separate deities who rose simultaneously.

Guanyin is by far the most popular Chinese deity, considering the entirety of China. She is worshiped by those who otherwise have no direct relationship with Buddhism. Her special qualities are diverse; for example, she is worshiped by those desiring children, and she is the patron of merchants. She is commonly known through her role in the highly popular, traditional novel, *Journey to the West* (Xiyouji).[7] Her image is omnipresent; images placed on or above the family altar are usually of her, and she is the statue most frequently bought in local department stores.

When a temple is dedicated to her—and there is one in virtually every county—it is not necessarily Buddhist. In Buddhist monasteries and Daoist temples, she is often an image off to the side. However, in major monasteries in central China, her image has a more central location; e.g., Lingyinshi in Hangzhou and Xiyuanshi in Suzhou. In the large Buddha halls of monasteries, the major images, usually centered on Shakyamuni (Gautama Buddha), are backed by a high screen to increase their presence. On the backs of the screens, facing the rear doors, of the above-mentioned monasteries, there are images of Guanyin at least as tall as that of the Buddha. She is surrounded by attending figures and before her is a full complement of paraphernalia for worship: braziers, candelabra, kneeling pads, etc. The antiquity of the paralleling of the image of Guanyin with that of the Buddha, literally back to back, remains a question. However, there is no question that, at least in the Jiangnan region, even in Buddhist monasteries, the female deity achieved equal status in the popular mind to the male Buddha.

There are many pilgrimage sites devoted to Guanyin, including a temple on the hill above Lingyinshi mentioned above and Puto Island off the coast of Zhejiang Province, where Hangzhou is located. In 1987, during the four month pilgrimage season to the Upper Tianzhu temple above Lingyinshi, the government estimated that over two million pilgrims visited; on Guanyin's birthday alone, there were forty thousand pilgrims visiting this small temple. Over eighty percent of the pilgrims are women.[8]

Guanyin is so popular that excuses are found for pilgrimages several times a year; at her temple on Mount Nanfeng in Wangcang County in Sichuan Province, her birthday is celebrated three times a year. As with Mary in southern Europe, she is multiple. There is a different Guanyin for each of her major functions: she is known as Songzi Guanyin (a fertility deity for children), Daci Dabei Guanyin (who protects people through her great mercy), and Qianshou Qianyan Guanyin (portrayed with a thousand hands and eyes, indicating her ability to save all people at once).

At this temple on Mount Nanfeng, worshipers, primarily women, pray to Guanyin for health, wealth, children, etc. Food, steamed bread and chicken, is placed before her statue and then given to the sick to eat. Those who are healed or otherwise have their wishes granted are expected to repay this food multifold. This is typical of the Chinese sense of reciprocity, both among humans and in interactions with spirits. In 1992, her image was crudely made of local clay; obviously, the destruction of the Cultural Revolution had not been properly repaired. But it also seemed that local people were more comfortable with the simplicity of the crude images than they would have been with refined ones.

Typical of pilgrimage sites, there are many shrines on the path to the summit. The first set is of two pairs of Grandmother and Grandfather Earth in a crude shelter. They were placed together because their shrines had been destroyed. Of the various images in shrines along the route to the summit, there are the typical host of deities, some clearly identified, others variously identified by different persons. But all received offerings and were covered with new and bright red cloths, the most auspicious color in Chinese culture.

Many worshipers have specific requests, but others merely wished to meet general family and individual needs. Chinese tend to be quite pragmatic about offerings: they cannot hurt and may be beneficial. On being asked the purpose of their journey, young, educated people, who were just becoming aware of traditional religion after decades of suppression, offered responses such as, "People all say worshipping is effective . . . It doesn't take a great effort but can provide one more way to solve one's problems. Why not try?" A common expression in this regard is "Burn incense more and suffer grief less."

Mazu

As with Guanyin, there are varying biographies of Mazu as a human. The literary accounts, relevant to her state titles, agree in that she was the daughter of a

minor official, surnamed Lin, with a distinguished lineage; among other accomplishments, she subdued evil demons and protected the countryside around
her. More popular accounts understand her to be the daughter of a poor fisher-
man; she dreams of saving her brother(s) and, in some versions, her father, who
are subsequently rescued in a storm. There are various accounts of her holiness
from Buddhist, Daoist, and more generalized spiritual standpoints, most versions combining all of these. Virtually all versions share an understanding that
she was unusually silent as a child, that she was associated with the sea, and that
she either did not, or refused to, marry.[9]

Mazu became the patron deity of seafarers, as well as a local Fujien deity. As
seafaring mercantilism developed, she also became a patron of merchants. She
is the most important deity in southeastern and southern China, and in Singapore and Taiwan, whose populations, in the main, came from the seafaring merchants and fishermen of coastal Fujien Province. By the late Song period, she
began to be incorporated into the state religion by being granted titles. Eventually, her prestige developed to the degree that the Ming emperor, Chengzu
(early fifteenth century) gave her the title of Holy Mother of Sky Above (Tien-
shang Shengmu); a century later, she further gained the title of the Empress of
Sky (Tienhou). She tends to be labeled by one of these two titles. Her image
wears archaic imperial regalia.

Given her titles, we would assume her to be a sky rather than a sea deity.
The construction of a modern temple in the suburbs of the southern Taiwan
port city of Gaoxiung indicates rather that, as a major female deity, she is understood as the Earth deity herself (sea deities are also earth deities in many
cultures).

Chinese temples traditionally are one-story affairs, although the roofs may be
multilayered. Modern ferroconcrete construction allows for an inexpensive vertical structure. The Lungcheng Guan in Fengshan, Gaoxiung County, has an
unusual two-storied main hall. The lower hall has a horizontal display of five
life-sized images; the upper hall has a two layered display of five images per layer.
In total, there is a massive display of fifteen deities ranged in three layers.

The upper layer, which cannot be directly approached, centers on the Jade
Emperor, with Shakyamuni and Guanyin at the ends of the row. The middle
layer, directly on the second floor, centers on Confucius and includes Laozi.
The lower layer on the main floor, from which the other layers cannot be seen,
centers on the Holy Mother of Sky Above and includes local protector deities
and the Goddess of Childbirth (the First Lord of Purple and Azure Clouds, discussed above). On asking one of the temple caretakers about the obvious
interpretation, he confirmed that the layout of the deities in three levels indeed

was intended to indicate, in physical ascending order, Earth, Humans, and Sky, the standard, tripartite Chinese cosmos.

Hence, regardless of her title and original specific function as protector of seafarers, a function that continues in importance in addition to a more recent one of bringer of rain, Mazu has become the Earth Mother. In other words, her title, Holy Mother of Sky Above, indicates rank and regard, not location. It seems that, in the Chinese religious mind, any powerful female deity, excepting the Buddhist Guanyin, is essentially an earth deity. This may be a universal human tendency; it has been argued that the Virgin Mary took on the role of the suppressed pre-Christian European earth-grain deity. Mazu as Earth is immediately approachable, so different from the distant Sky, and this characteristic, of a mothering female deity, she shares with Guanyin and Mary.

Local manifestations of Chinese deities are often understood to be related to each other on the model of the hierarchical Chinese family, and the images are annually brought in procession to visit the mother temple. Yet the annual visit is far more reminiscent of a woman making her traditional yearly trip to her natal home than the activities within the patrilineal family, particularly in the case of a female spirit. On Mazu's birthday, her images from many temples in Taiwan congregate at the primary Mazu temple in Beigang. As each palanquin carrying the deity approaches the temple, Mazu becomes increasingly excited. The palanquin jumps around, and the bearers have a difficult time controlling it. Finally, as she reaches the temple's courtyard, the palanquin moves to and fro in a frenzy, while masses of firecrackers are set off for the auspicious reunion. Her excited mediums become possessed by her and, in the Chinese mode, begin to beat themselves with spiked balls or sharp swords, causing bleeding that quickly stops. Using the bodies of the mediums, she heals the afflicted who have come for this spiritually charged moment. It is a pandemonium of holiness.

Summary

Were the above not focusing on Chinese female spirits, far more deities would have been discussed. Particularly important are the Gods of Walls and Moats that protect one's immediate territory. Of equal importance are Guan Gung, the patron of merchants, and various healing deities. The list could be considerably extended. Sex is involved as it is among humans, for many of the deities were humans. Protecting deities and deities of education for the civil-service examinations, now university-entrance examinations, are male, as they would have been in traditional times. Deities of nurture, succor, and childbirth are female;

they are mother images even if unmarried and childless in their lifetime. Fertility deities are commonly understood to be married couples; human fertility and fertility of the soil are understood to result from the conjoining of female and male energies, of *yin* and *yang*.

Nonetheless, the most popular deities are females. They are females who died unmarried and became unsupported ghosts who, on possessing humans, demonstrated their powerful beneficence. Among East Asian Buddhists, male and female, Guanyin functions much as Mary does in Roman Catholicism, as an approachable mother image, who is less forbidding than her male counterparts. Within Chinese religion as a whole, her mercy extends to all who call on her, but her ability to assist women in conceiving sons renders her particularly important to women. Similarly, Bixia Yuanjun and Nüwa are again especially important to women because of their role in procreation. Mazu, on the other hand, has many functions and, in that quarter of China in which she is the major deity, appeals equally to females and males.

FEMALE RITUALS AND RITUAL ROLES

Female Rituals

There are few rituals today that are specifically female, and none, except for certain of the ancestral rituals, for males alone. One set would include those that are associated with giving birth, and these vary regionally. For example, in northern China, in the Beijing area, before birth, sacrifices are directed towards Zhixun Niangniang (To-have-descendants Mother), Cuishen Niangniang (Timely-birth Mother), and Songsheng Niangniang (Giving-birth Mother). Aside from burning incense daily to these deities during pregnancy, they are also offered delicious sweets. Three days after the birth, after the Xisan ritual (a childbirth ritual involving three washings of the infant), the paper images of the deities are burned; that is, the deities are sent away with gratitude for their assistance as they are no longer needed. Pregnant women are assisted in these rituals by mid-wives, who are females, as in virtually all cultures. Childbirth rituals for the infants, of course, apply to infants of both sexes, although specific details vary for female and male infants.

Rituals that are primarily female, although not exclusively so, are pilgrimages to the holy sites of those female deities, discussed above, who are potent in bringing about pregnancy. It is common for groups of females to travel together on these pilgrimages, particularly to famous temples dedicated to Guanyin and Nüwa.

Mixed Gender Rituals

Sacrifices

The sacrifices that take place in the home are primarily carried out by the women of the family. The senior woman in the household or a female delegated by her daily offers incense to the ancestral tablets and other deities on the altar. But if no woman is available, a male will perform this ritual. When meals are offered, women are involved with most of the preparation and the offering itself, but often men will also cook and otherwise prepare the food—there is no assumption in Chinese culture that cooking *per se* is a female task, but nourishing and nurturing are understood to be female roles.

In the clan temples, however, only males take part in the ritual offerings. Similarly, at the sacrifice to Confucius, which still continues at the Confucian temple in Taibei, only a male descendant of Confucius makes the offering assisted by male ritual specialists (university faculty), musicians, and dancers. But at the end of the sacrifice, when the gates are opened to the general public, both female and male students rush in to pluck a hair from the sacrificed animals for luck in the examinations, since, in the twentieth century, both males and females are involved in higher education.

Hence, it is not the activities themselves that are gendered, but the place. These rituals are still imbued with the tradition, discussed in the previous chapter, that the females of a family are responsible for what takes place within the home, and the males for that without. While this orientation follows for clan and family ancestral spirits, this is not the case for non-family spirits. It is primarily women who bring the uncooked food to the local temple for offerings to the spirits whose images are in the temple, before bringing the food home to be cooked and offered to the family dead. But men will be involved when whole animals are offered, in part because of the physical task of carrying and arranging the heavy carcasses. Often women on passing the temple after their daily shopping at the market will stop and offer the purchased food to the deities before bringing it home. In Taiwan, this is usually fruit, which is available year-round on this semi-tropical island.

Ritual Roles

Mediums

From at least three thousand to two thousand years ago, females had important religious roles as mediums between the realm of spirits and deities and that of humans. Not only did they offer themselves to be possessed by these numinous beings who could then speak to and heal humans, but these same individuals served priestly roles as exorcists and purifications specialists. Males also served in these functions, but the majority seem to have been females.

During the Song dynasty, social theorists became increasingly concerned about the breakdown in cultural values and social structures during the shift to an urban culture, concerns generally similar to those expressed in the twentieth century West. A slowly adopted solution was to reinforce the concept that the female role was in the interior of the home and the male role exterior to the home. Foot-binding was fostered (but not started—it being initially a female fashion) by the most important theorist; women were no longer offered governmental appointments as mediums; and wives seemed to function less as advisors to husbands who were officials.

At the same time, the intellectuals, while adopting many of the religious practices of the general population, particularly as Chinese culture spread into what is now south-central and southern China, also regarded many other religious practices as superstition. Especially those religious roles which involved ecstatic behavior were held in askance. The role of the Incorporator of the Dead, in which both males and females served to be possessed by the ancestral spirits in order to eat the food and drink the wine of the sacrifice, was dropped from the ritual. Non-family mediums were considered by the intellectuals, who controlled government policy in these regards, to be charlatans. Hence, mediums lost social status, and over time, women were forbidden to practice as mediums, although many continued to do so to the present.

The ending of martial law in Taiwan and increased freedom of traditional religious practices on the Mainland in the 1990s led to an enormous increase in public functioning by mediums, particularly female mediums. In Taiwan, mediums, following contemporary social practices, formed a society offering mutual support and training workshops. Within a year, thousands of women were functioning as light-trance mediums (lingji).

Often with limited education, but some from middle-class homes, these women gained self-esteem and public functions that had not been available to them for literally a millennium. Obviously the knowledge had not been lost for this period of time else so many could not have so readily taken on these roles. These extrafamilial roles can raise problems for families. Often these women will be away from their homes for days at a time, leaving young children in the care of their husbands, and, as they do not accept payment for their services, their expenses can be a drain on the family economy. But as one husband expressed to me, "She is my wife (what can I do?)," belying the Western misperception of female subjugation in China.

Buddhist Nuns and Lay-nuns

Some pre-modern Chinese women were disinclined to surrender themselves to the complete loss of independence that marriage meant: being subject to their husbands in-law, at least until they themselves became the oldest females in the household and had daughters-in-law of their own to subjugate. One way out was to become a nun; Guanyin herself is the model for an unmarried female within the Buddhist tradition, as is Mazu for either the Buddhist or the Daoist traditions.

Different from Buddhist nuns in the South Asian traditions, Chinese nuns are relatively equal in status to monks. Monks and nuns often live in the same monasteries, in opposing wings to the main worship hall. And for the last one hundred and fifty years (since the loss of monastic lands following the destruction of the eighteenth-century Taiping movement, see Chapter 13), both made their livings by saying masses for the dead in the monasteries and in homes during special memorial services subsequent to funerals. Nowadays, nuns also function as social workers, health service providers, etc.

Widows with financial resources of their own (from the Song dynasty on, women of upper-class families did not have remarriage as an option), who for any number of reasons did not have a satisfactory place to reside, could purchase a place as a nun in a monastery with exemption from physical and religious work. Men too, particularly retired generals who would be safer out of the public eye, at times also availed themselves of this culturally acceptable option.

Older widows, who do not have the comfort of the religion of familism available to them, may become lay-nuns. They continue to reside in their homes, particularly if they have a son and his family at home, but live a vegetarian life of devotion, sometimes having their heads shaved and wearing the garb of nuns. Those I met living this life were Mainlanders living in Taiwan; they were cut off from clan and extended family and felt their security after death would come primarily from Chinese Buddhist practices.

In this regard, it must be understood that death is not a subject to be avoided, as in the West. There was no concept of a permanent hell, although Buddhism brought to China concepts of temporary hells as purgatories. All who have male children will be cared for after death by being sent food, luxuries (as paper models to be burned), and money, gold and silver ingots and bonds (again as paper replicas forwarded to the spirit realm by burning), enough for a comfortable existence in the world of the dead, its understanding patterned on this world. Buddhism added the Pure Land, created by Amida Boddhisattva, but entry to the Pure Land is facilitated by Guanyin. Faith is sufficient for admittance into the Western Paradise; hence, the appeal of Chinese Buddhism, particularly to women who are never directly part of the patrilineal clan religion.

Women in Daoist Institutions

Women continue to serve as Daoist priests, although little has been written in this regard, particularly in the modern period. In the twelfth century, a monastic form of Daoism, loosely based on Buddhist models, developed: the Quanzhen sect. Different from Buddhism, it seems to be totally egalitarian with regard to sex. Monks were termed *qiandao* and nuns *kundao*. Both practiced an inner alchemy designed to lead to extreme longevity (usually termed "immortality") through making the body ethereal. Since the Cultural Revolution in China, the sect has been revived with some support from the government.

The numbers of *qiandao* and *kundao* are approximately equal in most areas—some areas may have more males, some more females—and there are as many female heads of monastery-temples as males. The practices are virtually the same for males and females except for sexual differences. When Yin Mingdao, the elderly female head of a temple, was asked in 1984 about the differences in practices between women and men, she replied:

> When we worship in the temple, when we chant sacred texts aloud, it is exactly the same [for men and women], there is really no difference. The difference is in the physical and meditative practice [of inner alchemy]. What a [male] *Daoshi* (Daoist initiate) practices is "making the white tiger submit" [that is, not releasing semen but circulating it back up the spine to the head]. For a [female] *Daoku* (Daoist initiate), the practice is "cutting off the head of the red dragon" [causing the menses to cease].[10]

These practices have been reported in several different locations, and modern versions of texts on these female practices are now being published in Beijing.

Other Religious Roles

Over the last few centuries, women had equal roles to men in popular religious movements; women served as heads of congregations, military leaders, and teachers of both males and females. Today in Taiwan, new religious sects are constantly arising, usually based on visions and dreams, and women are very active as founders and leaders, as well as forming a substantial part of the congregations.[11]

FEMALE SELF-UNDERSTANDING

Before proceeding to an analysis of the hermeneutics of femaleness in modern Chinese culture, it is necessary to discuss two related topics that have been misunderstood in Western treatments and in Chinese writings informed by Western theorists: female pollution[12] and subservience. Regarding the former, on being asked to enter a temple or home where rituals are taking place, a menstruating woman may say, "I cannot come in now, because my body is not clean," or "Today my body is not clean." The term is a euphemism for menstruation. This is often interpreted, from the standpoint of Western theories of purity and pollution, that Chinese women are assumed, by their nature, to be polluted and polluting. But this is not the Chinese understanding.

In traditional Chinese culture, all bodily waste discharges from both males and females, including the body itself after death, are considered unclean, dirty. But three of these substances are considered particularly harmful, because they are the fluid of life and directly connected with human procreation: menstrual blood, semen, and post-partum blood discharges.

Blood itself is a powerful substance: blood dripping from possessed mediums, who cut their tongues for this purpose, is used as a powerful medicine. Red, the color of blood and life itself, is the most auspicious color. Red is common in temple decor, for the color of doors, for the lightbulbs used in lieu of red candles on altars, and, traditionally, for the marriage garb of both males and females. (In modern times, the bride wears a white Western wedding dress for the mandatory wedding photo and the signing of government marriage papers, a Western custom, and a red Chinese style dress for the banquet that is the essential traditional ritual, while the groom will wear something red, either a tie or a carnation, with a Western style suite.) White, or more precisely unbleached hemp, is worn by the immediate family at funerals to indicate the absence of blood, of death. Pre-discharge menstrual blood was understood to combine with semen to form the foetus at conception. Menstrual blood, then, is triply potent: first, by being blood which has an inherent power; secondly, by being involved with procreation; and thirdly, by not being used for procreation and discharged as waste fluid.

Hence, a menstruating woman will avoid going to temples, or at least approaching the deities in the temples, and avoid mediumistic rituals. The very presence of the powerful menstrual blood disturbs the deities, and she has no desire to reduce the efficacy of the offerings being made by her family and neighbors nor to place in harm's way those involved in difficult and potentially dangerous rituals. This is not because she is polluted, but because of her being temporarily the bearer of a powerful, and therefore potentially harmful, substance. (Menstrual blood is used by specialists for certain spells, both harmful and beneficent.) Otherwise, she does not avoid social contacts and continues her normal activities while menstruating.

Similarly, a woman ideally remains confined for a month following birth, as she has been made dirty by the discharged, powerful, birth effluent (and, if economic circumstances permit, because the rest is considered beneficial to her and the infant). Her husband too, whom it is assumed will come into contact with his wife and baby, is also temporarily contaminated and avoids temples, rituals, etc. Indeed, anyone who has come into contact with the birth process or with the new mother, male or female, as well as the infant, is in a similar unclean state.

Therefore, from the standpoint of hermeneutics, the dual features of the discharges, both positive from the standpoint of power and negative in their ability to cause harm, cancel each other out to a degree. In any case, the sex of those rendered unclean is irrelevant; it is the fluid discharges that are understood to be tainted. Chinese women are not polluted, nor are they denied entrée to rituals for that reason; rather they voluntarily exclude themselves from these activities because they are temporarily "dirty." The same terms are used for anyone, male or female, coming from the fields sweaty and filthy. (Similarly, intercourse in even a deserted temple is considered sacrilegious because of the discharge of semen.) Nevertheless, essential as childbirth is to the continuance of the family, sons arrange for a Buddhist ritual following the death of their mother to free her from the sin of pollution due to her having given birth to them and the resultant bloody discharges. Since this "sin" leads to a particular torment in the purgatory "hells," we can but wonder if this concept flows from the synthesis with Buddhism.

This latter understanding of sin and pollution is so completely contradictory to normative Chinese myths and religious understanding that the reason for its arising is most puzzling. Terry Wu, in examining the meditation texts that describe the female body in early Chinese Buddhism, seems to have found the solution. These texts, which originated in India, in order to emphasize the meaninglessness of lust, provide meditation exercises for monks that describe the female body as a bag of puss, urine, etc. They teach male monks to look at the female body with revulsion rather than delight. Theoretically, these descriptions would be applicable to the bodies of both males and females, but, for practical reasons, given that the texts were written for male monks, the focus was on the female body.[13] Over many centuries, these texts could have led to a misogynistic attitude towards the female body in general; it seems to be the only plausible explanation for the development of attitudes towards the discharge of female fluids in popular culture that are contradictory to general Chinese ideology.

Although Buddhism in China has long been noted for its difference from Buddhism in India in the more egalitarian treatment of nuns vis-à-vis monks, the attitude in original Buddhism in this regard should not be forgotten. It is well known that, according to early sutras, the Buddha is supposed to have resisted accepting females into the monastic orders. When he finally did so, he is supposed to have said that Buddhism would consequently not last as long as it would have if nuns were not accepted. The early rules for nuns make them subject to male monks. Conversely, in China, one finds nuns meditating and praying in the prayer halls equally with monks; this is not the case in forms of Buddhism that received direct influence from India. When the anthropologist Anna Grimshaw spent a winter in a Ladakhi nunnery, she found the women treated as virtual slaves of the monks, excluded from rituals and given no time for meditation, for women's "bodies were deemed weak, impure and unsuitable for ritual manipulation."[14]

With regard to female subservience to males, a gross misunderstanding has occurred, leading to Chinese feminist anger towards Western feminists who see themselves as saviours to the poor, suffering Chinese women. This attitude in essence is little different from that of most nineteenth century Christian missionaries, who were at the forefront of Western imperialism, towards the Chinese people.

From a distance, Chinese culture can be perceived as the epitome of a patriarchal culture. Because of the patrilineal and patrifocal socioreligious order, women's religious roles as well as family allegiance were theoretically to be directed to their husband's lineage. The basis of Chinese religion and society was the patrilineally defined family and clan, and all state rituals were founded on this conception.

As a result of the patriarchal sociopolitical order discussed in the previous chapter, women could not gain elite status, particularly after the changes of nearly a thousand years ago, discussed above. Aside from the imperial family, which was outside of and superior to the social order, the elite was predominantly composed of those who passed at least the first of the three civil-service examinations, open only to males, based on an education that was theoretically, and usually in practice, reserved for males. Traditional Chinese elite culture was highly androcentric, and women received but minimal protection from a patriarchal governmental structure that reinforced a patriarchal social structure. Women of middle-class and higher status families were effectively imprisoned in the family compound, physically hobbled by the practice of footbinding and legally bound by societal norms.

As in a number of other cultures, patriarchal Chinese culture continued, in part, through females subordinating women. The practice of patrilocality in China determined that women suffered, not at the hands of men, but at the

hands of other women, their mothers-in-law. Older sisters-in-law too could be
oppressors. The pattern of abuse became cyclical. Only by living long enough
to become the matriarch within the family compound could a woman seek her
revenge against her treatment by her mother-in-law by mistreating her
daughter-in-law, who by custom was her servant. A husband who defended his
wife against his parents could be thrown out of the house and disinherited (or
even executed in the past) for being unfilial, the most severe crime in traditional
China. Shen Fu, the author of a rare autobiography and biography of his wife,
Six Records From a Floating Life,[15] was forced to leave his family home for this
very reason.

In the past, polygyny, although not a practice of the vast majority of Chinese
families, meant that secondary wives and, especially, concubines (who did not
have the status of a secondary wife) had virtually no control over their own lives.
Polygyny was limited to wealthy families and theoretically existed to ensure the
production of male heirs, essential to the basic religious value: the continuation
of the patrilineally defined family. Polygyny became a form of conspicuous con-
sumption among wealthy males. It was also considered a virtual necessity by
government officials who were not allowed to serve in the locale of their family,
yet whose primary wife was expected to remain in the family home to care for
his parents. Away from the family home for years at a time, the male officials
would have no marital life without a second wife; of course, the reverse, equally
true, was not a matter for cultural consideration.

In theory, a male had to receive the permission of his first, the primary, wife
before taking another. Secondary wives and concubines were under the juris-
diction of the first wife, and all the children they bore were officially hers.
Again, the abuse of secondary wives and concubines predominantly came from
both the mother-in-law and the first wife; i.e., other females. Hence, the very
nature of the male-dominated and male-oriented culture led to women perse-
cuting each other, where persecution existed, particularly in multi-female residences. This statement, however, is not intended to imply that husbands
themselves did not abuse wives in Chinese culture, a pervasive cross-cultural
problem, or, for that matter, that wives in working-class families did not physically beat their husbands, as still not infrequently occurs in lower-class families.

The above theoretical structure has been understood from a modern Western feminist perspective to illustrate the total subordination of women to men.
But are Chinese women dominated by males and do they consider themselves
subordinate?

The traditional term for a Chinese wife is *tai-tai* ("great-great," meaning
"the great one"). The term is understood literally. That husbands are *pa tai-tai*

("afraid of their wives") is a normative supposition in China. This term does not in itself signify that Chinese males are "henpecked," although their being so is far from uncommon. It does denote that a Chinese wife expects to dominate many features of family life, particularly economic aspects. Observation over several decades of a number of Chinese families indicates that the term, *tai-tai*, is indeed a descriptive one.

In traditional elite families, women dominated the interior of the home and controlled the family finances.[16] In peasant families, both women and men farmed. A pervasive image, when one is travelling through the countryside, is of couples working together in the fields. Chinese wives rarely fit the Western stereotype of them. Indeed, in Taiwan, Chinese males dream of having a Japanese wife rather than a Chinese one, because of the non-Japanese stereotype of the Japanese female as utterly subservient to males.

It is naive to assume that any theoretical socioreligious system is absolute, particularly if the interpretation assumes a narrow range of possibilities, or that a patriarchal sociopolitical order *ipso facto* means that females are powerless. Cultures are highly complex, and the gross simplification that frequently occurs in Western writings on China (and other cultures) and Chinese religion can be highly misleading. As a Chinese female, one of the authors of this chapter is continually perturbed by the assumption she frequently encounters in the West that Chinese women are weak and powerless. As a Western male, the other author can assure the reader that the reputation of Chinese wives, as depicted above, is well earned, Chinese females being culturally disposed towards an egalitarian family life.

In any case, the lives of females in China, in many respects, are quite different now as compared to the previous century. The fashion of footbinding ended several generations ago, and, for nearly a century, it has not been assumed that the female role is limited to the interior of the family compound. Modern light industry has reversed the dowry system in Taiwan; now the groom's parents are more likely to lavish expensive gifts on the bride's parents in compensation for the loss of her income. Educated women have been entering the professions for many decades and, in their professional capacities, keep their maiden names. Women have not achieved the higher political positions, and this is recognized. A women's college has been created in China to address problems of political and social equality, and procedures have been devised to require dual male and female heads of institutions. Just this year (1996), a law was passed in Taiwan allowing for bilateral inheritance and for women to keep their maiden names after marriage, if they wished.

As discussed in the preceding chapter, the traditional ideology and religious practices were based on the concept of complementary opposition, the sexes assumed to be equal and utterly essential to each other. With the ending of the state religion, which focused on male deities, there may now even be an imbalance towards female deities. These deities are independent; they are not married, and they have no male peers, excepting Fuxi in the case of Nüwa. Women need but look at Guanyin, a large image of her dominating most family altars, for a model of female autonomy. Once married, they can look forward to becoming revered ancestral spirits upon death; and if they remain unmarried, as is increasingly prevalent among educated women, there are alternative options within the Buddhist and Daoist traditions, or they may turn towards Christianity.

With regard to rituals, the female's role dominates within the household as the male's does in the clan temple. In local temples, female roles are at least as important as males, their activities relating to the particular festivals and deities involved. Women are reasserting themselves in the major role of spirit medium and will soon be the majority in that activity, if they are not already. From the above, we trust it is apparent that a patriarchal sociopolitical structure and a patrilineally oriented religion do not necessitate a patriarchal religion, as assumed by Western scholars.

From the standpoint of religion, women understand themselves to have an inherent power of their own, as they embody *yin* power, different from but equal to the *yang* power of males. Both perceive marriage as a means of bringing these complementary powers together to create a whole life that will lead to the creation of new life that, in continuing the family, ensures the continuity of their own lives after death.

Women constantly perceive many models of female superhuman power in the many female deities, along with male deities, with which the culture as a whole is imbued. Women daily interact ritually with both the ancestral spirits, half of whom are female, and female deities. Ordinary women, as spirit mediums, serve both males and females as mediators between the realms of the spirits and the living. While their tasks as spirit mediums may at times be difficult, they have the satisfaction of helping other people and the realization that a deity has chosen them to be their means of appearing to humans. Rural women, at times, may travel together, under the leadership of a female, to sacred sites, experiencing not only intense religious feelings during the journey, but also fun, camaraderie, travel to new places, and a vacation from their hard, work-filled lives, no different in that regard from their men. Finally, most women, like men, can expect to become upon death, revered ancestral spirits, sent sufficient wealth by their family to live a very comfortable life in the afterworld, where they are in a position spiritually to benefit their living children and grand-children.

When I asked You Meiling, the articulate and analytical Executive Director of the new professional association of *lingji* (mediums) mentioned above, why she thought more females were mediums than men, she responded that females were *yin* (that is, females have both *yin* and *yang*, but, being females, have a greater proportion of *yin*). This simple statement has multiple meanings. The realm of spirits of the dead is considered *yin*, and an old term for the dead is *lingyin*; hence, females with a *yin* nature are more receptive to spirits from the *yin* realm. But this interpretation in itself would not account for possession by deities (*shen*); other meanings flow from the statement that females are *yin*. To function as a medium, one must be receptive to the entry of a spirit or deity into oneself and be willing to yield oneself to the control of this deity. This requires a *yin* nature, as discussed by Ban Zhao in the preceding chapter, which females have more readily than males.

Furthermore, according to You, to function as a medium, one must be empathetic. Empathy is essential for one to feel and be able to respond to the needs of the patient/client. Again, females are understood in China to be more empathetic than males, due to their nature. Mothering requires being in tune with another, and this innate ability renders females more readily empathetic than males. Nevertheless males have a *yin* as well as a *yang* nature, and some males are very empathetic, as well as the reverse. That females are *yin* explains why females are more prone to functioning as mediums.

Women who choose not to marry, or young women before they marry, are in an anomalous situation upon death, as are males who die in war and other forms of violence, or who die young. But parents may arrange for a spirit marriage so that their souls will find a home with the family of their husband. Or their remains may be placed in a Buddhist monastery where masses will be said for them to assist their entering the Western Paradise. If completely uncared for, their souls will lead a miserable life, but a few will become powerful deities, as did Mazu and Miaoshan (Guanyin). Educated, modern, unmarried women also have the option of becoming agnostic towards traditional religion and ceasing to concern themselves about life after death; they can live a rich, full life in a profession or in business. And if they are familiar with Daoist ideology, they are aware that nothingness (*wu*) is at the basis of everything, and death, as life, is essentially without purpose (a joyous not a nihilistic understanding).

In summary, Chinese women today, in the main, do not feel themselves dis-advantaged vis-à-vis men, except in the case of gaining the top echelons of business or government, where patriarchy is most evident. The religious lives of women are little different from those of men, and religious ideology is founded on a system of complementary opposition, a set of concepts based, in part, on an unstated assumption of equality between the sexes. Even the socioreligious structure of the patrilineal, patrilocal family is weakening, given the attempts to control overpopulation, equal educational opportunities for females, and the contemporary economy.

6
EFFECTS OF CHINESE RELIGION
ON NEIGHBORING TRADITIONS

A S A MAJOR CIVILIZATION AND EMPIRE in Eurasia for over two thousand years, even larger than the contemporaneous Roman and Parthian empires at its beginning, China influenced all the kingdoms around it. To the west and north, the influence was primarily on material culture: dress, architecture, weapons, household utensils, etc. To the east and south, additional influences also included written language, literature, socio-political structures, and religion. As is clear from the residue of the more recent European and American colonialism, as well as late twentieth-century economic imperialism, what is actually imparted to other traditions is not always the best aspects of the expanding cultures. With regard to the subject of this book, we shall look at two countries that voluntarily incorporated major aspects of Chinese culture into their own: Japan and Korea.

Neither tradition originally had its own system of writing, and at first, those who would be literate in these two countries in the making had to learn Chinese. This was a more difficult task than it might seem, for Korean and Japanese, both being Altaic languages, belong to a different language family with nothing in common with the Sinitic language family to which Chinese belongs. Eventually, both cultures, independently and in different ways, converted the logographic written Chinese into syllabic symbols in order to write in their own respective languages. More important, together with the written language, they assimilated Chinese literature and ways of thinking into their own cultures as well. The focus of these borrowings was the Chinese system of government, which, being patriarchal and replete with *rujia* ideology, had important influences on cultures where women had, and then to differing degrees lost, important social, political and religious roles.

ASPECTS OF JAPANESE RELIGION
with Marilyn Nefsky

Exactly three decades ago, as I write this section in the summer of 1996, I was residing in Kyoto (the imperial capital until replaced by Tokyo in the late nineteenth century). The Americans refrained from bombing it during the Second World War, and it remains a conservative city, in architecture as well as attitudes. I experienced two incidents revolving around gender that were so striking to me at that time that I still recall all the details.

Once, on boarding a crowded streetcar at a time when most males would be at work, a quite elderly woman dressed in the traditional kimono that most older women then wore in Kyoto stood up to give me her seat. Being raised in the different androcentrism of North America in the 1940s, I had been well trained to give my seat to women, the elderly, and the infirm (an interesting statement on the Euroamerican conception of females). I was at the time in my mid-twenties and in the peak of health, for four hours every evening intensively practicing *kendo* (Japanese fencing with an approximation of the two-handed battle sword) and *iaido* (solitary practice of drawing an actual sword and killing an imaginary attacker from any position). Now here was a very old woman giving me her seat. And I took it, for to have done otherwise would have insulted her. I understood the cultural reasons for her action; it was just hard for me to accept.

At the *kendo dojo* (training hall), I was quite anomalous, not just for being the only foreigner. I had been studying *kendo* for only an academic year, as a member of the Taiwan National University *kendo* team, while Japanese males of my age often would have had two decades of training. School and college age males received their training in their schools. The students in this evening class were either too young for school or highly advanced males—the *sensei* (teacher), in his mid-seventies, was considered one of the best teachers of swordsmanship in Japan. When it came to the various types of lessons and practice routines, there was no problem. But learning *kendo* requires practice in full combat. I could hardly go against babes literally carried into the *dojo* in their mother's arms, and sparring with those highly advanced would have been pointless for both of us. Fortunately, there was a simple solution. A young woman had been training there for several years, and we were set against each other every day. In armor, helmet and *hakama* (floor-length culottes), sex was invisible, and swordsmanship requires quickness, finesse, and stamina far more than strength.

In pre-modern times, women of the samurai clans were trained in the use of weapons. While they did not go off to war in the feudal period, they were expected to die in defense of the home or slash their throats prior to capture if defeated. I have observed a number of formal *kendo* competitions between males and females. Usually, in these combats the women wield an approximation of a halberd, the preferred weapon for household defense, and the men, one or two swords; women won these competitions at least as often as men. Yet prior to the end of the Second World War, women were trained to defer to males, also a development of the samurai period (*bakufu*), hence, the giving up of a streetcar seat to a male. Seemingly, these two values with regard to gender are contradictory: female subservience and female equality vis-à-vis males. This contradiction may illustrate one of the effects of the Japanese selective borrowing of Chinese ideology. To understand it, we must go back as far as we can in Japanese history.

The few references to Japan in the early Chinese histories are brief and enigmatic, but indicate that at least one of the regions was ruled by a female. About fourteen hundred years ago a leading clan of the main island's central plain, in order to solidify its control over the other leading clans, introduced Chinese language, culture, and political institutions. At that time, the second major Chinese empire, the Tang, was being instituted in a period when Buddhism was still quite influential. Within a century, the result was a Japanese imperial clan using the terminology of the Chinese government and ruling from a capital town that was a miniature model of the Chinese capital city—Japan, as a country, then being barely the size of a Chinese district, let alone a province. The powerful clans were allied to powerful monasteries of armed monks in the hills surrounding the capital.

One of the consequences of the cultural fusion was the written recordings of myths, manipulated to legitimize the hegemony of the ruling clan over the other elite clans. Two versions come down to us: one in literary Chinese written by a male, and one recording the version of a woman elder written with Chinese characters used for their phonetic sounds to approximate spoken Japanese. Within these renditions, there is one of the most fascinating accounts of creation: Following the arising of some of the primordial *kami* (spiritual entities), a brother and sister pair of *kami*, She-Who-Invites and He-Who-Invites, decide to create some land. They take a long sky-spear of red coral and push it into the briny deep, stirring it around. After a while, they lift it out, and from its tip droplets fall to the surface of the sea where they coagulate into the main islands of Japan, with its peak being the *axis mundi* of Mount Fuji. The two *kami* descend to the new land. He-Who-Invites, looks at himself and notices that he has a piece of seemingly superfluous flesh hanging from the middle of his body; She-Who-Invites notices that she has a void in the middle of her body. Observing the antics of a wagtail bird, He-Who-Invites says, "How would it be if I put that extra part of my body into the place where you have a gap?" She-Who-Invites thought that sounded rather interesting and agreed. So they went around the sacred pillar, Mt. Fuji, in opposite directions. When they met on the other side, She-Who-Invites said, "Oh handsome youth." He-Who-Invites was upset. He said, "That is wrong. I am the male and should have spoken first." But she ignored him, took him by the hand, and off they went to procreate other *kami*, including the lesser islands and other sacred places. (In another version, one preferred by Western scholars, they go around the sacred pillar a second time, when he speaks first.)

In the ancient myths and legends, disregarding later patrifocal manipulation, we find females as deities, empresses and rulers, priests, ritual dancers, founders of sects, and mediums. Called *miko*, the latter served as mediators between the *kami* and the people. Not only those women who functioned as priests and mediums, but all women, played an important role in the religious life of the Japanese people. Females were perceived to be in direct contact with *kami*, announcing the divine will to humans. These pronouncements were then articulated and managed by males. As illustrated in the early Japanese chronicles, the priesthood can be understood as embodied in a complementary female-male relationship. The establishment of Buddhism and *rujia* ideology in Japan added an overlay of patriarchal beliefs, values, and norms that had for centuries served to define these traditions in China. As long as the ecstatic elements remained a central focus of religious life, women remained important. References in the chronicles to female rulers, such as Pimiko, and priests, such as Tamayori-hime, demonstrate the early prominence of females, soon to be lost with the adoption of Chinese institutions.

With the Taika Reform thirteen hundred years ago, the government, following the Chinese model, became a centralized absolute authority. Rituals directed towards specific local deities were organized into a single central system of an official and national character which came to require a male-dominated priesthood. Hence, the religion can be seen as being transformed into the rationalized concern of bureaucrats rather than consisting of the spontaneous acts of naturally religious persons. In other words, the deities once summoned by a charismatic personality would now appear only at predetermined specific times and places. Each step of the rationalizing process pushed women further away from significant positions in official Shinto, the name given to the unnamed indigenous religion after the introduction of Buddhism. The move to male-dominance engendered a hierarchically structured cosmology of *kami* who visit the priests in revelatory dreams and speak to, not through, them. The development of a chasm between priest and *kami*, as compared to the possession of mediums by *kami*, devitalized Japanese religion by diminishing the intimacies of spirit and flesh, wisdom and emotion, person and nature. Despite the rationalization process, charismatic women continued to relate to a non-hierarchically structured cosmology of *kami* who guided their wisdom and spoke intimately through them.

In the first several centuries of the patriarchalization of Japan, while males nominally ruled, women and women's families continued to hold enormous social and political power. We are aware of the situation of the elite women, because they were highly literate and wrote most of the literature of the period, perhaps because they did not hold official positions and had more leisure time. This is unusual in the study of early civilizations, where in virtually all other cases, what we know of the culture we know almost exclusively through the eyes of men. In this period of Japanese culture, we know that elite women had the same sexual freedom as males; husbands and wives equally had affairs and lovers. (In indigenous Japanese culture, sexual behavior in and of itself is considered neither of ethical nor moral concern, so long as a pretense of discretion is maintained.) Women exercised political power, literally, from behind screens. The imperial family soon fell under the control of another powerful family that maintained control over many generations of emperors by forcing emperors, as soon as they became physically mature, to marry daughters from their family and then retiring when a son was born. Hence, the *de facto* ruler during this period (Fujiwara) was always a regent who was the maternal grandfather of the child emperor.

This system of government slowly decayed as layers of family upon family came to dominate the political realm and the elite slowly lost contact with the rest of the population. At the frontiers of the realm, in the area of present-day Tokyo, a new elite of hereditary, professional warriors was emerging. This led to a second wave of cultural borrowing from China, a China where Buddhism had since lost its dominance and survived in the Pure Land sect among the populace and in Chan (Japanese: Zen) among the male intelligentsia. It was a time when a revised form of *rujia* (called Neo-Confucianism in the West), which sought to stabilize society by limiting females to the interior of the household compounds, became the dominant and then official ideology. The new militaristic Japanese elite found these practices and ideologies ideal. In Japan, Zen was a new sect of Buddhism that was as yet unallied to any political faction, and the new, powerful military families made it their own. Moreover, the Zen focus on meditation and the sameness of everything (all being "empty, void"), including life and death, was found most useful in the training of warriors. The new *rujia* ideology could be interpreted by them to stratify society by power/function and sex. Through force, they instituted new regimes (*bakufu*), in which the military clans dominated the imperial institution, which lost all but its ritual

role, and developed a class system that allowed a *samurai* (hereditary professional warrior) to kill a non-*samurai* at will, that held males superior to females
in all regards, and that made absolute loyalty to one's superior the primary value.

Several centuries ago, one of these military clans came to dominate the
others and all of Japan until the late nineteenth century. It enforced a peace and
an isolation from the rest of the world by officially adopting its own interpretation of the revised *rujia* ideology. The only remnant of female power was in the
subservient imperial court, where the priest of the great imperial shrine at Ise
had to be a female who is a close relative of the emperor. The Ise Shrine is
devoted to Amaterasu, the most important Japanese *kami*, who is the female
sun deity and the ancestress of the imperial clan, which remains unbroken to
this day from the beginning of the Japanese historical period. When the American navy forced Japan to open itself to international trade over a century ago,
a new political order developed under the banner of reinstituting the power of
the Emperor. In actuality, these political developments led to a new, modern
military regime, modeled on Prussia, dedicated to mastering the new Western
military technology to demonstrate the superiority of Japan. When conquered
by the United States at the end of the Second World War, Japan underwent a
fourth period of selective cultural borrowing, this time from the United States,
orienting itself towards economic rather than military superiority.

This brings us back to the seeming contradictions I experienced thirty years
ago in Japan. Prior to Chinese influence, that culture in Japan which expanded
to eventually conquer all of Japan seems to have had a strong female component: women served as rulers, priests and mediums. In the initial state of borrowing, women lost most of their institutional roles, retaining some of the
priestly positions, but none of the political ones. Nevertheless, from the
description of elite women's lives that we have from the early female writers,
women seem to have retained a degree of autonomy and power. Women maintained their roles as mediums, but apparently with less status than before. The
second wave of borrowing was far more detrimental.

Chinese Song dynasty *rujia* theories, when interpreted through the eyes of
Japanese male warriors, led to a rigidly structured hierarchy which included
sex. All public social intercourse involved status signals between two or more
individuals, none of whom would be precisely of the same rank. Females
deferred to males of the same or higher social status. This is why the old woman
gave me her seat on the streetcar. Nonetheless, Japanese women retain to the
present close ties with the numinous. Most mediums and ecstatic healers are
female, and women are often at the heart of new religious sects. Once established, however, these sects then tend to be taken over by male institutional
leaders.

This public behavior of female subservience to males has led to a gross misunderstanding of Japanese women by non-Japanese males. In the 1960s, older Chinese male friends in Taiwan would tell me that their ideal life would be a Western (upper middle-class) house, Chinese cuisine, and a Japanese wife (their wishing for a difference from their female-dominated households). Any Japanese male could have told them that they were being naive; Japanese women have at least as much control over their households as do their Chinese counterparts. Deferential they may be in public, but the home is the women's domain. Males turn their paychecks over to their wives, to receive a small allowance in return, hence, the practice of companies paying for the entertainment of Japanese middle and upper-class employees. Males have little involvement with the home and spend most of their time outside of it. Indeed, husbands and wives are not used to being with each other. Most divorces occur after the male spouse retires and begins to hang around the house. While women have few institutional ritual roles, they perform virtually all of the rituals which take place in the home, and, as in China, these are the most common and important ones; women also have major roles in local festivals. Female mediums function primarily in their homes.[1]

The development of a militaristic culture, however, did not lead to Western romantic chivalry, which in any case developed after the end of feudalism in Europe. A current of egalitarianism, both sex and class, underlay martial values: a sword could kill regardless of who wielded it. It should be noted in this regard that swords in Japan are holy. They are made by Shinto priests, with religious rituals at all stages of manufacture, and are understood to have a sacred life of their own. In performing *iaido*, we always kneel and fully bow to the ground before our swords before sliding the ensheathed sword into our *obi* (sash). When Musashi, the famous swordsman, killed one of his rivals, he was challenged by the dead opponent's mother. Not wishing to kill an old woman, he was advised he had no choice: he must kill or be killed by anyone who challenged him; there was no place for sentimentality nor sex or age differences.

When a *samurai* woman took up a weapon, the archaic Japanese egalitarianism reasserted itself. To fail to understand that would lead to immediate death. When I was paired against a Japanese woman with a sword, it was the sacred sword that was important. Sex differences disappeared in the symbolic life-and-death struggle to score killing strokes against each other. Hence, my two seemingly contradictory experiences were two sides of the same coin, so to speak, both modes of behavior resulting from the second wave of borrowing from China. Giving me the seat reflected the 1930s militaristic interpretation of *rujia*; fighting a woman in *kendo* reflected Zen theory, which underlay the *dojo* training: female and male, life and death, all were the same in undifferentiated reality.

ASPECTS OF KOREAN RELIGION

Korea is a peninsula that points to Japan from the northeast corner of China. Both countries have at times conquered Korea, yet, throughout, Korea has maintained its own language and culture. Korean is an Altaic language, and the culture at one time would most likely have had many similar aspects to those of the other Altaic-speaking cultures of Northeast Asia. A series of adaptations of Chinese culture over nearly two millennia ago as well as the possibility of southern influences from the sea has led to an unusual development of different but parallel religions differentiated by gender.[2]

The basic religious pattern in Northeast Asia is shamanistic, but the situation in Korea is complex and the early period confusing. Korean scholars tend towards the view that the early rulers were also shamans, that, for example, the earliest crown found is related to shamans' headdresses in some southern Siberian cultures. In Korea, at least for the last few hundred years, however, all those termed shamans are females or, if male, dressed as a female while practicing. Moreover, the term "shaman" in the Western literature is universally used for a plethora of Korean terms for female religious functionaries. Some clearly fulfill the role of ritual leaders or priests; others are ecstatic religious functionaries, but function as mediums; that is, they are possessed by spirits. Few, if any, actually function as shamans. While the Altaic Tungus word *saman* is found in Chinese, I have not found it among the lists of Korean terms translated as "shaman."

How did mediumism begin in a culture that at one time was most likely shamanistic? The answer may be found in relevant myths. Chang Chu-kun has analyzed twenty motifs within sixty myths collected from three hundred shrines on Cheju Island, which many scholars consider the area that has continued most unchanged with regard to this aspect of Korean religion:

> The important ones are: a) the emergence of male gods from the earth [elsewhere in Korea they descend from the sky], b) the hunting and flesh-eating life of male gods, c) settlement at the place of an arrow's fall, d) the entry of a female god into the island after drifting on the sea, e) the marriage of male god to female god, f) the female god's encouragement of, and recommendation of agriculture to male gods, g) the rice diet of the female god, h) the conflict between male gods and female gods arising from a difference in tastes. . . .

These mythic motifs may well explain the complex nature of the situation. Prior to the introduction of horticulture, shamanism was the norm and practiced by males and females in relation to hunting, as is typical of circum-polar cultures. As wet-rice agriculture spread into Korea from the south, possibly introduced early by sea, so too did female mediumism, often found in conjunction with horticulture. Males continued to practice shamanism in relation to hunting and warfare, while females, who carried on horticulture, practiced mediumism. As Chinese elite culture was adopted in conjunction with governing, Chinese elite practices displaced the shamanism of the males, while the females continued to practice mediumism. Such an interpretation is in accord with other myths pertaining to mediumism and with the historical and current situation in Korea.

The term "shamanism" appears to be used in the Western language literature for indigenous aspects of Korean religion in general and would correlate to the use of the term "Shinto" in Japan, except that Shinto, to a degree, became institutionalized, especially after it became an official state religion in the late nineteenth century. In Korea, the borrowing of Chinese culture was more complex and continuous, given the land connections between the two cultures.

Aspects of Chinese culture would certainly have been present in Korea when Han dynasty China conquered the northern part two thousand years ago. With the formation of Korean kingdoms in the fourth century, aspects of the Chinese mode of government, including *rujia* (confusingly called "Confucianism" in the West), were clearly in place. Later kingdoms oriented themselves to Buddhism, which at the time was closely connected to the Chinese government. It was not until the last Korean dynasty, the Yi, which began in the fourteenth century, that a revised form of *rujia* thought and practice (called "Neo-Confucianism" in the West) became mandated by the state. Indeed, it is only in Korea that one can accurately deem *rujia*, essentially a bibliographic convention in China, a religion.

With state sponsorship and promulgation, the central aspect of Chinese religion with its focus on sacrifices to the dead of the family became the only approved form of religious practice. Buddhism, once a quasi-state religion, was officially downgraded and viewed with the indigenous religious practices as low-class superstitions. Since the Yi mode of *rujia* practices was patrilineal and patrifocal, males oriented themselves to this aspect of religion. Females continued the indigenous aspects of religion both for themselves and the males of their families. During the Yi reign, there were repeated attempts to eradicate the indigenous female-led religious practices. Since the late nineteenth century, Christianity in Korea, the only East Asian culture in which Christianity took hold and became important, but reinforced, if not exacerbated, the devaluing of female rituals and female ritual leadership.

This split of religions between the sexes may have been reinforced by Yi policies but certainly did not originate at that time. As we will see, mediumism everywhere involves females more than males, but is not exclusively female. Moreover, it is to be noted, that in the neighboring Manchurian culture, also Altaic, is was common practice for a daughter of the family to not marry and devote her life to being the family shaman. One of the characteristics of Korean "shamanism" is that it is home and family centered; the rituals take place in the home of the family to be benefited or in the home of the medium, if the ritual is for the benefit of an individual. Among that group of "shamans" who are not ecstatic religious functionaries but rather priests, the position is passed on from mother-in-law to daughter-in-law, given that families are patrilocal. Hence, the religious roles of females in Korean culture would seem to go back in time to its very origins; it is the split between male and female religions that would be much later. The effect of the adaptation of Chinese religion, although not as practiced in China, has been the split into parallel religions divided by the sex of practitioners and differing greatly in social prestige.

Those who function primarily via spirit possession are termed *mudang*. They frequently come to the profession through long-term illness that is diagnosed by divination as due to their need to function as *mudang*. Although they may resist for a time, many such women will then undergo training in the profession under an experienced *mudang*. The initiation involves a knowledge of the proper ritual, identification of the possessing deity, so that the proper costume can be worn and appropriate rituals followed, and dancing while in trance on knife-blades (climbing a ladder of upturned sword-blades is common in Northeast Asian shamanism and can be found in northern Chinese mediumism).

The ritual performed by the *mudang* is called a *kut*. It is an elaborate ritual that involves the whole family in whose home it will be enacted for a variety of needs and benefits. The complex ritual involves the preparation of a sacred space, sacrificial rites, and dances by the *mudang* accompanied by drums, leading to her possession by deities or spirits of the dead, at which time prognosis and healing will take place. Males of the family sponsoring the *kut* tend to stay on the fringes, but at times need to be involved. Some do so enthusiastically; others make it quite clear they would rather be somewhere else. There are male mediums as well, but when they officiate at a *kut*, they wear the garb of females; that is, it is acknowledged that they are taking on a female role during the time of the ritual.

By far, the most articulate analyses of the female aspect of Korean religion are by Laurel Kendall, from which the following brief passages are taken, but the reader is highly recommended to consult the whole work:

Public powerlessness and private strength, this contradiction permeates a Korean woman's entire life. She follows a few steps behind her husband on village lanes, but once inside the house she uses a sharp tongue and managerial acumen to good effect. In *kut* she transmutes this contradiction into high drama and comedy. She acknowledges the powerful with flattery and an occasional treat, but she shouts back at the gods when they presume too much.

The system of ritual and belief . . . implies a housewife, usually the senior woman of a household, who deals with the supernatural on behalf of the house, and a professional shaman [medium] who can, when the need arises, invoke and become possessed by the gods, ghosts, and ancestors of client households. Women hold this corner of life in an overtly Confucian society where, as my male informants would remind me, "Man is respected and woman lowly," where men hold public power and prerogatives. . . .

The *kut* is a woman's party, but total exclusivity is neither necessary nor desirable. The male house head must greet his gods and ancestors, and each spirit delivers a divination to each member of the family. . . .

Korean shamanism is a professional elaboration upon Korean household religion. Shaman and housewife perform analogous tasks and deal with the same spirits. A *mansin* [*mudang*] claims the capacity to trance, to envision and become possessed by the gods and ancestors of all her client households and to muster the power of supernatural generals and warriors against ghosts and noxious influences. . . .

The male-led religious practices promote the continuation of the patrilineal family line and the power and public prestige of the family. The female-led religious practices promote, not so much the well-being of the family, but of the household, all those who live in and are influenced by those residing in the home. This may include neighbors; it will certainly include married daughters. This aspect of Korean religion, proceeding as it does from the females of the family, is not limited to the patrilineal family but includes the woman's daughters and their families. Hence, there is a tendency for these gendered complementary religious traditions to differ in gender orientation as well. In a sense, Korean mediumism is matrifocal, and the "Confucian" rituals from China are patrifocal and, outside the home, supportive of patriarchy.

Part III
Native North America

When the first Indian maid reached adolescence, Grandmother Moon,
hiding her face (it was the time of the new moon), peered down at her
and whistled, saying, "follow me." For some days the girl remained
dreamy and wished to play all by herself; but when a fortnight had
elapsed and the moon was past full, she heard the call of her grandmother and tried to reach the place from which the whistle sounded. A
large tree blocked her path, and the girl did not try to leap over it but
looked back. Grandmother Moon then taught her to redden her cheeks
with the juice of the bloodroot as her own cheeks were reddened, and she
bade her go and fast on the hide of a "lion" (mythical giant lynx) to prepare herself for a blessing. Afterwards Grandmother Moon taught her to
fashion a pot of clay and to smooth its surface with a stone. The grandmother herself provided the food for the pot as soon as it was finished.

—Mary Sugedub (Anishnabe) of Wasausink,
as recorded by Diamond Jenness in 1929

7
INTRODUCTION: FOUR VIGNETTES

NATIVE AMERICAN TRADITIONS are numerous, encompassing all degrees of socioeconomic complexity and a multitude of environmental conditions. They share certain commonalities, such as pervasive shamanism. South of the Arctic there are further common features, including the use of tobacco as an offering to spirits and a focus on the number four. In Mesoamerica and South America there is a further commonality in the orientation towards the use of psychotropic plants in vision questing and shamanizing.

To introduce the detailed studies of the following chapters in this section of the book, four brief vignettes of aspects of Native American religious traditions will be presented, vignettes to indicate commonalities in highly diverse traditions, as well as the fatal flaws of the androcentric literature. The first discusses an image of what is probably the Earth Mother found both in Eurasia and the Americas; the findings are based on my own research. This is followed by discussion of a people that spans both Asia and the Americas, the Inuit, one of the few cultures to gain their subsistence primarily from hunting; it focuses on their understanding of the Earth and Sea Mothers. The discussion is based on the work of my former student, Daniel Merkur, and our many dialogues on the topic. The third vignette concentrates on an area with the opposite climate from the Arctic, the Amazonian rain forest to the east of the Andes, and the concept of the Earth Mother in relation to gardening; the study is excerpted from the work of Michael Brown and Margaret Van Bolt, the first ethnologists seriously to consider the ideology and rituals of the women of the Amazon. Finally, the opposite type of culture from the egalitarian Aguaruna is briefly introduced, the imperial civilization of the high Andes and its west coast, with particular reference to the Earth Mother and the Moon and their relationship to female rulers; this discussion is indebted to the analysis of the ethnohistorian Irene Silverblatt.

BRIDGING THE CONTINENTS: A FEMALE IMAGE

The first European to record his impressions of the Americas on landing on the east coast of Cuba noted female images in the homes of the local people, the Tainos, and entertained the possibility that they were objects of worship: "They found many images made like women and many heads like masks, very well worked. He did not know if they had them for beauty or whether they worship them." Christopher Columbus recorded his impressions in a diary completed in 1493. An abstract made by Bartolomé de las Casas, the priest who argued in the Spanish court that Native Americans had souls, is still extant. The sex egalitarianism of the culture was also noted if not understood: "Afterwards the men went out and the women entered, and sat in the same way round them, kissing their hands and feet, fondling them, trying to find out if they were of flesh and bone like themselves. . . ."[1]

A half millennium later, near where Columbus landed, in the town of Bane in eastern Cuba, there is a tiny museum of Native American archaeological artifacts. I was astounded to find on the second floor a case of small, ceramic female figurines of every shape imaginable and unimaginable. There were no curator, catalogue or labels, but I was given to understand that the museum was in the small town because the artifacts were found in the vicinity. Undoubtedly, among these figurines were those similar to the ones seen by Columbus.

On his second voyage to the Americas, Columbus commissioned Father Ramón Pané to study the Tainos. Pané identified the female images as those of Atabey, the mother of Yúcahu, the spirit of cassava, the mainstay of the diet. Pané understood Atabey to be the goddess of human fertility; women prayed to her for success in childbirth. However, as the museum collection in Bane makes clear, there was not a single image, but many. While one was of Atabey, another must have been of Itiba Cahubasba, the Earth deity.

The Tainos had images of both female and male deities or *zemi*, a term applied to both the deities and their images. The images were kept in small shrines in the homes; major ones under the care of village chiefs were placed in special structures, functioning as small temples. The most common ritual seemed to be the offering of food to the *zemi*.

In preparation for communicating with the *zemi*, the Tainos would purify themselves by inducing vomiting using a small stick placed in their throats. After purifying themselves, they inhaled through a forked tube inserted in the nostrils a snuff, called *cohoba*, made from the crushed seeds of the piptadenia tree. *Cohoba* is psychoactive and produces visions, through which the *zemi* communicate to the ritual participants.

The Tainos were matrilineal, matrilocal, and egalitarian with regard to sex. Either women or men might serve as village chiefs, and both participated in the ritual ball games.[2]

Some of the female images at the museum in Bane are of a shape found throughout the Americas, from the southern Andes Mountains, through Mesoamerica and the Caribbean, through the Great Lakes area of North America, to the coast of Alaska. There are also Maori examples, from the North Island of New Zealand, the westernmost Polynesian culture. The image is of a slim, standing female, legs slightly apart, with clearly depicted breasts and vulva, but neither emphasized. The diagnostic feature of the image is the position of the arms. The forearms are held across the chest, between the breasts and the diaphragm, with the fingertips or knuckles, if the hands are clenched, just touching. The upper arms are tight against the sides or at an angle with the elbows jutting outward. It is to be noted that, of all the ways humans can hold their arms, this posture is neither comfortable nor a natural configuration. Nor is it a posture that simplifies the carving of the image (or of molds for cast images), since, in the case of those examples where the elbows jut outward from the body, it is far more difficult to hollow the space between the angle of the upper arm and forearm than to carve the arms straight down at the sides.

The earliest datable examples are from sites in Turkey, Greece, Bulgaria, Sardinia, Iraq, and China from 8,500 to 6,500 years ago. Later examples abound in the eastern Mediterranean area. A prototype may be represented from figures from Mal'ta in Siberia, dated to 18,000 to 15,000 years ago. The only factor making the relationship of these Upper Paleolithic period figures to the later figures uncertain is that the hands are held or touch across the lower abdomen.[3]

Returning to the Americas, areas with demonstrable continuity of these images over a considerable period of time include Mesoamerica and the Andes. In the Andes, a further diagnostic feature is the representation of the figurine's hair, which is depicted as long and straight, cut square where it touches the upper back, with a noticeable part in the middle from the forehead down to the back. The earliest known figurines with this characteristic are small ceramic ones found in large numbers at a coastal side in Ecuador known as Valdivia Phase, Period B, dating from 4300 to 4400 years ago. These images are identical to those found in metal—gold, silver, and a gold-silver-copper alloy—common in Inca sites to the time of contact. They range in height from five to twenty-five centimeters. Given that the Spanish melted down all the gold and silver they came across, the large number that survived indicate that these images were quite numerous before contact. Hence, the image has a remarkable time-depth of nearly four thousand years, perhaps the longest continuous use of a complex religious symbol in human history (obviously, the simple vulva symbol discussed in the next chapter has a considerably longer time-depth—at least 30,000 years).[4]

Due to the dryness of the climate, both along the coast and in the high altitude of the mountains, one of the Inca period figurines, dressed in a mantle and headdress, was found *in situ* with the mummy of a young girl. Were all of the Inca figurines originally dressed? This is an unanswerable question. In the later period there are also male figurines of similar manufacture. But certainly the Western art historical interpretation that these were dolls for little girls to play with can be given little credence. Would the same be said for images of the Virgin Mary in Catholic cultures? Moreover, gold and silver were sacred substances in Inca culture and not for mundane use.

But what did this image represent in Andean cultures? Indigenous religion was ruthlessly suppressed by the Spanish following the conquest of the Andes, and so we must rely on the recordings of the oppressors or of assimilated Incas for what little information we have. Father Bernabe Cobo notes that the Incas "imagined that the Moon looked like a woman, and the statue of the Moon that they had in the Temple of the Sun was in the form of a woman." Over a century earlier, Miguel de Estete recorded finding life-sized gold and silver statues of females in temples in the suburbs of the capital city. Irene Silverblatt convincingly argues that the Incas, to solidify their empire building, created a hierarchy of sex-paralleled deities and replaced Pachamama, the Earth Mother, with the Moon Queen. Hence, in the Andes alone, during the reign of the Inca in the century preceding the Spanish conquest, these female figures may well have represented the Moon, paralleled by the similar male images that represented the sun (to be further discussed in the last segment of this chapter). Prior to that time, and without the parallel male images, the image more likely represented the Earth Mother.

Many of these same images in Mesoamerica are larger than the extant Inca metal ones; some of stone are the size of an adult human. What would have been the purpose of these small silver, gold, and gold alloy figurines? The Spanish chroniclers do mention life-sized ones, but all those found were melted down as booty. Cobo noted that "it was very common for them to make offerings of silver and gold, sometimes in small lumps of different sizes, and at other times they offered these metals in the form of human or animal images, some small and others large." The small images that are still being found are undoubtedly from sacred sites of the kind Cobo describes: "And the sacrifice was made by burying the things at the *guacas* [burial places; sacred places, such as springs, special stones representing Pachamama placed in the fields, etc.]

and places consecrated to the gods in whose honor the sacrifices were made. . . ." Given Moon was worshiped in imperial-sanctioned temples and Pachamama was worshiped in the fields and other natural sites at the time of the Inca empire, the female images are more probably of Pachamama created both as offerings to her and, perhaps, as representatives of her to which *chicha* (corn beer) and food offerings could be made in the home.[5]

The Spanish conquistadores observed images of women sculpted in gold in ceremonial buildings of Cuzco, the Incan capitol. "These statues, which Pedro Sancho described as goddesses whom the Incas fed and talked with 'as if they were women of flesh,' were 'dressed in beautiful and very fine clothing'."[6] Whether these images were similar to the ones being discussed in this chapter can no longer be known, but it is likely.

In Mexico, similar figures of pottery are found in many areas and from every archaeological period, the earliest dating to approximately three thousand years ago, and the most recent of this century. I had long assumed that these images were specific to Mesoamerica and the Andes and that the paralleling of these images in early Europe, west Asia and Siberia was but coincidental. Discovering that this image had been found north of Lake Ontario, in the vicinity of the Peterborough Petroglyphs discussed in the next chapter, gave me pause. I recently travelled to Alaska on the offchance that I might find something of relevance to this topic. At the Sheldon Jackson Museum in Sitka, I found a drawer full of the kind of figurines under discussion but made of ivory. No data were available on their provenance, nor were tests done with regard to their age. However, their manufacture from walrus tusk certainly indicates that they are coastal Alaskan and the patinate on the ivory, all being brown and some very dark brown, suggest they are quite old. Similar sized pottery figurines from Manchuria with the same arm placement, as discussed in Chapter 4, would date to between four and six thousand years ago. The distribution from the southern part of the Americas through Alaska to Siberia to eastern Europe and western Asia indicates a continuity of human experience, of a specific image of a numinous female, through diffusion and/or migration bridging Eurasia and the Americas. (I am uncertain as to how to explain the Polynesian examples in this regard.)

If this female image with a specific and unnatural placement of arms and hands, however, does indeed represent the Earth Mother, then the use of similar male figurines during the Incan period in the Andes, and nowhere else, is perturbing. Surely, the male image does not represent the Earth Mother, although it might represent the Sun Father with the female image transferred to the Moon Mother. After completing the initial draft of this book, I was studying the collection of the Museo de América in Madrid, when a solution to the enigma came to me. The museum houses a number of gold and copper objects from a cache found in Columbia a century ago from the Quimbaya culture of about a thousand years ago. In this collection there are eight relatively large gold figures, either alone or applied to gold vessels. Most are male, and, except for those holding objects in their hands, all have the hands in the above described position. Rather than deities, they may represent aristocrats. If there was originally but a tradition of creating anthropomorphic female images of deities, then when it became desirable to represent aristocratic humans, the hand position for representing deity may then have been used to designate the semi-divine ruling class as well. This is a possible explanation for the many Incan male figurines with the similar hand position at a relatively late time, the century preceding the Spanish conquest.

SEDNA: FROM EARTH MOTHER TO SEA MOTHER

Not only do images bridge Eurasia and the Americas, but so does a people: the Inuit reside in extreme northeastern Asia and far northern North America and Greenland. Until the United States and the former Soviet Union stationed troops on each side of the Bering Strait to shoot at those attempting to cross, Inuit on both sides regularly traversed the channel between North America and Asia to visit and intermarry. And until a few decades ago, when, at least in Canada, Inuit were forced to live in permanent settlements on threat of having their children taken from them to attend school, they maintained a nomadic life style. For the last thirty to forty years, the Inuit have suffered illnesses from unsanitary conditions due to permanent settlement in the Arctic (only the White administrators were given clean water and sewage facilities) and a diet which shifted from hunted animals and fish to store-bought sugars and carbo-hydrates, and the alcoholism and suicide that follow cultural destruction. For this reason, the following analysis of an aspect of Inuit religion is based on the culture prior to 1950.

Before this time, Inuit culture was one of the few to subsist almost entirely on hunted meat and fish. The far northern Inuit, in particular, developed a sophisticated technology to enable themselves to live in an area that for all other humans was utterly inhospitable, a technology so advanced and detailed that males and females were required to specialize in different skills to the degree that neither could survive without the other. Females created complex, tailored, warm, waterproof garments that enabled males to engage in sealing on frigid waters and over frozen seas. Although women were not directly involved in certain major subsistence activities, their contribution was considered equally important by all. Bogoras quotes an Inuit male: "It is a mistake to think that women are weaker than men in hunting pursuits. Home incantations are essential for success in hunting. In vain man walks around, searching, but those that sit by the lamp are really strong, for they know how to call the game to the shore."[7] The culture is egalitarian; both men and women function socially as shamans, the only traditional occupational (part-time) specialty.

Inuit religion enables us to understand a transition that often takes place when a terrestrial culture becomes a maritime one: the supplanting of the Earth Mother by a Sea Mother. (In Chapter 5, we had the example of a Sea Mother who additionally takes on the characteristics of an Earth Mother when a sub-culture shifts its emphasis from fishing to farming.) The Chugach Inuit, who reside on the southwestern coast of Alaska, an area with forested mountains, understand the earth as *Nunam-shua*, the "Indweller of Earth," as well as the "Indweller of the Alder Tree." She is understood to be a woman, her body encased in a bright light; she wears a garment from which are suspended all the terrestrial creatures. She dwells in the mountain forests.

Among the more northern Inuit, who inhabit the treeless tundra, Earth is particularly associated with caribou, the terrestrial mainstay of the diet. Both caribou and muskoxen are understood to have originally emerged from holes or eggs (depending on the particular sub-cultural myth) in the ground. Earth may be referred to by circumlocution, out of awe and respect, through allusion to caribou. The Caribou Mother, of major importance among the northern Inuit, derives from the Earth Indweller, as Grain Mothers derive from the Earth Mother in horticultural and agricultural situations.

Earth is more than the mother of the hunted animals; she is also the mother of humans. A number of myths from different Inuit sub-cultures concern human beings originally born from the earth and only later from human females. As these myths were garnered from males, it is quite likely that the women have myths that directly related themselves and birthing to Earth.

Given the wide distribution of these myths as well as their great variety, Daniel Merkur concludes,

> The Earth Indweller of the Inuit may definitely be counted among the circum-polar goddesses of the earth, birth, and hunt that derive *ex hypothesi* from the mother goddesses of the Upper Paleolithic of Eurasia and its eastern variant, the Advanced Paleolithic of Siberia. The derivation does not imply a lack of change. Indeed, it is by demonstrating a sequence of changes that we may be certain of the Earth Indweller's high antiquity.[8]

The development of the hunting kayak allowed maritime hunting of seals, in addition to whales, hunted from the much larger skin boats also used for transportation. The development of the dog-sled allowed migration when the seas were frozen. A few thousand years ago, these new technologies allowed a shift from a semi-nomadic life with stone residences to a fully nomadic life utilizing ice-homes, igloos, in the winter and skin tents in the summer. These developments allowed the year-round exploitation of the far northern environment and a subsistence shift from the seasonally migrating caribou to seals and walrus. The sea became more important than the land; the Sea Mother became more central to life than the Earth Mother.

The Inuit in Asia call the sea *Nulirahak*, the "Big Woman"; she is conceived as an female elder controlling the sea animals from the sea bottom. The Chugach in Alaska and the Inuit in West Greenland understand her as *imamshua* (*imap-inua*), the "Indweller of the Sea"; and they conceive of her as do the Asian Inuit. She is seen at times by hunters appearing as a sea-otter transformed into a human female, just as, as will be discussed in the next chapter, Anishnabe may see Deer as a woman, and the Lakota, Bison as a woman.

The far northern Inuit tend to merge the Earth Mother with the Sea Mother. Called *Nulijajuk*, the "One Who is Wife," among many of the far northern sub-cultures, she controls both the sea and the earth and all the animals on both. She is involved not only with hunting, but with childbirth and death, that is, all the essential aspects of life. As well, she controls the weather and earthquakes. Her name implies that she may appear as a spirit called *nuliayuq*, a spirit who appears as a human female and may marry an Inuit man. Again myths of humans marrying spirit bears, deer, bison, beaver, etc., that is, those animals important to human well-being, abound in Native American cultures to the south. There are probably parallel myths with regard to human women, but again the gathering of data from primarily males precludes our understanding Inuit female spirituality from the literature.

Typical of the awe and respect accorded spirits in the Americas, the Sea Mother is usually not referred to directly, but indirectly as *Kavna* (*Qavna, Kana*), "the One Down There," or *Arnaluk takanaluk*, "the Woman Down There." On Baffin Island, she is known by the dialectal variant, *Sedna* (the "One Down There"), and it is by this name that she is discussed in Western studies of myth and religion. She is also known in the far north as *Nerrivik*, "the Food Dish," and *Arnaquassaaq*, "the Old Woman." In East Greenland, she is known as *Imap-ukua*, "the Mother of the Sea."

As in all hunting traditions, hunting is successful only when the animals give themselves to humans. In return, people treat them and their remains with respect and honor them with appropriate rituals. When this is not done or when humans transgress the appropriate behavior taught them by these spirits, then these animals will turn from humans, and the people will starve. Hence, when the hunted animals disappear or when severe weather prevents hunting for a long time, the Inuit seek to appease the Sea Mother. In different parts of the Arctic, this may be done in different ways: Shamans may send their helping spirits to the abode of the Sea Mother to learn from her what offenses have been committed so that the negligent person can confess the misdeed and the animals return. Shamans may summon the Sea Mother from the ocean depths, hauling her up with a rope, as they do seals, to just below the ice floor of the igloo. There the shaman pleads with her to release the animals. Shamans may journey to her home on the sea bottom, there to overcome many obstacles to reach her and overpower her, she having turned her back due to her anger towards the people. The shaman then combs from her tangled hair the misdeeds of the people. This pleases her; as often understood in the form of a humanoid seal, she has no fingers and is unable to grasp a comb. Placated, she returns the animals to the sea, where they can again be hunted.

The far northern Inuit live in a difficult environment; when the hunted animals are not found, there is no backup source of subsistence as there often is in more southerly regions. Without the ability of shamans to appease the Sea Mother, on whom their lives depend, the people would die. In the far north, human life is utterly dependent on the Sea Mother's beneficence, as those living off the land are dependent on the Earth Mother.

THE AMAZONIAN EARTH MOTHER AND HER RITUALS

There is an extensive ethnological literature on the Native Americans of the Amazonian basin; all but one ignore the religious lives and understanding of women. Many are written by male anthropologists, and it is understandable that they were not privy to this information. Less acceptable is the conviction that that to which they are not privy does not exist. Unfortunately, the androcentric orientation of anthropology meant that female anthropologists took the same attitude. I will never forget a book by a budding female ethnologist, who shall remain here unnamed, who on finding that males would not associate with her and considering females far too unimportant to speak to, ended up with nothing of interest to report. Out of the plethora of publications, four will be discussed.

The earliest general English language work of importance is Irving Goldman's *The Cubeo: Indians of the Northwest Amazon*, based on fieldwork carried out in 1939–40, and published in 1963. Understanding horticulture to be the female occupation, Goldman notes: "Women give birth in their manioc gardens and during male cult ceremonies they may take shelter in the garden." But he fails to understand why they did so: "Manioc is a strictly secular crop for which there are no rites, despite its overwhelming nutritive importance and the usual hazards of cultivation." Durkheim's dichotomy reigns supreme in Goldman's analysis: "Women are not barred from the front plaza, but it is definitely a male zone with sacred connotation . . . By contrast, the rear plaza is a female zone and is secular."

Goldman provides one of the earliest detailed descriptions of the use of long flutes and trumpets as male sacred instruments; they are employed in male initiation rituals and not to be seen by women, and they are found in a number of Amazonian cultures. He reports the Cubeo origin myth of the flutes that accords with others: either the flutes are taken from the women in mythic times and given to the men by a deity, or the men steal them from the women in mythic times. He describes the women's reactions to the male secrecy: "The women at their chores near the river bank paused to listen to the low, mournful notes of the oncoming horns. A shot from the canoe was a warning signal that sent the women running for the house, *laughing* and shrieking at one another to hurry . . . Now the women . . . ran off together to the manioc gardens, their traditional sanctuary, those in the lead calling to the laggards to hurry" (emphasis added). To my mind, it seems that the women are amused at the men's secrecy, and they repair to their sacred space, the manioc garden (see below), so as not to embarrass their husbands and brothers. More important, analysts have failed to note the implications of the mythic origin of the flutes; surely, it signifies a reverse of the Durkheimian thesis. It is women who are innately sacred; it is men who have to steal sacredness from them in order to have some of their own. The women cannot be allowed to see the flutes, because they may take back their power.

Yolanda and Robert Murphy studied the Mundurucú from 1952 to 1953 and published their *Women of the Forest* in 1974. Due to the popularity of the work, a second edition was published in 1985. Studying the women of the culture was a laudable and important work, particularly at the time it was done. As a couple, the Murphys would be able to learn from both men and women and bring the two different parts of the culture together into a meaningful whole. Alas, the entire work is so imbued with androcentrism that it assumes the male ideology is *the* cultural ideology. Not only does female ideology remain unexamined, but the work implies there is no such thing.

The work on Amazonian ideology most frequently referred to is Gerardo Reichel-Dolmatoff's *Amazonian Cosmos: The Sexual and Religious Symbolism of the Tukano Indian*, first published in English in 1971. The work is based on a *single* male informant acculturated to modern urban life! Reichel-Dolmatoff notes that a substantial proportion of the daily food supply comes from horticulture, but that the activity is "contemptible and of low prestige." We have a major section on "The Creator and His Creation," but it seems there are no major female deities. There are chapters on "The Master of the Animals" and "The Spirits of the Forest," but none on the spirits of the garden. There is a section on "Man and Nature," but, of course, none on "Woman and Horticulture." Yet this book remains the major reference for Amazonian religion!

From 1976 to 1978, Michael Brown studied the Aguaruna. He was joined in 1977 by Margaret Van Bolt, who was pleased to be able to learn from the Aguaruna women. They present a picture of Amazonian religion radically different from any before theirs; the book does not just include the neglected women's side of things, but, more important, there is an analysis of how the women's and men's understanding, rituals, symbols, and life-styles interrelate to create a meaningful whole. While there are linguistic and regional differences among some of the four above-mentioned Amazonian cultures, surely the Aguaruna are not atypical, even if they do not have the male initiatory flute ceremonial. That manioc is the main staple for all of these cultures, that the occupational specializations by sex are the same, that the hallucinogenic substances utilized are the same, and that many of their symbols are similar argues for a fair degree of commonality in the basic concepts described in the following.[9]

The Aguaruna are a Jivaroan-speaking people who live at the western end of the Amazonian rain-forest in northeastern Peru. Typical of these cultures, males are hunters and warriors and females, horticulturists. As we shall see, there is overlap in both occupational realms.

The two most important deities are similarly divided. Women relate to Nugkui, the Earth, while males relate to Etsa, the Sun. The other major spirits include Tsugki, a deity who may be understood as either male or female and is particularly related to shamanistic activities. Both men and women may have visions of the *ajútap*, the ancient warrior spirits. More recently, among Christian converts, a new deity, Apujui (Our Father), has become important.

Nugkui lives in the topsoil as well as caves, and she controls the garden plants. It is she that women address in rituals of gardening, potting, and caring for domestic animals. Her daughter brought horticulture and ceramic pots to the people.

As the spirit realm, the Aguaruna life-style is imbued with complementary sex opposition. Females bear children; males go on headhunting raids (at least in the past) to bring back the shrunken heads that add to the life of the community. (A pair of stone figurines at the Museo de América in Madrid from a tropical forest culture of Costa Rica parallels a woman cupping her breasts with her hands and a male holding a head on his chest with both hands.) Females garden; males hunt. The female realm is the swidden (slash-and-burn garden) and the home; the male realm, the forest. Males may plant above-ground crops—maize, plantain, tobacco; the women, below-ground crops—manioc, sweet potato, etc., the staples of subsistence. Women manufacture pottery; males work wood. There is overlap between the two: young couples may hunt together, and women care for the hunting dogs; and men clear the forest in the swidden horticulture. Both sexes depend on the other: men gain prestige through the hospitality of manioc beer, the production of which is dependent on their wives' horticultural skills; women rely on men for defense, for clearing the gardens, and for animal protein.

Male hunting rituals are paralleled by female horticultural rituals. These are of two types: power songs and the offering of blood analogues. Sacred songs, *anen*, are central to hunting, horticulture, and courtship. *Anen* are received from elders in a ritual involving the transfer of consumed tobacco, either orally or nasally. The song is learned with the recipient intoxicated by the sacred tobacco; a song learned without the ingestion of tobacco would have no power. Learning songs also requires special dietary restrictions and sexual abstinence for a period of time. Before using *anen*, the person ingests an infusion of tobacco water to become intoxicated; it is this intoxication that enables the recipient of the song—plant, animal, or person—to hear it. Songs may be sung aloud or silently; as in other parts of the Americas, courting songs may be played on a flute.

As animals are spirits, so too are the plants; both are understood to have similar feelings to humans. Sometimes the largest plant in the garden is understood to be the Manioc Mother (*mama dukuji*), who walks about the garden. Margaret Van Bolt was told:

> When you hear a twig snap on the edge of the garden, you shouldn't look in that direction because it's the manioc mother. If you look at her, she gets angry and shits weeds. The whole garden fills with weeds. If you don't look at her, she is happy. She shits manioc and the plants grow quickly.

It is to the plant spirits that the sacred songs are sung. These songs should be sung day and night during the most vulnerable time of the manioc plant's life-cycle, the first three to six months. Of the many songs recorded by Van Bolt, the following is directed to Nugkui rather than to the plants as are most gardening *anen*:

> In worn-out soil I make a garden
> In the thicket of the bird *chuchumpiú*
> I make a garden
> Mother Nugkui, mother Nugkui
> Let me know your manioc

I am an orphan among enemies
Almost dying I live
In worn-out soil I make a garden
In the thicket of the bird *chuchumpiú*
I make a garden
Mother Nugkui, mother Nugkui
the children of others cry like bird's offspring
"Chianana" they cry, suffering
My child does not do this
Mother Nugkui, mother Nugkui
Let me know your manioc.

This song contains aspects typical in supplicating spirits throughout the Americas. One makes oneself pitiable so that the spirits will take pity on oneself, a weak human being, and make manifest the requested benefit. That women identify with the Earth Mother is clear from the usual ending couplet of songs, "I am a Nugkui woman / I am an Uwanchváu woman" (see Brown's book for an explanation of the latter spirit, a complex topic).

The second type of horticultural ritual involves the use of sacred stones called *nantag*. These stones, often red in color, are originally acquired through visions and dreams and passed on matrilineally. Many of these visions involve Nugkui informing women where a stone will be found.

The stones are used in planting rituals, together with pods of the red-staining achiote plant and other plants. On arriving at the garden, the woman will crush an achiote pod and paint lines on her cheeks, those of her children, and of anyone else with her. This is to let the stone and the manioc plants recognize her as a friend. The *nantag* are unwrapped from their cloth coverings and placed in a bowl with mashed achiote pods, other special plants and water, creating a red liquid. This liquid, referred to as "blood," is poured on the root cuttings to be planted and on the hands of the women. Sacred songs will be sung, for example:

My child has hair cut in bangs
My child has blood
The enemy's child has an oval face
Drink his blood
My child has blood
Drink, drink the blood of the paca
Drink, drink the blood of the agouti
Don't drink the blood of my child
Let the manioc of my enemies come to me
Come, come.

Here we have an explicit paralleling between the blood of hunting and raiding and the "blood" involved in manioc gardening.

Young manioc plants are understood to be thirsty and if the thirst is not assuaged they will "drink the blood" ("eat the souls"), that is, drain the life-force of those passing by. The *nantag* ritual provides the new manioc plants with "blood" and the power of the sacred stones to ensure the manioc's growth and meet their need for "blood," so that their families will be safe from the plant's thirst. The *nantag* also require "blood" and are fed the achiote-pod liquid once a month, also protecting their families from the stone's thirst for blood. A thirsty stone may appear in a dream as a young girl pleading for something to drink.

The involvement of blood in horticultural fertility rituals is linked to the Aguaruna understanding of menstrual blood. Women menstruate because "Etse cuts their wombs." Etse (different from Etsa, Sun) is a spirit in the form of a woman who is irresistible to men. She is the epitome of womanliness: fertile, seductive, and potentially dangerous to men. As women control their fertility through menstrual blood, so they control the gardens through their sacred songs, *nantag,* and symbolic blood. Blood is also understood as the means for thought to circulate through the body; hence, the "blood" of the planting rituals is a means for the thought of the sacred songs to be conveyed from the woman planter to the plants.

Menstrual blood, the fertility of Mother Earth and human woman, and the needs of Mother Manioc are all interconnected in the domain of female sacredness. It is this domain, essential to the life of the Amazonian people, that ethnologists ignored until the work of Michael Brown and Margaret Van Bolt.

INCA GENDER PARALLELISM[10]

The blindness of the medieval Spanish to the importance of female spirits and to female leadership roles, as well as the adoption of Christian androcentrism by assimilated part-Inca writers, such as Garcilaso de la Vega, has led to an understanding of Inca religion and the Inca sociopolitical system that is closer to the European experience than that of Native America. Inca society is generally described as headed by a male ruler and the religious system by a male supreme deity, with human females servile to males and female spirits subordinate to male spirits. This understanding, except for specific Christian tenets, was and is identical to that of Spain and surrounding countries, but is it true of a Native American empire?

Irene Silverblatt, in a brilliant ethnohistorical analysis of the medieval Spanish texts, finds a very different picture, one that accords with sex relationships in non-hierarchical Native American cultures:

Andean peoples interpreted the workings of nature through an ideology of gender complementarity. Male and female interdependent forces were also ancestor-heroes and ancestor heroines of the mortals whose gender they shared. Constructing the supernatural with familiar materials, Andean women perceived kinship and descent to follow lines of women, just as, in parallel, men saw themselves as descending from and creating lines of men.

Andean culture was one of gender parallel descent and leadership. As elsewhere in the Americas, occupations tended to be structured according to gender symbolism as well as anatomical differences; for example, men plowed the fields, and the women dropped in the seeds. Within the communal agrarian villages, a male led the men, and a woman led the women; women cared for female spirits, and males cared for male spirits. Both women and men functioned as diviners, healers, and shamans. Similarly, deities were understood as opposite-sexed pairs. Pachamama, the Earth Mother, according to Silverblatt, was paired with the thunder deity. However, as elsewhere in the Americas, this may have been more a pairing of Earth with Sky, the latter represented by both Thunder and Sun. Father Bernabe Cobo, in several places in his text, points to a pairing of Earth and Sun: in raising food, in people making a oath, and in their being the most common recipients for sacrificial offerings. Be that as it may, although both males and females made offerings to spirits of both sexes, females felt a special relationship with the Earth Mother, the Sea Mother, the Maize Mother, the Potato Mother, and other female spirits, as males did with Sun, Thunder, and other male spirits.

In creating their empire, the Inca added a hierarchical component to every aspect of Andean life within the gender-paralleled structure. The Spanish themselves realized that the supreme deity of the Inca was a concept they created to reinforce their imperial governmental structure. Cobo writes,

> Although this god Viracocha was much venerated before the time of [the person Viracocha] Inca and sacrifices were regularly made to him, [the deity] Viracocha was not held to be superior to the Sun until the time of this Inca who adopted his name.

Of course, Father Cobo assumed the deity, Viracocha, was male.

To the contrary, Silverblatt demonstrates that the Inca did not shift out of a gender-paralleled mind-set by placing a single-sexed deity at the head of a now hierarchically structured pantheon, rather Viracocha was androgynous. An indigenous author, Pachacuti Yamqui, in a 1613 text, drew a chart of the Inca pantheon. Silverblatt writes of this text and chart:

> Pachacuti Yamqui leaves no doubt as to Viracocha's sexual duality, for above his/her image are the inscribed words "whether it be male, whether it be female."

Viracocha incorporates the opposing forces that each gender represents: "the sun, the moon, day, night, summer, winter."

A further ideological shift fostered by the Inca was to replace Pachamama, the Earth Mother, with the Moon as the female counterpart of the male Sun. This allowed for a semidivine pair of human rulers with matching celestial connections. For the empire of the Inca was not ruled, as is generally assumed, by a single male king, the descendant of the Sun, but by a couple, the descendants of the Sun and the Moon. The male Inca ruled the males of the realm, and the female Inca ruled the females; the male Inca sacrificed to the Sun, and the female Inca to the Moon. When the male Inca was leading the armies in conquest, the female Inca ruled the conquered realm from the capital.

As in life, so in death: the mummified bodies of deceased male rulers were placed in the Temple of the Sun and of deceased female rulers in the corresponding Temple of the Moon. Both sets of mummies were cared for and worshiped equally.

Although female and male symbols, spirits, and rulers were equal from an ideological standpoint, it is not being suggested here that males and females in a hierarchically ordered empire based on the conquests of male armies were equal in practice. Silverblatt presents a complex argument to indicate how females of the conquered territories, albeit in a mode of honor and respect, were brought to the capital and other imperial centers, as a means of maintaining control over the conquered realm.

In summary, the Inca empire indicates the pervasiveness of the sex egalitarianism ubiquitous in Native American cultures. Even in a complex, socially stratified, imperial realm, both rulers and deities continued to demonstrate the structuring of sex and gender into complementary pairs.

8
ANISHNABE RELIGION

INTRODUCTION

A NISHNABE (PLURAL: *ANISHNABEG*) IS THE NAME by which peoples of the Great Lakes region of North America who speak versions of the Algonkian language family denote themselves. In this chapter, the focus will be on the culture designated in the literature by the following appellations for language dialects, the spellings for each varying considerably: Ojibwe (Chippewa, Salteaux), Odawa, Potawatomi, and Algonkin. The analysis, however, in many respects, would also be pertinent to the woodland Cree, Menomini, Mesquakie, and Sauk, who are closely related, both linguistically and culturally.

Prior to contact with Europeans, the Anishnabeg were semi-nomadic over a fixed seasonal range, travelling by birch-bark canoes and snowshoes, according to the season. The Great Lakes region is rich in many plant foods, including wild rice and maple syrup, and many useful plants for healing, structures, containers, bindings, and so on. Many types of fish and other edible water animals were once abundant. Deer in the southern parts and moose in the northern parts were plentiful, as well as the woods bison and elk. A limited amount of horticulture was carried on where the terrain and climate allowed: maize, beans and squash, and tobacco for ritual offerings. The people lived in wigwams and tipis covered with birch bark.

Undoubtedly they were involved in the vast trading networks of the region. Those in the northeastern region traded smoked meat and fish and hides for maize with the more settled Iroquoian-speaking peoples to their south. But the peoples all along the Great Lakes must have been indirectly connected by trade with the cities on the upper Mississippi from the eleventh to fifteenth centuries, cities larger than those then present in Europe, built by the junction of major

127

trading arteries where Euroamericans later built their cities, such as St. Louis at the confluence of the Mississippi and Missouri rivers.

The Anishnabeg continue to be organized into exogamous clans called *dodem* (totems), symbolized by an animal (which is not "tabu"—early anthropology confused the *dodem* symbol with individual guardian-animal spirits and created a fictitious structural model, with no reference to any lived culture). The people lived in family groups of varying sizes depending on the season and the region. Those south of the Great Lakes, where the climate was favorable to horticulture, lived in more permanent and larger settlements. Politically and socially, the Anishnabeg were egalitarian. Leadership, when necessary, was temporarily and voluntarily vested in those individuals who had demonstrated special powers in the tasks at hand; for example, warfare. Women as well as men could act as chiefs and express opinions at council meetings. Advice and guidance was sought from elders, male and female.

Sex played no role in these regards; all were equal. There were, however, gender-oriented economic activities, as is normative to human cultures, due both to physiological specialization and symbolic connections. Females gardened, where it was carried on, and gathered wild plants, fish, and small game. Males hunted larger animals and engaged in trade and raiding—all activities that involved danger and extensive travel. These specializations, nevertheless, were not absolute. Depending on individual predilections and visions, those from either sex could take on any activity. Women, by necessity for survival, given that men could be away for long periods, knew how to hunt.

Anishnabe religion fits into the model of democratized shamanism. All individuals were expected to have visions, guardian spirits, and at least limited shamanic abilities. These connections and abilities were considered absolutely essential for survival. The Anishnabe world was, and remains for traditionalists, imbued with numinous powers. Everything to some degree has power, and everything is interconnected, related. Humans, being weak compared to many plants and animals, require their assistance to survive.

Hence, the Anishnabeg, from childhood, were, and many continue to be, taught to point out their pitiable condition to the spirits, so that individual ones would come to them—to teach, to empower, to protect, and to give themselves for food, clothing, shelter, fire, and other necessities. Plants are not gathered as much as asked, with tobacco offerings, to contribute themselves when needed for human life; animals are not killed but asked to give their flesh to humans so that they may survive. All are relations and involved in familial giving and taking, in a circle of life. And so the spirits, animals, plants, and stones are addressed and understood with love and respect, as grandmother and grandfather, mother and father, sister and brother.

There are four primary means for forming connections and communicating with spirits. From an early age children are trained to fast for longer and longer periods to elicit visions. Those fasting have their faces blackened with charcoal; wear old or little clothing; variously stay in a small dwelling constructed for that purpose, in a nest built in a tree, or in other modes which accord with the spirits with whom they have developed a special relationship; and refrain from food, water, comfort, and sleep for a specified period or until the desired vision is had. Visions need not come from a special ritual; spontaneous visions and significant dreams are equally important.

A second means, also common for all the Anishnabeg, is the ritual of the spirit-lodge, known in the literature as "sweat lodge." In a special structure, similar to a dwelling, the size depending on the number of participants, those taking part entered naked (nowadays towels, shorts, or terrycloth gowns are worn), into a powerful symbolic realm where the heat and steam generated from red-hot rocks, understood as Grandfathers, numinous powers, physiologically assist in eliciting individual and communal visions.

Relations with the spirit world are continued through offerings. Of particular importance is the offering of tobacco, one of four sacred herbs. Food also, especially first fruits—berries, wild rice, etc.—are offered in ritual feasts to the Grandparents in thankfulness for their blessings.

Finally, those, both females and males, with unusual talents in interacting with the powerful spirits utilize special rituals, including what is called in the literature, the "shaking tent." A small structure is constructed in which the individual is placed bound (and later leaves unbound). Those outside the structure can hear the person talking with the spirits and the spirits themselves. As the spirits enter the structure, it shakes violently. All of these rituals, save for the use of tobacco, were found throughout the northern part of the northern hemisphere, in Asia as well as in North America.[1]

Contact with Europeans had profound effects on this people and culture. Europeans brought with them diseases for which the native people had no immunity, and massive numbers of people died from smallpox, influenza, measles and other communicable illnesses. Waves of epidemics over several centuries weakened the ability to resist intrusion and conquest. The second major impact was due to the nature of the trade that developed between Europeans and the native peoples.

The primary interest of Europeans in northern North America was in trade with the native people for furs, in contrast to raising tobacco in the southeastern part. Europeans added to this trade their own regional conflicts, and trading alliances between various European countries and native peoples engaged these peoples in the wars between Europeans that they continued in North

America. Not only were native people the providers of the furs, but various peoples also sought to monopolize the trade, especially as the desired fur-bearing animals, particularly beaver, were decimated in their own areas by the expanding trade.

Iroquoian-speaking peoples south of the eastern Great Lakes, who had created their own alliance among themselves (The Five, later Six, Nations), allied themselves first with the Dutch and then with the British. Iroquoian-speaking people to the north of the Lakes allied with the French. In the mid-seventeenth century, those from the south, supplied with firearms by the British, attacked those to the north and disbanded the survivors of the diseases brought by French Jesuit missionaries. Within a century, Anishnabeg from further north and west routed the Six Nations and drove most back south of the Lakes.

West of the Great Lakes, to secure a monopoly on the furs coming from the west, Anishnabeg drove Siouan-speaking peoples from their homeland. In migrating to the western plains, some of these people joined the emerging plains horse-based cultures and created a new life-style. This large-scale warfare, new to the native peoples in North America, further decimated the populations and weakened their ability to resist European intrusions.

The fur trade led not only to the Anishnabeg dominating most of the Great Lakes region but also to major changes in life-style. The shift from foraging to trade for beaver pelts, previously not of economic significance, led to the notion of ownership of trapping areas inherited patrilineally; to the development of mercantile towns by the Great Lakes at the confluence of trade routes where Europeans built trading forts; to reliance on European goods, such a metal pots and tools, firearms, woolen blankets, flour and other foods; and to the use of distilled alcohol, for which there was no traditional use (as there was for fermented beverages by native peoples in the southern part of North America). The increasing reliance on trade for non-meat food, clothing, and utensils possibly led to the devaluation of females by males caught up in the fur trade trapping, trading, and warfare, especially between the French and English.

Britain's taking of Canada from France, followed by the American revolution, had disastrous consequences for the Anishnabeg. Britain, not particularly interested in expanded colonization, in order to keep native allies, blocked Euroamerican emigration west of the Appalachian mountains. With the end of British control south of the Great Lakes, Euroamericans flooded the area, driving most of the surviving native peoples west of the Mississippi. British loyalists took over the land north of the Great Lakes, and they were soon augmented by English, Scots, and Irish driven from their homes by the land clearances and famines in Britain. The Anishnabeg were reduced to living on ever smaller, economically non-viable reserves in western Quebec, Ontario, southern and central Manitoba, eastern Minnesota, and northern Wisconsin and Michigan.

Forced into poverty and reliance on government hand-outs, and politically subject to the changing whims of Euroamerican governments, native peoples were also subject to a deliberate policy of cultural genocide. Reserves were placed under the control of Christian missionaries, who were given the authority to call upon the military or police to enforce their will. Native religions were criminalized and practitioners jailed. Children were forcibly taken from their parents and placed in missionary controlled boarding schools, where those that survived epidemic diseases were subject to physical and sexual abuse. The children were tortured for speaking their own language or following their own customs. The net result was generations of alcoholism, despondency leading to what has been termed by coroners "suicide epidemics," and overall cultural malaise. By the second half of the twentieth century, Euroamerican anthropologists were reporting, some approvingly, that Anishnabe religion was dead, that all Anishnabeg were Christians.

But Anishnabe religion had not died; it had gone underground. While virtually all Anishnabeg were nominally Christian, the Euroamerican governments allowing little choice, a core of Anishnabeg kept many of the traditions alive in a number of reserves, but for fear of police raids, these practices were kept secret from government agents, missionaries, anthropologists and even natives from other communities. The co-author of the central segment of this chapter, for example, underwent the traditional menarche ritual to be discussed later.

By the end of the 1960s, revitalization movements wedded to the struggle for political rights began at both ends of the Great Lakes. At the eastern terminus of the Lakes, Mohawks on the Akwasasne Reserve began political action to reassert authority over their own land, began their own school led by traditionalist elders who were rejecting Christianity, and started a newspaper, *Akwasasne Notes*, that developed a continent-wide circulation. At the western terminus, Anishnabe and eastern Dakota, formerly enemies, joined to form the American Indian Movement (AIM) to protect native people in the Minneapolis-St. Paul area. AIM quickly spread to other urban areas with native populations and gained the support of traditionalists on reserves, particularly of the Lakota. These youths, bypassing the assimilated middle-aged generation, joined with traditionalist elders to reassert native rights and traditions. After the first few years of political activism, some of the AIM leaders founded nativeway schools in urban areas: the Red School House in St. Paul and the Wandering Spirit Survival School (now the First Nations School) in Toronto. Some of these same leaders were at the heart of the revitalization of the Anishnabe Midéwiwin religious complex, which in turn stimulated the reemergence into the light of other aspects of Anishnabe religion throughout the Great Lakes region.

By the early 1990s, some Anishnabe reserves were gaining limited control over their economic and political lives; by 1995, a few had their own police forces, schools, medical facilities, and stores. Traditional rituals are now held openly, and pow-wows are regaining spiritual components long denied by missionaries. Although, in most communities, the majority of people remain Christian, the number of people adhering to some aspects of traditional practices is continually growing. The depictions of female aspects of Anishnabe religion in the central part of this chapter focuses on twentieth-century practices, particularly as they are understood today.

PRE-CONTACT FEMALE SPIRITUALITY

Prologue

For every part of the world, Western scholars assume that early historical cultures are related to late pre-historical ones in the same locale, save Native North America. South of Canada and the United States, Mexicans, and to a lesser extent Peruvians, celebrate the indigenous civilizations that existed prior to contact with Europe as their country's origin (although this has been of little benefit to the native peoples themselves). Simple logic requires the assumption that what is radically different from European or, at a later date, African cultures, must be indigenous and that pre-contact archaeological finds dated near the time of contact must be connected to the people at the time of contact, and all we know of human beings tells us that no one has a blank mind. Yet these presuppositions fail under the need of many Euroamericans in North America to understand the indigenous peoples to be "savages," whether noble or treacherous. To be a savage is to be without culture (as all females are in the Durkheimian frame of reference).

American culture is based on the myth of the New Jerusalem of the Puritans. As the Israelites were understood to have driven the Canaanites from the land given them by God, so the Europeans were brought by God to this new land of "milk and honey," an unused wilderness, plagued by subhuman savages who were to be cleared from the land as the trees from the forests. The Puritan myth was reinforced by early American novels and nourished by the Hollywood image. The romantic literature focuses on speeches, placed in the mouths of Native leaders, implying that these children of nature are so natural that they would not conceive of planting crops or mining metal.

I was taught in the American public schools that the brave Euroamerican pioneers, led by Daniel Boone, crossed the Appalachians and cleared farms in the wilderness, in spite of the depredations of the ignorant savages who knew but to hunt, both deer and White people. I certainly was not taught that these "pioneers" stole the farmlands and towns of horticultural peoples while slaughtering their women and children. Nor was I taught that, before the coming of the Europeans, these people had cities at the junction of trading waterways, such as Cahokia at the junction of the Mississippi and Missouri rivers across the river from where St. Louis now stands. Somehow it was forgotten that it was the introduction to Europe and Asia of New World cultivated plants, such as maize and potatoes,[2] that led to the population explosions in those continents. And it was not well known that the native peoples of the Great Lakes area had finely wrought copper weapons as early as anywhere else.

This continuing denial of indigenous American cultures includes religion. Early Christian missionaries insisted that Natives had no religion; more recently, a number of scholars have taken the position that the pan-Indian rituals of the revitalization of the last several decades is a modern "New Age" phenomenon—that there could not have been shared rituals—and that the importance of female spirituality is a result of modern Western feminism. Somehow, it never occurred to these scholars that circum-polar rituals such as "sweat lodge," "shaking tent," bear sacrifice, and pyroscapulamancy, would necessarily be pan-Indian. Moreover, the widespread trading networks that can be archaeologically documented as several thousand years old required common rituals to enable travellers to be accepted as relations rather than enemies. This was the impetus for the ubiquitous ritual of the separate-stemmed sacred pipe. Finally, the types of female spirits and spirituality present in Native cultures have no parallels in the androcentric, monotheistic Western religions, including modern feminist rituals.[3]

Most incredible of all, some contemporary scholars deny Native female spirituality its ideological basis; a relatively recent book published by a major university press argues that the concept of the Earth Mother was stimulated by Euroamerican culture (see Chapter 1). Such attitudes verge on being racist. When I showed photographs of the caves to be discussed below to a feminist scholar of American history and friend, I was flabbergasted to hear the interpretation of the glyphs as vulvaform challenged. These same symbols when in a European cave context were accepted as vulvaform without question. Was it assumed that Native women are physiologically different from Caucasians, as American soldiers once did of East Asian females?

In other words, this segment of the chapter should not be necessary. It is insulting to Native Americans to need to argue that their understandings of females spirits, female symbols, female rituals, and female ritual roles are their own and not borrowed from the West. Nevertheless, I hope the reader finds the caves and rock described below as fascinating and exciting as I did and worth discussion in and of themselves.

Some Caves in Northeastern Iowa[4]

Just south of Iowa's border with Minnesota and just west of the Mississippi River, in an area replete with human-made mounds formed in the shapes of sacred beings (Bear, Thunderbird, etc.), are rock shelters, caves, and rock faces painted and incised with petroglyphs. Due to the weathering of the soft sandstone, accelerated by acid rain and vandalism, many sites have lost all traces of the images or they have become difficult to discern.

Two relatively well-known sites are Paint Rock and Indian Cave. The former is a sheer, bald-faced promontory, over 100 meters high, that served as a landmark along the upper Mississippi River. Up to a height of approximately 10 meters, it was covered with incised and painted images, the latter no longer visible, that Euroamerican travelers in the early nineteenth century noted as annually repainted by Native people. Indian Cave is a few miles up the Mississippi from Paint Rock and consists of two crevices in the sandstone layer of a steep bluff about 75 meters high. Again the site is badly weathered and the images recorded in the late nineteenth century are rapidly disappearing. Among the incised images are three that were once described as female figures but are no longer sufficiently distinct to be read clearly.

In contrast to the two Mississippi River sites, there are two nearby along Bear Creek that, being difficult to access and better protected from the weather, have retained their markings. A friend, the late R. Clark Mallam, who was professor of archaeology at nearby Luther College and a specialist in Late Woodland effigy mounds, with the permission of the landowner, took me to see the one called Malone Rock Shelter (also know as Blake's Crevice) in 1985. Not far from the cave, the area between the creek and the bluff widens, where an Oneota village once stood, and there are burials in the vicinity of the same period.

The crevice, in a bluff a few meters from the creek and at the level of the creek bank, is tall and narrow and tapers to a size just sufficiently high and wide for a person to stand. It is long enough for a person to lie down out of the weather. A sandstone layer on both sides is inscribed over and over again, the glyphs often overlapping, with the same symbol: two facing ellipses with a vertical line between them, often descending past the ellipses. There appears to be no other symbol. Potshards of the Oneota type with worn edges were found on the floor of the cave; microscopic examination and testing indicate that these shards were probably used to make some of the engravings.

At the time I visited the cave, I was given no information about it or the surrounding archaeological sites; I was not even given the name of the creek. I now believe that Clark wanted my uninfluenced impression. On entering the cave, I immediately had a clear and confident intuition of its employment:

Young women at menarche utilized the cave during their menarche fast (discussed in the next segment of this chapter). The cave being distinctively vagina shaped was understood to be the vagina of Earth. There the girls becoming women sat with their menstrual blood flowing from their vaginas to mingle with the soil of the ur-mother inside her own vagina. As they sat or lay down to dream, they could hear the coursing of the creek, the flowing of the blood of Earth as their own blood flowed. Each young woman celebrated and reified her experience by forming the vulva symbol indicating the vagina through rubbing the sandstone wall over and over again, either making a new sign or going over a previously made one. As a girl, she enters Earth, the mother of all life, through the focal point of Earth's creative energy, her vagina; she leaves Earth a woman, her own vagina having become the source for the flowing of lifeblood, now herself ready to bear life through her own vagina, to be a mother herself.

Of course, in the scholarly world, a subjective conclusion must be verified by objective data. First, my intuition assumed a nearby village, one close enough that a girl beginning to menstruate could reach the cave fairly quickly, could be protected by warriors if need be, and could be visited by her female relatives and village elders to assist her through her physical and spiritual transformation. Indeed, there is a nearby village site just around a bend of the creek. Although it has not been thoroughly excavated, a typical Oneota assemblage was found in the context of European trade goods. Of course, given the benefits of the location—flat areas for gardens, protective bluff to the rear, water from the creek—it may have been used off and on for a considerable period of time.

Secondly, there was the question of the symbol. As mentioned above, I was challenged as to whether it indicated a vagina (although it is so accepted without question in European caves) and how it could be related to the earth. A year after visiting the cave, I began to take classes in Ojibwe (an Anishnabe language) lessons in Toronto from Alex McKay, an Anishnabe from northern Ontario. In the first lesson, with no prompting from myself, he wrote a symbol on the board that was identical to the one in the cave: two facing ellipses with a vertical line between them descending past the ellipses. The sign indicated both the female vagina *and* Earth. The Ojibwe word for Earth (at least in his dialect) is *aki* and for vagina, *akitun*, the suffix indicating motion. Hence, Earth is a motionless vagina, as indeed is the cave, or the human vagina is a moving Earth. In either case, the linkage is direct and unambiguous.

Third, there was the question of menarche ritual practices. Would inscribing on the walls of a cave accord with Native menarche rituals? As detailed in the next segment of this chapter, Ron Geyshick, in a 1989 publication, recounts the tradition of his Anishnabe culture in northeastern Minnesota that girls, during their menarche fast, created petroglyphs with their own menstrual blood or mixed their blood with berry juice (the blood of Earth) for painting on rocks. Hence, not only is the practice of creating petroglyphs during the menarche fast known, but it is quite possible that the fasting young women at the cave colored the rubbed grooves in the sandstone with their menstrual blood or a paint made with their blood in combination with some other sacred substance, such as bear grease. No record would continue because the cave is subject to periodic flooding, when the creek overflows its banks, which would wash the paint away. When I attempted to revisit the cave in the spring of 1993, the flood waters were unusually high in that part of Iowa, and the cave would have been under water. (But my timing was perfect, because the archaeological survey of the county, necessary for this study, unbeknownst to me, had just been completed the month previous.)

Finally, is this site unique in its symbols or are there others? For it is less than likely that a single village would have a unique ritual; although given the exceptional shape of the cave, it is plausible in this instance. A few months after visiting the cave, Clark wrote me of another nearby cave, or, more precisely, overhang, he had recently visited, Bear Creek Rock Shelter (also known as Burke's Rock Shelter) that abounds with petroglyphs. At the entrance to the shelter is an explicitly delineated bison, with another two further inside. On the back wall is a clearly depicted turtle, the only one known for northeastern Iowa. Similar to the previously described cave, the walls where they narrow are covered with repeated vulvaforms. The vulva glyphs are slightly different in the shelter from those of the cave, for the vertical lines are balanced within the ellipses and do not extend beyond them—this is the more common design worldwide. On the rear wall of the shelter, Clark was particularly impressed by three incised images that are unmistakable bear paws. He pointed out that, if one sat on the shelf of the rear wall facing the entrance, by extending one's arms, one could place each of one's hands into two of the bear paws.

Aside from the vulva signs, all of these symbols reflect female images in Native North America. While the bison bull signifies warrior bravery and strength, of more cultural significance is the bison as nurturing mother. These caves are not that far from the original extent of the prairies, and the people of the local cultures surely hunted either prairie and woods bison. Bison provides humans with the sustenance of her flesh, shelter and clothing from her hide, sewing thread from her sinews, spoons from her horns, and so on. For the Lakota who moved from Minnesota to the Plains, as White Buffalo Calf Woman, Bison gave the people their most sacred pipe and their rituals—she gave them life. In Lakota myths, she is connected with Earth: she arises from its dust.

Turtle also represents the earth. In the traditions of the Six Nations, it was on her that Sky Woman landed and on whose back the earth was created, giving North America the name of Turtle Island. She is also the primary spirit of the Anishnabe "shaking tent" shamanic ritual.

As the bison bull, the grizzly bear of the western plains and mountains is symbolic of warrior ferocity, but the black bear of the area is understood in most Native North American traditions as a healing, female spirit, intimately linked with the Earth. For Bear enters Earth in the late fall and comes forth when the snow melts with new life, her cubs. Her annual resurrection within Earth signifies her power to give life to the ill and needy, as Earth gives life to us and sustains us.

Hence, all of the symbolism repeats the understanding of Earth as life-giving and life-supporting. The shelter too must have been used for menarche rituals. Nearby is another village site, a mound, and the New Galena enclosure. The latter is an unusual earthworks consisting of two embankment-ditch ellipses between steep bluffs, approximately 40 by 30 meters, that at first was understood to be a fort, although the walls would not have been high enough for defensive purposes. Given its east-west orientation, with openings at each end (similar in shape and orientation to Anishnabe Midéwiwin ritual lodges), it was more likely a ceremonial center.

There may have been many more of these menarche ritual sites. Appropriate caves, particularly with soft sandstone walls to enable easy engraving, would have been rare. More common would have been fasting shelters by a rock wall, if available near the village. Given centuries of weathering and vandalism, it is most unlikely that any of the markings would have survived. We are indeed fortunate to have these two protected examples. At present, they are on private property, and the landowners keep the curious away from them. It has been recommended by archaeological surveyors that plans be made for their protection.

As an afterthought, one must note the name of the creek by which these caves are found. Unfortunately, it is not known whether Bear Creek was originally a Native or a Euroamerican name. Should it be indigenous, the implication should now be transparent.

To which contemporary cultures would this culture, vibrant before the decimation caused by the introduced diseases—smallpox, measles and influenza—be connected. The pre-historic and early historic archaeological complex is termed Oneota, and Iowa archaeologists tend to assume that the Oneota are the ancestors of the Iowa. Nonetheless, the area was at the interface of several cultures. To the northwest were the Siouan-speaking Dakota, to the southwest the Siouan-speaking Iowa, to the east, just across the Mississippi, were the Algonkian-speaking Misquakie, and to the southeast were the Algonkian-speaking Sauk, the latter two cultures closely related to the Great Lakes Anishnabeg. Hence, it is difficult to be certain which people or peoples are their descendants; Native peoples can speak for themselves.

A Rockface in Southeastern Ontario[5]

Diagonally across the entire Great Lakes region of central North America from these northeastern Iowa caves, north of the north central shore of Lake Ontario, and directly north of a group of large theriomorphic mounds (Serpent Mound Provincial Park) is a large, horizontal, rock surface at the southern edge of the glacier-scoured Great Shield. In a part of this crystalline limestone rockface is an area with numerous fissures and holes and three hundred identifiable glyphs, plus over six hundred others too weathered to be deciphered, known as the Peterborough Petroglyphs. Now an Ontario provincial park, to protect the site from both acid rain and potential vandalism, the rockface is covered by a modern, glass-walled building, with interior walkways around the rock and a moveable, overhead catwalk.

The largest, most impressive image of the many figures is of an anthropomorphic female, vertically centered on a straight, red-mineral seam. Along the seam are natural holes in the rock. The female image was pecked around a large, deep, oval hole that forms the vagina of the figure. The figure also has a clearly delineated breast so that her sex is unambiguous. There are two other smaller images of fully featured females with the vagina formed by a natural crevice and many other anthropomorphic images that may be female, some possibly pregnant, although their sex is less certain. There are also seven vulvaform images, most pecked around natural holes in the rockface, similar in form to those in the Iowa rock shelter described above.

The anthropomorphic images are not exclusively female. Two frontally depicted male images have proportionally very large, clearly depicted penises and testicles, similar in form to those found in other areas of North America, from Utah to Arizona. There are also four male figures in profile that are ithyphallic; in one, a line from the foot of the male figure connects to a vulvaform image. None of the male figures involve natural holes or fissures in the rock, as do the female images.

Other petroglyphs at the Peterborough site include many turtles (some with eggs), horned herbivores, horned and hornless serpents, bear and moose tracks, lizards, cranes, thunderbirds, a semi-anthropomorphic solar image, etc. Of importance to this study is the particular relationship of female images and symbols to holes in the rock, undoubtedly linking the vagina of the human to the vagina of Earth.

Other artifacts found at the site include thirty gneiss hammerstones, some worn, that were used for pecking out the designs and seven tiny pottery shards. The site is near a waterway that was heavily traveled both in pre-contact and in contact times. There are two archaeological sites nearby. One site, four kilometers to the southeast, seems to have been a campsite of Laurentian hunters from over five thousand years in the past. The second, eight kilometers southeast, is of a large Iroquoian village of some five hundred years ago. Neither is assumed to have been linked to the creation of the petroglyphs. Joan and Romas Vastokas conclude that the "petroglyphs were engraved by prehistoric Algonkians at the latter end of the Woodland period, sometime between 900 and 1400 A.D." But the significance of these glyphs remains vibrant today; Ansihnabeg continually visit the site and leave tobacco offerings on the glyphs (only Native people are allowed by the park personnel to walk on the protected part of the rockface).

Conclusions

With the same symbols in pre-contact archaeological sites to the east and west of the Great Lakes Anishnabeg, symbols still in use by the people today, can there be any reason to doubt the importance of female spirits and spirituality prior to the arrival of Europeans? Certainly there is overwhelming evidence for the aboriginal understanding of the earth as a numinous being of primordial and continuing creation and the direct linkage of human females to her, as well as the cyclic rhythms of the moon.

Hardly new or unusual is the correlation between menstrual blood and fertility, as well as the flowing waters of streams as the blood of Earth; between the human vagina and fissures in Earth, there being worldwide cultural myths of the release of game from caves; between the female menstrual cycle and the cycle of Moon, which surely is not a matter of coincidence; and between human mothers as birthers and nurturers and other mammalian mothers, all animals being theriomorphic spirits where hunting remains a substantial cultural element. Vulvaform symbols are found in caves throughout the inhabited world. The earliest known, in caves of the Dordogne area of France, are generally assumed to be of Aurignacian date, ca. 30,000 B.P.; that is, the symbol is among the earliest used by humankind. Mother Earth is hardly a new term invented by Euroamericans. As indicated in other chapters, the term exists in many languages including Native American ones, from the ancient Mediterranean world to the Andes and Caribbean, as noted by the Spanish at the time of contact. Probably the concept and term existed among the earliest human cultures, albeit we can have no record of it. We are here considering a fundamental human understanding, even if Western cultures have lost the emotional bonding between humans and Earth, Moon, Sun, and Thunderstorm. The modern Western concept of "Mother Earth" is an intellectual one; it lacks the impact of a true relationship, of the awe, respect, love, and gratitude a child feels for his or her mother. But this is what the Earth Mother means in many cultures around our planet.

CONTEMPORARY ANISHNABE FEMALE SPIRITUALITY[6]
with Jacqui Lavalley

Female Spirits

The Anishnabe world is imbued with sacrality. All beings, save humans, are invested with numinous power, but the concept of being is far more inclusive than in the Western world view. For plants, animals, rocks, waters, the earth itself, and all sky phenomena are other-than-human persons[7] or *manido*. All beings are related, and humans turn to their more powerful relations for all those things necessary to sustain life and for life itself.

Every individual requires a special relationship with at least one other-than-human person to live. These relationships are usually obtained through isolated fasting experiences, when one makes oneself pitiable in the hope that a *manido* will appear and become a guardian spirit, as well as through dreams. For this reason, the Anishnabe understanding of the spirit realm is individualistic, although such understanding would necessarily accord with cultural expectations to be validated. Hence, the following depiction of spirits is intended to be suggestive of possibilities rather than definitive; all individuals, to a considerable degree, have their own understanding, based on their experience of the numinous and instruction from particular elders, within this range of possibilities.

Anishnabe words do not, as in Indo-European languages, denote gender, and the spirits do not in and of themselves have sex. However, due to function or symbolism, spirits may be understood with gender connotations. Whether the spirit is called *nokomis* (Grandmother) or *mishomis* (Grandfather) is often a means of realizing a particular individual's understanding of a spirit's sex.

Cosmic spirits occur in opposite-sexed pairs. Earth is invariably female and linked to human females, as was discussed in the preceding segment of this chapter and will be further discussed in the following. She is variously called Grandmother or Mother and is sometimes understood to be the daughter of Grandmother Moon. Earth was probably paired with Sky, but given generations of boarding-school experience, which emphasized Genesis creation myths, she is now more usually paired with, or considered subsidiary to, the Creator.[8] (Native American myths give priority to migration and emergence myths, the equivalent of the biblical creation myth being re-creation myths of a preexisting world.) All the aspects of Earth are also understood to be female, such as water and vegetation.

Grandmother Moon is paired with Grandfather Sun. She is also specifically linked to women and their physiological cycles. She is the kindly grandmother to whom women can always bring their problems. She plays a major role in the Nanabush culture-hero/trickster myth cycle, although Western analysts tend to focus only on the male hero. Nanabush's mother, Beautiful Woman, who in some versions is Earth and is impregnated by the powerful West Wind, dies on giving birth to Nanabush. He is raised by his maternal grandmother, who is often understood to be Grandmother Moon; she teaches Nanabush all he needs to know to accomplish his achievements.

Earth and Sky are the recipients of two of the six offerings, the other four offered to the Four Directions (or Winds), invariably made when tobacco is offered, either directly via fire or through the sacred pipe. Zenith and nadir and the four directions delineate the spiritual as well as physical cosmos. Each direction has its own complex of symbols: colors, animals, functions, seasons. Often South is portrayed as a pregnant female, South epitomizing warmth, sustenance, growth, and becoming.

Various theriomorphic spirits tend to be understood as sexed. For example, Deer is usually understood as female and may appear in dreams as a human girl, while Moose, along with other humped herbivores, is often understood as male. Owl, the most powerful bird of the female night sky, may be understood as female, while Eagle, the most powerful bird of the male day sky, is generally understood to be male. Bear (the black bear), the major healing spirit as previously discussed, is often understood to be female and may also appear in dreams as a woman. It is probably because of this same-sex relationship with this powerful spirit that women, in at least some Anishnabe cultures, do not eat the tongues or the hearts of bears. This list could be extended considerably, but it should be clear that the Anishnabe world is imbued with powerful and helpful female and male spirits.

One of the effects of misogynist Christian missionaries disparaging traditional religion for centuries was the imputation of evil sorcery to relationships with female spirits. Among many semi-assimilated Anishnabeg, Grandmother Owl came to be understood as a fearful sign of the dead, and "bearwalking" became a term used to designate the practice of evil sorcery.

Female Rituals

Most rituals are the same for females and males; for example, naming ceremonies, which are essential for young children to gain relationships with spirits until they are old enough to engage in vision questing to engender such relationships themselves. When ritually requested to do so, elders dream, fast for from four to eight days, or utilize the shaking-tent ritual to gain a name from the spirits for the child (or older person). If the name is from an animal spirit, one avoids killing that animal; although, if one is desperate, the animal will give itself to that person. Ron Geyshick points out: "For a girl, ask that she'll have a decent husband and be good at skinning, even killing, so she will be a hunter herself. If you're helping a boy, it's different. Bless him for hunting, thank all the animals he will shoot, fish he'll eat. . . . If he's a hunter, ask that he won't kill anything. A moose will give up his meat. . . ."

Children are taught from an early age to fast for visions. From the age of six or seven, children are encouraged to blacken their face with charcoal as a sign of fasting and, in isolation, abstain from food and water. Beginning with a sunrise to sundown fast, as the children become older, they fast for longer and longer periods, until completing the traditional four-day fast. Later in adolescence, they will be encouraged to fast for seven, eight or ten days. All aspects of this tradition are the same for boys and girls, including the types of visions that may be experienced. For example, women as well as men may receive war visions from powerful, male spirits. Ruth Landes' female informant received a series of visions from the Thunderbirds, leading to a communal ritual for the overseas soldiers during the First World War.

Turning into a Bear

What is special for the female is the menarche ritual, for, in contrast to females, there are no male puberty rituals or fasts *per se*; that is, rituals to celebrate an explicit transition from child to adult. A boy becomes a man on the change of voice. Normally sometime during adolescence, the youth engages in a major fast, ideally for ten days, when he is limited to only a half-cupful of water a day. More recently, perhaps due to modern Midéwiwin influence, a seven-day complete fast is more common.

The usual anthropological interpretation of Anishnabe menarche rituals follows from Christian misogynist attitudes towards menstrual blood, understanding this essence of womanhood to be evil. For example, in Ruth Landes' 1930s study of Ojibwa women, all of the features of the menarche ritual discussed below are noted but cast in entirely negative terms, leading to her viewing assumed male adolescent rituals positively and the female ones negatively: "Unquestionably her puberty ceremony has a different import from that of the boy's. His is a hopeful striving for broader horizons, hers is a conscientious withdrawal of her malignant self. While obsessed and saddened with this terror of herself, she is supposed to seek a vision." While one may feel sorry for Landes in her devaluing, in effect, her own womanhood, one must note that such interpretation has led to the devaluing of Native women in the scholarly literature.

In 1929, Mary Sugedub of Wasausink gave to Diamond Jenness the following origin myth of the menarche ritual:

> When the first Indian maid reached adolescence, Grandmother Moon, hiding her face (it was the time of the new moon), peered down at her and whistled, saying, "Follow me." For some days the girl remained dreamy and wished to play all by herself; but when a fortnight had elapsed and the moon was past full, she heard the call of her grandmother and tried to reach the place from which the whistle sounded. A large tree blocked her path, and the girl did not try to leap over it but looked back. Grandmother Moon then taught her to redden her cheeks with the juice of the bloodroot as her own cheeks were reddened, and she bade her go and fast on the hide of a "lion" (mythical giant lynx) to prepare herself for a blessing. Afterwards Grandmother Moon taught her to fashion a pot of clay and to smooth its surface with a stone. The grandmother herself provided the food for the pot as soon as it was finished.

When a girl has her first period, her mother or other female relative will immediately take her into the bush and return with the necessities for a temporary residence. The girl will build a small shelter where she will stay until her bleeding ceases. Each day a female elder will spend the day with her, imparting the knowledge and sharing the wisdom she will need as an adult. Ideally, for her this will be the major seven-day fast undertaken by both females and males around the onset of puberty. If it is not possible to have the major fast at the first menstruation, fasting will continue until the menstrual flow stops, and the major ritual fast will be held as soon after as possible. Ron Geyshick notes: "Her family is proud, because it means the girl has grown up and become a woman."

Girls tend not to be provided information about menstruation until their first menstruation; hence, it may come as a surprise. This seems to be a deliberate instructional technique. The shelter is a small wigwam the girl makes for herself away from other residences, where she stays for from four to ten days, with seven days now preferred. But nowadays, girls may stay by themselves in the basement of the house or in their own room for four days and nights. In at least some regions, the period of isolation is called *makwa* or *makwawe* ("turning into a bear"), Grandmother Bear being a powerful healing spirit and understood to be closely connected with Earth. The girl blackens her face with charcoal and wears old clothes. She is not to touch or scratch herself, but can use a special scratching stick. She will not wash until the end of the fast.

Either the fast may be total, which is preferred, or a small amount of simple food may be brought to the faster every evening, but she will eat no food of the season, only dried or smoked food from previous seasons. She uses her own dishes, traditionally drinking from a special birch-bark cup, often for a full year following the onset of menarche. She is so powerful at this time that, if she enters a lake or stream, the fish could die. If she touches a plant, it could die. This is why she does not eat any of the food currently being gathered. She is not to gaze at anyone, except female elders, her mother, older sister, etc.; nor is she to look at flying geese, and so on.

During this time, the girl is not idle, but may be involved in handiwork of some sort, and she is instructed with regard to women's roles, expectations, and so forth, by her mother, grandmothers, or female elders. Girlfriends, particularly those menstruating, may visit her at night. Girls usually have vision-dreams during this fast that empowered them for the rest of their lives.

Girls sometimes receive visions that greatly influence their communities as well as their own lives. In 1929, for example, the people of Wasausink told Jenness of a young woman who, at the time of the wars with the Mohawks in the early eighteenth century, during her menarche seclusion had a powerful vision from Grandmother Moon, who gave her martial leadership skills and a relationship with one of the most powerful spirits. Her visions and resultant power led to victory over the Mohawks in several major battles and the taking of central and southern Ontario from them.

At the end of the fast, the new "old woman" washes herself and her clothes, or puts on new ones, and may walk on a bed of cedar boughs (cedar being an especially sacred plant with healing and purifying qualities) back to her home for a ritual feast of an animal, preferably hunted by her father. (This is reminiscent of a ritual for females only that centers on walking on four cedar boughs.) Female relatives burn the seclusion hut and old clothes.

The period of isolation, the wigwam made by the faster, the face blackened with charcoal, the old clothes, the ritual feast at the end of the fast, the removal of all elements of the fasting wigwam are all identical with fasting in general, as well as the major fast of male adolescents. Not only are the menarche seclusion and male fast procedures virtually identical, but there are parallels in the "first fruits" rituals of the young woman in the year following menarche (see below) and the feast ritual of a young man on bringing back his first major hunted animal (deer or moose). The feast for the young woman emerging from the menstrual hut traditionally focused on the animal brought back by her father, while males on emerging from a fast proceed to a feast that must be ritually prepared by a female and should include foods gathered by women: "(wild) rice, berries, corn, fish." More specific features vary regionally. Ron Geyshick writes,

> There's a story that the rock paintings here were made by girls with their own blood while they were on their puberty fasts. Those girls got a lot of powers from fasting out there. They discovered weapons that our warriors used . . . Painted Rock is one of the very secret places for our young girls to fast and receive guidance and wisdom. So this girl came. She stayed there as long as eight or ten days, and received powers. Spirits came to her. They gave her all kinds of berries [berries symbolizing the blood of Mother Earth], some of them non-edible. She was told to mix these with her own [menstrual] blood, and to go and make her own mark on that rock.

There are exceptions to the avoidance of others, particularly males, during the menarche fast. Under certain circumstances, the girl can use her powers to heal. For example, if a middle-aged man were suffering from back problems, he might be placed face-downwards in the girl's fasting wigwam, so that they could not see each other's faces, and she will walk up and down his spine. Her enormous power at this time can cure his affliction and enable him to rise and walk with the strength of a youth.

Berry Fast

For the year following menarche, the young woman engages in a set of practices intended to encourage her physical and spiritual development. She avoids certain foods. Berries are not eaten, hence the name of the practice. Berries are linked to the blood of Mother Earth; thus, they are too powerful for her to eat at a time when her own female powers are developing. No humped animals—moose, bison, mountain goat—are eaten because these animals have masculine qualities and should be avoided while the young woman's female aspect is being nurtured and developed.

Alternatively, in some areas, following the menarche fast, the young woman is not to taste any of the berries as they come into season, the strawberry being the first fruit of the spring, or other fruit or vegetable, until a feast is held for each food and she ritually eats it. The ritual, as with ending any fast, involves refusing the proffered food until the fourth offering before eating it.

In some areas, she is not to pick berries for a year or swim or walk on ice. Berries, as well as lakes and streams, are understood to be the blood of Mother Earth. For the year, she is also not to drink from another person's cup, or she eats only from her own dishes; her power still consolidating and coming under her control.

Moontime

While some sources of the 1930s note that women did not seclude themselves when menstruating after the menarche seclusion, other sources imply that it was a traditional practice. It is one that is current among some traditionalists and a set practice when there are large gatherings for seasonal Midéwiwin rituals, the menstruating women residing together in a Moon Lodge.

Menstruating women do not now usually isolate themselves after the menarche fast, but are expected to avoid ceremonies, to stay around their home, to use special dishes and not touch food for others, and not step over people, clothes, sacred objects, etc. Since hunting is no longer the primary male occupation, there is no longer a functional need for males to avoid the odors attendant on menstruating females. As well, urban life does not readily allow for physical separation. Speaking of the traditional period, Marilyn Johnson points out:

> . . . women went off and stayed by themselves in a moon-lodge set aside from the rest of the community . . . They would do beading and quillwork . . . They did not have to look after the children or do the cooking. Another woman brought them food every day (as well as water and firewood) . . . whatever they needed. The men did not go near them. It was a "time-out" period.

The avoidance by menstruating women of stepping over males, their possessions and sacred paraphernalia undoubtedly arose from functional necessity, when the family's survival, especially in winter, could be dependent on hunting success, but there are other reasons as well. Not only will the woman's power at this time drain the power of sacred items and the power of most males, but she will draw their power into herself through her vagina. Secure in her own power, she is not likely to want someone else's power, power that may be deleterious or otherwise undesirable. So the avoidance is not only out of concern for others but for herself as well. For this reason, men and women have their own pipes, drums, and other hallowed articles.

Menstruation, then, is a monthly renewal of a woman's powers by Grandmother Moon, which she also does for the medicine power of male shamanic healers, whose power must also be periodically renewed through fasting and

Spirit (sweat) Lodges. Some male healers limit their shamanizing to once a month because of this periodic renewal. Hence, for a man, this renewal comes from others; for a woman, it comes from within herself and her own intimate connection with Earth and Moon.

Moon Ceremonies

The Moon Ceremony is usually held during the full moon, but, if the ceremony is needed, it can be held at any time in the moon's cycle. Women, including those who are menstruating, come together to speak to Grandmother Moon. The basic requirements are fire, purifying herbs, tobacco, and water, but often berries and cloth are also used.

The details of the ritual will vary with the leader of the ceremony, but a typical one would be as follows: A fire is built in a sacred way by the ritual leader. The women, who each bring with them a square meter of pale yellow cloth (the color of the rising, full moon), tobacco and cedar leaves (a sacred herb with healing power linked to Moon as well as Bear), gather in a sacred manner. They sit in a circle about the fire, hold the tobacco offering in their left hands for a while, so that it absorbs their thoughts, and then tie it into a corner of the cloth, which they drape about their shoulders. After a song inviting the spirits, the leader will explain to those not familiar with the ceremony its purpose, the nature of Grandmother Moon, and the relationship of women's physiological cycles with those of the moon. A song invoking Grandmother Moon is sung. The berries are offered to the spirits through the fire and then passed around the circle, everyone sharing the special food. A copper (copper is native to the northern Great Lakes region and has been used by the Anishnabeg for thousands of years) bowl of water, the blood, the life fluid of Mother Earth, is prayed over and passed around the circle to be shared. The shaker (rattle) is passed around the circle, and those that feel the urge to share a sacred song can do so. Then each woman around the circle speaks to Grandmother Moon. Each speaks for her family and for herself.

The Moon Ceremony is special as, in this ritual, one can ask of the spirits for one's family; in other ceremonies, one more usually asks for the people as a whole. Grandmother Moon is gentle, listens to all who speak to her, and grants the requests. One can speak of one's problems and one's joys; tears can be shed and shared. After one speaks, one places the tobacco offering with the cloth into the fire. Fire is the medium for the transmission of the offering to the spirit recipients. Each person in the circle speaks in turn. When everyone has spoken, a song of thankfulness to the spirits is sung. Usually a feast is then shared and enjoyed.

Recently, men have also been attending what had been an exclusively female ceremony. They may do so, for example, to speak for the women of their family who, for any number of reasons, cannot or will not take part.

Female Roles in Mixed Gender Rituals

Of the many rituals that involve both females and males, all are equal in the rituals. Both men and women, who have earned the respective privileges, may have sacred pipes, shamanic drums, and Midéwiwin water drums; serve as ritual leaders and teachers; and lead songs. There are, however, specific gender responsibilities in these regards. These specific responsibilities flow from the spiritual connections of females and males. For example, females prepare the food for ritual feasts and pray with the water, food, and nurturing being the gift of female spirits and water the lifeblood of Earth; males collect wood and tend the sacred fire, which is linked to Sun. However, if a person of the appropriate sex were not available, a person of the other sex could carry out the task.

Men and women, during rituals, sit at polar halves of the sacred circle about the sacred fire. The ritual leader normally sits at the West facing East, the Direction of the rising sun, of beginnings. Females sit in the northern half of the circle, facing Grandmother South, while males sit in the southern half of the circle, facing Grandfather North. The complementary sexes together form the sacred circle, the circle of life, each being necessary to the other for the continuation of life.

In modern pan-Indian ceremonies led by those who were not raised in traditional cultures, there may be an attitude, adopted from Christianity, that only males may interact with the spirit realm, which they understand to be predominantly male, and lead rituals. But the teaching of the elders, both men and women, of the tradition that females and males are spiritually interdependent and equal is increasingly being heard. Where, at the beginning of the revitalization, the spirits were addressed in prayers as Grandfathers only, now with increasing frequency one can hear addresses to the Grandfathers and Grandmothers, as in the past.[9]

Female Self-Understanding

Two centuries of intensified colonialism had numerous deleterious effects. Enforced patriarchalization—for example, government requirement of patrilineal lineage, even for matrilineal cultures—reduced the power and prestige of women. The ending of traditional male means of gaining prestige as warriors and the reduction in traditional male economic roles—due to government controls on hunting, reduced amount of game with end of semi-nomadic life, and the reduction of the value of furs, as trapping replaced hunting—led to males both devaluing females and becoming jealous of the continuing economic roles of females. Required Christianization resulted in the notions of a male high god superior to the female spirits, of male-only priestly roles, of secularization of female rituals and ritual roles, and the use of terms for female spirits to connote evil sorcery. For example, the well-known Anishnabe artist, Norval Morrisseau, who is often assumed in Euroamerican culture to represent indigenous traditions, has been recorded as stating: "I firmly believe that there are female goddesses. But according to Ojibway customs and beliefs the male is superior to all life and the female is set aside." Basil Johnston, the native consultant at the Royal Ontario Museum, writes that obtaining a vision was necessary for males to achieve "self-fulfillment; for women a vision was not essential. By giving life through the first mother, women were fulfilled."[10] It seems that Western androcentrism, epitomized in Durkheim's dichotomy of male/culture/sacred and female/nature/profane, at least by the mid-twentieth century, had suffused through native males no longer living a traditional life-style. Under these circumstances, it is remarkable that so much of female spirituality has survived and is reemerging in the lives of Anishnabe women.

Traditionalist women do not consider gender consequential. They have been taught to do all the things a man could do—hunt, prepare furs, etc.—because in traditional small groups, when males were away hunting, females had to be able to carry out all tasks to survive. These women consider themselves as empowered as males. They control their home. If a wife is fed up with her husband, she places his belongings outside the door as a message to him and the community. A husband cannot do the same. Upon the dissolution of a marriage, children remain with the mother.

Females are spiritually empowered by their physical maturity—being able to conceive. Once a female menstruates, the mark of her physical maturity, she is careful to avoid stepping over males, their ritual objects, etc., even when not menstruating. This is because she would weaken their power by drawing their power into her. Hence, she avoids this type of contact not only out of respect for others, but because she may not want to draw that power to her.

Because female humans share the creative power of Mother Earth and the cycles of Grandmother Moon, they have an innate connection with two of the most potent spiritual powers. As discussed above, the word for the human vagina and the earth are the same in some Ojibwe dialects and share the same symbol. Menstrual blood and Earth's blood, as found in the strawberry, are symbolically the same. Women and Grandmother Bear, closely connected to Earth, share symbolic aspects of their lives, as is clear from one of the names for the menarche ritual. As Marilyn Johnson observes about the spiritual conditions of women:

> We are born connected to Earth, since we are born from another woman. We just have a natural relationship with Earth, whereas men do not. They have to work at it; they go to sweats and fast to *earn* their connection. I have heard drummers talking about how they have to beat the drum so they can make the connection to the heartbeat of Earth, to that female energy. We already have it. The men I know are usually doing sweats, pipe ceremonies or sunrise ceremonies; they are doing something for the information to come to them or for their spirit guides to show up.

Here, in contradistinction to Basil Johnston's statement above, Marilyn Johnson is stating that obtaining visions is more natural for females than males. Basil Johnston has confused actively seeking visions with the visions *per se*.

Female power is different from that of males. Speaking from her experience as a shaman, Marilyn Johnson notes:

> When women are on their cycles, it's hard for them to channel energy. Power can be very erratic at that time of month. It can be very powerful, but it sort of has a mind of its own; it can just shoot off and do its own thing. The power surges and does not seem to mesh well with male energy.

This is why males, when leading sacred rituals, are concerned about the immediate presence of menstruating females—not because they are polluting, but because they are so powerful at that time that their power can overwhelm that of males. Sacred pipes held by males have been known to break when passed to a menstruating woman at a pipe ceremony, because her power at that time surpassed that of the pipe-holder.

Hence, traditional Anishnabe women understand themselves to be empowered physically, socially, economically, and spiritually. Traditional Anishnabe males respect and celebrate this empowerment, because all humans need spiritual power to survive, and the entire community benefits from the combined power of its members.

TRADITIONS COROLLARY TO THOSE OF THE ANISHNABEG

The Lenape'wak

To the south and east of the Great Lakes Anishnabeg, Algonkian language family speaking peoples were more oriented towards horticulture, living in settlements surrounded by cultivated fields. Among these people were the Lenape'wak, more commonly known in the literature as the Delaware (from the third Lord de la Warr, Sir Thomas West, governor of Jamestown in 1610, who had never met them!). Both Anishnabe and Lenapé mean, with controversial modifiers, "the people." The Lenapé homeland, prior to dispersion due to European encroachment, was the area that now includes southeastern New York, Delaware, New Jersey, eastern Pennsylvania and northern Maryland.[11]

They lived a life-style similar to the Iroquoian speaking peoples to their northwest and the Algonkian-speaking Powhatans and Nanticokes to their south. The women grew corn, beans, squash, and pumpkins, and gathered fish and shellfish; the men hunted. Extended families lived in longhouses, which archaeological excavations indicate could be over thirty by seven meters. Their religious understanding was similar to that of the Anishnabeg, with more complex rituals enabled by permanent dwellings, and greater importance accorded deities that flow from gardening, such as the Corn Mother.

What is of interest in comparison to the Anishnabeg is that inheritance of clan affiliation and leadership is matrilineal, not unlike that of the Six Nations in Ontario and the Cherokee in Oklahoma, to whom most of the Lenape'wak dispersed. This form of inheritance is typical of mixed-economy cultures in which the women do the gardening: matrilineal families "own" (in the sense of use and care for) the fields and the longhouses. Most likely, Lenapé longhouses were matrilocal, matrilineally related multifamily dwellings. Early eighteenth-century literature also describes female shamans ("prophets") among the Lenape'wak.

The Anishnabeg north of the Great Lakes did little if any gardening, and, until the fur trade and later forced relocation to reserves, did not live in fixed settlements. Hence, there was nothing to own and nothing to inherit. Leadership was volitional and *ad hoc*. Eleanor Leacock has convincingly argued that family hunting territories among the Algonkian-speaking "Montagnais" of Labrador developed in relationship to the fur trade and did not exist prior to contact.[12] The fact of the Algonkian matrilineal Lenapé culture brings into question the age of the Anishnabe practice of patrilineal clan descent. Did this precede the fur trade and the Euroamerican insistence on patrilineal family designation? Given the gender egalitarianism of the traditional culture, why would descent have been limited to one sex, one that had no other prerogatives? Could descent have been bilateral, as among the north-west coast cultures, albeit less formal, and as among the Algonkian-speaking Plains cultures, for example the Tsistsistas (Cheyenne—see below), who moved to the Plains from the area west of Lake Superior? Analysis of other Algonkian-speaking cultures suggests that gender egalitarianism was probably complete among the Anishnabeg prior to contact. Certainly, the Jesuit *Relations* indicate that this was the case for the Montagnais, the gathering-hunting Algonkian-speaking people to the east of the Great Lakes Anishnabeg along the St. Lawrence River.[13]

The Nitsitapi Tribes

To the west of the Anishnabeg bordering the Rocky Mountains in present-day Alberta and Montana live three Algonkian speaking inter-connected native tribes collectively named Nitsitapi: the Apikuni, Kainai and Siksika (known in English as the Peigan, Blood, and Blackfoot, respectively). Prior to being forced on reserves, they lived a nomadic life following the bison herds within a large defined range. In the late eighteenth century, elderly Apikuni people spoke of living near the Eagle hills of present-day Saskatchewan, before the adaptation to a horse-centered life, of hunting the bison on foot. Typical of the equestrian Plains cultures, Nitsitapi tribes have a rich ceremonial life focusing on large-bundle complexes, age-graded ritual societies, and a yearly renewal ritual, Okan, termed the "Sun Dance" or "Medicine Lodge" by Euroamericans. It is on these aspects of the religion of the Nitsitapi tribes, not found among the woodland Anishnabe, that this section will focus.[14]

Ritual Bundles[15]

Ritual Bundles are the most precious possessions, both in the sense of cultural importance—the lives of the people are based on the care of these sacred items—and material value—as a sign of their importance, those to whom their keeping is transferred pay a large sum in the currency of the day (horses and robes in the past). Of importance to this study is that the bundle complexes, which include the rituals and songs, are held by a married couple, the daily care usually provided by the woman. The rituals of opening the bundles, as well as transferring them, require the leadership and participation of female-male pairs.

Grinnell quotes an 1879 description of a healing ceremony that involved the opening of a sacred pipe bundle. After purifying themselves,

> The man and woman [the keepers of the bundle] now faced each other and again began the buffalo song, keeping time by touching with the clenched hands—the right and left alternately—the wrapping of the pipe, occasionally making the sign for buffalo. . . . After singing this song for about ten minutes, it was changed to the antelope song. . . .

Following further purification, both wife and husband, separately and alternately, undertook healing rituals, the woman with the special pipe-stem of the bundle and the man with a general-use sacred pipe.

Some women became renowned as powerful healers. Beverly Hungry Wolf's great-uncle, Willie Eagle Plume, told her of his grandmother, Otsani:

> She was a very powerful person. She knew all our religious ceremonies and she doctored the people. Among her doctoring methods she used cactus spines and porcupine quills to perform what is now called acupuncture . . . She had the power to communicate with ghosts, and I once saw her do this.

Eagle Plume then relates a shamanic ceremony that Otsani undertook to discover the location of a lost knife, which, if found by others, could have placed the owner in considerable trouble. When the ceremony was over and the lights were back on, the knife was lying on the floor. She had not merely discovered its location as asked; she had had a spirit retrieve it!

McClintock presents detailed descriptions of bundle ceremonies and transfers. In all cases, males and females carry equal and indispensable roles, paralleling the relationship between Sky and Earth. One of the introductory songs of the major Beaver Bundle ceremony includes the verses:

> The Heavens provide us with food.
> The Heavens are glad to behold us.
> . . . .
> The Earth loves us.
> The Earth is glad to hear us sing.
> The Earth provides us with food.

Two Beaver songs maintain this balance:

> The Old Man (chief male Beaver) is coming in.
> The Old Man has come in.
> He sits down besides his medicine.
> It is very strong medicine.
> . . . .
> The Old Woman (chief female Beaver) is coming in.
> The Old Woman has come in.
> She sits down and takes the medicine.
> It is very strong medicine.

Throughout these songs and the various lifting of the bundles and their components, husbands and wives sit facing each other and hold the sacred items together, or the woman might sing while the male performs ritual gestures and vice versa. There are also women's songs and dances, in which all the women take part. When there is a pipe smoked by men in a bundle, there is usually also a second pipe smoked by the women, a fact which androcentric writers simply ignore.

The necessity for couples in these rituals is not a dispensable feature. When a ceremonial bundle was ritually transferred to the Alberta Provincial Museum in the 1960s, as documented in the film *Iyahknix: Blackfoot Bundle Ceremony*, a woman had to stand in as wife for the curator, John Hellson, who was not at the time married. When Mrs. Rides-At-The-Door's husband died (see below), she engaged in rituals with her brother as her "partner."

Ritual Societies

Women were involved in the secret ritual societies in two modes: female societies and membership in male societies. The male Horn Society is paralleled by the female Motokiks Society. Paula Weasel Head, a Kainai elder, told Beverly Hungry Wolf that when she was an advisor for newer members of the Motokiks Society, her husband, Mokakin, was doing the same for the Horn society. Both societies put up their own lodges during the annual Okan ceremony, which brings the tribe together. For four days the Motokiks have initiations and ritual dances, many of which are private and esoteric. Within the Motokiks, there are four sub-groups, each with its own ritual paraphernalia, songs, and dances.

A woman may become a member of the male warrior societies in two ways, by joining, and sometimes fighting, alongside her husband and by living the life of a male warrior. Beverly Hungry Wolf writes of her great-aunt, Hate Woman, who was the wife of the famed warrior, Weasel Tail. He said,

> My wife said she loved me, and if I was to be killed on a war party [raids to capture horses for prestige] she wanted to be killed too. I took her with me on five raids. Some of them I led, and my wife was not required to perform the cooking or other chores. She carried a six-shooter. On one occasion she stole [desirable war exploit] a horse with a saddle, ammunition bag, and war club.

Hate Woman was asked to recite her war exploits during the Okan ceremony, an honor only accorded warriors.

George First Rider says of those women who become members of the warrior societies:

> A woman becomes a member — her life is better, her social status will rise, she becomes a leader. She's a [bison] Bull, aggressive and courageous, a defender of the people. She's a woman, physically weak, but should her husband be threatened, she'll come to his defense. No one will show disrespect for him in her presence.

Mrs. Rides-At-The-Door spoke to Beverly Hungry wolf of her daughter's full membership in the Horn Society:

> My daughter that nearly died—the one I put up my first Sun Dance [Okan] for— she was also a member of the Horns Society . . . she is one of the few women that

ever joined as a full member. Usually women only join with their husbands, except those who put up Sun Dances may not join at all [because of the nature of their sacrality]. My husband was a member without me, and he also made the pledge for our daughter to join, when she was so sick . . . I made her a new beaded outfit of buckskin to wear during the society's public dances. You couldn't even tell that she was not a man. She was pretty slim, anyway.

A few women lived as male warriors. Running Eagle, who was killed in battle in the mid-nineteenth-century, became so famed as a warrior that she led raiding parties. She preferred the activities of boys as a child, although she did household work when her mother was ill. When her father died, she had a dream that she should follow the male life-style. She was not interested in relations with men and never married, taking a widow into her lodge to perform the household chores (their relationship is unclear). Many in Running Eagle's community did not take her seriously, until she went on a fast vision quest and the spirits gave her warrior power that was acknowledged by her community. She was honored with a new warrior's name and invited to join the young warrior's society.

Okan

Okan is the major community ritual of the Nitsitapi tribes. In early summer, when there is sufficient grass for the large gathering of people and their horses, the tribes come together for this ritual and the subsidiary rituals of the various ritual societies. All the societies have important roles, as well as being the keepers of the major sacred bundles and pipes.[16]

The origin myth of Okan found in the literature is the story of Scarface, a poor young man with a scar on his face (who in some versions is the Morning Star). He was in love with a beautiful young woman from an important family. He went on a journey to find the Sun and seek his aid. After a series of adventures, he achieved his goal and was given the ritual and many presents. He returned without the scar, married the girl, and they carried out the first Okan.

George First Rider, a Kainai elder who was initiated into the tradition when a youth, told a different origin myth in 1974, when he was seventy. This myth, with the length and details of ritually told myths (seventeen typescript pages of translation for the first part alone), covers all the major ritual features of the Okan. Briefly, the story begins with a poor young woman who married an older man, who in misplaced jealousy physically abused her repeatedly. She attempted to hang herself but the rope broke; she fell asleep and had the first of a series of powerful dreams. She tried to tell her husband, but he beat her again. "This time a woman came in to help her. This woman grabbed the man by the hair and threw him all over the place." She listened to the girl's dream and told her own husband, who notified the people. The sacrificial ritual of her dream was carried out at the tree from which she tried to hang herself. In a series of visions, she learned further details of the ritual, including the center pole, the lodge, the buffalo tongues and the self-inflicted flesh offerings. Her husband reformed and assisted her with carrying out the rituals.

Ben Calf Robe, a Siksika elder, tells part of another Okan origin myth, the story of a young woman who marries the Sun. Transported to the sky world, she gathers prairie turnips but is told not to dig an especially large one. Eventually, out of curiosity, she does. When she gets it out of the ground, she finds a hole through which she can see the earth (this relates to the Iroquoian creation myth). Because of her act, she must return home to earth, but she is given the Okan to take back with her.

Central to the Okan is the Sacred Woman, the term for a woman who vows to Sun, sometime in the preceding year, to put on the ceremony. Only a woman who has the respect of her community can make such a vow, and only if a woman makes this vow can the ceremony be held. In the past, the vow was often taken in a request to Sun to aid a husband or son away on a raid; in this century, the vow is usually given when requesting Sun's aid for a seriously ill member of the family. From the time the vow is taken until the completion of the Okan, the woman and her husband live a ritually prescribed life. Traditionally, the woman's family would gather a hundred dried buffalo tongues as a food offering for Sun, to be shared by the people during the Okan. (To try and stop the Okan, the government once forbade Native people from gathering buffalo tongues.)

When all the people gather at the Okan grounds, the Sacred Woman's lodge is put up, where she will fast during the four days of the ceremony. This lodge, which only the ritual leaders enter, along with the four sweat lodges and the main Medicine Lodge, are the foci for the Okan. Meanwhile the Sacred Woman's husband will engage in a series of sweat rituals. The Sacred Woman will wear the Natoas (Sacred Turnip) headdress, kept with the important Beaver bundle (the keepers of the Beaver bundles function as the head priests in the ritual). The Sacred Woman and her husband will request the ritual passing of instructions for carrying out the ceremony from a couple experienced in this ritual; this couple will serve as their ritual grandparents.

The Okan is rich and complex, and a proper description would take many pages; moreover, there are several detailed descriptions in the literature. The point being made for this study is the role of the Sacred Woman, who retains this status for the rest of her life, for it is a female that sponsors the most important ritual of the Nitsitapi tribes, and it is her ritual activities that are at the heart of the Okan.

Nor is this centering of the "Sun Dance" on a woman unique to the Nitsitapi tribes, for a similar situation exists among another Algonkian-speaking Plains people, the Tsistsistas ("People"), known in the literature as the Cheyenne. Their ritual, called Oxheheom ("New Life Lodge," the meaning of the Anishnabe Midéwiwin), centers on a male Pledger and a Sacred Woman. She is the focus of the complex ritual and leads the processions of sacred objects, of dancers, etc. In the past, as part of the Oxheheom, her ritual intercourse with an older male priest chosen by her was the sacred act which led to the renewal of life.[17]

In Their Own Words

Beverly Hungry Wolf recorded the words of several female elders (see her book, *The Ways of My Grandmothers*, for the complete texts). The following is from the thoughts of the Sacred Woman, Mrs. Rides-At-The-Door:

> My Husband and I lived by our Indian religion through all our many years together, and I am still living by it today. We went through many ceremonial transfers. We were given a medicine pipe bundle which he took care of for many years. . . .
>
> I have had a beaver bundle for many years. It is the biggest medicine bundle of all the ones among our people. There is a very long ceremony for its opening and they used to sing several hundred songs during it. The men and women all join together to sing these songs and dance with the different parts of the bundle . . . We used to have a really happy time with this beaver ceremony, but now there is no one left who can lead it. . . .
>
> I was very young when I first started with this holy business, and now I am an old woman [had been given a very long life], on account of it. It has been a very trying life, especially during the medicine lodge ceremonies [Okan]. Sometimes when I had to go out [from the Sacred Woman's lodge] during the four days of rituals my assistants would have to hold me up, I would be so weak [from fasting]. I have always been devoted to my religious duties to help my family and people. All the younger people are like my children.

From Paula Weasel Head, Beverly Hungry Wolf received the story of her initiations, from which the following is extracted:

> I'm going to tell you a little bit about the holy initiations that I have gone through in my lifetime of over seventy years, to show what a woman can take part in with our tribal culture . . . I was also initiated to join with a medicine pipe bundle

when I was very small. Each of those bundles has a man and a wife for a owner, and a child goes with them to wear the special topknot wrapping and fur headband that is kept with the bundle. That is what they transferred to me, and I sat right up front with the main people, each time the bundle's opening ceremony was held. . . .

Mokakin and I got married in 1921 . . . We were still very young when we made a pledge to take that bundle called Backside-to-the-Fire Medicine Pipe. We treated it very well. I was very scared to do something wrong to it, there are so many rules and regulations to follow. The ones who initiated us for it were the real old-time people, so we were initiated in the old-time way. The ceremony took a couple of days. . . .

We lived very good by that medicine pipe bundle. I used to take it outside every morning, before the sun came up, as was the custom. I always had to start a fire in the stove so that I could make incense before I took the bundle out. I watched it during the day so that nothing would happen to it while it hung outside . . . Then I made incense again before the sun went down, and I would bring the bundle back inside. I made incense once more before we lay down to sleep. That is when we really learned to pray . . . Since then I have been praying steadily, and up to this day I am still praying. . . .

Mokakin and I joined the Horns Society several times. First, we had that membership called Has-a-Rattle, which is one of the leading ones. These membership bundles come from long ago. We went around with this bundle for several years, and I treated it good, too, just like our pipe. . . .

The Horns are the secret society for men, and the Motoki are the secret society for women. I belonged to this society for many years. I had one of the leading memberships . . . In recent years a younger group of women has taken over the society. Like Mokakin with the Horns, I serve as the adviser to these newer members. I am their grandmother. This is how Mokakin and I have been rewarded for our faith in the holy ways of our people.

These are remarkable women. I feel privileged to have been a guest in the home of the Apikuni Sacred Woman, Josephine Crow Shoe, and her husband, Joe, who have lived through virtually the entire twentieth century. They have kept important bundles since 1934 and have worked for most of their lives to keep the traditions of their people alive and to stop the desecration of their sacred Old Man River by damming. In 1992, they were both awarded the Order of Canada, Canada's highest honor. This indicated unexpected insight on the part of the government in recognizing that all of their work was as a couple. And it is ironic, because they were given the award for preserving Apikuni culture, when the government had been trying for over a century to destroy it!

9
HOPI RELIGION[1]

BACKGROUND

WHEN THE SPANISH REACHED what is now the Southwest of the United States four hundred and fifty years ago, they found indigenous peoples, speaking widely diverse languages, living in permanent agricultural settlements. These peoples are still called in English by the Spanish word used to designate them, "Pueblo," meaning simply "town," referring to their living in agricultural settlements. Most of these complexes of towns are to be found in the Rio Grande valley, and all but one are in present-day New Mexico. On being reconquered after a successful revolt against the Spanish, an accommodation was reached in which both the Catholic Church and traditional indigenous religious traditions played important roles. Again in all but one pueblo.

The Hopi are the most distant from the others of the Pueblo peoples, and reside in a series of villages on three mesas in northeastern Arizona, surrounded by the large Navaho reservation. Their villages are the closest to the ruins of the early large settlements of a millennium past—a vast cultural complex that included major ceremonial centers, large-scale irrigation, and extensive road networks for trading and/or ritual purposes—to which pilgrimages are still made, some being under the protection of clan ancestors. The Hopi, alone of the Pueblo peoples, speak an Uto-Aztecan language, as do the Papago and other peoples to their west and various peoples in Mexico. To the present, Christian churches have made relatively little inroads on the Hopi.

The traditional Hopi socio-economic system occupied an interesting niche in the range of possibilities: a matrilineal and matrilocal, egalitarian society in which the men did most of the farming as well as the weaving. Women owned the residences (and the matrilineal clans, the fields) and spent much of their time grinding maize, which is the food staple, and carrying water. While the rituals still involved elements of a male hunting and warrior culture, game other than rabbits does not abound in the semi-arid area, and the traditional villages were built on high mesas for defensive purposes. At least two factors seem to be involved in the male economic focus on farming: the sparsity of herbivores and the adoption of sheep-herding from the Spanish reduced the opportunities and lessened the need for successful hunting, and the agricultural fields being far from the villages made it difficult for the males as warriors to protect the women if they were to do the farming, perhaps leading to the males taking on the agricultural role.

Because subsistence was dependent on the crops—particularly maize, although squash, melons, beans, cotton, and tobacco, for rituals, were also grown —in a semi-desert area, virtually all of the rituals focused on rain and germination to varying degrees. Being settled in villages, some of which are centuries old, the Hopi have a rich ceremonial life. Although there are ceremonies throughout the year, from the end of the harvest to the beginning of the planting season, there is a near constant round of ceremonies, the responsibility for which rotates among the ritual societies, which belong to the matrilineal clans.

The Hopi live off the major trade routes of the now dominant culture in an area not seen by the dominant culture as desirable, and there was little impact by Euroamericans on Hopi culture until the end of the last century. Since then there has been increasing pressure and domination, including violence, by the American government; a factional split between the "traditionalists" and the progressives; a prophetic eschatological movement appealing to non-Hopi;[2] inroads by evangelical missionaries; and a blurring of gender roles with an economy increasingly oriented towards salaries from federal governmental agencies, a government imposed by the dominant culture; etc. Accordingly, the following depiction of female aspects of Hopi religion is more oriented towards the past of a century ago than the present. Nevertheless, much of the following is relevant to the contemporary Hopi, who number about ten thousand in twelve villages.

FEMALE SPIRITS

As in all the Pueblo traditions, the Hopi world is imbued with many powerful beings, some portrayed symbolically and many, the Katsinas, appearing in the form of masked dancers throughout the late winter, spring, and early summer ceremonies. The Hopi spirit realm is complex and can be confusing to those outside of the tradition. There are different understandings, at times compatible and sometimes contradictory, to be found in the Hopi mesas, villages, and clans. Hence, the following generalizations will not hold for all the differing Hopi versions of the spirit realm. In general, among the most important female spirits are Huru'ingwwuuti ("Hard Beings Woman"), seemingly paired with Sun, as well as her children, Muy'ingwa (Deity of Germination) and Tuwapong-tumsi ("Sand Altar Woman"), and Kookyangwso'wuuti ("Spider Woman"), a culture-hero/trickster/fertility figure (these last terms are used quite loosely).

While in some of the other Pueblo traditions earth and maize fertility deities are explicit from their names, the lack of names for Hopi deities that exactly coincide with European language words should not necessitate the seeming confusion among some Western scholars regarding an assumed want of these deities. As we shall see, Hard Beings Woman is certainly an earth (and sea) deity. And the concept of a maize mother certainly exists in Hopi culture. For example, the *tsotsmingwu* ("maize-mother") is a perfect ear of maize used in the baptism of infants and of initiates. Since the *tsotsmingwu* is considered to be the mother of the child or initiate, with the Sun being the father, the maize-mother is presumably, if not explicitly, connected to Hard Beings Woman. Hence, the virtually universal mother-daughter relationship of Earth and a grain-mother as daughter of Earth is also present in Hopi traditions, albeit in a somewhat attenuated form.

Earth Mother and Fertility Deities

Huru'ingwwuuti ("Hard Beings Woman") is usually spoken of in connection with shell, coral, turquoise, and other beads, symbolizing the hardness, the solidity of the earth. White Shell Woman of the Apache, their earth deity, is probably connected to her. It is around Huru'ingwwuuti and the small piece of land on which she resided earlier in mythic time that the earth grew. Although an earth deity, she is also associated with sky powers. She "owns" the moon and stars, and her house is a kiva (see below) in the Western Ocean which Taawa ("Sun") enters every evening, journeying under the earth to rise in the east in the morning. Hence, Huru'ingwwuuti is also a sea deity. (On Third Mesa, Huru'ingwwuuti is dual, being in the east and the west.) In one myth, a young man travels down the Colorado River to her realm, where he meets a young maiden. He sleeps with her after Sun, a young man dressed in the Flute cere-monial costume (see below), rushes past. When the young man of the story wakes in the morning he finds her an old woman, perhaps symbolizing the phases of womanhood, of which Huru'ingwwuuti is the epitome. She herself is only indirectly a fertility deity as she gives birth to two children, female and male, who are the primary fertility deities.

Her son is Muy'ingwa (Deity of Germination and Growth), the fertility deity of the crops, as well as the central figure in the initiation of children into the Powamuy and Katsina societies. The Powamuy ceremony is the first of the spring fertility ceremonials. Muy'ingwa resides at Tuuwanasavi ("Center of the World"); he comes from the direction Atkyamiq ("below, nadir"). Of importance in this study, according to Geertz, "is that he is a male deity with androgynous characteristics in a role normally assigned to female deities." (Indeed, as Muy'ingwwuuti, the deity is female.) Muy'ingwa's costume is the female wedding blanket and he wears female make-up. On First Mesa, his counterpart is Aalo'saka, who in one legend is born as male and female twins and, at the turn of the century, was represented by male and female stone images, both named Aalo'saka.

Huru'ingwwuuti's daughter is Tuwapongtumsi ("Sand Altar Woman"), an earth deity who nourishes all plants. She is the wife of Maasaw, the ruler of the Fourth (present) World and deity of the realm of the dead (who has become virtually an all-powerful deity in the modern period), and patron deity of the Aa'alt (Al Society). In one of the Third Mesa villages, Orayvi, Tuwapongtumsi is conflated with Tiikuywuuti ("Child Sliding-out Woman"), mother of the game animals and deity of birth. Elsewhere on Third Mesa, however, the deity of childbirth is Taalawtumsi ("Dawn Woman"), patron deity of the Taatawkyam (Taw Society). Taalawtumsi carries small wooden images of babies in Her womb. She sends these figures into the wombs of women desiring children.

In the Hopi variation of the typical Native American cosmology of six directions (the four horizontal directions, zenith and nadir), as elsewhere, the zenith is represented by Taawa ("Sun"). Huru'ingwwuuti and her two children, male and female, together represent the nadir. Each of the three is an earth deity, by name and/or by associations; combined, they fulfill the normative nadir powers of plant fertility and human birth.

Trickster/Culture-Hero

Kookyangwso'wuuti ("Spider Woman") is an alternative creator deity to Tiikuywuuti-Tuwapongtumsi, but she is not primarily a fertility deity. Rather she is, in part, a "trickster" figure, similar in certain respects to the male Coyote and Rabbit of other Native American traditions. In one myth, learning of the creating of Tiikuywuuti and Tuwapongtumsi, she creates a human pair. But they are Spaniards who plague the Hopi. She makes more pairs of humans, each pair speaking a different language. Finally, she creates a mateless female and tells her to seek a single man. Eventually, the single woman finds the single male, but they do not get on well. They fight, separate, come back together, and continually repeat the cycle. They mix with other humans and are the progenitors of strife.[3]

Kookyangwso'wuuti is not always a troubling creator. The Leenangw ("Flute Ceremonial") was brought from the Underworld by her during the Emergence. This ceremony focuses on rain and abundant germination; the Flute ceremonial costume is related to Sun (see above), and the flute is a courting instrument throughout Native North America.

Kookyangwso'wuuti is the keeper of tradition; she speaks for the old ones, the ancestors. Tiny and difficult to see, she may appear on one's shoulder when one is in trouble, offering advice and admonition. An object of visions, she is powerful and must be dealt with cautiously and respectfully. As owner of salt, she is also central to a major pilgrimage ritual.

When Kookyangwso'wuuti was making the trail for the Hopi to reach Öngtupqa ("Salt Canyon" [Grand Canyon], the place of emergence into the present world [Sipaapuni]), she became weary and changed herself into a stone marker to guide the Hopi (the trail was completed by her grandchildren, the Pöquangwhoya ["Warrior Twins"—the sons of Taawa outside of Third Mesa]). The small, black stone is vulva-shaped, with a hole about five centimeters in diameter and sixteen centimeters in depth. During the ritual pilgrimage by Hopi males to gather salt, the pilgrims leave offerings of prayer feathers and sacred cornmeal in the hole. Naked and covered by a wedding blanket, the pilgrims insert their penises into the stone and have symbolic intercourse with Kookyangwso'wuuti, who in this instance is known as Salt Woman. The intercourse promotes the life and health of the participants and leads to their wives having children.

A Few Other Female Deities

Of other female deities, also important are Hahay'iwuuti (Hahay'i Woman), the Mother of the Katsinas, and the Hee'e'wuuti (Hee'ee Woman), the Katsina who leads the Katsina processions. Hahay'iwuuti, present in many ceremonies, urges on and tends to the Katsinas. She may bless the people at ceremonies by patting water on their heads, water that comes from Kiisiwu, the summer home of the Katsinas. This water is especially significant since Hahay'iwuuti is the mother of the rain-bringing Katsinas. As another form of blessing, she also hands out *somiviki* ("tied piiki"), a special blue cornmeal preparation and a gift particular to the women's domain.

Hee'e'wuuti is a female warrior Katsina (in the version of one village, a berdache transvestite), who, followed by two Hotootos (guard Katsinas), leads the Katsinas on their ritual circuits in several major ceremonies. According to her myth, once while still a human when her mother was preparing her hair, she saw enemies approaching her village. Hair done up into a whorl on one side only, she grabbed a bow and arrows and led the attack which defeated the enemy. Her costume includes hair in a dressed whorl on one side and hanging free on the other.

FEMALE RITUALS AND RITUAL ROLES

Life-cycle Rituals

Among the Hopi, life-cycle rituals for females concentrate on two interrelated foci: human fertility and change of status. The former consists of puberty and childbirth rituals, which, to a degree, are equated; the latter is the primary import of the marriage ritual, which, for females, is also connected to death rituals.

Prior to the American domination of the Hopi country a century ago, adult males were not only farmers and ritualists, but they were also hunters and warriors. Becoming an adult male is a matter of incremental physiological changes leading to the physical ability, with the knowledge gained from initiations, to take on adult roles. For the female adult Hopi, in traditional times, all roles centered on life: the providing of food for sustenance and the bringing to life of new human beings. While the male role in reproduction is clearly understood and there are affiliated responsibilities, it is the female that births and nurses.

The preparation of food is a major element of both female puberty and marriage rituals; indeed, it is central to female participation in all rituals, as it is central to life itself. While the ability to prepare food is not marked by physiological change, the ability to bear children is. Hence, female puberty is marked by a private ritual, for which there is no corresponding male ritual. It is to be noted, however, that there are parallels and interconnections between female and male rituals; for example, rituals for scalps brought back by successful warriors, which are treated like newborn infants, are equated with menarche and childbirth rituals.

Around the time of menarche, or after American government enforced enrollment of children in boarding schools in the first half of the twentieth century, several years later, adolescent females engaged in a ritual that marked their changed status and eligibility for marriage. As with all rituals, details vary considerably from mesa to mesa, and even among villages on the same mesa.

At the home of a paternal aunt or grandmother, singly or in small groups, eligible females continuously grind maize throughout the daytime for four days in a room darkened by the placing of rabbit-skin robes over the windows. During this time they follow the traditional Hopi fasting practice of abstaining from meat and salt and limiting the intake of liquids. The girl remains secluded, except for a few companions who had themselves recently undergone the ritual, and she uses a scratching stick prepared by the husband of her host. On the last day, the girl bakes *piiki*, the thin, flat bread important in many rituals, and has her hair dressed for the first time in the large whorls on each side that are emblematic of an unmarried maiden. In the meantime, men hunt rabbits in preparation for the feast held on the evening of the last day.

The ceremony is preceded by a ritual several years earlier in a girl's life, when at around ten years of age, she goes to a paternal aunt's or grandmother's home to ritually grind maize for a whole day, after which her hair is trimmed in a particular style. This preparatory ritual is reminiscent of the one-day fasts that pre-pubescent girls and boys underwent in the Woodland regions prior to the four-day or more fasts of adolescence.

There are many aspects of these rituals to be found in other Native American cultures: the four-day (or longer) seclusion, the use of a scratching stick, the baking of a special bread (in the Southwest), and fasting. Of particular interest with regard to the Hopi ritual is the focus on grinding maize, a major activity of women, and the pairing of the activity with male hunting. Clearly, the crux of the ritual is the production of prepared food, signifying the transformation of the girl into an adult female able to carry out the food-preparing role of womanhood as she physically becomes able to fulfill the reproductive role of women. The ritual is considered an essential preliminary to marriage.

Different from many other Native American traditions, there is no female seclusion, nor is there male avoidance of females during menstruation. Sexual intercourse can take place during menstruation, particularly by infertile couples, as this time is considered particularly effective for conception, the foetus understood as formed from the combination of female blood and male semen. One woman told Alice Schlegel that intercourse is avoided during heavy menstrual flow as it might be harmful to the woman, not the man. The reason for this difference from the normative gathering-hunting pattern may very well be the male occupational shift from hunting to primarily farming. Not only would contact with a menstruating female not be inimical to farming as it is to hunting, but it may even have a positive value from the standpoint of fertility symbolism. Hopi men do avoid sexual contact with women, menstruating or not, before a hunt, as do other Native Americans.

The major ritual in a typical Hopi female's life is the wedding ritual, for it is the married state that enables the Hopi female to fully realize her personal power and social roles within the matrilineal and matrilocal cultural context. The female initiates the ritual by proposing marriage to the male. Acceptance of the proposal leads to the first stage of the elaborate marriage ritual, which is patrilocal.

The bride temporarily moves into the groom's home, where, for the first four days, she is secluded and fasts in the Hopi fashion. On the last day of the fast, women of both the bride's and groom's families are involved. Bride and groom are bathed by the females of their respective families, and the groom's mother washes the couple's hair and twists their hair tightly together into a single knot (with the groom's aunts ceremonially trying to interfere). After the hair-washing ceremony, the bride is taken out of the house by the groom's mother and exhibited to the rising sun (as is the infant after the naming ceremony). The bride then continues to reside in the groom's home until the groom's family (the males do the weaving in Hopi culture) completes the manufacture of the bride's wedding garments. During this time, the bride cooks for her in-laws.

When the bride's garments are finished, a feast is held. On the next day, the couple move to the matrilocal residence. After a couple of children are born and the marriage is stable, the husband builds a house for his wife by her family home, a house which she will own and, should there be marital strife, from which she can kick out her husband. (The youngest daughter of a family, however, remains in her parents' home after marriage and inherits the family house.) The husband now farms the fields assigned him by his wife's clan and assists his father-in-law in providing for the family. However, the wedding is not entirely complete until the bride's family accumulates the payment for the wedding garments and delivers the payment to the groom's family; the payment includes the making by the bride of a special wicker plaque for the groom,.

These wedding garments are very significant in the final rituals of the life-cycle, those of death, for the wedding-garment bundle is essential for females on their after-life journey. Without it, they will be forced to grind grain halfway to the Underworld; with it, they will swiftly reach the Grand Canyon, where is located Sipaapuni, the place of emergence and the entrance to the realm of the dead. In turn, the *hahawpi* ("instrument for descending"), the wicker plaque woven by the bride for her husband, is essential for his smooth journey to Sipaapuni.

For this reason, Geertz and Lomatuway'ma have equated the wedding ceremony for females with the male's initiation into one or more of the ritual societies:

> The equation is unavoidable: the status of womanhood and the appropriation of rights in the Underworld are attained exclusively through the wedding and the

garments, whereas the status of manhood and the appropriation of rights in the Underworld are attained exclusively through initiation and the knowledge that it offers.

Alice Schlegel (personal communication) notes that "it is at her wedding that a girl (*mana*) becomes a woman (*wuhti*) (whereas a boy [*tiyo*] becomes a man [*taka*] at his second initiation)."

Not only do the women's wedding garments and the payment of the *hahawpi* directly affect the afterlife fate of both women and men, but the wedding is further connected with death in that marriage continues in the Underworld. A first husband and first wife remain so forever. Should a person marry again, that marriage is temporary, lasting only until the death of one of the partners, who will again be with the first spouse.

The equation between the wedding ceremony for women and the initiation ceremonies into the ritual societies for men should not be understood as exclusionary. Obviously, men are also involved in the wedding rituals, and women are initiated into either or both of the all-important Katsina and Powamu societies. As well, some women take part in the rituals of the male societies and there are three female ritual societies into which they may be initiated.

Female Ritual Societies

The Hopi ceremonial year is elaborate, one of the most complex to be found among human cultures. Traditionally, all the Hopi, female and male, were initiated into at least one ritual society, and usually several.

Most of these societies have their own kivas, the underground ceremonial chambers that are the only non-family, non-dwelling buildings in the traditional Hopi villages. The kiva has a long history, being found in, and central to, the oldest archaeologically known towns in the Southwest. Every part of the kiva is of symbolic significance; overall, its import derives from the the basic myths of emergence, as well as birth. The earliest structures in the Southwest were pit-dwellings; undoubtedly, the kiva reflects the long habitation of the area by horticulturists. Near the center of the kiva is the *sipaapuni*, which represents the *sipapu*, the entrance to the Underworld, the realm of the dead, and the symbolic entrance from the realm below to the present, Fourth, realm into which the Hopi emerged. Offerings are placed in the *sipaapuni* for the spirits of the Underworld. The Kiva itself functions as a womb in which new or transformed life—initiates, Katsinas, sacred objects—is created. The narrow exit, through which one climbs up a ladder to reach the outside, serves as the vagina, from which life emerges. (The kiva also functions, when not in use for ceremonies, as a men's clubhouse—a space for the men, given that the house is the women's domain.)

From the beginning of snow in November well into the spring, there is, with short breaks, a continual round of ceremonies. Since most of the activities of these ceremonies, which often last sixteen days, take place in the underground kivas, the public aspects involve but one or a few days, and, since only the relevant societies and clans are active in specific ceremonies, the Hopi individually are not continually involved in rituals during this period. Moreover, some ceremonies alternate with others in two-year cycles. The literature on these rituals is voluminous and cannot be meaningfully summarized in a short essay. Moreover, most aspects of these rituals are esoteric, and the ethnographic data were not always gathered in ways that would meet contemporary ethical standards. Accordingly, the brief exposition that follows is merely suggestive for the overall analysis and should not be understood to completely describe the ceremonies to which reference is made.

Along with the dozen or so primarily men's ceremonials, there are ceremonies carried out by three female ritual societies: Maraw, Lakon, and Owaqöl. Although these are female societies, as with the male societies, there are usually a few members of the other sex. These men, most often brothers of the female leaders, take part to assist them.

Most important of these ceremonies is the Marawtikive. The Maraw is the only one of the female societies to have its own kiva, and it is a sister society to the male Wuwtsim society. This female society contains within itself all the elements that are dispersed among the four male fraternities: crop fertility, human fertility, animal fertility and hunting, and warfare. It is said that, in earlier times, all females belonged to the Maraw society. Females can be initiated at any age; often infants or young children are initiated.

The Wuwtsim society, together with three others, puts on the Wuwtsim, the first of the great winter ceremonials. In the origin myths of the Marawtikive and Wuwtsim, the societies were founded, respectively, by a sister and a brother. The Marawtikive is concerned with the production of rain, the growth of maize, the fertility of women, and caring for the dead. As well, the ceremony has martial and healing components. With regard to the latter, the ceremony is especially efficacious for the "twisting" sickness, as is the Wuwtsim.

The ceremony is held in the fall and winter but, in many villages, takes place in alternate years. The pattern follows the general framework of all the major Hopi ceremonials. The ceremony lasts for eight days (the leaders of ceremonies may be involved with rituals for the preceding eight days). The first four days involve various ritual preparations in the kiva, including bringing in of sacred items for the ceremony, ritual smoking, manufacture of prayer sticks, construction of the altar, announcement to the dead of the ceremony, etc.; specific to Marawtikive is the preparation of food and other offerings for the dead. At Orayvi, during the fall ceremony, a women is dispatched to a shrine several miles from the village, along the road taken by the dead to and from the Underworld. There, she removes her clothes and invites the spirits of the dead members of the Maraw society to come to the ceremony.

The second set of four days includes various public performances that involve the participants leaving the kiva to dance in the village open areas. For the Marawtikive, this includes dances in which women put on men's apparel and mock the men in song, including sexual humor. The men retaliate by throwing water, urine, and filth on the dancers. These dances reverse, from the standpoint of gender, some of the rituals of the Wuwtsim. In one record of the ceremony, the final ritual of the winter ceremony was a public dance focusing on the mythic male and female progenitors of the ceremony. The female roles were danced by members of the Maraw society, and the male roles by members of the Wuwtsim. On the penultimate day of the fall ceremonial, the women danced with prayer sticks bearing corn tassels and painted with corn, germination, cloud, and rain symbols. At night, they carried ears of corn instead. On the last day, several women dress in men's clothing, carry weapons, and wear elaborate headdresses. These women join the other dancers, shooting their bows and throwing their spears. The archers and lancers then make balls of sweet cornmeal and water which they toss to the spectators.

Lakontikive and Owaqöltikive take place in the autumn, put on respectively by the Lakon and Owaqöl female societies. Both share a number of features, particularly the use of coiled baskets made by the women which are thrown to the spectators. The latter ritual, however, is generally understood as a relatively late arrival in the Hopi ceremonial calendar.

The rituals of the first half of the Lakontikive are similar to those of the Marawtikive, except that the society does not have its own kiva; at Orayvi, these rituals take place in the Hawiwvi kiva. On the evening of the eighth day, the women of the Lakon Society race from a shrine to the village. The next day, the winner is dressed as the Lakon Maiden, the major deity of the ceremony, and, with the male Lakon chief, proceeds to the starting point for a race by young men. Carrying a basket, she begins the run, passing the tray to whoever passes her; he in turn passes the tray to anyone who passes him.

Meanwhile the Lakon Society women, led by the female chief, enter the plaza, each carrying a basket. There they dance awaiting the winner of the race, who pushes his way through them and proceeds to the Hawiwvi kiva, where he is joined for breakfast by the women when they finish their dance.

Throughout the day, the women return to the plaza to sing and dance. At each of these occasions, two women, dressed as the Lakon Maidens (different women taking turns), carrying a bundle of gifts on their backs and ears of corn with feathers attached in their hands—each ear a different color representing the four directions—approach the circle of dancers. They are preceded by a male member of the society who draws cloud symbols on the earth with pollen and cornmeal. The Maidens throw the corn ears onto the cloud symbols. The male ritualist returns to the kiva, and the Maidens, from within the circle of female dancers, toss the gifts into the crowd of spectators. The males in the crowd ritually fight for these gifts laden with significant symbolism.

The difference between female and male society dances is of interest with regard to gender symbolism. While the men form straight lines in their dances, the women dance in a semicircle, the various activities taking place within this circle.

Female Roles in Male Society Rituals

As the female society rituals discussed above included a small number of male ritualists, usually relatives of the female leaders, so the male society rituals usually require the participation of some females. For example, during the Soalangw, two to three female relatives of the ritual leaders take part as Soyal Maidens. During the Leenangw (Flute) ceremony, two maidens from the clan which "owns" the society are involved in aspects of the ritual; at Third Mesa, women, one from each family, race to a spring where parts of the ritual take place. At the Tsuutsu't (Snake[-Antelope]) ceremony, a man and a woman are dressed in the regalia of the two major deities of the ritual. As discussed earlier, Hee'e'wuuti, the female warrior katsina (albeit embodied in a male dancer), leads the katsinas on ceremonial circuits during the katsina rituals. The list could be considerably extended.

While these are examples of specific roles, women as a whole play a central role in all the rituals, including those of male ritual societies, for no ritual can take place without major elements of female participation. The most important female ritual role, as in other Native American cultures, is to provide food for the ceremonies, without which they cannot be held. For the Hopi, this particularly means grinding the sacred cornmeal, used in the preparation of sacred food, and in blessing the ritual participants and the deities. Geertz and Lomatuway'ma quote the words of a Hopi woman:

> . . . And these women did not have any bad thoughts within themselves when they prepared food for the performers and took it to the kiva. They will earn a (good) harvest through their hard work, and they will have this in mind as they do

it. . . . They will become enriched with all that produce, and take it into the kiva, still keeping this (intention) in mind. All of these things come to one end (i.e., a bountiful harvest).

FEMALE SELF-UNDERSTANDING

Traditional Hopi women consider women more important then men, with the proviso that men are still important. The major Hopi value is life (*tiita*, "to give or have given birth," "to multiply"), in both aspects of generation and continuity. Women know that they mirror the Earth Mother by birthing and nurturing children, by nourishing the community with prepared food, and by sustaining the sacred items by feeding them. They understand that they embody the life-force in all aspects. But traditional Hopi men too understand they have a role in providing life. Not only do they farm the fields of their wives, but they are cognizant of a more important role in conception than that found in modern Western culture. For they understand conception to be an ongoing process rather than a single incident; intercourse is continued during pregnancy to help the child grow.

Hopi women are raised in a world imbued with female numinous beings as well as male. They celebrate this world and continue it with daily rituals, the feeding of sacred household and clan items with cornmeal, and periodic complex ceremonials. All ceremonies require their participation to varying degrees. Men play the dominant role in most ceremonials, save those of the female societies. But without the women, the ceremonies could not be held. It is they who grind the sacred cornmeal, essential to virtually all rituals, and sprinkle the cornmeal on the masked male dancers. Women prepare the food that is necessary to all ceremonies and, in some, distribute it to the spectators, who value this food as particularly sacred. Women as well as men may sponsor Katsina dances, the sponsor said to "stand above the *kikmongwi* [village chief, see below]."

Alice Schlegel (personal communication) notes a further reason for the greater involvement of men in rituals. Much of the ritual activity involves contact with the ancestors, and sustained contact with the dead is both spiritually powerful and dangerous, particularly to women in their child-bearing years. Hence, men take on most of the risks of this important but precarious activity.

While both female and male children are desired, both males and females clearly prefer the former. For a female, the birth of a daughter means the continuation of her own matrilineal lifeline. For a male, it means the birth of someone who, with her future husband, will support him in old age. A son will live with and support the family into which he marries rather than his natal family.

A female has twice as much "heart" (life-force) as a male. For example, "witches," malevolent shamans (male or female), are understood to lose life-energy in gaining power. To continue to live, they must steal the hearts of children, killing them in the process. If "witches" steal the heart of a boy, they gain four years of life, but if they steal the heart of a female, they gain eight years.

In the socio-political realm, women indirectly control the community, as well as own the homes, ceremonial objects, fields, and the produce of the fields. A man must receive his wife's permission before undertaking ritual obligation. Male political leaders are cognizant of the wishes of the Clan Mothers. As older men state: "Women always get their way."

But the power of women, their spiritual, political, and economic superiority, does not exist in isolation, but in dyadic relationships. Geertz and Lomatu-way'ma emphasize that a

> . . . dichotomy remains throughout all the institutions of Hopi society. The women own the sacred objects which give the clan its authority, but it is the initiated male who effectuates them. The women make the food, while the men perform the rituals, with the exception, of course, of the two or three exclusively female ceremonials—which, by the way, are presided over by the clan's initiated male leader. The women grind the corn which the men use to make their prayers and rituals heard, and so on.

As on the cosmic plane the male sky phenomenon of rain fertilizes the female earth to bring forth life, so on the human plane male semen mixes with female menstrual blood to create life. Males farm the female earth (both in ownership by his wife's clan and as the female Earth) to produce maize which is ground and cooked by women into food. The matrilineal clan is led by the Clan Mother, not alone but paired with the Clan Uncle, her brother. As discussed above, the Hopi fertility deity is Tuwapongtumsi-Muy'ingwa, a sister-brother pair, the children of Huru'ingwwuuti, the Earth Mother, herself paired with the Sun. This brother-sister dyad, found on all levels of Hopi society, is itself paired by a second dyad, that of husband-wife. These two dyads lie at the heart of the two essential Hopi social structures, respectively, clan and household.

The gender dichotomy is also reflected in spheres of activity, domestic for the female and public for the male. The Hopi say that "the man's place is on the outside of the house." His realm is the kiva, the fields, the hunt and defense, while the woman's realm is the home, which is hers and hers to control. A male is in charge of the village, called the *kikmongwi* (*ki*: house; *mongwi*: leader), together with a council of male clan elders (*mongwi*), but his primary role is the maintenance of harmony between the village, the human realm, and the realm of the spirits. The *kikmongwi* is addressed as "father"; his wife, "mother." As the female is leader in the house of the family, so the male is leader outside of the home, in the "house" of the community.

This dichotomy is further reflected in the Hopi understanding of the cosmos. For while the Earth always connotes peacefulness, harmony, birth, and nurture, the fertilizing sky phenomenon of rain is often accompanied by the dangerously violent thunder-lightening, and Sun not only promotes life but also death if the rains do not come. Rain too can become so abundant that it washes away the young plants and causes flooding of the fields. So the male human not only fertilizes the female for reproduction and farms the female fields for maize, but also is able to harness an innate violent aspect, uniquely male, to defend the core of the community—the women—as well as protect the plants.

As depicted above, all the rituals, whether female or male, contain elements of the other gender for balance; harmony is a key Hopi value. Ritual elements tend to be expressed in gender pairs; for example, the *paahos* (prayer sticks) are made and used in female-male pairs.

Traditional Hopi religion, then, is one in which women, as part of male-female pairs, are fully cognizant of their worth in every possible respect. Their understanding themselves to be the superior aspect of these dyads is similar to the understanding of Papago women. (The Papago also live in Arizona and are probably distantly related in time to the Hopi.) When, in the 1930s, Ruth Underhill was doing fieldwork among the Papago and was perturbed at the seeming secondary role of the women in religious ceremonies, she received a very different interpretation of their situation from the women themselves:

> "You see, we *have* power. Men have to dream to get power from the spirits and they think of everything they can—songs and speeches and marching around, hoping that the spirits will notice them and give them some power. But we *have* power." When I looked a little surprised, the answer was: "Children. Can any warrior make a child, no matter how brave and wonderful he is?"
>
> "Warriors *do* take a little part in starting children."
>
> They sniffed. "A very little part. It's nothing compared to the months that a woman goes through to make a child. Don't you see that without us, there would be no men? Why should we envy the men? We *made* the men."

This cultural valuing of females is not limited to women alone, but is also recognized by males. In a 1950s test of values among Zuni children, a Pueblo culture southeast of the Hopi, ten percent of boys on being asked who they would like to be if they could change themselves expressed a preference to be their mothers or sisters. No girls chose males.

10
FUSION: DINÉ MENARCHE RITUALS

BACKGROUND

A FEW YEARS AGO, I was in St. Petersburg, just before the city reverted to its old name, Leningrad, to do some research at the Museum of Anthropology and Ethnography. This museum is particularly rich in early northwest North American artifacts because of the Russian presence there before Russia sold Alaska to the United States in the mid-nineteenth century. As I was kindly being taken through the galleries by the curator of Native American cultures, we came upon a mannequin wearing the clothes and other appurtenances of a young Dené woman from what is now the Canadian northwest. From her neck, on a decorated thong, hung a long bird-bone tube. I was asked if I knew what it was, given that it was shaped like a bird-bone whistle, but did not have the appropriate notches. Although I had never seen one before, I immediately knew what it was, for the Dené are famous for their elaborate menarche customs and rituals. One of these customs is that cold water should not touch the girl's lips at that time; a bone tube for drinking is worn around the neck. The bone tube in question was not a whistle but such a drinking apparatus.

The Dené, the northern Athapaskan speaking peoples ("Athapaskan" meaning "stranger" in some Algonkian languages), are generally acknowledged to be the last Native American group to arrive in the Americas, although this was many thousands of years ago.[1] A gathering-hunting tradition prior to the development of the fur trade, those cultures towards the western part of their territory are matrilineal, while those to the east practice bilateral inheritance similar to the neighboring Algonkian speaking peoples. Essential to life is gaining shamanistic "power" through dreaming and vision-questing, practices which involve both males and females. Although all of the Native peoples of the northern North America have menarche rituals, theirs is perhaps the most elaborate.

174

Typical of the Anishnabeg discussed above, indeed of all gathering-hunting traditions, Dené menstruating females avoid and are avoided by males, as well as those weapons and tools used in hunting. Again similar to these cultures, the Dené do not have male puberty rituals, but do have a major period of seclusion and vision-questing at the time of the first menstruation. Unusual in regard to other cultures were elaborate features such as a long fringed hood worn by the menstruating young woman, to which were added many symbolic features, and the swan or goose-bone drinking tube mentioned above.

When June Helm, who has studied northern Athapaskan speaking cultures for several decades, asked her male informant about women and *ink'on*, spiritual power, she was told:

> Oh yes, women can have *ink'on*. They say that a woman's *ink'on* is stronger than a man's . . . some, women cure with it . . . A woman gets *ink'on* the same way a man does. When a young girl gets her first monthlies, got to build a little spruce tipi . . . Out of the camp. Nobody should see her . . . The girl lives by herself till she gets older. And if she's lucky she going to get *ink'on*. That's the time.[2]

At various times Dené peoples split from each other. Some moved to the coast and adopted Northwest Coast cultural patterns. Some moved onto the Plains; a few stayed in southern Alberta, others continued a southward migration. From archaeological and historical evidence, in conjunction with the people's migration myths, these Dené—Diné in the southern dialects— reached the southern part of the Plains by five hundred years ago. They would have been nomads, hunting bison, with their possessions carried on dog-travois. They began to trade with the Pueblo peoples of the present-day southwestern United States, and, when horses became available with the arrival of the Spanish shortly thereafter, began to raid as well. By about four hundred years ago, there was considerable social and cultural interaction between these Diné and the Pueblo peoples.

In 1680, the Pueblos jointly revolted against the Spanish colonialists and were successful in driving them out of the Southwest. However, the Spanish returned. In 1696, the Spanish retook the area, and many of the Pueblo populations fled and joined their Diné trading partners. Some of these Pueblo people never went back to their old way of life and intermarried with the Diné. One group of Diné—known as the Navajo—adopted horticulture, sheep raising, and became semi-sedentary. Others—known as the Apache (being the Chiricahua, Jicarrila, Mescalero, etc.)—continued a foraging-raiding existence, particularly against, first, the Spanish and, then, the Mexicans and Americans. Indeed these were the last groups of Native peoples to be conquered by the American army. A Chiricahua band under the leadership of the great war-shaman, Geronimo, did not surrender until 1886. The Navajo reservation is the largest in the United States (and engaged in a major territorial dispute with the Hopi, whose reservation they surround) with the largest population of an indigenous people north of Mexico.

In these cultural and religious syntheses we find a fascinating fusion of settled rituals, as described, for example, for the Hopi in the preceding chapter, and hunting-gathering cultures, as described for the Anishnabe (see Chapter 8). These two cultural forces when combined led to one of the most remarkable menarche rituals in the human experience, in which the young woman-to-be becomes the Earth Mother herself.[3]

CHANGING WOMAN/WHITE PAINTED WOMAN –WHITE SHELL WOMAN

In the long ago, when the spirit beings were emerging from one realm to another, Talking God and Growling God instructed one group of beings to place two living figurines, of turquoise and of white shell, on a buckskin with a yellow and a white ear of corn. Over this the gods placed another buckskin. As the spirit beings sang a sacred song, the gods lifted an end of the top buckskin so that Wind could enter. On the fourth entrance of Wind, the turquoise figurine had become transformed into Changing Woman and the white shell figurine into White Shell Woman; the ears of corn had become White Corn Boy and Yellow Corn Girl. After four days, White Shell Woman, impregnated by a waterfall, gave birth to the one who came to be called Born for Water, and Changing Woman, impregnated by Sun's rays, the one to be called Monster Slayer. The twins—for Changing Woman and White Shell Woman are understood by many elders to be one—instructed by Spider Woman and armed by Sun, after many trials and adventures, killed dangerous monsters.

After these mythic events, Sun returned to Changing Woman, and tried to embrace her, since he wanted her to marry him and make a home for him in the West. She would have none of it. Sun claimed that their son, Monster Slayer, promised her to him, but to no avail:

> What do I care for promises made by someone else in my behalf? I make my own promises or else there are no promises to be made. I speak for myself or else I am not spoken for. I alone decide what I shall do or else I do nothing.[4]

Sun pleads with her, tells her he is lonely, and asks what is the use of male and female apart from each other. After silent reflection, she says to him that she wants him to build her a house in the west as nice as his house in the east. She wants it built out on the water, so that when the Earth-Surface People (humans) are produced and multiply they will not bother her with their petty quarrels. She wants the house surrounded with the many types of gems so that she can live in beauty. She wants the various animals—those that will be eaten by the Earth-Surface people—around her, for she will be lonely while Sun is making his daily journey across the sky. He asks why he should give her all of this, and she certainly tells him: He is male; she is female. He is of the sky, and she of the earth. He is constant in his brightness; she changes with the seasons. He constantly moves across the sky; she must remain solid and unmoving. More important, she gave her body to him, endured the trouble of pregnancy and the pain of birth, nurtured the child and raised him to serve the people, and what had he done?

> Remember, as different as we are, you and I, we are of one spirit. As dissimilar as we are, you and I, we are of equal worth. As unlike as you and I are, there must always be solidarity between the two of us. Unlike each other as you and I are, there can be no harmony in the universe so long as there is no harmony between us.
>
> If there is to be such harmony, my requests must matter to you. My needs are as important to me as yours are to you. My whims count as much as yours do. My fidelity to you is measured by your loyalty to me. My response to your needs is to reflect the way you respond to mine. There can be nothing more coming from me to you than there is from you to me. There is to be nothing less.

Sun accepts. On the fourth day of their journey westward to her new home, as they crossed a sacred mountain, Changing Woman lay down at its very top facing west. Her body was massaged and her limbs stretched. This was to be the model of a ceremony for Earth-Surface maidens when they reached woman-hood; their bodies were to be molded into the perfect shape of Changing Woman prior to marriage.

After Changing Woman left with Sun for the west, White Shell Woman was lonely. After wandering a bit, Talking God returned. She asked him if he was also lonely, but he lived with other gods in a special place. White Shell Woman, being Earth, could not leave the earth. Talking God told her to wait for four more days, and he would return with Changing Woman and some other gods. Talking God returned with Growling God, Changing Woman and other Holy People. They were carrying various sacred items and two ears of corn, one white and one yellow. After a complex ritual, the two ears were placed between sacred buckskins, and Wind entered. Wind gave life to the ears of corn; the white ear became a man, and the yellow ear a woman. These were the five-fingered Earth-Surface People. White Shell Woman happily led them into her home, and the gods departed.

The preceding is a very brief synopsis of a beautiful, elaborate Navajo myth.

A number of related similar myths have been recorded, and, while details vary, all center on Changing Woman. Among the understandings that are expressed, we find the creation of Earth. For both Changing Woman and White Shell Woman are Earth in her varying relationships to people. The Navajo singer (ritual leader and shaman) Slim Curly said: "White Shell Woman is in reality the earth which changes in summer and becomes young again, then relaxes and dies off in winter, but remains the same woman."[5] "Changing" refers to the changing seasons of Earth and the changing aspects of Woman: the changing of Earth from a child (spring) to a young, fertile woman (summer), to a mature woman (autumn), to an old woman (winter), and back again to child (spring). "White Shell" refers to the substance of the earth, but also to the vagina, the shape of many shells, particularly the cowrie, which is sacred in many cultures: "Next she [First Woman] made a vagina of white shell. Into the vagina she placed a clitoris of red shell . . ." Changing Woman represents the aspect of Earth in its cosmic relationship to Sky/Sun and the ongoing cycle of the seasons; White Shell Woman represents the material Earth. Another Navajo elder understood a historical transition from Salt Woman (see preceding chapter on Hopi religion) to White Shell Woman to Changing Woman. Regardless of name, it is she who longs for humans, the Diné, to inhabit her. All human females, on reaching physical maturity and prior to marriage, are to undergo a ceremony to be molded into the shape of Changing Woman, the cosmic Earth, indeed to become temporarily Changing Woman herself.

Finally, we learn from this myth that in this matrilineal, matrilocal culture, women are the center and males, if they want to live with them, must acquiesce to their needs. In all respects, males and females are equal; but the women have the harder task, and the men recognize this by producing for them. A Chiricahua (Apache) friend of mine, a war-shaman, told me how it was the women who instigated raids. If the women needed flour or other things, they would send the male warriors off to obtain it.

Apachean myths are available only in truncated, reordered form. Non-native authors have a propensity for removing the oral aspects of Native myths and reordering them to fit European linear logic. Nevertheless, there is sufficient data to indicate that there are few, if any, essential differences between Navajo and Apache understandings:

> Sky is our father, Earth is our mother. They are husband and wife and they watch over and take care of us. The earth gives us our food; all the fruits and plants come from the earth. Sky gives us the rain, and when we need water we pray to him. The earth is our mother. We came from her. When we came up on this earth [the Diné, as the Pueblo peoples, preface migration myths with emergence myths], it

was just like a child being born from its mother. The place of emergence is the womb of the earth.[6]

In these myths, White Painted Woman, the white clay with which the pubescent girl is painted at the menarche ritual (= Changing Woman), sleeps with Sun, and White Shell Woman sleeps with Water. Thereupon White Painted Woman and White Shell Woman begin to menstruate for the first time. They both underwent the menarche ritual to be discussed below. White Painted Woman has the child, Killer of Enemies (= Monster Slayer), and White Shell Woman, the child, Child of the Water (= Born for Water).

After Killer of Enemies slays monsters, he returns to the people at the point of emergence. White Painted Woman and White Shell Woman, in the presence of other deities and the people, sing of the past and of how they came to be who they are. At this time, some girls were having their first menses, and, in this myth, White Painted Woman and White Shell Woman provide the details and assist the girls in the menarche ritual.

KINAALDÁ / ISANAKLESH GOTAL

The name for the Diné menarche ritual is Kinaaldá among the Navajo and Isanaklesh Gotal among the Mescalero (Apache). There is no agreement with regard to the meaning of the first term, although it seems to refer to sitting alone in a lodge. According to Inés Talamantez, Isanaklesh means Clay or White Clay Woman, the Earth Mother, and Gotal means a "ceremonial sing." Hence, the term means the ritual to transform the girl into Isanaklesh, and into a mature woman at the end of the ritual. The ritual is the last of a sequence of rituals that mark the transitional steps of a girl from infancy to adulthood.[7]

Two descriptions will be used for this discussion. One, from the Chiricahua, was recorded in the 1930s and contains some details that have changed in modern times, but it is handicapped by the ethnologist's being a male with an androcentric perspective. His informants were primarily males; it would be far preferable to have the female understanding of the ritual. Moreover, his terminology, typical of the times, exemplifies the Eurocentric assumption that priests are necessarily male. For example, he calls the female ritual leader the "assistant," even though, as we shall see, his own description makes clear that not only is her role at least as important as that of the male "singer," but often she has more personal spiritual power. The Navajo description was recorded in the 1960s by an ethnomusicologist, after major influences on the Navajo from American culture and the adoption of a more normative, from a Euroamerican perspective, North American life-style. Furthermore, the ritual was filmed, and the presence of cameras, along with the presence of a number of outsiders, undoubtedly had its effects, including resentment by a number of Diné. There were also serious delays during the four days of the ritual while waiting for the film crews to arrive ("comfortable" hotels tend to be far from Navajo dwellings) and for setting up the equipment. Nevertheless, the author is female and was privy to discussing the ritual with Navajo females. Unfortunately, she also persists in calling the female of the two ritual leaders the "assistant."[8]

Isanaklesh Gotal

Long before the Chiricahua menarche ritual takes place, the family of the girl who is approaching womanhood will be gathering the many materials needed for the ceremony. For example, her dress and boots alone require the hides of five deer. These garments are decorated with many relevant symbols and dyed yellow, the color of pollen. They must, of course, be beautifully made and blessed, usually by a female singer; she might sing over them for several months.

Two elders will be asked to lead the ritual: a female, who dresses, leads, and sings over the girl, called "she who makes the sound," and a male singer, who superintends the erection of the sacred tepee and sings the public songs. A woman who learned a ritual directly from Moon or had a vision of White Painted Woman is preferred. A male who sang for women-to-be who subsequently led a good life is sought after.

A third leader who must be asked is one who prepares and arranges for the masked dancers. He must have the power to make the costumes and decorate the males, who will then be imbued with the essence of the mountain-dwelling spirits. It is the power of the elaborate mask, created by a person of power, that transforms the humans into deities. Here we find a pattern found worldwide (see, for example, the following chapter on African religion), where it is understood that women are innately powerful spiritually and do not need to wear masks, but males need external assistance to become holy; hence, only males are masked dancers. However, among the Chiricahua, it is not understood that the masked dancers become the Mountain Spirits, only that they temporarily have the power of the Mountain Spirits and can thereby heal: "The dancers do not turn into the real Mountain Spirits while they are dancing. They stay men but just get more strength [power]." Before the masked dancers approach the place of the menarche ritual, on each of the four evenings, but after they are dressed and essentially transformed into deities, people might approach them for healing in their encampment towards the mountains.

In contrast, the girl to be transformed into woman during the ceremony is called White Painted Woman (or White Clay Woman). The ritual structure that is erected is called "the home of White Painted Woman"; the clothing made for her is understood to be the clothing of White Painted Woman, and she is painted with the white clay for which White Painted Woman is named. But she wears no mask, for, throughout the four-day ritual, she is, in every respect, White Painted Woman, and so she shall be called in this description of the ritual. This is why during the four days of the ritual she can heal and control the weather.

Because of the elaborate preparation necessary for the menarche ritual, the major communal celebration of the culture, all will not be ready when a girl has her first menstruation; ideally the ritual should take place four days after her first menses begins. Family and neighbors will gather for a truncated version of the longer ceremony, which takes just a morning, as in this Mescalero elder's description of her menarche in 1912 spoken to Inés Talamantez:

> When I was became a woman, my parents conducted a feast for me, but there was no dance and no Big Tipi. An old woman made "medicine" for me. I ran four times, so I would be strong, just as they do in the Big Tipi Ceremony. My buckskin dress was not finished yet; it took my aunt and grandmother two years to make that dress . . . In the morning, about 4:30 or 5:00, they took me out and prayed songs for me as the sun came up, and painted me with pollen to represent the sun's rays. The sponsor said, "I want this maiden to get old like me with all the good luck."

The full ceremony takes eight days: four days of public ceremony, followed by four days of private withdrawal. The following description is only a brief synopsis that skips many of the details and the richness of the elaborate ceremonial.

Before sunrise on the first day, the female ritualist places pollen on the girl as a blessing and prays for her. She arranges the initiate's hair and dresses her, while the girl faces the rising Sun (the husband of White Painted Woman), all the while praying and singing. Only women may be present at this time. When the initiate is dressed and otherwise ready, she has become White Painted Woman; men may now enter. She is now given her first meal of ritual foods. From a fringe on her dress a reed tube is suspended, for she may not drink water directly with her lips for the eight day; here we have a continuation of customs prior to the move from northern North America to the Southwest.

While the girl is being dressed, the male ritualist directs the erecting of the sacred tepee. As the songs for the construction are being sung, whenever a deity is mentioned, the woman ritualist makes a sacred cry; hence her name, "she who makes a sound." When the framework is completed, the women bring out a feast which is blessed with pollen and sung over. After the feast, the structure is completed, being the abode of White Painted Woman.

The female ritualist now leads White Painted Woman into her dwelling. She lays down the skin of a four-year old deer on which White Painted Woman kneels; a basket of ritual implements is placed before her. She is marked with pollen by the female ritualist, and she then marks the ritualist. The people line up to do the same: paint her with pollen and, in turn, be painted by her. This is a blessing from the deity; those who are sick will be healed.

When everyone has been blessed, the female ritualist lays the initiate down on the deerskin and "molds" her, praying, "May this girl be good in disposition, good in morals. May she grow up, live long, and be a fine woman." White Painted Woman then rises and walks on a trail of pollen from fruit and nut-bearing trees. She then runs to the four directions. Young boys and old men run behind her, praying for long life and good health. Meanwhile, the initiate's family throw gifts to the crowd of onlookers.

It is now mid-day, and the sacred rituals are replaced by social activities: visiting, gambling games, racing, etc. Although her ritual obligations are over until the evening, she may be asked to cure young children. It is said, ". . . the girl can take a very young child, pick it up under the arms, and hold it to the directions. This is done to give the child long life and good luck." "If your arm is crooked, go to the girl at the time of the ceremony. She can work it and make it straight." Towards evening, White Painted Woman or the male ritualist lights a fire in the sacred tepee with a fire drill, a fire which will be kept burning through the remaining days of the ceremony.

Meanwhile the masked dancers are becoming Mountain Spirits, and, when all the requests for curing have been accommodated, as the sun sets, they approach the sacred tepee from the east while all the people pray for their needs. The masked dancers are treated in a sacred manner: they are not touched nor pointed to, nor are they called by the name of the dancer. They circle the fire four times from the four directions. As the Mountain Spirits dance, men beat out a rhythm on a rawhide skin, as is done on the Plains, and on skin-covered pottery drums, as are used in the Pueblos, and the drummers sing.

The male ritualist leads White Painted Woman out onto the dance area with an eagle feather, singing all the while. Symbolic objects are brought by the fire. Again typical of Plains ritual practices, for several hours, the initiate dances in place to sacred songs that are to guide her to a long, full life. White Painted Woman retires, and the Mountain Spirits return to the direction of the mountains. The people in attendance then engage in social and courting dances through much of the remainder of the night.

During the mornings and afternoons of the following three days, the initiate is free of specific ritual obligations, although she must remain cognizant of who she is, while the people gamble, feast, and have social dances. Each evening at dusk, the Mountain Spirits return and White Painted Woman is led out to the sacred tepee. The songs throughout these evenings continue the songs dedicated to her life-journey; for example,

> White Painted Woman's power emerges,
> Her power for sleep.
> White Painted Woman carries this girl;
> She carries her through long life,
> She carries her to good fortune,
> She carries her to old age,
> She bears her to peaceful sleep.

On the fourth evening, the masked dancers do not leave after their sacred dances, but remain for the social dancing. Four of these dancers chase the people in from each of the directions. At dawn, even the initiate is brought out for the social dancing. The masked dancers ask each unmarried woman whom she would like to dance with and then bring the named man over to her. They will also dance with any woman who asks. Every male must give, for the privilege, a gift to each female with whom he dances.

As Sun again enters the sky, the social dancing stops, and special songs are sung. Kneeling on the sacred hide, the initiate faces emerging Sun. As in the Plains "Sun Dance," no one crosses between the sun and the sacred tepee; no one is between White Painted Woman and her husband. The male ritualist puts pollen on his face and the initiate's; the female ritualist prepares white clay paint, and the male ritualist paints the initiate's face. After further decoration of the initiate, the people line up and are painted with the remaining sacred substances.

After the sacred songs, the ritual items used are put away, and the initiate retires. Food is brought out and blessed. After the feast, the ritual structure is dismantled, except that the four main poles are left standing. Footprints of sacred substances are then made on the sacred hide, which the initiate steps on. After the fourth song, she stands at the head of the hide, while children, the sick and the elderly walk this same path. Again she runs in the sacred directions. As she completes the fourth run, the main poles are pushed to the east, where they will lie undisturbed until they decay, and gifts are thrown to the crowd. This marks the end of the public part of the ritual.

Most now leave, but the initiate and her parents remain. For four more days, she continues to wear the sacred garments and does not wash. She continues to use a scratching stick and to drink from the tube. At the end of the fourth day, still in her ritual garb, she brings a horse as a gift to the male ritualist. At the following dawn, before sunrise, the female ritualist shampoos the initiate's hair with yucca soap and washes her body. After this, the initiate, no longer White Painted Woman, although embodying her essence for the rest of her life, is now a mature woman.

Kinaaldá

Among Navajo "singers" (the term used in the literature for priests/shamans), Kinaaldá is part of the great ceremonial, Blessing Way; others say it is the very beginning of Blessing Way. Regardless, it is considered in and of itself the most important ceremony of the Diné.

Given time, thirty years, and the cultural differences, there are noticeable differences in detail from the above descriptions. Rather than the sacred deerskin on which the initiate lies for the molding, a blanket of the type manufactured by the Pendleton Company for sale to the Navajo is used. The girl dresses in typical Navajo finery—velvet blouse and silver-turquoise jewelry—rather than specially made deerskin clothing. The ritual takes place in a traditional Navajo dwelling, the log and earth hogan, rather than a special tepee. There are no masked dancers or drums, as there are for some other Navajo ceremonies, perhaps because Kinaaldá is understood to be part of a longer ritual. There is an additional feature: the initiate makes a special cornbread, baked on corn husks laid in the sacred directions in a pit of coals, a cake which represents the Earth Mother herself. Aside from these differences, much else is quite similar.

On the first day, the girl's hair is combed and she is dressed by a ritual relative, who then "molds" the initiate as she lies on a Pendleton blanket with her head to the west. The blanket is on several blankets lent by people, so the lenders might receive blessings. After the molding, she ritually returns the blankets to those who have lent them, who thank her, calling her "Changing Woman." The initiate then stands in the center of the blanket facing east, while the people in attendance circle the fire in the center of the hogan and form a line before her. One after the other, they turn their back to her, and the initiate puts her hands on the back of the neck and lifts upward. If those lifted are children, the purpose is so that they will grow properly. It is unclear from the description whether the initiate is understood to have become Changing Woman or represents Changing Woman; what is clear is that at this time she has the power of Changing Woman.

When the healings are completed, the initiate begins the first of a series of runs, always towards the east. Throughout the ceremonial, each run must be further than the previous one. The longer the run, the longer will be her life. Those of any age may run with her, but most that do are children and young teenagers.

In the evening, the initiate grinds corn with a *mano* and *metate*, the traditional southern North American stone roller and rolling tray. She then, after removing only the jewelry lent by holy persons, goes to sleep.

At dawn on the next day, she runs the first race of the day. A second race is run at noon, and a third towards sunset. During the day, she grinds corn. The third day (due to delays, this was actually the fourth day of the filmed, described ritual) also begins with a race at dawn. The male and female ritual specialists prepare the pit for baking the special cornbread; when the two differ, it is done as the female directs. During the day, with the runs continuing, a fire is lit in the pit, and the batter prepared. A feast is served to all those present. Towards the end of the day, the fire is removed from the pit, the prepared corn husks laid, and the batter, all eleven buckets prepared by elder women, poured into the pit. The female ritualist blesses the batter with sacred cornmeal, and it is covered with layers of corn husks, newspapers and earth. The coals are then raked on top. A large fire is kept burning by the men throughout the night.

Towards midnight, the hogan is prepared for a ritual sing. A blanket with the sacred ritual objects is placed at the back of the hogan, facing the sacred eastern entrance, with the male ritualist at one end and the initiate at the other. The females sit on the north side of the hogan and the males on the south side (a pattern used for rituals by many Native American cultures).

The structure is blessed with pollen, and the initiate circles the fire. The ritual objects are blessed with pollen, and then, beginning with the initiate, each person blesses her or himself with pollen. Ritual singing starts and continues until dawn. Towards dawn, the initiate's hair is ritually shampooed as is the jewelry she has been wearing; there are special songs for this purification.

At dawn, the initiate races for the last time. While she is gone, racing songs are sung, and the pit is uncovered for the bread to cool. A female elder prepares a paint of white clay. When the initiate returns from her run, a final song is sung, and pollen pouches are again passed around for blessings. Everyone then gathers around the fire pit. The bread is cut according to the ritual directions and passed around. A meal of traditional foods is served to the men in the hogan and the women in the cooking house; the initiate does not eat.

After the meal, the initiate's hair is combed, during which combing songs are sung, and she is then ritually painted with the white clay, again with the appropriate songs. The initiate then stands facing east and puts a dab of the white paint on all those who wanted a blessing. A final molding of the initiate takes place outside of the hogan, while the initiate lies on a pile of blankets and garments that people have brought for the blessing. Afterwards, she ritually returns them, each again thanking Changing Woman for the item. This ends the public, four-day ceremony; traditionally, there is a private continuation for a further four days.

INTERPRETATION

Among analysts of Diné culture, there is agreement that the religion changed in a number of important ways after the Diné lived with and among Pueblo cultures. Because of the Western scholarly tradition of focusing on males and hunting, while ignoring the more important activities of females with regard to subsistence in general, as well as their ritual and other roles with regard to hunting, assumptions are made about the culture prior to their migrating to the Southwest that lead to grossly exaggerated conclusions. For example, it is assumed the northern Athapaskan-speaking cultures are male centered: that only males are shamans, that puberty rituals are for males, that there were no matrilineal clans, etc. As discussed in the introduction to this chapter, it is probable that the Diné had matrilineal clans prior to leaving the north, that women and men equally were oriented towards gaining spiritual power, and that there were elaborate menarche rituals. It is not that contact with the Pueblo cultures introduced these features, but, given that the Pueblo cultures had similar features expressed differently, the combining of elements of these cultures greatly reinforced, and led to an elaboration of, these traditions.

Among the Apache, we can see the continuation of the northern culture, as well as features picked up during the generations of migrating southwards through the Plains: the continued use of the drinking tube in the menarche ritual, the importance of both male and female spiritual power for both the female and male ritualists, the importance of hides, and the use of a tepee structure to create a ritual space. Added from Pueblo cultures were the use of masked dancers (from the *katsina*), running to elicit ecstatic religious experience, the tossing of gifts to the onlookers, the use of pollen for blessing and purification, the molding by massage, the ritual hair-washing with yucca suds, and, most important, the conceptual shift, not absolute but in emphasis, to anthropomorphic spirits from theriomorphic ones. Among the additions to Navajo culture, we find perhaps an increased importance of the clan structure, also the importance of running, masked dancers (although not for the menarche ritual), and the adoption of different features suggesting closer ties to Pueblo traditions: the use of a permanent structure, the hogan, for rituals; the substitution of woven blankets (although the Navajo sell the blankets they weave and buy Pendleton machine-woven ones); and the importance of grinding corn and making a sacred cornbread.

What is striking from cross-cultural perspectives is the primary feature of the menarche ritual that seems not to have been a part of either set of cultures prior to synthesis: the initiate temporarily becomes the Earth Mother. Undoubtedly, this is due to a fusion of fortuitous cultural features. In the chapters discussing northern woodland Native American cultures, it was pointed out that the menarche and menstrual rituals and understandings encourage an identity of human women with Earth and Moon. Northern shamanism, relevant to both males and females, enhances an identification between humans and spiritual entities. Pueblo traditions emphasize formal, elaborate rituals, as well as stress the importance of Earth and her daughter Corn. The adoption of masks to transform humans into spiritual beings brings in a new mode of spirituality to the Athapaskan-speaking peoples in the south. But partially identifying with, and being transformed by, masking is not the same as being a deity. Nor, in the mediumistic traditions discussed in East Asia or in Africa to follow, are those possessed by deities understood to be themselves deities. The Diné menarche ritual may well be unique.

In the traditional Diné cultures, before massive influence from American culture, all females would have undergone the menarche ritual; all females would have become Changing Woman/White Painted Woman and would have retained a residue of that identity for the rest of their lives. All men knew, from experiencing the healing power of female initiates at the time of the menarche ritual, that their mothers, sisters, and wives, had been, and to a degree continue to be, divine. Could any human experience be more awesome?

What does it mean to become or have been a deity? A Mescalero female elder told Inés Talamantez,

> We must always remember Isanaklesh, her name means "our mother," she is sacred Mother Earth. We depend on her for all of our needs. We ask her for our food both from the plant world and the animal world, as well as for shelter and healing. Because of her power, we have been given life, we are shaped and molded by her. All of our life we are protected by her; we experience her as we see with our eyes, hear with our ears, smell with our nose, as we touch, as we grow old and become wise like her. . . .

An elder instructs the Isanaklesh Gotal initiate in the meaning of becoming deity as follows:

> When you become Isanaklesh in the ceremony, you will have her power to heal because it is Isanaklesh who handed this knowledge to us. There is a sacred story about this. Since you will be Isanaklesh, you will be asked to heal and bless people who come to see you. You must always remember how you felt during your

ceremony, when you were the living goddess; then, later in life, you can call on
her for help whenever you face problems; you will remember how you felt when
you were her, when you became her.

Elbys Naiche Hugar, an Chiricahua elder, still clearly recalls her own menarche ritual:[9]

> I had mine back in 1944 at the old ceremonial grounds. It's something good that
> a girl goes through. The parents and the godmother and the godfather talk with
> the young girl before the puberty ceremony. The girl will know what to do and
> she'll know about it before she can enter the ritual . . . It's for four days and
> nights. A girl has to fast, and sometimes you lose weight. That's what I experi-
> enced. It's still part of me and it's going to be that way for the rest of my life. I'll
> never forget the good it did for me and how it helped me over the hardships.

By the time Elbys Naiche Hugar had her ceremony, the culture was changing. Not all girls had the full ceremony; some had a shorter substitute version.
Kathleen Kanseah recalls her own sense of loss in this regard:

> That was terrible. I regret it. I really regret it. But old man Eugene Chihuahua
> gave me his blessings for two days down at the house there by the community
> center. I can still hear him. He said, "You're my granddaughter now. For two
> nights I'll sing for you and bless you and get you going because you're going to be
> a very strong woman." I was twelve or thirteen years old when he said that, and
> he had me sitting on the ground on a tarp. My father put the sacred pollen on
> him, I put the pollen on him, and then he put the pollen on me. I can still hear
> his songs. He was a very powerful man, and he told me I would be a strong
> woman. And I find that I can be strong in a lot of things.

Over the last several decades, American values, required attendance at
schools, Christianity, etc., have made deep inroads into traditional culture.
More recently there have been gains in indigenous control over schools, revival
of the language where it had been lost on the smaller reservations, and the continuation and reintroduction of traditional rituals. The menarche ritual is difficult in modern times: young adolescent females tend to be shy and reticent and
resist being made the center of a major public ceremony, particularly when it is
different from the ways of the dominant culture; the ceremony, which requires
feeding a large number of people over four days and the giving of gifts to everyone in attendance, and large gifts to the ritualists, requires the family to save for
years; and the full four days of public ritual, followed by a further four days, do
not fit into modern school and work schedules. But at least there is less chance
now of Christian missionaries complaining about, and the U.S. military accordingly stopping, the ceremony. A Chiricahua woman, Ruey Darrow, who had

been acculturated to and extensively educated in the dominant tradition, succinctly states the contemporary understanding:

> If the girl believes it's going to mean something to her, then I believe in it—for her. I think she can go in and out of that world and be the better for it. There are a lot of things that Apaches teach their girls in those ceremonies. It's eight days of concentrated teaching. Some of the woman of my age who had the ceremonies have profited, I think, not only because they learned something of how to present themselves to the world, but also it's just a way of life . . . It's kind of like you have to get far enough away from the puberty ceremony to be able to go back. And then you've developed a great appreciation for it. Some of these people have not gone far enough away.

Part IV
Sub-Saharan Africa

It is wonderful to be able to receive another being in yourself, a being who comes to say something, a being who comes to heal . . . this force that uses your body to heal somebody else, to warn us of something that is going to happen. . . .

—Zeze, a young Daughter of the Deities,
speaking Portuguese in the film,
Candomblé: A Religion in Brazil with African Roots (1989)

11
GLIMPSES OF TRADITIONAL
WEST CENTRAL AFRICAN RELIGIONS

PREAMBLE

O N VIEWING COLLECTIONS OF CENTRAL WEST AFRICAN TRADITIONAL ART, one
cannot but notice the many examples of female images, either alone or
with a male figurine of equal size and, if alone, often with children. Among the
contiguous Dogon and Senufu, these paired figures represent the primordial
couple. Among the Dogon, the pair may be seated or standing, often with the
male's arm about the shoulder of the female. Of Senufu pairs, the female is usually larger than the male. Ibibio sculptures also depict couples, representing
Mother Earth and Father Sky. In Igbo sculptures, the female earth deity is
shown alone. Most common are images of females holding or nursing babies,
usually representing fertility powers and deities; among the Akan, they will
often represent the "Queen Mother," who holds power equal to if not greater
than that of the king. Images without children may be protecting deities or used
in divination rituals. Both male and female images will have clearly depicted
genitalia and, for females, breasts, leaving little doubt as to their sex.

Given the importance of female images in these cultures—a visual celebration of female fertility, sacredness, and power—and given the importance of
female ritual leaders in the religions of these cultures when they were involuntarily transplanted to the Americas (see the following chapter), it is quite surprising to find most descriptions of the religions of these regions downplaying
female spirituality. There seems to be a disjunction between the visual evidence
and descriptive rhetoric; it is this contradiction that the present chapter will
explore.

I approach this chapter with considerable trepidation, for this is the one
complex of cultures and geographical region covered in this book with which I
have had no experience. Yet not only does Africa comprise a large part of the

inhabitable planet with many peoples, it is now generally understood to be the womb of humans and human culture. Moreover, the two large culture areas with which I am most familiar, aside from areas dominated by European and Euroamerican cultures, are East Asia and Native America. Given that these two sets of cultures, particularly with regard to religion, probably shared some tenets and practices tens of thousands of years ago, any shared traits could be seen, whether actual or not, as due to this common substrate. Such assumptions could hardly be made about Africa, since all contact between East Asia and Africa began well into the historical period. Hence, it is necessary, in spite of my qualms, to present a discussion of relevant aspects of religion in Africa.

Africa, of course, is a huge continent, inhabited by different peoples of many cultures and speaking diverse languages; it would be impossible to apply the method of this study to Africa as a whole. Since the Afroamerican religions are derived from those of central West Africa, the homeland of most of those enslaved and forcibly brought to the Americas, it is this area on which the discussion will focus. But an analysis of the religious traditions of even this delimited area is still highly complex. Aside from the wide variety of cultures, there has been considerable influence from Muslim and Christian missionaries over many centuries, as well as from the former European colonial governments. Frequently individuals adhere to a combination of traditions, and many new religions have developed in the past half century. Accordingly, the discussion will be limited to what is known of the traditional religions, rather than the contemporary situation, a topic controversial in itself.

For coherence, only two cultures will be covered, the Yoruba of Nigeria and the Akan of Ghana. The former was chosen both because it is the most important influence on the Afroamerican religions of Brazil and the Caribbean, and because of the availability of the relevant scholarship of Jacob K. Olupona and Margaret Thompson Drewal. The latter culture was selected because Elizabeth and Paul Adjin-Tettey from Ghana kindly offered to prepare a précis of Akan female spirituality for this work. Furthermore, as Yoruba culture is nominally patrilineal and Akan culture is matrilineal, we have two different types of societies, in a major regard, represented. Those who are interested in a general study of women and religion in sub-Saharan Africa as a whole are highly recommended to Rosalind J. Hackett's exemplary introduction.[1]

YORUBA RELIGION

"Yoruba" is a name originally used by Europeans to designate a group of cultures sharing a language and many, but far from all, cultural features. Originally, there was no single name for the entire group of cultures now subsumed under the term, "Yoruba." For this reason, it should not be assumed that any particular social or religious feature to be discussed will be identical, or even found, in all Yoruba sub-cultures. As examples, Jacob Olupona's study focuses on the Ondo people at the eastern part of the Yoruba area and Margaret Drewal's on the western Yoruba cultures. The major focus of each study is specific to those particular areas.

The Yoruba comprise more than forty million people who inhabit the western part of Nigeria and parts of Benin and Togo. They have been an urban people (more than half the population) since at least the earliest European reports; and one of their major cities has an archaeological depth of at least a thousand years. Their economy is based on farming and trading. The language is part of the Niger-Congo branch of the Congo-Kordofanian language family, which covers most of West Africa.

Each Yoruba group has its own king and a complex system of chiefs and other rulers, aspects of which will be important in the discussion of rituals and ritual specialists. The society has both patrilineal and bilateral features, and arguments have been made that the culture was originally matrilineal. Individuals belong to patrilineal clans, but inherit from both mothers and fathers; clans and families are headed by the eldest male (the *bale*—"father of the house") and senior wife (the *iyale*—"mother of the house"). Marriage is patrilocal and polygynous.

Economic roles are gendered: males farm, females trade. Women, even in polygynous compounds, are economically independent, and each wife has her own household. The marketplace is the center of female activities, and women may be wealthier than their husbands. Within the marketplace, there is a female ruler, and she creates the king of the country.

Female Spirits

The Yoruba spirit realm is highly complex and difficult to encapsulate. Most of the divinities are termed *orisa* and were humans who became divinized. A second group are the ancestors of the family, of major importance for the welfare of families and clans, and deified clan founders and other important clan personages, who are important to the history of cities and cultural attributes. Then there is Olorun, the center of a scholarly controversy.[2]

Creation and Migration

There are a number of contemporary creation myths. All begin with Olodumare, also known as Olorun ("owner of sky"), who is genderless, whose abode is in the sky, and who decides to create earth by converting a marshy plain to solid ground. In one version, it sends Obatala (King of the White Cloth), the chief male deity, to scatter some soil to create the ground. Obatala falls in with a group of divinities drinking palm wine, gets drunk and falls asleep. Oduduwa, the chief female deity, aware of Obatala's mission, picks up the earth given him by Olodumare and creates the world. In another major version, Olodumare sends the primary deputy, Orisanla ("Great Divinity" = Oduduwa), to create the world. She comes down from the sky and tosses earth on the water, then looses a five-toed hen to scatter the earth about, creating the world on which we live. Subsequently, she creates the Yoruba people. In either case, it is a female deity that creates the world (unless one follows many written accounts which present both versions of the divinity as male). Some scholars understand Olodumare to be a late addition to the cosmogonic myth, perhaps paralleling the shift from a female to a male king, which the next myth indicates. Oduduwa is interpreted variously "as 'container or author of existence' or 'that which creates existence.' The term iwa in the polysyllabic Odu-du-iwa means existence."[3] Regardless of the version, it is a female deity, superior to all the male divinities (Olodumare is literally above the divinities and is not understood to be an orisa), who creates the Earth, as is the case with most, if not all, Central African traditions.

The various Yoruba sub-cultures have migration myths, stories of how they came to reside in their present localities. Each sub-culture has its own king and attendant political structure. In the Ondo myth, Onduduwa is understood to be male (probably a sex shift relating to the gender shift of kingship in the myth), and one of his wives gives birth to twins. Originally, it was Oduduwa who most likely gave birth to the twins, given her similarity to the female ancestress of both the people and kings of many other African traditions. One of the twins, a female named Pupupu, leads the people from the central Yoruba city of Ile-Ife to the Ondo's present locale. She becomes the first osemawe (ruler). When she became quite elderly and lost most of her hearing, the people begged her to give them a substitute king (oba), and so she made her first son king in her place. He became known as Airo ("replacement") and, after his death, functioned as a divinity. The above version is common among the people; the palace version is more patriarchal. In this version, the female king neglected her state duties for domestic ones, so that the state assembly decided that, ever after, it would only appoint male rulers. After her death, they appointed her son, Airo, as king. Given the meaning of Airo's name, the former seems more likely the original myth.[4]

The Orisa

The orisa are the effective deities, humans who on death became divine, and are those to whom offerings are made, with whom humans maintain relationships. Each individual dedicates her or himself to an *orisa*. Usually this *orisa* is inherited from one's clan or mother, but events may happen to one that indicate, determined by divination, that one should be connected with another deity. Most of the important *orisa* are male—Ogun, the deity of iron, war, and hunting; Sango, the king and deity of storms; Esu, the trickster; etc.—but there is an important set of female water deities. As Olatunde Lawuyi points out, these female *orisa* as human females are all linked to flowing: "among the Yoruba there is a tendency to characterize women as an object [sic] that flows." Water is the essence of life, as are child-bearing women, and women are the containers of water. Women flow when menstruating and when giving birth (menstrual fluid and amniotic fluid). Rivers flow, and, as the power of women (to be discussed in the concluding section), this flowing can be life-giving and life-destroying, as nourishing water and raging floods and the *aji* of older women (to be discussed below).

Yemoja (Mother of Fishes) is the progenitor of all the water deities, including Osun, the Osun River deity; Oba, the River Oba deity; and Oya, the Niger River deity. Oya, as an example, is far more than a river deity; she is also a weather deity, the buffalo deity, and transporter of the dead to their realm. Her name means "she tore," and her power is indicated in praise songs to her (from different sources):

> Tornado, quivering solid canopied trees
> Great Oya, yes.
> Whirlwind masquerader, awakening,
> courageously takes up her saber.
>
> . . . .
>
> Insatiable vagina
> Wizard's medicine
> Child who carries the corpse
> Fighting Oya will come into her own.
>
> . . . .
>
> Mother, Oya
> She's the one who employs truth against wickedness
> She stands at the frontier
> between life and death
> Custom officer of multitudes!
>
> . . . .
>
> Oya had so much honor
> she turned around and became Orisha.
> Oya guards the road into the world
> and out of it.
> Oya, respect to the awesome.[5]

Oya is linked by marriage to two major male *orisa*, Ogun and Sango. First married to Ogun, she ran off with Sango. Given that Oya and Sango are both storm deities, it is a marriage literally "made in heaven." Her role regarding the dead follows from a general West African understanding (also found elsewhere) that the dead are ferried across three rivers that separate the realm of the living from that of the dead. Oya owns this fleet of canoes and functions as the deity of the flow between life and death.

Female Rituals and Ritual Roles

Female Chiefs and the "Woman King"

Among the Ondo, while there is a hierarchy of male leaders within each Yoruba sub-culture, there is also a hierarchy of female leaders, called *opoji*. At their head is the *Lobun* ("owner of the market"), also called the *Oba Obinrin* ("woman king"). Lobun derives from the term for market (*obun*), indicating dual spheres of authority: the court for males and the market for women. All the titles of the various female chiefs have the word *lobun*, preceded by a modifier. Contrary to normative cultural patterns (e.g., as in China), the interior is the male realm and the exterior, the female realm. The Lobun's major function is to install a new king. Should a Lobun die, the office will not be filled until the Oba (king) dies. At this time, it is essential that a Lobun be appointed in order for the king to be installed; only she can perform the sacred rituals which install the one chosen to be Oba into his sacred role as mediator between the people and the *orisa*. The Lobun is in charge of the Ondo markets and is the priest of Aje (deity of wealth and fertility). Being a Lobun is a sacred role, and there are many rituals involved in her daily life; she is understood to be continually in a sacred state.

According to a Lobun interviewed in 1965, in the investiture of the Oba she represents Pupupu, the female who was the first king, while the Oba represents Pupupu's son, Airo, to whom Pupupu turned over the throne when she was too old to rule:

> This building we are in (Lobun's titled residence)
>   was owned by the first person to be king in this town.
> She reigned for 220 years.
> Her ears were already dried up . . .
> So we approached her one day and called her "Great Mother,
> Find someone who will be king for us since you are too old . . ."
> So she agreed and called her first son Airo
> That is the one we call, *afiparo* (a substitute) . . .

She made him kneel down,
Her crown on her head,
She removed the crown and placed it on his head,
Three times . . .
When she arrived at where he would ascend the throne,
She made a few rites for him.
That is how the story goes.

Hence, between the Oba and the Lobun there is a ritual relationship, of which the Lobun said: "The king is my son."

Menarche

The female puberty ritual is called *obitun* ("maiden"). It is generally held at the death of a senior member of a patrilineal clan and during the installation of chiefs. At these times, all those females who have reached puberty, but have not yet undergone the ritual, and their families prepare to take part.

The ceremony begins on a major market day, which is a day auspicious for women. On the day before the ritual, the bodies of the initiates were covered with a black pigment to indicate that they were in a liminal state. Their hair was also prepared in a special way, and they wore special clothes and decorations, featuring white undergarments and red garments over them. With their relatives, they went to the house of the nearest *opoji* (female chief), to make offerings at her shrine to Aje, and then to their female sponsor, who would make offerings for them. The sacrificial offerings throughout the ritual are red (kola nuts and baked beans) and white (coconuts and walnuts).

Each initiate plants a *peregun* tree in the yard of her natal home. The leaves of this tree are a major ingredient in preparing "love potions," and the tree exudes a white sap that is understood to be symbolic of semen. (That the tree is planted at the natal home has been interpreted by some scholars as indicating that the culture was once matrilocal.)

On the evening of the first day of the ritual, all gather for a number of ceremonies at the house of the person organizing the ritual. On the second day, an elaborate mock betrothal is enacted. On the third day, there is a rite of exorcism to expel malignant spirits found in pubescent females and a ritual mock marriage. On this day, red paint is added to the black with which the initiate was painted on the first day. As an old woman explained, "[The black paint] is to make her look different from the others. Only on the third day can we treat her as a royal person." The red signifies royalty. Of interest is that, in certain other rituals, red signified menstrual blood when in conjunction with white, which signifies semen.

Throughout the ceremony, except for the specific ritual events, the initiates are secluded and fed rich foods. Toward the end of the seclusion period, there will be a feast. On the last day, the ninth, a final exorcism of the malignant maiden spirits takes place. That night, the initiates again put on the special clothes they wore the first day and dance as adults, visiting the various shrines of the community, making offerings at each. When an initiate returns home, her parents sacrifice a chicken to the guardian spirit in the *peregun* tree which their daughter planted at the beginning of the ceremony.

The elaborate ritual incorporates all aspects of the transformation of a girl to a woman. The exorcist rituals remove the dangers of uncontrolled power of the first menstruation of a girl, allowing the controlled power of the mature woman to be manifest. After the ceremony, the young woman can participate in the ritual life of adult females and is eligible to become an *opoji*, a female chief, a royal role, and custodian of a shrine to Aje. The ritual mock betrothal and marriage rituals, combined with the repetition of the colors of red and white, signify that she is now fertile, indeed, symbolically pregnant with new life. The planting of the *peregun* tree, symbolically a "tree of life," to which she will offer sacrifices for the rest of her life, ritually links her forever to her natal home in an otherwise patrilocal social setting. She is now ready to take up the traditional triple female roles of wife, mother, and trader.

Festival of the Deity of Wealth and Fertility

The Odon Aje, celebrated to honor Aje, the female deity of wealth and fertility, is a woman's festival held every November. Each *opoji* prepares her portable Aje shrine, the Igba Aje: a brass bowl containing cowry shells (the former money), coral beads (symbolizing royalty), native woven cloth and china plates (symbols of wealth), and a white bird figurine (symbolizing female power to be discussed below).

During the evening ritual, the Igba Aje is placed on the head of a prepubescent girl, dressed as an *obitun* initiate. All taking part travel to an *opoji*'s house overlooking the Oba's palace and sing praise songs to Aje; for example:

> Aje excreted on my head;
> Whoever Aje touches is made human.
> Aje slept on my head;
> Whoever Aje touches acts like a child.
> Aje elevates me like a king;
> I shall forever rejoice.

Aje is happy, so am I.
Aje is happy, so am I.

(An infant excreting on the person carrying it is understood to be a sign of fecundity, and only Aje elevates an Oba to his station.)

When each *opoji* and her retinue reach the festival site, the Igba Aje is removed from the girl's head and set on a long table. Later, the Idoko priest-chiefs arrive; they are the chiefs of an Odon sub-group who, during the installation of an Oba, promise to perform rites for the well-being of the Ondo people as a whole. They offer prayers for each of the *opoji* for profit in trade and for fecundity of women in general. The *opoji* then dance back to their dwellings with their followers to continue the joyous celebration. Hence, we have females blessing males, in singing before the palace, and males, priests acting for the king, blessing females and their special roles.

"Our Mothers"

Female power, rather than potential, is understood to be actual. This is denoted by a collective term for all *opoji* and other female title holders, mediums and priests (see below), and all elder women: "Our Mothers" (*awon iya wa*). The term for their power, and also used for them, is *aje*, as the deity for wealth and fertility, but they would never be directly called by that word. In virtually all the literature on the Yoruba, reflecting the Eurocentric fear and dislike of elderly women, *aje* is translated as "witch" or "witchcraft," depending on use. One day of the four-day Yoruba week is devoted to Our Mothers.

These women are also known as the "owners of birds" (*eleye*), for these powerful elderly women are able to transform themselves at night into birds to fly into the forest and hold secret meetings among themselves. Because of their power of transformation, they are also known individually as "one with two faces" or "one with two bodies"; they can transform themselves not only into birds, but bats, rats, and snakes as well. The *eleye* have three kinds of power, not depending on the individual but on the particular activity: beneficial (white) *eleye* which brings prosperity, harmful (red) *eleye* which brings suffering, and destructive (black) *eleye* which brings death. They are more powerful than the deities, because it is they who actuate the deities. For these powers, Our Mothers are not detested, as in European Christian culture, but reverenced, loved, and given deference. Needless to say, one does not anger or cross these women, for, while they may not indicate their displeasure in their demeanor, they can quietly and secretly cause illness, even death, to those who treated them disrespectfully. More important, however, are the continued blessings they bring to the Yoruba people.[6]

Placating the Great Mother

The preceding descriptions of rituals have focused on the those found among the Ondo of the eastern Yoruba sphere. Among the western Yoruba groups a ritual, called the Gelede, is carried out primarily by males to honor the females:

> Gelede is the "secret of women." We men are merely their slaves. We dance to appease "our mothers."[7]

Although the ritual is not a female one *per se*, in that it is done in honor of female spiritual power and female ancestors and in awe of "Our Mothers," the ritual is an important aid in our understanding the hermeneutics of femaleness in Yoruba religion.

In each town where the ritual takes place, it is related to the founding foremother, an earth or water deity, and founding forefather. The focus is on the Great Mother, a term for the ancestral mothers as a collective. But the ritual is understood to honor and placate all spiritually powerful females: deities, ancestors and the powerful elders (Our Mothers). Women as a whole are understood to be more powerful than the deities; according to a female Gelede leader: "No orisha can do good without the mothers." Without the sanction of women, there can be no healing, no rain, no plant food, and no children.

The ritual takes place in the marketplace, the realm of women's economic and social activities, as well as the domain of the spirits. Usually the marketplace is at the center of the town, where the main roads cross. It is at the crossroads where one finds the shrine to Esu, the "trickster" *orisa*, and where sacrifices are frequently offered.

While women do take part in the ritual, far more important is their attendance, for a primary purpose of the Gelede is to entertain the elder women. Indeed, the purpose is more than to entertain; it is to propitiate the elder women, who, as all beings that flow or once flowed, have both the power for good and for harm. Those that share the "flow of blood"—the mothers of the present, the ancestral mothers of the past, and the female deities—are at the root of life and death:

> Gelede thus mediates between the owners of society—those who generate, manage, control and also punish it—and the community. Through praise and criticism, prayers and curses, Gelede spectacle carries out the perceived will of the mothers. The community is responsive, in turn lending its support. The art forms that make up spectacle thus become instruments for regulating society . . . The art forms of Gelede touch upon different concerns in different ways. They con-

stantly reinforce and revitalize each other to reach all segments within the community.

Gelede is a ritual involving complex masks, costumes, and dances, as well as offerings. Rather than attempt a brief synopsis, those interested in the details are recommended to the Drewals' superb study, *Gelede*.

Mediums and Priests

In sub-Saharan African traditions, people know their deities through directly experiencing them via mediums. Mediums allow their bodies to be taken over by the deities, so that the deities can be physically present temporarily among their worshipers. In Yoruba religion, as in central West African religions generally, both males and females can become mediums, but most are female. Men who so function are known as the wives of the possessing deity and frequently wear female dress and hairstyles.

It is understood that the deity enters the medium's head, displacing the animating spirit of the possessed. Equestrian terminology is commonly used; the deities are said to mount their mediums. But is it also understood that mediums to a degree control the deity who rides them. They receive the deity; they are receptacles for her or him; but they also are able to influence the deity to help or harm people and society. Moreover, there is an identity between the medium and the *orisa* who possesses her. Although the deity is not present until possessing the medium, there is always an aura of the deity about the medium. The mediums are also the priests for the rituals directed towards the relevant deity. Hence, the mediums are not understood to be passive in their relationship with either the *orisa* or human society; mediums, as persons of power, are highly respected in their communities.

To become a medium requires a complex initiation ritual during which the deity is installed in the medium's head. The initiate is secluded in a dark shrine for several weeks, with her normal clothes taken away and her head shaved. The head is ritually bathed and painted in designs featuring a combination of leaves, blood, and minerals; these designs signify the vital energy of the particular deity. With the deity now fixed in her head, she is known as *adosu* ("one who had received in the head"), the *osu* ("ball of medicine") of the deity, and she acquires a new name.

Miscellaneous Roles

Women have many other ritual roles than those described above. They function as priests in rituals directed towards various *orisa* and hold a major role with regard to Itefa ("establishing the self"), the male initiation ritual. The central part of this ritual takes place in an enclosure known as Odu's grove. Odu is understood in various Yoruba regions as the female deity who controls all other deities and as the wife of the first diviner, who was taught how to divine by her. Women are not allowed to enter Odu's grove, perhaps because as the ceremonial area itself is female, it is felt that the presence of human females would overwhelm male potency. Nevertheless, in some areas at least, only male transvestite priests enter the grove with the initiates.

An important part of Itefa, as well as Yoruba life in general, is Ifa divination, divination using palm nuts to create numerical combinations, to which are attached oracular verses. These nuts are kept in a sacred container that is Odu. (Females are understood to be containers, while males are the contained.) During the divination part of Itefa, while a woman dances holding the calabash containing the palm nuts, the diviners seek the spiritual support of the women through songs and incantations. Margaret Thompson Drewal observed that, in one such ritual, the diviner prostrated himself before the female dancer, to demonstrate his respect for women's power, from which, as a diviner, he received his own.

Female Self-Understanding

Because the public governmental leadership roles are male, early Western theorists assumed females had no power; they were oblivious to the role of the "Woman King" and the female chiefs. Because males headed the families, these analyses appear unaware that the status of a female was not dependent on that of her husband but on her reputation as a trader and from her wealth, which was independent of, and often greater than, her husband's. Because the clans are patrilineal, again these analyses did not reveal that inheritance was bilateral and the society matrifocal. Matrifocality developed because, in the polygynous compound, with each wife having her own household, children were far more influenced by their mothers than their fathers.

Not only are there major female divinities, but women themselves are in various respects divine. The mediums-priests, mostly female, are imbued with the divine qualities of the *orisa* who reside in their head. They and the elder women are Our Mothers, whose powers precede those of most divinities. As a female priest told Margaret Thompson Drewal,

> If the mothers are annoyed, they can turn the world upside down. When an herbalist goes to collect a root at the foot of a tree, the mothers put it up. And when he climbs up for a leaf, the mothers put it down.

A female Gelede leader said,

> No orisha can do good without the mothers. The mothers could spoil any good action if they wanted to. Therefore Sango himself cannot help his worshippers without permission of the mothers. The prophesies of the Babalawo (diviner) will come to nought, if he had not appeased the mothers. Oro and Egun cannot kill without the mothers.

Our Mothers, the Owners of Birds, possess *aje* as depicted in the following invocation:

> . . . .
> Honor, ooooo, honor today, ooooo
> I honor you today
> Old bird did not warm herself in the fire
> Sick bird did not warm herself in the sun
> Something secret was buried in the mother's house
> A secret pact with a wizard
> Honor, Honor today, ooooo
> Honor to my mother
> Mother whose vagina causes fear to all
> Mother whose pubic hair bundles up in knots
> Mother who set a trap, set a trap
> Mother who has meat at home in lumps

In certain rituals, women may not be present, because menses can render male priestly power impotent. Although this is put in terms of danger to women, it is more likely that the males are the ones in danger. The women go along as a means of cooperating with the men. Margaret Thompson Drewal records the following experience that she had when sitting with women secluded in their house during a ritual:

> For them closing themselves in demonstrates solidarity with their father or husband, as the case may be, since they have the ultimate power to undo his works. These women seem to enjoy the excitement of the men parading by outside. Sitting inside with the senior wife of an Agemo priest while her husband's procession was in progress, I asked her why they do not want women to see Agemo on the road. She exclaimed in Yoruba, "because they will go blind!" At that point, the junior wife, who was about my age, quite literally fell out of her chair laughing. That was all part of the play.

In Yoruba rituals only men wear masks. From an external viewpoint, it could be understood that only men are worthy to wear ritual masks. Indeed, it is the opposite. Women are in themselves sacred by their very nature, and, when they are possessed, the deity is directly in their head. Men must be transformed to represent the divine, and this is the function of the mask, symbolically to make one into another. Only men wear masks because women have no need to do so. That the power of the masks comes from the women is most clear from a myth concerning Odu and Obatala, from which the following is excerpted:

[Olodumare says to the orisha when they first go the earth] "Whatever you want to accomplish, I'll give you the power, that the world may be a good place."

Ogun marched ahead, Obatala followed, Odu lagged behind . . . "down there Ogun will have war power. He has saber, he has gun, he has everything for fighting. Obatala also has authority to accomplish anything. What about me, the only woman among them? What can I do?"

[Olodumare said,] "Yours is the power of motherhood to sustain the earth. The bird-power is yours. I gave you a big gourd full of it. . . ."

Since that time, because of Odu, women have the power to say what they please, for in the absence of women, men can do nothing . . .

"Let's live together," [Odu] said to Obatala. "That way you can see everything that I do . . ."

[Obatala said,] "But how about those things you have? those things you do?"

I'll share everything with you!" Odu replied. When she went to worship Egungun [the ancestral spirits that appear in masquerade form], though he said he was frightened, Obatala went along too. In the sacred wood she put on the costume but didn't know how to sound like Egungun. Later, Obatala added a net face to the cloth, took up the whip, and spoke with the voice of Egungun . . .

[Obatala, masqueraded as Egungun, comes into town.] Seeing he wasn't home, recognizing her costume, Odu stayed where she was and sent her bird to perch on the masquerader's shoulder. From then on everything Egungun was able to do came about by bird-power. When Obatala did everything as Egungun, he came home, took off the cloth, laid down the whip, and went to greet Odu. Before her he placed all the gifts he received.

"You can have Egungun," she said: "no longer will woman dare to put on the cloth, but the power you will use belongs to us, and when you go out I will dance before you. From now on, only men will take out Egungun. But no one, neither children nor old men, will dare make fun of women. Woman-power is greater. Women give birth, and whatever men want to do, women must help them or it won't come to anything."

So they sang together, and Obatala said that every week [the four-day week] everyone must praise women so the world will be peaceful.

Bend your knee, bend your knee before women, for women have brought you into the world; women are intelligence of the earth, women have put us into the world; reverence women.[8]

As in myth, so in life. "Yoruba say that the mothers (*aje*) conceive a plan and their male counterparts (*oso*) carry it out." As for the Gelede, as in other ritual performances, "the males are masqueraders but the elderly women are the source of their power."

When women are depicted in sculpture as deities (or possessed mediums—the same thing), they are most frequently depicted nursing children or offering their breasts. (In Yoruba culture, children are nursed for three years.) Women offer themselves. The nurture and power they offer are from themselves; from them comes the nourishment that is the foundation of life. The male corollary is the offering of blood in sacrifice. Only men make blood sacrifices; their offering is a life taken from another through death.

Another important sculptural mode are the paired brass sculptures that are the emblems of society. The pair, female and male, are of equal size and often joined by a chain. These are ritually prepared and understood to symbolize social unity. Their presence is essential in judicial proceedings, indeed legitimizes them, for they bring the ancestors and the earth to witness the oaths taken.

This essential unity, implicit equality, recognition of differences, and interdependence of males and females was communicated by a Babalawo:

> . . . you see, men and women, they all came to the world at the same time. There has never been a time when we have men and we don't have women. And there has never been a time when we have women and don't have men. So everybody comes to play his role successfully. If you leave men, then the role of women cannot be played successfully. If you leave women, the role of men cannot be played successfully. That's how they have been mixing every issue, and everyone had his own secrets, too. Men have the secret and women have the secret, just to trouble each other, just to add more spice to the world.

AKAN RELIGION

with Elizabeth and Paul Adjin-Tettey[9]

The Akan comprise nearly half the population of contemporary Ghana, over five million persons, and also reside in the neighboring Ivory Coast. This linguistic-ethnic family includes a number of groups, the most commonly represented in the literature being the Ashante. The culture has a long history of powerful kingdoms and acquiesced to European colonialism only in the early twentieth century.

The society is divided into seven matrilineal clans, each traced from a single female progenitor. In the words of Madam Yaa, a member of the royal circle at Kumasai, the ancient capital,

When a wife and husband come together in love, the wife will lie on her left side and honor and caress the husband with her right hand. When she gives herself to her husband in ecstasy she receives his seed, and the two bloods come together. It is a great climactic moment that seems to involve the whole universe, bringing into oneness so much that is not one. It is obvious that the main giver is the woman, though our menfolk like to talk of a woman as a mere mold into which man pours everything. The mother gives the mogya, the "blood." This immediately connects the person conceived with the mother and her ancestors, both female and male. The child's descent and inheritance are for us determined through the mother's ancestors in the female line (*abusua*). As our proverb says, "Everyone knows a person's mother."[10]

For Akans, the link between one generation and another is provided by the *mogya*, which is transmitted through the mother. The tracing of matrilineal descent is important in almost every aspect of Akan life: establishing personal status (as royalty, commoner, or slave), validating the right to succeed to political office, claiming citizenship of a particular state, legitimizing the use of lineage farmland and houses, and determining the inheritance of property. The matrilineal clans are the major groups found in a community; they have important religious, political, legal, and economic functions. Its members are corporately responsible for each other's debts and wrongs, and borrowing between members is not considered a debt. The often quoted saying which expresses the corporate unity of the lineage is "One lineage, one blood; a lineage is one person." The significant place of women in the Akan matrilineage cannot be overemphasized, and this extends to other religious spheres.

From the father, the child receives *ntoro*, connected with a person's personal deity (Bbosom); other Akans say the child receives *sunsum* from the father. *Sunsum* refers to the individual's spirit, including character and disposition. Either term reflects inheritance of the spirits of the father's ancestors, complementary to the inheritance of blood from the mother's ancestors.

Female Spirits

Virtually all descriptions of Akan deities begin with *Onyame* (or *'nyame*, *Nyame*). The word means "sky" but is commonly translated as "God" or the "Supreme Deity," often described in monotheistic terms. Some scholars have noted that the peoples along the coastal areas of West Africa have been in intimate contact with Europeans since the fifteenth century and understand the present concept to be due to synthesis with Christian (and probably Islamic) notions.[11]

Another scholar points out that Nyame also can refer to Moon, a female deity, who alone gave birth to the universe. The waxing moon indicates her ability to give life and increase, and the waning moon, her ability to take life. The round head of an *Akua'ba*, the female fertility figurine used to induce pregnancy and a healthy baby, represents the moon, and a similar figurine with upraised arms is placed on the graves of clan headwomen, symbolizing the *kra* (life-giving power) of the moon and of the dead leader. Since the rituals related to the life-giving "queen-mother" (see below) reflect an identification of her with Moon, it is argued that Moon, as mother-goddess, was earlier understood by the Akan to have given birth to the universe.[12]

Whether as Moon or Sky, diagrammatically placed opposite Earth, it is more likely that Nyame was originally a celestial deity, rather than the contemporary God, to whom no offerings are made, nor rituals directed. Other spirits are natural features—rivers, lakes, mountains, forests—and the blackened stools of deceased "queen-mothers" and kings. Of major importance are Earth and the Grandmothers.

Asase (Earth)

One sub-group of the Akans, the Ashante, refer to the earth deity as *Asase-yaa*, while another, the Fanti, use the name *Asase-fua*. "Asase" literally means "Earth." "Yaa" and "Afua" are both Akan names for females born on specific days of the Akan week.

Libation is poured to Asase-yaa on appropriate occasions, and sacrifices are also offered to her periodically. For example, a libation is poured to Asase-yaa before a grave is dug. The following is a prayer that normally accompanies the libation on such an occasion:

> Earth, whose day is Yada [4th day of the week],
> Receive this wine and drink.
> It is your grandchild [name of deceased]
> that has died.
> We have come to beg you for this spot . . .
> So that we may dig a hole for her/his burial.

The earth deity resents tilling and digging the land on the fourth day of the week because it is her special day. Misfortunes are understood to fall on those who act contrary to her will. She is prominently mentioned in many invocations, and she forbids, among other acts, vicious spilling of human blood, incestuous practices, burying a dead pregnant woman without the removal of the foetus from her womb, and, most important, sexual intercourse in the bush. She must be propitiated if a woman delivers in the bush.

There is a profound sense of dependence upon the earth among Akans. This is not merely because the corporeal elements, whether alive or dead, rest on the earth, but also because the earth provides food, water, trees, etc., on which human beings so much depend. Madam Yaa points out, "As our drums say: 'O earth, earth, at birth we depend on you. At death we repose on you. O earth, earth, condolences.'"

The earth deity is regarded as the spirit of fecundity and the epitome of the fertile female. No land can be cultivated without seeking her permission, and sacrifices are offered to her before new land is cultivated. Sacrifices are also offered in gratitude to her when there is an abundant harvest. There are popular accounts among Akans of particular individuals who died because they failed to sacrifice to the earth deity after good harvests.

The earth deity is also understood to guide and protect morality. Individuals swear oaths in her name, and she punishes immorality. In the cosmology of traditional Akans, Asase-yaa is a controlling agent; she is the cause of prosperity, fertility, and health, as well as retribution for misdeeds. She is held in utmost awe.

Nananom 'samanfo (Grandfathers and Grandmothers)

Those who live a proper life on death become revered ancestors, the spirit Grandmothers and Grandfathers. In most written accounts of traditional Akan religion, there is a tendency to neglect the Grandmothers even though, among the matrilineal Akan, "queen mothers," as other female dignitaries, have their stools blackened after death, as those of kings, and accorded veneration coupled with all the necessary religious rituals, sacrifices, libations, etc. In Akan culture, the ancestral focus is so important and elaborate that the religion of the Akans may well be described as primarily oriented towards the veneration of Grandmothers.

The Grandmothers are understood to be alive (being the living dead) and residing at a place called *Asamando* ("the land of the dead"). The exact geographical location of Asamando is vague. Akans refer to the location variously: "a far away place on earth," "an uninhabited part of the wilderness," "far beneath the earth," or "the underworld." Wherever it is, Akans do not describe Asamando as a paradise; it is more or less a replica of this earthly existence.

The Grandmothers are spirits principally concerned with the welfare of humans. Having once been living humans, they are familiar with human needs: numerous children, especially daughters to continue the matrilineal line; good harvests; long life spans; peace; and the continuity of the socio-cultural pattern.

Roles in Akan society are determined and enforced by the Grandmothers, who are the guardians of the living. Proper demeanor on the part of human beings is rewarded by the Grandmothers in the form of numerous and healthy children, good harvest, and prosperity in all aspects of life. Departure from the norms of society is considered as acting contrary to the precepts of the Grand-mothers and carries with it negative consequences. Improper behavior is pun-ished by the Grandmothers with calamities such as infertility, infant death, droughts, excessive rainfall, or other plagues.

Female Rituals and Ritual Roles

Akan female rituals and ritual roles primarily relate to fertility. The quest for fertility is explicit in life-cycle rituals (birth, puberty, marriage). Akan traditional religion can be described as a life-affirming religion, seeking to ensure the fer-tility and vitality of human beings. An important aspect of the religion requires that the spirits and memories of famous Grandmothers be venerated and pro-pitiated. The extinction of a lineage would be a calamity too horrible to con-template. Grandmothers often desire to be reborn into their lineage to finish uncompleted tasks. If a lineage were to cease, that would end all hope of return for those Grandmothers who wish to do so. In reproducing human life, females play an essential role in the continuity of lineages and, consequently, religion.

Akan religious practices solemnize biological changes in life through rites of passage. The principal officiants and participants during these rites of passage are females. The cooking and advice that accompany such rites are also pro-vided by females. The symbolism of the rituals regarding birth, puberty, and marriage vividly portray the essential cultural meaning of mature womanhood and its place in Akan religion. In this section we will discuss the first two of these life-cycle rituals.

Pregnancy and Birth Rites

Madame Yaa notes:

> The mother's religious devotion, her peace of mind, and tranquility of soul all affect the child—as well as what she eats and drinks, and even what she thinks, for there are things a woman must avoid at those times because their spiritual and physical influences may be contrary to those that benefit the child. The woman's body and her food come from earth; the physical constituents she is giving the child come from earth. The mother's regard and reverence for the earth is of first and last importance to the child.

Rites regarding birth commence with pregnancy. Custom demands that a pregnant woman protect herself with charms and amulets and that she receive medical attention from a herbalist, who, in some cases, is also a traditional female priest. Libations and prayers are constantly offered to the Grandmothers and the earth deity for the spiritual protection of the expectant woman. It is common for a pregnant woman to visit traditional shrines to offer sacrifices and make promises to spirits for the purpose of ensuring safe delivery at birth. Special herbs may be burned in the bedroom of the pregnant woman to drive away bad spirits, in particular witchcraft spirits directed towards harming her.

A pregnant woman has to observe ritual avoidances, especially those of her husband (*ntoro*). Should the expected baby be a "gift" from a spirit, the expectant mother would have to observe the rituals particular to that deity.

The woman returns to her parents' home when it is time for her to give birth. In her mother's home she will receive the necessary care, and she can be assured that any confession which she might utter during her labor will be kept secret. Unfaithfulness on the part of a woman is understood to be the primary cause of extremely difficult labor. It is traditionally understood that, if a pregnant woman does not confess her wrong doings, she will not survive her labor. Consequently, women tend to make a number of confessions before delivery. A pregnant woman's death during delivery is considered an accursed death; it would not have occurred if the pregnant woman had not committed some horrible crime. Hence, she is unworthy to be honored with the normal funeral rites. A dead pregnant woman is not buried with the foetus or baby. The corpse is sent to the cemetery, and the chief executioner of the village (*abrafohene*) extracts the foetus from the corpse and buries it separately. The earth deity hates burials where the foetus is not removed from the mother's corpse. This could cause famine, drought, epidemics, or other calamities.

Traditional midwives play an important role in the rituals of childbirth by administering medicines and sometimes inducing labor. Immediately after the baby is delivered, the placenta is removed and ritually buried by a female. The woman who buries the placenta urinates on it as that will make her fertile, especially if she is barren.

The newborn is then bathed by the grandmother with specially prepared water and the "ghost hair" is removed. Some Akans put bones of animals such as leopards or lions in the bath water so that the bones of the child will be strong. In Brong-Ahafo, the bone of the bear which symbolizes strength is used.

Menarche Rites

Among the Akans no elaborate puberty rites are performed for males. Females, however, undergo elaborate puberty rites which commence with their first menstruation.

Akan custom requires that a female who menstruates for the first time be sent to the "queen mother" for examination. This is to ensure that the female in question is not pregnant. A female who becomes pregnant before the puberty rites has committed an offense against the spirits, who may punish the entire community with disaster, such as floods, unless purificatory rites are performed.

In some Akan areas, a female who menstruates for the first time is obligated to come out of her house at dawn crying. She then informs her mother of her condition. She is given an *asesedwa*, a white stool which is a seat of honor, to sit on at the entrance of the house. The mother announces the news to the community by taking any old implement, such as a hoe, and beating it to make noise. The older women then assemble to sing special songs. This is one ceremony at which only females, usually old women, play drums. The mother then pours libations of wine to the spirits to ask for blessings for the girl.

The hair of the initiate is ritually shaved and preserved. The shaving of her hair symbolizes the death of her old state of life; she is regarded as reborn into a new life. Should she die and be buried away from her homeland, funeral rites would be performed over this hair.

The initiate is then taken to the riverside where a young girl and a young boy stand on her left and right, respectively. The heads of all three are immersed in the river three times. Three, among the Akans, is a symbol of life, signifying the beginning, middle, and end of life. The meaning of this ritual is that if she gives birth to either a boy or a girl it will be appreciated, since the religiocultural preference is for daughters. In order to ward off evil spirits and for the good luck of the woman to be transferred to the initiate, she is then washed by a woman whose children are all alive. After bathing, the sponge with which she has been bathed and some eggs are placed in the river. The spirits of the river are invoked to ask blessings for the girl, to reward her with many children, long life, and a successful marriage. White clay is smeared on her forehead, and she is taken home with her head covered.

Mashed yam or plantain is prepared with palm oil and eggs. In addition a stew made of palm oil and blood is prepared. The grandmother or a woman who has reached menopause takes a little of each of these dishes and offers it to the girl. The girl is offered the food three times, and each time she lets the food fall on the ground. An egg is touched to her mouth three times (eggs are a symbol of fertility and life); she swallows it without chewing or biting through it. A female from her clan then brings three roasted pieces of an elephant's ear and touches the mouth of the initiate with them three times. This is done so that the girl will develop a womb similar to an elephant's in order to bear many children.

The initiate then eats *eto* (a sacrificial dish made from yams) and eggs while her head is covered with a white cloth. In some Akan localities, young children try to snatch the food while the initiate tries to grab their hands. If she first grabs the hand of a girl, then her first born will be a girl.

Akan menarche rites normally take a week during which the initiate receives many presents. At the end of the rites, the initiate is dressed in her best clothing and goes around the community thanking all those who attended the ceremony. She is led by two girls dressed only in beads, gold jewelry, and a long female loin cloth. The initiate herself is dressed in *kente* cloth (worn by royalty on ritual occasions) with many gold ornaments.

The performance of the puberty rites establishes a relationship between the female and the spirit realm through the libations and sacrifices offered to the spirits. It also enables an individual to be recognized as a mature member of her community.

Priests and Mediums

Early twentieth-century texts on Akan religion assumed, in an uncomprehending manner, that all major religious functionaries were male and that female religious functionaries served these males, but this hardly fits Akan religion. There are many female, as well as male, religious functionaries in Akan traditional religion; they occupy important social positions as well. They are called *obosomfo* or *okomfo*; the latter refers to possession by spirits. In the literature, they are variously termed priestesses, prophetesses or spirit mediums.

Female priests perform several religious duties, mostly in shrines and sacred groves. They are regarded as the servants of the spirits. They are the mouthpieces of the spirits and act as intermediaries between the spirits and human beings. Akan priests are chosen to perform their duties in various ways. Most Akan priests are "called" by various spirits because of the spirits' love for them. They become possessed by these spirits through entering a trance when carrying out daily activities alone or during religious ceremonies. The spirit possession is interpreted by diviners, and in most cases the interpretation is expressed in terms of "marriage" to the spirits.

Parents sometimes make vows to the spirits in order to be granted children, especially daughters. In gratitude, they dedicate the child born under these circumstances to the spirits. These children wear white and black beads, and their hair is left uncombed. The names given them signify that they are dedicated to the spirits. Dedicated daughters live in the shrines with elderly female priests and start training from infancy. On the ceremonial days of the relevant spirits, novices remain without food throughout the day. They are initiated when they reach physical maturity.

Ceremonial ablutions occupy the first year of training in the priesthood. These consist of bathing with mixtures of leaves, herbs, and bark of trees sacred to the particular spirit; they are gathered by the trainer. Leaves of the *krampa* tree are used to strengthen the ankles of the neophyte priests for dancing. Leaves of the *asoa* tree are used to enable them to receive a "second sight" to "see" the spirits. Some of the leaves are also used to arouse the spirit possession if the ecstasy is slow in recurring.

The plants are gathered from a graveyard. An offering of a fowl and eggs is placed in the pot and sent to the graveyard, whence the plants were taken. The novice must go alone to that place at midnight and bathe with the herbs for seven nights. The bathing at the graveyard is to enable the novice to come into contact with the spirits of the Grandmothers.

During the second year, the novice receives further instructions, and the various requirements of the spirits are revealed to her. She wears certain charms (*asuman*) and is informed of special practices attached to each. She is, however, not yet taught how to make the charms. There are a number of restrictions which have to be observed by the novice. These observances "set apart" the novice for the work of the spirit. Since she is separated from the mundane life enjoyed by her friends and relatives, her life becomes sacred.

In the third year, the novice is taught how to make spells and incantations, to hear and salute trees, and sometimes how to cure various diseases. At the end of the training, a ceremony is performed, and the novice becomes a full priest.

The ceremony starts in the evening when the novice is dressed in a white calico skirt with charms on it, and white clay is sprinkled on her. There is drumming, and the priests who are present dance. At midnight, the novice is sent to the river. She carries a large pot containing dried chewed sugarcane pieces, with a torch set on top so that she can be seen. This rite is known as *wonhyia*, which literally means "should not meet." It is considered unlucky for the novice and her attendants to meet anyone while she is being led to the riverside. If she meets someone accidentally, the novice's face is covered, and she leaves the path. At the bank of the river, the novice is bathed with water and given new clothes to wear. The following morning is one of rejoicing, and sacrifices are offered by the new priest to the spirits.

Noel King describes a mediumistic ritual he witnessed in Ghana:

> The orchestra and the choir were already assembled, the prophetess—powdered in white, wrapped in white, and holding a broom and a stick—had gone through all the preliminaries [the academic observers were late] . . . I presented my bottles of schnapps. The spokesperson poured a great libation . . .
>
> > Spirits of the above, come drink.
> > Spirits of earth, come drink.

Ancestors, spirit grandfathers, spirit grandmothers,
   come and drink.
Remember the needs of those travelling,
   —those in childbirth
   —those under compulsion
   —those in need of money
   —in need of children.

I found it deeply moving and prayed silently.

The prophetess danced as the orchestra played, and we all sang. The head drummer was inspired . . . the next invocation would be to the gods of the town. It was rumored that the spirit of the lady possessor was that of a woman who had died giving birth to simultaneous twins . . . Various people posed their questions and made their supplications, and the spirits spoke to them. Much later, the exhausted prophetess was carried out. . . .

Other related ritual roles include diviners and healers, with their own modes of training, rituals, and initiations.

"Queen Mothers"

One of the two most important religio-political roles is that of the ɔhenemmaa, generally translated as "queen mother." Because of the presence of a Queen Mother in the British monarchy over the last four decades, it is all too easy to assume for Akan traditions the same meaning as the term in England. The British Queen Mother is precisely that, the mother of the ruling monarch; she has no power of her own. The ɔhenemmaa is utterly different. She is a co-ruler with the king; she is neither his biological mother nor his wife, but a ruler in her own right. As is the king, she is chosen from the appropriate matrilineage. Both she and the king have sacred stools, emblems of their office, of the same size but with different designs. When a "queen mother" dies, her stool is blackened with eggs and soot, as is the stool of a dead king, and placed in a special shrine with the stools of the previous "queen mothers." The stool then is the locus for her spirit, which can enhance the prosperity of the kingdom. One of the primary ritual roles of "queen mothers" and kings is to make offerings in the respective royal shrines. In a diagram of the Akan cosmos made by Madam Yaa, Onyame (Sky/"God") and the natural deities are shown in the upper part; Asase (Earth) and the spirit Grandmothers and Grandfathers are shown in the lower part. At the center are shown a male and female human, and to their left and right, respectively, are shown a stools for a "queen mother" and a king, of equal size and importance.

Images of "queen-mothers" are carved and housed in the shrines of major deities important to royalty. They are shown seated on their royal stools, holding a child on their lap, and pointing to their breast, signifying that they are the mothers of the kingdom, both symbolically and spiritually.[13]

Female Self-Understanding

The above sub-section title is used to maintain conformity with the rest of this book, but is somewhat of a misnomer here. There is insufficient material in the literature to discover how women understood themselves in traditional Akan culture prior to the major influences from the monotheistic religious traditions. All too often, cultural phenomena are given a European androcentric twist. For example, Akan women are not to create anthropomorphic and zoomorphic figurines; this is a male prerogative. Stories are told of women who do so and become barren.[14] From a Western perspective this could be understood as indicating the inferiority of females; from an Akan perspective it more likely indicates the inferiority of males. Males cannot produce children, the most important task of humans. At best, males can approximate reproduction by carving or casting figurines. If women took this mode of creation from them, they would have nothing, and women out of kindness and compassion support males.

Matrilineal cultures are egalitarian with regard to sex, far different from some patrilineal cultures which become patriarchal. Madam Yaa's diagram and discourse clearly indicate the equality of females and males, and the two rulers, "queen mother" and king, rule equally, one over the males and one over the females. Without the medium-priests, most being female, people could not come into direct contact with the spirit realm, their assistance being essential for life and comfort. Without mothers to produce daughters, the matrilineal clans could not continue, and the world, as the Akans know it, would fall apart. Surely individual women understood and appreciated their importance and power.

COMPARISON

Although different cultures, albeit in the same part of the world, Yoruba and Akan traditions share a number of general features and interpretational problems, all based on the nature of the synthesis with the monotheistic cultures. This to a degree is obscured in the above descriptions, because the available data for each culture had different foci. Christian missionaries have had a major impact on both cultures, and Muslim missionaries have been equally important in Yoruba culture, although the cultural response has been to develop new, African modes of Christianity. European colonial powers dominated both until independence, and the modern governments have maintained semi-European patriarchal systems, although side by side with traditional forms of government on the local level.

The first question is whether the Yoruba have always been patrilineal. Given the similarity of the traditional government with dual male and female rulers among both Akan and Yoruba culture, as well as other social and religious features discussed above, a number of contemporary scholars have argued that the culture was probably matrilineal prior to European and Islamic influence.

The second question revolves around the history of the understanding of Olodumare among the Yoruba and Onyame among the Akan. There can be no question that they are now understood as Supreme Deities within a polytheistic structure, but was this always so? The internal logic in the respective traditional theological systems is that the sky deity is equal with the earth deity. A similar phenomenon can be seen in those Native North American cultures that have had as long an interaction with European Christians as have Central African ones. But this development did not take place in those Native American traditions with comparatively little interaction with Christianity. Hence, some scholars understand the quasi-monotheism in Akan and Yoruba religions to be an overlay, albeit a significant one, of the last centuries.

12
CANDOMBLÉ: AN AFRICAN RELIGION IN THE AMERICAS

I N THE AFRICAN DIASPORA, when millions of central West Africans were cruelly and involuntarily transported to the Americas, religion served as a means for personal and cultural survival. In the Protestant colonies, black slaves were not considered human and were prevented from practicing religion. In the Catholic colonies, slaves were considered human and, accordingly, forcibly Christianized. This led to syntheses between Catholicism and central West African religions that continue to the present: Vodou in Haiti, Shango in Puerto Rica, Santería in Cuba, Candomblé in Brazil, etc.[1] It is on the latter that this chapter will focus.

The heart of African-Brazilian culture is found in northeastern Brazil, in the city of Salvador in Bahia. From its very beginning, the religion centered on women, focused on ecstatic trance, and attracted those of European origins. A satire from the seventeenth century, the first literary reference to Candomblé, points to these three features:

. . . .
Teaching by night
Calundas [Bantu term suggesting possession] and fetishism
Thousands of women
Attend them faithfully
So does many a bearded man [a Portuguese] . . .
This much I know: in these dances . . .
Can teach such ecstasy.[2]

Although persecuted well into the twentieth century, Candomblé, which means "ritual" in the Yoruba language, persisted among the black population until the slaves were emancipated in 1888; from which time it continually expanded. Priests were brought by the involved populace from Africa to Brazil, and African-Brazilians went to Africa to study the traditions. As Brazil increasingly became a mulatto (mixed) population, so the religion, in new forms, spread throughout much of the populace. Some have suggested that, in its various forms, Afro-Brazilian religion is the national religion of Brazil. Certainly, much of the popular culture, such as samba music and dance, derives from it, and, in the major southern cities, many adherents are from the light-skinned middle class.

In Rio de Janeiro, a more open synthesis of Yoruba and Bantu traditions is known by the Bantu word *Macumba*; in São Paolo, it is *Umbanda*, from the Bantu word meaning "of the cult"; and other terms are used in various regions of Brazil. Umbanda is a fusion between the Euro-Brazilian version of Spiritualism (see Chapter 13) and Macumba. As one moves from north to south, one finds increasing participation of white Brazilians and increasing participation of male mediums. For consistency, this discussion will be limited to Candomblé and the province of Bahia.

Although slavery ended over a century ago, the majority of Bahians are both black and poor. Women form the mainstay of community and family and are the merchants in the marketplace, as in the Yoruba world. Hence, not only is there continuity with regard to religion and culture, but also with regard to certain socio-economic aspects.

The synthesis with Christianity at first undoubtedly was a matter of necessity; the Yoruba deities had to be disguised as members of the Trinity or as saints to be openly worshiped. But as the centuries passed, this amalgamation became spiritually meaningful. Candomblé adherents are Catholics simultaneously, regardless of whether or not the Church accepts their synthesis. Initiation rituals for the various Candomblé roles include blessings in the churches, and many festivals also involve church visits along with rituals in the *terreiro* ("temple grounds"). The linkages of the Yoruba deities with the Christian ones is meaningful; each deity is at one and the same time both a nature spirit and a saint and is worshiped accordingly. A full description of Candomblé is not possible in a brief chapter; rather the concern will be with an examination of the effects of this synthesis on the role of women and the hermeneutics of femaleness. Do we find in Candomblé the Christian or the Yoruba understanding of women, given that the two are incompatible?

The sources for this analysis are primarily the works of Ruth Landes, based on fieldwork of the late 1930s and written from the more distant anthropology of that day; that of Jim Wafer, whose participant-observation fieldwork is limited for the purposes here only by his sex; and Serge Bramly's journalistic reporting of the words of Maria-José (from which all quotations by her are taken). Although her *terreiro* is in Rio de Janeiro, Maria-José is from Bahia and represents the Candomblé tradition. Also informative for the spirit of Candomblé is the novel *Shepherds of the Night* by Jorge Amado, albeit, of course, he writes from a male perspective.[3]

FEMALE SPIRITS

In the 1930s description by Landes and the 1980s description by Wafer, separated by a half-century, there is a consistent picture of the attitude towards the African deities. Some *terreiros* consider any spirits other than the Yoruban ones, the *orixás*, to be improper; others most happily incorporate *cabloca* (spirits of the Native peoples of Brazil) and *egums* (spirits of the dead, particularly old African slaves).

The *orixá* are those described in the chapter covering Yoruba religion (the orthography here follows the conventions of contemporary writings on Candomblé). Important female spirits are those connected with water: *Oxun*, also St. Catherine, the deity of fresh waters (lakes, rivers, streams, waterfalls), epitomizes culturally approved female traits—love, sensuality, flirtatiousness, etc.; *Iemanjá*, also the Virgin Mary, is the deity of salt waters, the ocean that links Brazil to Africa, and the protector of all those of African origin who are in Brazil; *Nanã* represents the rain that is absorbed by the earth, becoming mud; *Iansã*, also St. Barbara or Joan d'Arc, is an armed sky-deity warrior, the deity of storms and tempests, as well as of death.

Some of these *orixá* have become national ones. On Iemanjá's day, December 31, in Rio de Janeiro, as well as all the other coastal cities, well over a million worshipers will crowd the beaches as the offerings to her are made by all the *terreiros*.

A second group of Yoruba deities are the *exus*. They are trickster deities who can protect and yet disrupt. Offerings are made to them before all rituals, but outside of the *terreiro*, as they are not invited in. *Exus* can be female or male, but Wafer makes an interesting point regarding gender in the comparison of *exus* to *orixás* and an interesting reversal of the gender associations concerning religion in Durkheim's schema (discussed in Chapter 1):

> It is interesting that both male and female orixás, when they descend at Candomblé festivals, wear skirts that are variants of those of the traditional Bahiana costume . . . This suggests that the *orixás* are comparatively "feminine" entities, by contrast with the exus, who are comparatively "masculine." And since the *orixás* are closer, on the spirit-matter continuum, to the pole of spirit, while the *exus* are closer to the pole of matter, it suggests also a link between femaleness and spirituality, and maleness and materiality.

FEMALE RITUALS AND RITUAL ROLES

Given several centuries of enslavement to Christian owners, it is not surprising that no descriptions of African-Brazilian female rituals are to be found in the literature. On the other hand, given that Ruth Landes, although female, chiefly associated with a male academic informant, and Wafer, although a participant, being male, primarily associated with male adherents to Candomblé, no certainty can be attained in this regard. Virtually all the rituals described are mixed sex rituals. Fortunately, there are good descriptions of female roles in these rituals.

There are a number of leadership roles in a *terreiro*. Most *terreiros* are led by females called *mãe* (mother); often this role is passed on matrilineally, although the Mothers rarely marry legally. There will be a senior as well as junior Mothers. Male priests are called *babalaô*, but, if they are associated with a *terreiro*, they are called the "Mother's Brother." A female head of a *terreiro* is also called a *iyalorixá* ("mother of the gods"), while a male is called a *babalorixá* ("father of the gods"). Initiated males who are not mediums are called *ogã*; they play the sacred drums and serve as protectors of the *terreiro*. Initiated females who are not mediums are called *equede*; they support the entranced mediums during ceremonies and otherwise assist in the running of the *terreiro*.

Mediums are the central ritual functionaries, and most are female. Of the male mediums, many are homosexual; in any case, they often wear female clothes during the rituals. Mothers of the Gods do not ordinarily become possessed, according to Maria-José, on being asked if she went into trance,

> [After a sigh] I am a very attentive Mother. If I went into a trance, who would watch over the faithful? Some Mothers of the Gods can't resist the call of the drums. But I personally believe that my role forbids me to enter a trance. Before running the terreiro I, like all initiates, was possessed by my god. I too have known the ecstasy, my son; I too have known it. . . .

Potential mediums, once it is determined through their experiences and divination that the role is suitable for them, undergo an elaborate initiation, far more involved than those for *ogã* and *equede*; only the mediums are the full initiates in the religion. Since the initiation ritual is similar to those in central West Africa, described in the preceding chapter, it will not be described here. The initiates are known as Sons or Daughters of the Gods, depending on their sex. Mediums often have several spirits by whom they are possessed, often evenly divided between male and female *orixás* and *exus*.

In preparation for rituals, mediums and priests take ritual purification baths and sleep apart from their spouses. This seems to be a cultural universal; traditionalist female and male Native American shamans also avoid sexual intercourse for four days prior to shamanizing and ritually purify themselves with sweat rituals. As elsewhere, mediums avoid the *terreiro* when they are menstruating. Marie-José explains:

> My son, the body of a menstruating woman is a closed body. It can receive nothing, for it is already rejecting a part of itself. To be a medium is to agree to offer yourself, to open yourself in order to give yourself to the gods. When a woman loses her blood she is ridding herself of a part of her body that is choking her and which must flow out so that she can open herself anew. But during this period she is in a time of rejection and it is impossible for her to work.
>
> You can receive nothing from the gods, my child, if you aren't open to them. During a work, for example, you mustn't even cross your legs if you are seated; it would be a negative gesture, an attitude of refusal. The energy can't circulate, and nothing can happen.

In Bahia, the *terreiro* floors are earthen, and mediums divest themselves of their shoes. It is essential that their bodies, through their dancing bare feet, are constantly in contact with the earth, so that its energy can invigorate them. The mediums must be literally grounded. What it means to be a medium will be dealt with in the following section.

A typical ceremony involves considerable preparation. Throughout the day, birds and animals to be sacrificed, plant foods, and sacred herbs are purchased in the market. The *terreiro* is thoroughly swept, the room of images and sacred paraphernalia is cleaned, and offerings are made. Food is prepared, decorations of sacred herbs are made, ritual baths (with herbs) are prepared, etc. Most of the work is done by the women, which, although hard, creates a time for companionship, for communal activities. The young children of those involved will be running about and having a good time.

As evening approaches, an offering will be made to Exu. The drummers have been gathering and warming up their drums. Spectators have been filtering in and taking their places, usually along a rail surrounding the open, roofed *terreiro*. The senior *ogã* take their places on chairs of honor behind the chair of the Mother of the Gods. The mediums and *equede* enter; the drums begin, and songs invoke the *orixás* needed for that evening's ceremony. The mediums dance; those whose *orixás* are being invoked begin to go into trance. The Mother (or Father) circulates among the dancing mediums, stimulating those who are having difficulty entering trance, bringing those who should not be going into trance out of it if they seem to be going under, and, in various ways, controlling the ecstasies of the daughters and sons of the gods. When all who should be in trance are well under, they dance towards the Mother for blessing and then, assisted by the *equedes*, enter the room where the costumes and other ritual paraphernalia are kept. They are each dressed in the proper outfit and handed the symbols of their deity. When all are ready, they dance back into the *terreiro*: the deities are present. After each *orixá* (as well as *cabloca* and *eguns* in certain *terreiros*) is celebrated by a song and dance, people may approach them for healing, advice, succor, and blessings. The deities and other spirits then leave, people feast on the food that had previously been offered to the spirits, and the ceremony is completed.

FEMALE SELF-UNDERSTANDING

What does it feel like to be possessed? Since by far the majority of mediums in Candomblé are females, this is of major interest in understanding the hermeneutics of female religious functionaries in African and African-American religions. In a film made in Salvador, Zeze, a relatively young female medium addresses this issue (translated from the Portuguese):

> It is wonderful to be able to receive another being in yourself, a being who comes to say something, a being who comes to heal . . . this force that uses your body to heal somebody else, to warn us of something that is going to happen . . . I was ten when my *orixá* began to come forward. It was all very confusing; I didn't know what was happening with me when the *orixá* came. I knew I would have lots of aches in my body and I would feel terribly, terribly sleepy, and the other people, my colleagues and my friends, my sisters and saint, they would tell me like this, that they had seen me talking and dancing and doing other things, and I thought it was all very strange, but not all that strange because I had seen my mother in trance, with her *orixá*, Omulu, and today I consider myself a privileged person . . .
>
> . . . and I think that, although the saints, sacred things that the supreme god put in the world, like nature, men and women, that one of the most wonderful things is the *orixá*. . . . And we feel confused and grateful at the same time, with this process of having an *orixá* . . . And I feel very much this force, this major force, a force I can't explain. It exists between Heaven and Earth . . . There are mysteries that cannot be explained, and one of them is the *orixá*.[4]

Maria-José speaks in a similar fashion, although from her perspective as a Mother of the Gods, as a spiritual and community leader, she understands the broader implications:

> [On being asked how the medium feels in the aftermath of the trance—] She feels good. Very good. And tired, of course, especially if the trance has been

active. But she feels good because her head has been emptied and in a sense regenerated. And above all because the god has left behind a great strength.

[On being asked about the larger benefits of trance—] No, the trance benefits the community most of all; how the medium feels is unimportant since she voluntarily offered her body to the gods. The essential thing is that the gods be able to become incarnate. It is a great honor to receive a god. I think that once the trance is over the mediums think only of their luck in having lent their bodies to the gods.

Sociologists have posited many reasons for why the majority of mediums, worldwide, are females; these theories tend to be based on the assumption that women are socially, if not actually, inferior to males. Being able to function as mediums, then, is compensatory for their otherwise low status. And since the culture understands that it is the deity that is present, not the possessed medium, she has no real status at all. Obviously, this is not the understanding of these female mediums and Mothers of the Gods. Nor is it the understanding of the male Candomblé adherents.

Ruth Landes' associate-informant, an *ogã* himself, speaks of a Father of the Gods in a Bantu version of Candomblé as having an inferiority complex. She asks why this would be so:

Why, he's a *man,* Dona Ruth, in a world dominated by women! A true priest of the cult should be a woman, and I think . . . is honest enough about his cult practice to wish he were truly a woman, instead of just a man acting like a woman. As it is, he has to delegate many crucial functions to a woman of the priesthood, and then it is she who is in command after all, instead of he. It makes fatherhood hollow at times.

Jim Wafer points to a different aspect of the female qualities involved in possession, whether the medium is male or female, although it should be remembered that male mediums are often homosexual (in Candomblé, not necessarily Umbanda):

. . . humans, who are equated with matter, are "female" in relation to all the spirits. Humans "give" offerings so that the spirits may "eat." "Giving" and "eating" are common Brazilian metaphors for the passive and active roles in intercourse.

There are many aspects to the reasons for these differences between male and females with regard to spirit possession. Some of these reasons, as the preceding are a matter of gender, others, of sex. Landes was told, "The women are sacred to the gods when in the temple . . . The blood of the men is supposed to be 'hot,' and that is considered offensive to the gods for whom the women have been preparing themselves."

As an introspective female on these matters, Maria-José is very precise on the differences between females and males with regard to possession:

> Masculine and feminine powers aren't the same. I don't mean one or the other is superior . . . Women aren't more intelligent than men, but it's true they understand more. It's not by chance that we are called Mothers of the Gods. Our children know this perfectly well. From the beginning women are more open to trances—they have fewer obstacles in their minds than men. I mean that their minds are always in harmony with their bodies . . . When they offer themselves to the gods they give themselves completely, more generously. And so their gift is worth more than that of men.
>
> Women have a much deeper relationship with themselves than men do . . . They truly exist on one level, a level of fullness, and have less of a tendency to fragment themselves. Look at the way a woman thinks: she doesn't analyze, she embodies. Her vision isn't fragmented . . .
>
> I think that women by their very nature, and by that I mean with their bodies, possess the means for penetrating certain realities that men can only guess at . . . I believe that women are naturally more able to pass easily from one reality to another, to the other side of things. For that is their nature. Men are less malleable, less receptive, less open . . . That's why women make better mediums.

Rarely does one find so clear an articulation of these gender and sex differences between males and females with regard to spirit possession. Marie-José's words are a fine place to end this chapter. Readers are warmly recommended to Serge Bramly's concise volume for a fuller exposition of her views.

13
ANALYSIS AND CONCLUSIONS

> ... What was the egg's upper shell
> became the heavens above
> what was the egg's lower shell
> became mother earth below
> what was the white of the egg
> became the moon in the sky
> what was the yolk in the egg
> became the sun in the sky
> what on the egg was mottled
> became the stars of heaven ...
> —from the Finnish epic, the "Kalevala"[1]

COMMONALITIES OF NON-WESTERN TRADITIONS

WHILE A NUMBER OF DIFFERENT CULTURES have been covered in this study, many have not. It would be impractical and lead to an impossibly massive volume to cover all the world's cultures with regard to any aspect of religion, let alone the religious practices and understanding of half the world's population. Most of the major regions of the planet have been covered: the eastern part of Asia, with some reference to the extreme western part; North America, with some reference to South America and the Caribbean; one part of sub-Saharan Africa; and the extreme northern fringe of Europe. Conspicuously absent are Europe, northern Africa, and the southern part of Asia.

Europe and north Africa, as well as much of western Asia, were not covered because this work is contrasting non-Western religions with the "Religions of the Book" (Judaism, Christianity, Islam), which are relatively well known in the West. It is important to see if there are any commonalities among non-Western

227

traditions, other than the simple fact that they are not Western. It is hardly controversial to posit that there are many similarities among the monotheistic traditions, due to common origins and continual mutual influence. Secondly, other than the Roman and Hellenistic traditions and their sparse, biased records of more northern traditions, we are aware of pre-Christian European traditions mainly through negative Roman and Christian overlays. This renders description and analysis difficult and tenuous.

South Asia has not been covered due to the complexity of the cultural development there and the desire to spend no more than five years in the writing of this book. To analyze adequately the development of Buddhism, Hinduism, Jainism, etc., we would have to delve into the complexities of Indo-European traditions, an endeavor which would entail study of pre-Christian Europe and Iran, as well as northern India. Beginning approximately thirty-five hundred years ago, this macro-tradition interacted with the indigenous traditions of South Asia for a millennium to engender the above named religious traditions. Islamic conquest and British colonialism also affected the sub-continent for many centuries and indelibly influenced these traditions, further adding to the complexities of the analysis. Moreover, the cultures of South Asia, West Asia and the eastern Mediterranean have continually been in contact with each other, from the trade between Sumer and the Indus Valley civilization to the interconnected, parallel development of Buddhism and Christianity.

Of particular interest with regard to female spirituality in South Asia is the Nāyar culture of Kerala (in extreme southwestern India), which maintained a matrilineal sociocultural structure, as well as an orientation towards Devī, the Great Goddess (also known as Amma, "mother"), in spite of being dominated by patrilineal and patriarchal Hinduism. Nāyar families consider the birth of a girl more important than that of a boy and have a major menarche ritual. Of interest in this regard is that at times the Goddess is perceived to menstruate, a particularly sacred event celebrated by females to enhance their own sacred/sexual power. However, a meaningful analysis of Nāyar traditions would be incomplete without describing the surrounding Hindu cultures for contrast. For feminist analyses of these traditions, readers are warmly recommended to the writings of Nancy Falk and other feminist scholars on Hinduism, and Rita Gross and others on Buddhism.[2]

From a religio-ecological perspective, however, the coverage has been thorough. With regard to primarily hunting traditions, rare in human cultures, there was some discussion of the Inuit. Gathering-hunting traditions were amply covered: The Saami and Nitsitapi were gathering-hunting traditions that, in very different ways, shifted to herding. The Anishnabe culture was a gathering-hunting tradition that engaged in the fur-trade after the influx of Europeans to northern North America. The Diné provide an example of a gathering-hunting tradition that, in moving into an area of settled agriculture, adapted to farming and raiding, and then herding.

The horticultural-hunting traditions are illustrated by the Aguaruna, and incipient agriculture is analyzed with the Hopi culture. With regard to agriculture, we have dealt with such cultures at varying stages of development: the Mesopotamian and Semitic kingdoms of the eastern Mediterranean; the Inca empire; Chinese, Japanese, and Korean cultures of East Asia; and two kingdoms of west central Africa. In the shift from agriculture to industrial developments, we have looked at China and at Candomblé in Brazil. Finally, with regard to post-industrial cultures, we briefly examined aspects of current developments in Taiwan within the chapter on contemporary China. The description of contemporary Anishnabe religion depicts the religion of those who dwell in modern North American cities, as well as reservations in more rural areas, and the analysis of Candomblé was of an urban religion.

In all of the above cultures, in spite of geographical separation, diverse languages, and different modes of historical development, a surprising number of commonalities can be found with regard to female spirituality. These commonalities suggest that the human species is indeed a mammalian species, with a common physiological structure including the brain, and similar responses to the complexities of living in the wide-ranging terrains and climates of this planet. Human beings share with all mammals (and many other biological phyla) an almost total bilateralness. We can be split down the middle into two similar halves with but a few exceptions: a single alimentary system, although the stomach is balanced by the liver; a single spinal cord and brain stem; a few single hormone-producing glands; and a single urinary tract, from dual kidneys, leading to a single sexual organ, albeit connected to either dual ovaries or testicles. In some cases, the bilateral halves do not have exactly the same functions, as in the heart and the brain.

Mammals are also divided into two somewhat different beings which must physically join together in order for reproduction to take place (granting the exceptions of parthenogenesis, in which a female may reproduce another female, given extremely rare circumstances, and "test-tube" conception). As with some parts of the body, these beings share many features and differ in others: examples include different but parallel reproductive parts; differences in skeletal structure and musculature, particularly in humans due to the need for a wide birth canal to allow passage of a large infant skull enclosing a big brain; differing proportions of behavior-influencing, as well as sexually-determinative, hormones; and differences in brain structure.

As the bilateral parts of the body work together in any functioning mammal, so the two types of mammals in each species must work together for reproduction to take place. Among the "higher" primates, including humans, the different types of beings—virtually different species—denominated by the terms, "male" and "female," also work together other than in direct action for reproduction; that is, males and females interact for long periods of time, seemingly for the advantage of each type. This means that culture develops as an efficient means to utilize the differences in physiological and mental structures of the two types of humans for the benefit of all the involved individuals. To continue the species and efficiently sustain the living are the motivation for individuals of the species to group themselves together.

As can be discerned in the preceding studies, the mammalian nature of humans profoundly affects their rituals and hermeneutics. The following analysis of the non-Western religions covered in this inquiry will be carried out with the tri-partite model utilized in all the major chapters.

Female Spirits

In every culture studied in this work, the creation of the world and/or the creation of humans is understood from the standpoint of the reproduction of mammals or birds. Either the progenitor is a cosmic egg, understood to have female connotations—males do not lay eggs—or the result of a cosmic pairing. When a sex is stressed, it is invariably the female. For although humans have always known the role of the male in mammalian reproduction—one need but observe the paleolithic cave paintings—obviously, it is the female that actually births. Although a few patrifocal myths shift birthing to males—for example, Zeus tearing the fetus of his son Dionysus from the womb of the dying Semele and placing it in his thigh in order to save it—male birthing is always presented as both extraordinary and unnatural, that is, divine.

The most common cosmic pair is male Sky and female Earth, sometimes represented by Sun-Moon, Morning Star-Evening Star, or other similar cosmic couples. To these spiritual entities are attributed male and female characteristics: Sky with lightning flash and thunder rains down life-giving fluid onto the receptive Earth, often conceived of as a cave. Earth does far more than receive the seminal fluid; she gestates and gives birth. Nor do her gifts end with birth, for she then nourishes the new life with water, her sustaining fluid, and sustains it with her animals and plants. This paradigm, sometimes simple, sometimes complex, is ubiquitous from the New Zealand Polynesians to the Arctic Saami, from Africa through the Americas and back to Africa. There seems to be but a single macro-cultural exception, and that we will examine in the next section.

For those who live, or whose culture is but recently derived from, a gathering-hunting existence, the deities tend to be of the natural world; the focus is on cosmic, weather, animal, and plant spirits. In Native North American religions, these are understood to be relations, all existing interdependently in a milieu of reciprocity. When those still living the tradition speak of the earth as Mother or the moon as Grandmother, this is not just lip service as is frequently found in contemporary Western rhetoric; it is felt emotionally. To observe Moon is to feel the welling up of gratitude and affection that one feels towards one's grandmother. It should be further understood that in these cultures it is often the grandmother that raises the children, the mature adults otherwise engaged in more directly productive occupations.

Reciprocity means that nothing is taken for granted. All that is received is understood to be from the spirits and requires recompense. Gifts are offered to plants and animals eaten or otherwise utilized. And as these themselves are spirits, they must be asked to give themselves so that humans may live. Their gift is their life, and, when necessary, for the sake of the community or family, all one can offer from oneself is one's body and, ultimately, one's own life. It is the one gift that each being alone can fully offer.

There is an intimate understanding of spirits, for the entire natural realm is numinous, and humans are never separated from nature by more than a skin or bark tent covering—and the coverings themselves as well as the supports of branches or bones are also gifts from the natural spirits. (Hence, the term "supernatural" has no meaning in this religio-ecological context.) One knows in depth the habits and life-cycles of the plants and animals around one, and these entities are both plant or animal and numinous beings at one and the same time. The numinous is never at a distance; it is the ground on which one stands, the air one breathes, the sounds and sights continually about one, and every being one encounters.

All of these cosmic, weather, plant, and animal spirits, as living beings, are gendered, when gender is meaningful. Some are female, some are male, some are both, as animal species, the gender focus shifting according to function. No sex is left out.

Paralleling mammalian sexual differences, all those deities associated with sustenance are addressed as female. For it is the females of mammals that nurse the young, and human females continue this nurturing role by taking responsibility for gathering the bulk of the food eaten and doing most of the food preparation.

But female deities are not only deities of life, for life and death are intimately connected. As Earth and her manifestations/affiliates are the source of life, of nourishment for the maintenance of life, so they are the source of death. As in many of the cultures discussed, Earth, Moon, or Evening Star is responsible for the abode of the dead. To give one of many examples not covered in this work, among the Siberian Nganasans, it is understood that the Moon-mother holds the threads of life, the "souls" of living people, that she determines pregnancy and is responsible for deliveries. When it is time for death, she tears off a person's thread.[3] To use Chinese concepts, while women may have more *yin* than *yang*, they do incorporate the latter as well; moreover, the *yin* realm includes the world of the dead. It us probably for this reason that in many cultures, the care of the dead is the responsibility of women. Those that bring us forth into the world prepare us for the next.

Female spirits often exhibit these dual characteristics or have opposing manifestations, as in the Hindu pantheon. Of theriomorphic spirits in other cultures, perhaps the clearest example is She Who Flies at Night (Owl). Commonly associated with the dead, as the great spirit of the night, she is often a helping spirit for female, as well as male, shamans. We have early portrayals of her in many civilizations; some of the finest Chinese sacrificial bronze vessels from more than three thousand years ago are of her. The women of the Kuna, a Native American culture of the San Blas Islands off of Panama, make designs from many layers of colored cloth that they wear in pairs of rectangular plaques on their blouses (*mola*), one in front and one on the back. The most impressive depiction of these dual characteristics of a female spirit I have encountered is found on a Kuna set of paired plaques of Owl: on one she is depicted as kindly and peaceful; on the other, she is terrifying in her ferocity. Aside from different appearances of the eyes and beak, the other changes in design are subtle. Among Native American cultures dominated by Christianity, Owl is now viewed as a negative spirit, contrary to nineteenth-century ethnographic data from these same cultures.

As humans exhibit a variety of emotions and personality traits, so too do the spirits. Again to use northern Native North American illustrations, the Winds are gendered; for example, male West Wind (the direction of most thunderstorms) is fierce and terrible but brings needed rain, while female South Wind is gentle, warm, and life-giving (of course, individual revelations through visions may lead to alternate understandings). In these cultures, the spirits are neither good nor evil. They are neutral with regard to these human values. It is humans, functioning shamanically, that can elicit the cooperation of spirits that may affect others as good or evil: to kill an enemy is good; to kill a neighbor is evil. The action is the same; the cultural perspective differs.

Moreover, the spirits do not, on their own, interfere with humans. It is humans who must placate and cajole the spirits to assist them in human enterprises, for they may not always do so. If they do not, no blame is placed on the spirits. That is their choice. But if they do assist, humans owe a debt of gratitude.

With the development of horticulture, the numinous realm is increased by the spirits of domestic plants. Plant spirits are almost always understood as female in any case, saving tobacco, which is often the only plant raised by males. The domestic plants are often conceived as the daughters of Earth. The sexes are equal in all respects in gathering-hunting situations, but the focus shifts to the female in horticulture-hunting situations. Males wander—hunting, raiding, or trading—from a semi-fixed center: the fields and more solidly structured homes that are the province of the female. Male and female rituals and ritual roles become more distinctly different, and so do the deities.

The semi-permanent residences, which move short distances every decade or so as the fields become exhausted, also lead to a different conception of the dead. People who are semi-nomadic—in the sense of moving to different sustenance resources over the course of a year—tend to place the corpses where they will decay by exposure or in shallow burials. The dead souls may return or are understood to travel to another realm, often in the west, the location of the setting or dying sun.

With horticultural residential patterns, the dead bodies remain buried in or near the settlement, often buried under the floor of the clan dwelling. Hence, the dead in horticultural situations are always present. When the settlements were shifted to new fields, the horticultural-hunting peoples residing around the eastern Great Lakes of North America took the bones of the dead with them and reburied them in communal pits in the new settlement. An understanding of clan with a past, the dead, and a future, by logical extension, becomes the socioreligious pattern. In horticultural situations, the clans tend to be matrilineal, and the preeminent dead human spirits would have been the leading elder females of each clan.

With the development of agriculture, this pattern is both enhanced and different. For in many, but not all, cultures, the clans became patrilineal. In the eastern Mediterranean, China and some African cultures, the clans are patrilineal, but, in other contiguous African cultures and in some southern parts of South Asia, the clans remained matrilineal. Then there is the matter of the Indo-European speaking peoples, who, thirty-five hundred years ago, appear as chariot-warriors with a herding economy, a strong patrilineal bent, but seemingly, perhaps being only semi-settled if at all, with no orientation towards the clan dead and few female deities.

The reasons for this shift from matrilineal to patrilineal clans is lost in antiquity. Two factors seem to be involved. First there is a switch from predominantly female to male farming, although, given that we now are discussing stratified societies as compared to the egalitarian horticultural ones, probably both sexes of the lower-ranked producing class worked in the fields. In these cultures' ideology, where we have the data, men produced the grain and women processed it into food. Certainly this is the situation with regard to the Hopi, although their clans have remained matrilineal; residential patterns, matrilocal; and socio-economic situation, egalitarian.

A second factor in the development of patriarchy is that the development of classes may be due to the felt need for professional warriors. Increased production would have led to increased raids from other cultures. As technology led to more sophisticated weapons requiring special training, particularly the war-chariot, and farming males no longer hunted and were by occupation unfamiliar with weapons, a class of weapons specialists developed whose occupation was protection of the society and its produce, as well as raiding against neighbors. The avocation of these professional warriors was hunting with the same weapons used in warfare. Clan social structure became the prerogative of this group, and, with its professional warrior focus, it was male oriented. No matter the reasons for the development, the above describes, as an example, the situation in China thirty-five hundred years ago, a situation which, according to the archaeological evidence, took at least a thousand years prior to that time to develop.

Before proceeding, however, one point needs be made clear. The above is not intended to suggest that patrifocal cultures are *ipso facto* more warrior oriented than matrifocal ones. In all the matrifocal cultures studied, males continue to serve warrior roles. Indeed, among the matrilineal, matrilocal Chiricahua, until quite recently, the economy was based on raiding (if not in the United States after Geronimo, then Mexico). There is no cultural evidence that matrifocal cultures are less warrior oriented than others, nor less prone to violence of other sorts.[4] In the matrifocal Iroquoian-speaking traditions, captured warriors were turned over to the women for disposal: either adoption or slow torture to the death over several days.

In this new social structure, patriarchy, with a new occupational role, the professional warrior, the dead of the clan, whether patrilineal or matrilineal, particularly deceased clan chiefs and their spouses, seems to have replaced the theriomorphic spirits of male hunters in horticulture-hunting cultures; the cosmic, natural, and grain spirits remain. The focus of religious practice becomes the continual care of the dead, particularly by offering feasts to the clan dead shared by the living members of the clan. The prerogative of the leading male and female of the clan to offer these feasts becomes the legitimization for kingship, when the elite warrior clans become organized hierarchically. The living, both males and females, can look forward to becoming the honored dead, to becoming virtual deities for their clan. We find this pattern in both China and Central Africa, and there are hints of rituals directed towards the dead at Ugarit and in Israelite times.

In the gathering-hunting cultures of the circum-polar areas and throughout the Americas, the means of communicating with the numinous is through shamanistic trance experiences, in which the religious functionary is able to achieve the cooperation of spirits, with whom a relationship has already been established, for hunting, raiding, and other community needs. In the horticultural situation, outside of the Americas, we find another mode of functioning in trance, through being possessed by the spirits and the spirits directly interacting via the body of the medium with the community. Probably the first possessions were by the dead of the clan. Allowing one's body to be used by one's dead parents or grandparents (or uncles and aunts) for the good of the clan would seem comfortable and create a closer bond between the medium, the community, and the dead. In the agricultural societies of southern and eastern Asia and sub-Saharan Africa, possessing spirits included not only the ancestors, but all divinities who assisted the communities. Alcohol, the major stimulus for settled agriculture—to provide grain or fruit for fermentation—became a major means for spirit possession and communication with the family dead to take place. This use of inebriation for these purposes occurred not only in Asia and Africa, but in the eastern Mediterranean as well, where there is also evidence of early possession by the dead.[5]

This means of interacting with the numinous became so basic to the culture of China, for example, that shifting from agriculture to industry and subsequently to the electronic post-industrial economy, as evidenced by the situation in Taiwan, has not led to any further change but rather an enhancement of the agricultural pattern. One reason is that the practices are so satisfying and so effective in enhancing family and community well-being that there is no perceived need to change them. A second factor is that the practices are not linked to any specific ideology. The understanding of the world may change, but the ritual practices continue. Hence, in Taiwan, with increasing wealth, we find a resurgence of temple building to various effective spirits—spirits who are not found to be effective find their temples being allowed to fall into ruin as people ignore them—and in homes an elaboration of the worship centers directed to the family spirits and other deities.

A logical question with regard to the above discussion in relation to the theme of this study is, What relevance does the acknowledgment of female spirits have for female spirituality *per se*? My study of religion has led me to the view that where only one sex is considered sacred, then only one sex is understood to have access to the sacred; hence, only one sex is considered important in both the sacred and the human realm. The examples I am most familiar with are the indigenous traditions of North America.

Native traditions in Canada and the United States suffered under the dual thrusts of legal prohibition of their practices under the penalty of incarceration and forcible removal of the children from the parents to reside in schools under the control of Christian missionaries. These missionaries were supported by the respective governments and their military and police powers. Children were usually allowed to see their parents only once a year, if then, and physically tortured for speaking their language, maintaining any of their traditions, and not according with the mode of Christianity required by the missionaries of the particular school (they were often sexually abused as well). Those who eventually returned to their cultures were thoroughly imbued with the simplistic form of Christianity forced upon them, including exclusive worship of a single, male, creator deity.

Hence, throughout the 1970s and early 1980s, in pan-Indian urban contexts, I continuously heard prayers addressed to, and religious statements focusing on, the Creator, a single male deity virtually identical to that depicted in Genesis as interpreted by Christian fundamentalists or as taught in simplistic catechisms. Where prayers were addressed in the only Native language in which I would be able to note the terminology, they were addressed to the Grandfathers, with no mention of the Grandmothers. At the same time, statements were made that females had no religious roles; it was then said by many that females never smoked the "sacred pipe" and females never engaged in "sweat lodges."[6]

When the second attempt was made to reform the Canadian constitution to assuage Quebéc, it failed in large part because it was condemned by Native women. Why? Native political leaders had long fought for recognition and received it in a statement referring to Native self-government. In the southeastern United States, where newly recognized Native tribes were given self-government, the males immediately removed all political rights from females, insisting that this was the Native way. These were cultures that in the past were matrilineal and matrifocal, where female elders chose male leaders and could remove them if displeased with their decisions. The new Native way was one of fundamentalist Christianity. Many Native women in Canada feared the same consequences if Native cultures, in their present assimilated state, were given self-government. The deliberate eradication of female spirits from religious consciousness can have far-reaching effects.

This extreme contradiction between the actual rituals, where offerings were always made equally to female and male spirits, to both the Grandmothers and the Grandfathers, and these Christianized utterances and their effects on female participation stimulated me to write the early paper, mentioned in the Prologue, which had the consequence of engaging me in women's studies. In it I wrote a sentence that has been quoted by others: "Of all the aspects of Christian influence, it is probably the excision of the female from the aboriginal concept of creation that enabled the concept of a single high god to emerge."[7] In the more than a dozen years since I wrote that statement—and here I use blunter language—I have become even more convinced that the exclusion of females from the spirit realm, in effect, is the equivalent of a clitorectomy on the religious life of females.

These effects tend not to be long-lasting if other aspects of the religious tradition continues. In the late eighteenth century, Ganeodiyo (Handsome Lake) instituted reforms of Seneca religion and society, with the advice of Quakers. He did so to save it from dissolution under the impact of Euroamerican culture and economy, but females were considerably affected. He shifted residency from matrilocal, multi-family, clan dwellings to patrilocal, nuclear-family, log cabins; he added to the religion a male high-god, the Creator, by changing the understanding of Sky; and he persecuted as witches powerful females in what had been a matrifocal culture.

Ganeodiyo's reforms led to the establishment among the Six Nations of the Long House Religion, which enabled much of the traditional religion to continue through a long period of Christian domination. But the common Iroquoian substrate was not lost. Although prayers begin with the Creator, they include all the numinous, female and male alike. Clan affiliation remains matrilineal, in spite of government insistence on official patrilineal family identity. Clan Mothers still choose male leaders, although these are not the leaders accepted by the Euroamerican governments.

A number of years ago, when I visited a Mohawk reserve to invite a Clan Mother to speak at an Elders' Conference being held at my university, I discovered an atmosphere in the home quite different from the environment in which I was brought up. The older male of the family deferred to the female. In doing this, he lost neither dignity nor his own power; it was simply the natural response within a matrifocal culture. When I invited the Clan Mother to come to the conference, she accepted and made it clear that the invitation, of course, also extended to her spokesman. Typical of cultures in which women hold leading political roles, they do not speak themselves, but a male speaks for them—the traditional warrior role. She did speak herself, however, in informal settings at the Elders' Conference. This mode of leadership is frequently misunderstood by those from Western cultures who assume that, because males do the public speaking, women have no power.

To return to the original example. Since the very late 1980s, after a decade and a half of revitalization, I have again heard prayers directed to *mishomis* and *nokomis*, the Grandfathers and Grandmothers. Simultaneously, one again finds women that carry pipes and lead sweat lodges, and there has been a resurgence in Moon rituals.

Female Rituals and Ritual Roles

Rituals

In the gathering-hunting traditions, or cultures derived from them, we find female power, in part, defined by the effects of female menstruation on male hunting. It is to the benefit of all, female and male alike, that this power be channeled into beneficial paths. Menarche leads to rituals that are similar to and part of striving for controlled shamanic power.

Among horticulture-hunting peoples, menstruation and menarche rituals remain important, although there has been insufficient research to comprehend fully the differences with gathering-hunting traditions. In agricultural traditions that are matrilineal or have maintained dual male-female political roles, menarche rituals remain an important or, more rarely, the major ritual event in a woman's life. In these cases, the linkage between actual first menstruation and the ritual that marks the transition to physical adulthood has lost its functional necessity, so that time may elapse between the actual and ritual events.

Adjusting to changed circumstances or new cultural environments seems not to lessen the religious significance of menarche. Among the Diné, as the gathering-hunting pattern changed through the stimulus of a settled agricultural pattern, the menarche ritual became the paramount ritual of the traditions. It is the single example of the young woman in the making not simply becoming more powerful (as among the Anishnabeg) or becoming mature (as among the Hopi), but becoming the Earth deity herself. This is neither possession nor shamanic power, but a full incarnation during the period of the ritual. The young woman, being the deity, can heal and assist the growth of children.

In those gathering-hunting cultures that have shifted but relatively recently into new patterns, where practices have not been suppressed or where they have continued underground while being suppressed, as with the Anishnabeg, menarche rituals continue. Under the circumstances of domination by Euroamerican cultures and the attempts at cultural genocide, many women did not undergo this ritual, particularly those forced into the Christian-controlled boarding schools. These women never had the opportunity to gain a strong sense of self-worth and have been plagued with alcoholism and other modes of substance abuse and the consequences of these addictions (as have the males who lost all means for social recognition and self-esteem). Moon rituals, particularly in urban areas, have become a means for women to rediscover the power and significance of femaleness.

With the shift from horticultural or incipient agricultural matrifocality to the patrifocality of agriculture, particularly with warrior-oriented patrilineal elite clans, the religious and social recognition of menstruation seems to disappear (gathering-hunting cultures tend towards being neither matrifocal nor patrifocal). In China, it is recognized that female power during menstruation can interfere with the relationships with the deities, and so menstruating women avoid temples and other ritual events. But it is only with the integration in China of aspects of patriarchal Buddhism from outside China that we find a negative attitude towards female bodily fluids; and even this is limited to a single culturally anomalous understanding of the need for sons to perform a specific Buddhist ritual on the death of their mothers. Among the elite in the early period, while there was no menarche ritual *per se*, in adolescence there was a ritual marking the transition to adulthood for young women parallel to the ritual for young men. In this regard, it is interesting that, in most cultures that celebrate, in various ways, menarche, there is no parallel ritual for males; that is, there is no ritual that specifically marks the physical transition of a boy into manhood, although there are initiation rituals into various adult ritual roles, as there also may be for females.

This book has focused on presenting new cultural data or reinterpreting old, rather than criticizing the many relevant theories regarding women and religion, save to make the point in Chapter 1 that many theories, particularly those of sociologists, have been based on flawed androcentric data. One comparative religionist, whose innovative studies I have admired, has presented interpretations of menarche rituals that need to be addressed. Bruce Lincoln has concluded that "women's initiation [cross-culturally] offers a religious compensation for a sociopolitical deprivation . . . it is an opiate for an oppressed class."[8] In an Afterword written ten years after the original edition, he strengthens this conclusion. As an example of his considering Kinaalda (see Chapter 10) to reinforce cultural oppression of females, he offers a quotation from a young Navajo woman who had just completed the ceremony:

Well if you're cheerful four days [the length of the ceremony] maybe you get the habit of it, doing it all your life. And if you put the food before the people all the time and try to help around the house, you'll be doing those things for the people wherever you go . . . You know, when you grow up, you got to learn sometime. You get most of those things out of the four days. As a woman. I mean most of those things you got to do as a mother.

From the perspective of this book, Lincoln's evaluation is based on one mode of Eurocentric-androcentric feminism. It is a feminism that assumes that any female role related to biology is *ipso facto* negative, and it is a feminism that values traditional male roles over female ones. What is missing is awareness that Diné culture is matrifocal; if any sex is oppressed—and I am not suggesting that it is—it is the male. That the ritual celebrates female birth and nurturing roles as the source of their power is dismissed because it is not a Western value. Hence, the corollary male role of warrior is posited as the only praiseworthy role. But could this value not be stood on its head? A Chiricahua male who as a youth participated in raids pointed out to me that females sent them out to raid and thereby risk their lives. One could argue that the Western idolizing of public power roles based on a warrior elite and the utter denigration of cross-culturally normative female roles simply confirms the patriarchal character of the West. Diné women have a choice of living a life expressing female or male power. Males do not have that choice; they cannot give birth nor nurse. So extremely patrifocal cultures can be seen as denying femaleness its sacred nature and power, relegating creation to a male deity and, as discussed in the next part of this chapter, attempting to steal birthing from females. Finally, because Christianity focuses on individual salvation, Western cultures tend to malign those many cultures that value community over individualism; the opposite is the case in Native American and many of the other traditions described in this study.

Ritual Roles

In all of the cultures examined, there is a complementarity of male and female ritual roles. An Inuit male is reported to have said: "It is a mistake to think that women are weaker than men in hunting pursuits. Home incantations are essential for success in hunting . . . Witchcraft [sic] binds up the animal, makes it wellminded."[9] In other words, the religious activities of the female, in a culture with extreme gender occupational specialization, are essential to the success of the primary male occupation.

In the Anishnabe gathering-hunting culture, at least in its contemporary form, females and males have both similar roles and complementary ones. For example, in the Midéwiwin rituals, males gather firewood and maintain the sacred fire, which burns continuously throughout the four-day ceremonies. Although males may carry heavy water containers to the women in the preparation arbor, women bring water into the Midéwiwin lodge and prepare the food for the ritual meals that are first offered to the spirits, and they pray over both. But highly respected males and females alike keep sacred water drums and carry sacred pipes.

In the agricultural Chinese empire, prior to the end of imperial rule in 1911, emperor and empress carried out most rituals as a pair, either together before the imperial tombs or simultaneously in different locations—in the outer and inner parts of the palace, respectively—for other sacrificial rituals. But the emperor sacrificed to the First Agriculturist and ploughed the first furrow of the agricultural year, and the empress sacrificed to the First Sericulturist and spun the first harvested silk of the year—ploughing considered a male role and spinning and weaving silk a female one. Of course, these symbolic connections broke down under peasant conditions, where everyone farmed, or industrial ones, with the development in China over two thousand years ago of a silk weaving industry, in which both sexes run industrial machines.

It is with regard to ecstatic religious functionaries that we find an interesting difference that may reflect both gender and sex differences: the overwhelming tendency for females to be mediums and males to be shamans, but not to the exclusion of either sex from either of these roles. Chinese historical texts suggest that most *wu* (most common word for medium in traditional Chinese literature) over the last several thousand years were female. As we have seen in the discussion of Korean religion, functioning as a medium is understood to be a female role; males who serve as mediums wear female garb during the rituals. In Japan, ecstatic functionaries tend to be female. Similarly, in African-Brazilian and African-Caribbean traditions, and apparently in Africa as a whole, most mediums are female. In Chinese culture today, there are far more female mediums than male ones. In contrast, in pre-contemporary Native American cultures, shamans who functioned publicly, as opposed to privately, tended to be male, particularly when shamanizing focused on raiding, defense, or hunting needs. From the standpoint of Native American democratized shamanism, however, females and males equally had shamanic abilities, and, given the modern socio-economic context, there are a large number of active female shamans.

There are two aspects to be considered here: cultural and neurological. From the cultural standpoint, it is plausible that spirit possession is linked to the development of horticulture. The earliest full possession may have been by ancestral spirits. All mediumistic cultures are, or were originally, economically based in horticulture/agriculture, politically based in clan-derived chieftainship/kingship, and ritually centered on sacrifices offered to ancestors. Horticulture leads to identification with particular locales: the relatively fixed gardens and villages. And it is only with the inception of horticulture that we seem to find ritual concern for the dead beyond the mourning period, however long that may be. With horticulture we tend to find reburial and sometimes moving the bones of the dead when the living shift to more fertile fields. A special relationship with a locale, one where the departed members of the clan are buried, could invite possession by the spirits of these ever present dead ancestors. Possession by the dead of the clan would cement a spiritual relationship between the living and dead members of the clan.

Horticultural societies, where the women garden and "own" the fields and clan, multi-family dwellings, are usually matrilineal and matrilocal. If spirit possession is linked to horticulture, then it would be expected that the possession was of the female clan leaders by the dead, both male and female, of the clan. For example, a Korean myth that seems to link mediumism with the introduction of wet-rice agriculture has been noted in Chapter 6. If this is the case, in Korea, mediumism then fused with the Siberian shamanism normative to Altaic language cultures. The connection of spirit possession with females may have continued as some of these cultures became patriarchal with the shift to agriculture and male farming, combined with the development of warrior elites in stratified societies.

This cultural memory, however, is insufficient in and of itself to explain the predilection for female mediums thousands of years after its inception. There may be biopsychological factors as well. Neurophysiological research, based on the most recent brain scanning devices, has established that female and male brains are structured differently. How these physical differences influence behavior has not, as yet, been determined, although the well-known comparative ease, in general, of language learning for females and comfort with spatial orientation for males is increasingly linked to differences in brain structure. Nonetheless, these findings coincide with the long-held Chinese, African, and other cultural understandings that male and female natures are different, a difference based not only on cultural determinants, but also on human nature in conjunction with the human body. This understanding of sexual differences, however, should not be confused with the Western understanding, particularly the Christian one, which posits values in regard to the differences.

The most reliable source for understanding the reasons for this gender predilection surely would be female mediums themselves. In the chapter on Candomblé, a source was quoted as follows: "The blood of the men is supposed to be 'hot,' and that is considered offensive to the gods for whom the women have been preparing themselves." The Mother of the Gods, Maria-José, spoke precisely on the differences between females and males with regard to possession, including the following statements from the longer quotation to be found in the preceding chapter (emphasis added):

> Masculine and feminine powers aren't the same. I don't mean one or the other is superior . . . Women aren't more intelligent than men, but it's true they understand more . . . From the beginning women are more open to trances—they have

fewer obstacles in their minds than men. I mean that their minds are always in harmony with their bodies . . . When they offer themselves to the gods they give themselves completely, more generously . . . I think that *women by their very nature, and by that I mean with their bodies,* possess the means for penetrating certain realities that men can only guess at . . . I believe that women are naturally more able to pass easily from one reality to another, to the other side of things. For that is their nature. Men are less malleable, less receptive, less open . . . That's why women make better mediums.

These statements, that men are "hot" and women more "receptive," are identical with statements made by Chinese mediums. In traditional Chinese cosmogony, humans receive their material form from *tiendi*—the male Sky and the female Earth—and their life-force from *yinyang*. Sky is bright and hot (sun), pulsing with aggressive energy (thunder and lightning), ethereal (air), and seminal liquid (rain); Earth is dark and cool (caves and ravines), tangible (soil), nourishing fluid (waters), and receptive (of the seminal rain). The female *yin* is dark, cool, yielding, and receptive; the male *yang* is bright, warm, assertive, and outgoing. A healthy human has both these energies in balance, but the balance is different for men and women. Females have more *yin*, and males have more *yang*, the proper proportions varying with each individual.

From a modern Western feminist perspective, it could be argued that this assumed nature of females was created by males to enhance their domination of females. However, Chinese females seem to have also understood themselves in this wise as well. As discussed in Chapter 4, Ban Zhao, the famed female scholar of two thousand years ago, understood *yin* and *yang* to exemplify the nature and appropriate behavior of females and males. The male mode of acting is to be forceful and unyielding; the female mode is to be gentle and yielding. This should not be understood as weakness. For Ban Zhao, by following the way (*dao*) of *yin*, a female fosters her natural power (*de*).

As discussed in Chapter 5, when I asked You Meiling, the Executive Secretary of the Chinese professional association of mediums, why she thought more females were mediums than men, she responded that females were *yin*. To function as a medium, one must be receptive to the entry of a spirit or deity into oneself and be willing to yield oneself to the control of this deity. This requires a *yin* nature, which females have more readily than males.

She, moreover, pointed out that, to function as a medium, one must be empathetic, and females are more empathetic than males, due to their nature. Mothering requires being in tune with another, and this innate ability renders females more readily empathetic than males. Nevertheless, males have a *yin* as well as a *yang* nature, and some males are very empathetic, as well as the reverse. That females are *yin* explains only why females are more *prone* to functioning as mediums; it does not mean that all females and no males have the requisite abilities.

Several years previous to my conversations with You, I had informal discussions with a group of female mediums in central Taiwan. With regard to differences between males and females in these respects, some felt there was absolutely no difference. Others felt that the greater proportion of female mediums was due to the present need for female qualities in the mediums; i.e., softer, more compassionate, more peaceful qualities. From a theoretical standpoint, all agreed that the spirit within (*ling*) was at basis without gender; the differences are due to the body. However, one did emphasize that women were the primary sex, because they give birth to men; without women, there would be no men (a statement virtually identical to that made by Papago women quoted in Chapter 9).

It is possible that this long-held Chinese understanding of the differences between the essential natures of females and males corresponds to the differences in brain structure. For the Chinese do not separate body and personality in their understanding of human nature as Christian culture does. Moreover, very recent genetic research confirms this Chinese understanding. The genes which apparently elicit an empathetic orientation are found on the "x"-chromosome received by females from their father; it is a gene or cluster of genes which males seem not to have.

This understanding equally explains why males are more prone to be shamans in many traditions, but again not exclusively so. For shamanic functioning seems to require, to a degree, a *yang* nature.

Shamanism is often involved with aggressive activities as war and hunting and deals with maleficent forces by attacking the perpetrating shaman (illness and accidents often understood to be caused by shamanic attack). Power contests between shamans are found in many shamanic cultures. When I was carrying out research on mediumism in Taiwan, I was introduced to a male head of a temple where mediumistic healing was practiced, although he himself is not a medium but heals through the power of his *ling* (spiritual essence/power). In the course of my visit, I intuited that he was contesting his *ling* against mine. I verbally warned him off when I discerned the attempt at spiritual domination, and thereafter he treated me as an equal. No female medium that I met engaged in this competitive behavior.

Female Self-Understanding

In all the cultures studied for this project, women in general have a strong sense of identity and self-worth as females. Certainly there would be some women who would prefer male roles, as we saw some males who preferred female roles. Even in cultures where women are suppressed or their roles are curtailed, such as in Brazil, those women who serve the spirits have a vital sense of meaning in their lives. Obviously, in matrifocal cultures, such as the Hopi, where the culture as a whole acknowledges the greater importance of females, there can be no question of the regard with which women hold themselves.

Particularly in cultures where menstruation is celebrated and the power of menstrual blood overtly acknowledged, women have a sure sense of their own power. Jacqui Lavalley, who coauthored the section on Anishnabe religion (see Chapter 8), has spoken of the strong feelings of self-worth and power she gained at her first menstruation ritual. From Marilyn Johnson, a contemporary Anishnabe urbanite (see Chapter 8) to Chona, living a traditional life in the 1930s (see Chapter 9), women speak of having an innate spiritual power that males must strive hard to attain. In Dené (northern Athapaskan) cultures, males acknowledge the superior spiritual power of females (see Chapter 10).

In Diné (southern Athapaskan) cultures, women at the menarche ritual become the major female deity; males have no such innate ability. Rather, males can don masks and represent, but not become, deities. So, too, in African traditions (see Chapter 11), only males wear masks to gain sacred power, because women have no need to do so. They inherently possess spiritual power and require no external apparatus for its manifestation. Indeed, it is the women who are understood to be the source of spiritual power for the masked dancers.

In the Luba culture of present-day Zaire in Central Africa, only women were considered to be sufficiently strong spiritually to contain and protect the spirits and sacred knowledge of kingship. On the death of a king, his spirit was incarnated into a female, and this woman inherited the former king's titles, dwelling, etc. He continued to be present when she was possessed by him. Throughout Central Africa, male kingship is based on and maintained by the spiritual power of females, a power which males lack.

That women have an innate spiritual power superior to those of males has been my own experience. The female shamans and mediums I have known enter trance immediately with no need for rituals; the male shamans and mediums I met all required some element of ritual preparation. Speaking for myself as a male, although at the time I had no conscious understanding of the preparation in which I was engaged coming from a non-shamanic culture, I was motivated from youth to spend time alone on remote mountains that were arduous to reach. Later I schooled myself in South Asian meditation techniques and underwent training in Japanese swordsmanship as a spiritual discipline. Finally, I was given the opportunity repeatedly to fast (vision quest) within Anishnabe culture. To enter a shamanic trance, I must go through a relatively complex ritual. Marilyn Johnson, an Anishnabe I have known since she first apprenticed as a shaman, has never needed to fast for this purpose, although she has fasted for other purposes since functioning as a shaman. She can enter trance without ritual preparation, though she does use rituals for a variety of purposes.

In addition to innate spiritual power, female ritual roles almost invariably include food preparation, extending from the female mammalian role in nursing infants and caring for the young. Although this is often interpreted in Christian cultures as relegating women to a subservient role, in other cultures it can be understood as a gender monopoly on a major aspect of rituals. For example, when I fasted within an Anishnabe traditional community, it was essential that I obtain the services of a female to prepare the ritual feast for the community on my completing the fast. Even in the Western tradition of Judaism, only a female can prepare the Sabbath meal, the major ritual which takes place within the home. This is the primary reason that traveling males were invited into people's homes for this ritual in traditional times, for they would have had no female with them to prepare the food and initiate the ritual with the lighting of the Sabbath candles.

One of the characteristics of all the cultures studied is that the concept of complementarity means that one sex does not infringe upon the spiritual prerogatives of the other. To do so would be to upset not just human relationships, but the harmony of the cosmos, of the world around one. In other words, to reject the complementarity of the sexes, where complementarity is understood, would be to invite disaster. Those cultures in which males have a mythic understanding of stealing their spiritual power from the females know that males have not stolen all of it. Rather they have stolen a part, so that there may be complementarity. I am aware of no such female myths because of the virtually universal understanding, except in Western cultures, that females have power by their very nature. They can afford to lose some to the males, so that the complementariness of spiritual powers can enhance the life of the community as a whole.

Finally, it is either explicit, or there are hints in the cultures studied, that women are one with the divine, with Earth. In at least some Anishnabe dialects, as discussed in Chapter 8, Earth and the human vagina share the same linguistic root; there is no corollary equivalency for males. In ancient Sumer, *ki* means Earth as in *an-ki* (Sky-Earth) and human femaleness as in *ki-sikil* ("woman"), while men are not equated with Sky—*lú* not *an* means "man." Other linkages include menstruation, as in Nāyar culture mentioned above, plant-animal food from Earth equated with nursing, common to many cultures, and so forth. In many cultures, females are simply closer to the divine than males. But in the Western tradition, it is the reverse in extremis; in traditional interpretations, only males are created in the image of God, as evidenced, for example, by the theological justification for the continued refusal of the Catholic Church to allow female priests.

COMPARATIVE SPIRITUALITY: WEST AND NON-WEST

A number of years ago, I presented a rudimentary version of this analysis to colleagues at the annual meeting of the Canadian Society for the Study of Religion. It was part of a panel I organized on comparative religion in which all the participants agreed to actually compare two or more traditions. When I finished my own presentation and it was time for questions and comments, one of the male panelists, a specialist on Islam and a friend of mine, stood up and, in an agitated, loud voice, said, "BUT YOU'RE WRONG, YOU'RE WRONG, YOU'RE WRONG!" There were few public comments, from males and females, all negative. Afterwards younger scholars came up to me and said how much they appreciated the analysis. None were willing to say this publicly. Many of you reading this will disagree with this section. I do not ask you to agree, only to read and perceive a possible comparative scenario.

In only one area of the world do we find a major divergence from the pattern described above. Spreading from the eastern Mediterranean two thousand years ago, a new conception of the numinous and a new pattern of interacting with the numinous had profound effects on culture and gender. Prior to approximately two and a half millennia ago, the kingdoms of Israel and Judah were polytheistic. In Solomon's temple a variety of deities were worshiped, including the deities of his wives. Among the populace, female as well as male divinities were the focus of offerings of divers sorts. We know of this only from archaeological remnants and the complaints of those "prophets" whose speech or ideas were recorded in the received version of the Hebrew Bible, but the very fact that these practices were railed against is clear evidence not only of their existence, but of their being common practices and understandings (see Chapter 3). For some reason around this time, the chief male divinity El came to be understood not as the king over all other divinities, or the only divinity for the Hebrews, but the only divinity to be worshiped: a single divinity with a single sex.[10] This divinity could not be approached directly but only through a patrilineally hereditary priesthood; hence, it is no wonder that mediums—female mediums—were condemned to death.

This change in the understanding of the numinous affected all aspects of life and perception. The cosmos was becoming different. Instead of all the directions being divine, only a single direction, above, was accorded divinity. The sky god was the single divinity, and the sky god's home was the single divine realm. God was in Heaven, and there was no counterbalancing, numinous Earth. Below had become the home of evil: Hell, the realm of the Devil, also male.[11] As male, at least the Devil was accorded spiritual powers, albeit they were inferior to the sky God's power. For some, God had a consort, the female Shechinah (Hebrew) or Sophia (Greek)—Wisdom—but she was only known to the practitioners of esoteric religious practices, predominantly male (at least according to the literature that has survived).

The lack of gender complementariness meant a fundamental change in the nature of dualism; all opposites were now understood as antagonistic and absolute: male vs. female, good vs. evil (presently understood as capitalism vs. communism, true religion vs. godlessness). Non-Western cultures tend not to have a concept of evil, other than recognizing the human tendency towards self-ishness, which, in the intrinsically communal societies discussed in the preceding chapters, was the epitome of antisocial behavior. Among Native Americans, those who were perceived to function shamanically for personal advantage were liable to be killed by their own relatives (to avoid vendettas). In classical Chinese philosophy, the opposite of the public weal, the determinative of the "good," is selfishness, natural, but undesirable, and to be eradicated through education. The concept of evil is different, for it requires the separation of humans from the rest of nature; the ability to choose between good and evil becomes the distinguishing characteristic of humans in Western theology.

In polytheistic religions, there tends to be no equivalent of the relationship between God and the Devil. The deities are morally neutral; although some may be capricious and a few dangerous, none are evil. For example, in China there is a concept of dangerous wandering ghosts (those dead who have no family to care for them or who died under anomalous circumstances—suicides, etc.). If they possess humans, they can cause illness or poor fortune, and an exorcist is needed to get rid of them. But sometimes they act beneficently and become deities. Temples are built for them in gratitude by those who have been aided by them. Some become nationally recognized divinities, as Mazu (see Chapter 5). Humans may elicit the aid of these neutral spirits to help or harm other humans, but it is then the human action which tends towards being approved (good) or disapproved (evil); that is, social or antisocial.

When there is but a single positive direction, as in the Western traditions (save for directing worship towards Jerusalem in Judaism and Mecca in Islam), so there is but one positive gender. If males, created in the image of God, are good, then females must be evil. And so the early Church Fathers, under misogynist inspiration, developed the unique notion of "original sin." Sin was committed by the first female and she infected all subsequent humans with her evilness. Only the male Son of God could redeem humans from the evilness of the female. A rudimentary notion of "original sin," and with it of hatred towards women, can be found at the root of Christianity. In the New Testament (First Timothy 2), we find the following statement:

> But I do not allow a woman to teach or exercise authority over a man, but to remain quiet. For it was Adam who was first created, [and] then Eve. And [it was] not Adam [who] was deceived, but the woman being quite deceived, fell into transgression. (NASB)

The notion of original sin is based on understanding a duality within humans. In the New Testament (Galatians 5), we find a dichotomy between spirit and flesh, the former being pure and the latter impure. This dichotomy within humans slowly became applied to the sexes. Males, being of the spirit according to late Hellenistic thought, are pure or good; females, being of the flesh, are impure or evil.

God, as generally depicted in the Hebrew Bible, is indubitably male. He is vengefully jealous, quick to anger, destructive in his wrathfulness, gambles with the lives and welfare of innocent human beings (Job), and bases his relationship with humans on contracts (covenants) with strict penalty clauses. While females, of course, are not free from these behaviors, they are the ones generally associated with males worldwide. All but missing are the usually acknowledged female attributes: compassion, kindness, gentleness, and succor. The New Testament, in a sense, sought to remedy this gap by introducing God's Son with these gentler traits. But his being male, there was still discomfort with the degree of his compassion. Hence, Mary, as the Mother of God, becomes for many Christians the favored intercessor with divinity. As a female spirit, she is approachable and accepting. It was hard for the male Church to divorce itself entirely from the female sex.

But as the Church constantly reiterates, Mary is not divine. Although in much of Europe, she has taken over the roles of the female earth and grain divinities, the Church has removed her from the female Earth and has had her taken bodily up into the male realm, Sky. Earth and females are understood to be equally evil; only by Mary's assumption into Heaven, removing her from the locus of evil, and by her virginity, removing her from the evil of flesh and female power, can she be perceived as an intercessor with divinity.

Although women were spiritual leaders in the earliest Christian churches, as were women in the early Diaspora Jewish synagogues and in the early development of Islam,[12] the misogynist view eventually dominated, and women were found to be too impure to serve as Christian priests. Only males could mediate between humans and God. Christian misogyny eventually infected Judaism and probably Islam. While there were noted women scholars in early Judaism, by the late medieval period in Europe, it became religious law that only males were to study Torah, the Word of God, the most important mode of interacting with divinity. Archaeology indicates that men and women worshiped in the early synagogues, although apart from each other as is the case in many religious traditions, but by late medieval times, women were placed outside of the main worship area, either on balconies or in side rooms. It is probably at this time that males began ritually to thank God for not being born a woman. Women were to remain in the home; the Torah study and ritual center, the synagogue, became a male realm. By this time too, of course, there were no longer any female religious leaders. This attitude towards female religious functionaries is virtually the opposite in almost all non-Western traditions.

The histories of Judaism, Christianity, and Islam are histories of taking from females the spiritual roles and spiritual natures they had prior to the full development of these traditions. Women were not passive in this monumental loss of power—many new Christian movements were founded by women—but in none of the mainstream modes of these traditions, until quite recently in some variants, have women achieved equal religious roles to those of males. Christian cultures further degraded women by attempting to remove every vestige of female spirituality and power, far beyond the attempts of Judaism and Islam.

As discussed in Chapters 2 and 7, among the Saami and the Aguaruna, the female activity of childbirth is paired with the male activity of warfare: both are dangerous, require spiritual power, and mark the epitome of gendered achievement with regard to social recognition. The same understanding is implied for other cultures. One confirming hint is that in many Native North American cultures, scalps were treated as babies. Brought back by male warriors, they were given to the women to nurture, as among the Hopi and Papago. Or war prisoners were given to women to choose for adoption or torture, according to their choice, as among Iroquoian-speaking cultures. For the Aztec civilization, texts modified by the Spanish have come down to us.[13] After a woman died in childbirth and her body was prepared for burial, she was carried on the back of her husband.

> The midwives and old women gather,
> They accompany her carrying shields, shouting war cries, beating their mouths with their hands and shouting.
> Shouting huzzahs to her, they are like the warriors following along.

She is buried before the images of the Cihuapipiltin, the Celestial Noblewomen. She herself becomes the deity Mocihuaquetzqui, as the midwives recite prayers to her. Warriors try to steal from her corpse some of her hair or a finger to place inside their shields to enhance their warrior power.

One of the signs of the extremes to which Western patriarchy has reached is that males virtually stole birthing from females. In the establishment of male physicians, who developed from barbers and their expertise with the razor in the late medieval period, women healers were forbidden to practice on pain of execution as witches. Many women healers, of course, were midwives. As physician guilds solidified in such institutions as the American and Canadian Medical Associations, physicians were able to gain government-supported monopolies. Those who practice outside the guilds, particularly female midwives, were until quite recently subject to arrest and incarceration.

This development enabled males to speak of "bringing babies into the world," even "to giving birth," statements I have heard made by male obstetricians. By the early twentieth century, when it was time for women in North America to give birth, they were drugged to semi-consciousness or even unconsciousness and placed in an unnatural position that rendered childbirth difficult and painful but was convenient for the male physician, who ripped the baby from the womb with forceps or induced labor. Male obstetricians, not wanting to interrupt their schedules, often prefer to cut the infant from the womb, rather than wait for nature to take its course. Babies, similar to cancerous growths, are surgically removed from females in numbers far beyond the statistical expectations of births so difficult that such operations would be medically advisable.

As the final reduction of female power, beginning in the Victorian period, the practice of bottle feeding of any substance other than human mother's milk was encouraged to remove even the nurturing function from women. Human milk was considered "dirty", "unsanitary," and breastfeeding "disgusting," "obscene." Until quite recently, women could be arrested and jailed if observed breastfeeding their infants; their babies were then taken from them, because having been jailed, they were deemed unfit mothers. As a standard practice, hospitals injected substances to stop the production of milk immediately after birth. Infants were removed from the presence of the mother after birth and kept separate, until brought in for brief, periodic feedings, bundled in layers of blankets. Skin-to-skin contact between mother and infant was not allowed, the normal human practice being deemed unsanitary. Those who insisted on breast-feeding were accordingly forced into circumstances that made successful breastfeeding most difficult.

Western males stole from women their sacred nature, their defining characteristic, the essence of their power; males made themselves birthers and "providers," the female relegated to cleaning the house, a task considered by society as a whole inferior and servile. One is reminded of the mythic stealing of the male power symbol, the sacred flutes, from the women of many Amazonian cultures. But in these cultures it was never forgotten that the males stole the only sacred power they had from the women, and the women kept the rest. It was necessary to steal that power to produce gender balance. In the West, the theft removed the last vestige of female power, all religious functions having been taken from women long before, with the establishment of the post-Augustinian Church and the assumption of Mary up to the male sacred realm. Durkheim was realistically reflecting his own culture when he assumed that females and religion were by definition mutually exclusionary (see Chapter 1). This extreme form of patriarchy is unique to western Christianity and those cultures it influenced, such as Orthodox Judaism, but to assume it a cultural universal is the epitome of ethnocentrism.

In comparison, it is instructive to look at East Asian versions of Christianity (not Christianity in East Asia). In the mid-nineteenth century, a Chinese Christianity, the Taiping movement, was founded by Hong Xiuqian; in the mid-twentieth century, a Korean Christianity, the Unification Church, was founded by Moon Sun-myung. Both share a number of similar understandings of Christianity, and both, in positing the second coming of Christ in a non-Caucasian, were, and continue to be, found anathema by normative Caucasian Christians.

Hong Xiuqian had a vision that, after learning the rudiments of Protestant Christianity, he understood to mean that he was the younger brother of Christ. In his visionary journeys to the Heavenly realm, he found himself part of a divine family. He met the Father, the Mother, Christ, and his Wife. Father, Son, and Holy Spirit were not a single deity, but individual spirits in a polytheistic milieu. His new religious movement rapidly spread in a period of dynastic collapse after the government lost several battles to Britain in its attempt to stop Britain from bringing opium into China. The movement succeeded in capturing the old capital of Nanjing, which Hung declared the New Jerusalem, marking the establishment of the Millennium, a reign of Heavenly Peace (the term and concept from a Chinese religio-political movement nearly two millennia previous). He carried out rituals with his wife, as did the Emperor and his spouse. He was the Sun (Great Yang), she the Moon (Great Yin).

Since mid-adolescence, Moon Sun-myung has had visions in which he met Jesus and many saints in Paradise. He understood Jesus to have been a failed messiah because he died before he had a chance to marry. Humankind had fallen because the original, perfect family was disrupted when Eve had intercourse with a serpent, Lucifer. This disruption can only be redeemed through the messianic creation of the perfect family, now realized through the union of Moon and his wife, called the Holy Mother (a term that goes back to the roots of Korean culture). Individuals become full members of the church by joining one another in a perfect marriage, determined and blessed by the original, perfect spouses. In forming a perfect marital union, Christ becomes the True

Parent who resurrects fallen humans by forming them into perfect marital couples. The mass marriages of couples brought together by Moon and offici-ated at by himself and his wife are well known, indeed, infamous.

In both cases, the theology is informed by ecstatic religious experiences and stresses divinity as a family. In the case of the Taiping movement, the Christian Trinity is replaced by a full, multi-generational holy family. In the Unification Church, the true Christ is a couple, male and female bringing to fulfillment God's intention for humans to live perfect lives as perfect couples. They thereby receive the Holy Spirit, repeatedly stressed as female in the Divine Principle, the equivalent of the Bible. Their children are automatically saved, for their marriage obviates the sin of Eve. Both modes of Christianity restore, albeit not completely, the female element lost in Western Christianity after the first few centuries.[14]

As discussed in Chapters 4 through 6, both Chinese and Korean cultures became patriarchal civilizations, the latter primarily through influence from the former. But a comparison between Christian European and East Asian Chris-tianity demonstrates that patriarchies are not all the same, although Western scholars tend to assume that an analysis of the development of patriarchy in the West is sufficient for an understanding of patriarchy in general.[15] In examining the history of Chinese religion with regard to sex and gender, we have seen how females slowly lost their power and prerogatives over a period of thousands of years, particularly in the last thousand years after major reformulations of the *rujia* (official ideology) tradition due, in part, to assimilation of Buddhist con-cepts. In contemporary times, what is holding back full sex equality in China is the conception of the patrilineal family as the basis of religion, and there are hints that this is slowly changing to a bilateral concept.

In the Western traditions, particularly Christianity, the ideological basis of patriarchy is not patrilineality, although this is present, but misogyny. Only Christianity, with the doctrine of "original sin," deems females to be the basis of fundamental evil.

Any situation, as in patriarchy, in which one sex rules another is undesirable from the standpoint of contemporary liberal values. But cross-culturally the sit-uation is complex, and simplistic ethnocentric assumptions can lead to mis-guided endeavors towards cultural imperialism. Only women within a culture can understand their own situation in their own culture's patriarchy, assuming in the first place that their culture is actually patriarchal. Western feminist mis-sionaries have at times only replaced Christian ones in seeking to "save" others for their own cultural perception of Paradise, or so I have been told by African, Chinese, Hindu, and Native American feminists. A major key to understanding the nature of patriarchy in a given culture is to examine the religious understanding of females and femaleness and then to observe the actual role of females in religious rituals, both gendered and non-gendered (confusing the two is one of the major factors in misunderstanding other religions). This, of course, is what this work has attempted partially to provide for those cultures fully discussed.

Similarly, it must also be recognized that many Western women do not find highly patriarchal situations undesirable. Many examples could be provided, but one needs but consider the present-day rapid growth of fundamentalist Protestant sects or the increasing shift, with smaller numbers of course, of Jewish women to ultra-orthodox modes to realize that some modern women seek out such religious situations as spiritually meaningful.

The discussion in this section has focused on the negative effects of monotheism on female spirituality, a cause and an effect earlier pointed out by leading feminist Christian theologians. But there is a complicating factor to this analysis: as discussed in Chapter 5, the original Buddhism of South Asia also evidences misogyny, albeit not to the degree found in Christianity. The more egalitarian Buddhism of East Asia (see Chapters 4-5) is probably due to Chinese influence, while the one hint of misogyny in Chinese religion almost certainly is due to South Asian Buddhist influence. Christianity and Buddhism share one common trait in their early development: an orientation towards celibacy by primarily male practitioners. In the New Testament (First Corinthians 7:1), we find celibacy the ideal, with marriage a necessary evil for those men who cannot control their desires: "Now concerning the things about which you wrote, it is good for a man not to touch a woman" (NASB).[16] Buddhism, of course, is based on male celibates (monks), while nuns were accepted into the tradition only with great reluctance and in a highly subordinate position to males, as are Christian nuns. None of the other religious traditions discussed in this book understood celibacy to have any spiritual value, save for the avoidance of sexual intercourse by female and male Native American shamans for four days prior to shamanizing. In these and many other cultures, sexual activity, aside from ritual intercourse, was also avoided during prolonged ceremonies; the placidity consequent on orgasm is probably inimical to attaining ecstatic states necessary for mediumistic and shamanic functioning.

Celibacy for spiritual purposes encourages the spiritual practice of focusing on the opposite sex as disgusting in order to void sexual desires. When practitioners find themselves straying from the celibate ideal either in practice or in imagination, there is a tendency to blame the opposite sex for their own lack of self-control. Hence, celibate practices for male-oriented religious traditions led to casting aspersions on female bodies as spiritual exercises to reinforce celibacy which, in turn over time, seems to have led to a misogynous orientation.

The above brief comparative discussion of Buddhism focuses on but one aspect, meditation practices surrounding celibacy. It does not typify, of course, Buddhism as a whole, since, as discussed earlier in this book, Buddhism theoretically and experientially in other practices, denies the ultimate reality of all non-enlightened understanding, including that of sex/gender.

A further factor, one that joins the early Buddhism of northern India and the Greek aspect of the Hellenistic-Semitic synthesis at the basis of Christianity, is the gender orientation of early Indo-European-speaking cultures. The Indo-European-speaking cultures that spread into the eastern Mediterranean, West Asia, central and northern Europe, and northern India around thirty-five hundred years ago, were herding cultures with a warrior aristocracy that introduced the war-chariot to the world—the war-chariot diffused into China one to two centuries later. The war-chariot is the first technological development that required a fully professional warrior class.

The war-chariot, invented long before the discovery of the yoke, required several horses to be controlled by individual reins, which demanded considerable strength and skill. Since the war-chariot was also a means for creating terror among an enemy, it was not simply a means for transporting warriors to a battlefield, but provided a platform for fighting at speed. As charioteer-warriors controlled the vehicle speeding on uneven terrain, other warriors fought with spears, halberds and bows from the unsprung, bucking platforms. Both activities required years of full-time training.

The early Indo-European deities were warrior deities, "city-destroyers." While there were female divinities as well, they seem not to have been equal in status or power to the male fighting deities. Nonetheless, on the cosmic plane, an earth mother was paired with a sky father. In cultures influenced by the Indo-European influx, as the Mesopotamian and Egyptian cultures were influenced by the Indo-European-speaking Hittites, male deities became even more powerful than female ones, and human females lost power to males. In contrast, the war-chariot alone diffused to China and seems not to have drastically altered the gender balance. It is only over three thousand years later, with the assimilation of aspects of Buddhism into the ideology of the elite (*rujia*), that we find the full development of Chinese patriarchy. (A corresponding shift in the Chinese depiction of female beauty takes place at this time—from robust ladies of the court playing polo to willowy, weak women.)

The above, of course, is most speculative, but it does provide the possibility of developing a tentative hypothesis. Perhaps a male-oriented monotheism combined with a predilection for male celibacy, influenced by a male-oriented cultural legacy from the earliest chariot-warriors, were the necessary elements for the extreme negative Christian orientation towards femaleness. Christian misogyny in turn introduced and/or heightened the misogyny in Judaism and Islam. No matrifocal tradition seems to teach male subordination, whereas some patrifocal traditions do teach female subordination, but all that do so seem to have been influenced by Buddhist, Christian, or Islamic misogyny. The unique acuteness of the patriarchy found in Christianity, when taken as a model, has led to gross misunderstandings of all other religions with regard to sex and gender.

TOWARDS A NON-EUROCENTRIC, NON-ANDROCENTRIC SCIENCE OF RELIGION

Western culture is so imbued with androcentrism that it is no simple matter to eradicate it from our thinking. As a case in point, when working on the chapters covering China in this book, I had already published several critiques of androcentrism in the study of Chinese religion. A book of mine attempting to revise a number of Western approaches to the study of Chinese religion, including sex and gender, had just been published. Yet, to my chagrin, a close reexamination of aspects on which I had already written indicated that I was still imbued with androcentric translations of Chinese religious terms and concepts from my graduate education. And when I reread my work of more than a decade ago, I shudder at some of the basic misrepresentations with regard to gender. Such androcentrism is not necessarily deliberate, it is imbibed with the basic study of any culture within our Eurocentric intellectual traditions, and it affects females and males equally.

On the Perversity of Androcentric Translations of Religious Terms

For devout Christian observers, the object of worship of a people they admire must be God, and, in the normative Christian understanding, God is a singular, anthropomorphic, male, supreme being: God the Father, God the King of Kings, God who gave His only Son, etc. Accordingly, when in the sixteenth to eighteenth centuries, Jesuit missionaries observed the Chinese emperor sacrificing to *tien* (Sky), they assumed that he was making the offering to an elementary notion of God, a God similar to that of Israelite religion prior to the inception of Christianity. The Jesuits promoted a favorable picture of China as a kingdom governed by philosophers, with a proto-monotheistic religion ripe for the Christian message. So as to differentiate their religion from that of the

Chinese, they termed their God in Chinese, *tienzhu* (Ruler of Sky). Later, Protestant missionaries, in translating the Bible, latched on to an earlier Chinese term for the object of sacrifices and used the archaic term, *shangdi*, as their translation for God.

Sinologists, who should have known better, took these translations as some kind of revealed truth and translated Chinese texts with these Christianized interpretations. Even a superb historical linguist and expert on Chinese etymology such as Bernhard Karlgren translated *shangdi*, and *di* alone, as God, although he knew that Chinese religion was very different from Christianity. Writers of world-religions textbooks, who knew of Chinese religion only from these translations, perhaps can be forgiven for finding what they called Confucianism to be a religion centered on a male, monotheistic deity. This finding allowed for the creation of grand schemes of a primordial monotheistic religion.

Four centuries of a Eurocentric interpretation of religion in China is hard to overcome. The realization that I was still using androcentric translations of Chinese religious terms allowed me to understand why my colleagues at my university, those who were not sinologists, could not understand my insisting that Chinese religion, at least the supposed "high religion" of "Confucianism," was not primarily oriented towards a male, monotheistic God, and that Chinese polytheism, particularly the worship of female deities, was not due to the ignorance of the uneducated masses.

Based on my research for Chapter 4, I was led to creating revisionist retranslations of those Chinese terms used for God and equivalents in virtually all translations into English, as well as these terms in compounds of religious import, and the term used for one particular female deity. Rather than the now usual focus on etymology and earliest usage in protohistoric divinatory fragments, whose interpretations are invariably quite controversial (e.g., is the glyph used actually referring to a person's name, the name of a place, etc.?), the procedure of analysis utilized is ethnolinguistics, borrowed from the study of nonliterate language traditions.

Although the following analysis solely concerns China, this is simply because Chinese is the only language for which I have translation competence. It is but meant to illustrate the point that translations into Western languages of terms of significant religious import have been seriously compromised by androcentric scholarship, that similar translations in all religious traditions need to be carefully reconsidered.

Tiendi

The Jesuits approvingly observed that the Chinese emperor sacrificed at the altar to the male Tien ("Sky"—normally translated as "Heaven"), but disapproved of his sacrificing at the altar to the female Di, "Earth." Over the course of Chinese history, the altars were more often a single joint one rather than separate. But in the late Ming dynasty, when the Jesuits arrived on the scene, the government had devised a grand array of altars in its new capital of Beijing, with altars to Tien, Di (to be distinguished from the altar to Soil and Grain), Sun, and Moon, respectively in the southern, northern, eastern, and western parts of the city. We know from the writings of Chinese critics of the Jesuits that the Jesuits castigated the Chinese for sacrificing to Earth; the Chinese understood that the Jesuits objected because Earth was female (see Chapter 1).

The emperor, with the empress, was not sacrificing to Tien alone but to the paired couple, Tiendi, "Sky and Earth." By the time of the first major Chinese empire, the Han dynasty, twenty-two hundred years ago, humans were understood to receive their material bodies from the cosmic pairing of Sky and Earth and their life-force from the pairing of the complementary, oppositional energies, Yin and Yang. The sacrifice to Tiendi was begun at this time, Di at first termed, in this regard, Houtu (Empress of Earth). This sacrifice was the prerogative of the emperor; for anyone else to carry it out was treason. Lesser rulers could sacrifice at an Altar of Soil and Grain.

Why did the Jesuits understand Tien as "Heaven" rather than "Sky" (the French *ciel* actually maintains the same ambiguity as the Chinese *tien*). Heaven is the abode of God; the Jesuits could interpret a sacrifice to Tien as a sacrifice to God and subtly shift the meaning of the term in their writings from "that which is above humans" to God himself. The opposite of Heaven in Christian thinking is not Earth, but Hell. Obviously, if the Jesuits were to promote China as a model civilization ready for the Christian message in order to ensure continued European support for the Jesuit mission, they wanted no mention of Chinese sacrifices to Hell. The fact that Earth was understood to be a numinous female cosmic force merely accentuated its hellish characteristics to these misogynist monks.

Thus begins the tradition that the Chinese sacrifice to Tien, a singular male deity. To obscure the equality of Earth in the compound Tiendi, most translations, even by feminist writers, capitalize the "H" in Heaven but not the "e" in Earth. Clearly, in the Western mind, only the male part can be a deity. I would suggest that "Sky and Earth" is a far more accurate translation than "Heaven and earth," as it more clearly delineates an equal bilateral split of the cosmos into a complementary pair and pairing.

Tienming

The most frequent objection I received to the above analysis, on which I have previously published in more detail, is that only Tien is mentioned in the compound *tienming*, almost always translated as the "Mandate of Heaven" in texts of political philosophy and the "Will of Heaven" elsewhere. These translations engender the notion that an anthropomorphic Heaven is causing historical events to occur and controls individual lives. Such understanding comes not from the texts or the Chinese term *per se*, but from the translations alone, which posit a Chinese deity similar to Yahweh of the Hebrew Bible.

Either term of this compound can be found alone standing for the compound; that the single word refers to the compound can be known from the context. *Ming* is still in use today as it was at the time of Kongfuzi (Confucius), as found in the older parts of the *Analects*. It simply means "fate." There is not an iota of evidence to indicate that Tien was ever understood anthropomorphically. There is, however, a virtually identical expression in English: "It is in the stars."

While *ming* means "command" when given by a ruler, it means "order" in the sense of "patterned order" when attached to Tien. Tienming means "Celestial Pattern" and relates to our concept of astrology. It is the ordering or pattern of moon, stars, and planets in the night sky and the sun in the day sky, and scholars of very early Chinese civilization have recently suggested that Tienming referred to particular conjunctions of the observable planets. In China, as elsewhere in the world, these patterns were understood to indicate destiny. When Kongfuzi bemoans his fate, he is referring to the celestial pattern, not a male deity willfully frustrating his ambitions. When a dynasty falls because of Tienming, it is not because a white-bearded supreme being so ordered it, as appears in world-religions texts, but because it failed to conform to the proper pattern of government and so lost its place in the destined order of affairs. To discover this order is why Chinese astronomy-astrology became so advanced at that time and why the Jesuits were later given positions in the Bureau of Astronomy/Astrology, since they brought Western astronomy to be added to Chinese astronomy.

Tienzi

The third term in which Western interpreters find a male anthropomorphic deity is *tienzi*, referring to a king and later emperor, always translated as "Son of Heaven," and, in effect, equating Chinese kingship with the then current notion in Europe of the divine right of kings. Divine right is not a Chinese notion; indeed, the Chinese theory of kingship in the *rujia* tradition was the opposite. This opposite ideology, of enlightened government in the hands of philosopher-officials, was its major appeal to the Jesuits, whose *Relations* from China influenced Voltaire and Leibnitz, among others. They in turn influenced Thomas Jefferson, as well as the instigators of the French Revolution.

To understand the Chinese concept, first we must understand that at least from the Han dynasty on, when the grand theories were created, the rulership of the world, China being understood as the entirety of the civilized world, was in the hands of a couple. Emperor and empress together had to carry out the sacrifices that were the prerogative and justification of imperial reign. Language fails here, for we have no term in English for a ruling couple. As the emperor represents the sun and Yang power (both the emperor and the sun are called the Great Yang—*taiyang*), so the empress represents the moon and Yin power (both the empress and the moon are called the Great Yin—*taiyin*). Hence, *tienzi* means "Sky's Child/Son," or, if a pun can be pardoned, "Sky's Sun." "Child of Sky" or "Son of Sky" presents a far more accurate statement of Chinese ideology than does "Son of Heaven," for Sky denotes half the couple, Sky-Earth, with the patrilineal, male aspect emphasized and the female part implied.

Shangdi

Shangdi or Di alone (different word from *di* meaning Earth) is a more problematic term. During the Shang dynasty, over three thousand years ago, when we have only enigmatic, fragmentary texts, the terms designated recipients of major sacrifices. Early nineteenth-century Protestant translators latched onto the term as their translation for God. Translators then read the missionaries' use of the term back into their own translations, rendering one or both as God. Since the object of sacrificial offerings must be God, this was considered an appropriate translation, ignoring the fact that Chinese culture is not monotheistic. Subsequently, since reputable scholars translated Shangdi and Di as God, writers of world-religions textbooks could comfortably state that in very early China, worship was directed towards a single male deity.

Fifteen years ago, I argued that the Di should be translated as nonanthropomorphic "Power" and Shangdi as "Supreme Power," *shang* meaning "that which is above," both in the physical and hierarchical sense. Robert Eno has since plausibly argued that the terms refers to the collective of ancestral spirits.[17] My own research confirms this interpretation.

According to the *Liji* (Record of Rituals), the Han dynasty manual of elite rituals that became part of the Classics, humans developed cooking and clothing in order to better serve the *gueishen shangdi*. China, typical of shamanistic cultures, as very early China was, understood humans to have two souls. In shamanism, a concept of two souls explains how one can travel in spirit leaving the body without the death of the body: one soul travels and one remains giving life to the body. Upon death, these souls become the *guei*, which resides with the corpse in the earth, and the *shen*, which ascends to join the collective of ancestors, to which *shangdi* probably refers. As the *shen* rose above and became the "bright spirits" (*ming shen*) which descended to possess the Incorporator of the Dead (*shi*) at the time of sacrifice (or the sacrifice was understand to ascend to *shen* in the sky in an earlier period), it would make sense that *shangdi* was a generic term for the ancestral spirits above. Hence, Shangdi should be translated "Power Above," assuming it must be translated at all. With regard to gender, it should be noted that the ancestral spirits equally include males and females (the women married into the patrilineal clans).

The above argument is supported by the later use of the same term, *di*, to replace *wang* (king) for the ruler of an empire, usually translated as "emperor." Di, as "emperor," is the equivalent of *tienzi*, "Son of Sky," meaning king or emperor, if it too referred to the imperial couple as the representative of all the ancestral spirits in their totality.

Xiwangmu

Aside from the ancestral spirits, Xiwangmu was the most important deity in Chinese religion during the Han dynasty (from twenty-two hundred to eighteen hundred years ago) and for several centuries thereafter. If we break down her title into its components, we have *xi* meaning "west," *wang* meaning "king," and *mu* meaning "mother." The middle term cannot mean "queen," for the Chinese term for "queen" as well as "empress" is *hou*. (For example, the deity Mazu has the title Tienhou—"Queen of Heaven"—among other titles [see Chapter 5].) So why is her title always translated as "Queen Mother of the West"? She was known well before the Han dynasty, but to continue the balance so important in Han ideology, there was added Dungwangfu, "King Father of the East." In Western values, when there is both a king and queen, they are not considered to be of equal power. The standard English incorrect translation automatically reduces Xiwangmu's power in comparison to that of the King Father of the East, yet the opposite is the case in actuality. Here we have a clear example of Eurocentric-androcentric values, whether conscious or not, belittling the importance of a female Chinese deity.

I decided to translate the term literally: King Mother of the West. *Wang* is a term for a male ruler; what right do we have to abrogate her holding a male title? In Chinese ideology, the male and female principles are equal, but in the socio-political realm, wives are to defer to husbands as ministers are to rulers. In the realm of deities, Xiwangmu is supreme; she defers to no one. Dungwangfu is at best her equal; he is not her sovereign. During the few times women were emperors in China, they held the male title of Emperor, not that

of Empress. I do not accept the objection from some of my sinological colleagues that the Chinese really meant *hou* rather than *wang*, and, because she
is female, we must translate her name with "Queen."

Conclusions

In conclusion, the Western understanding of Chinese religion is based on a
few shibboleths of Christian missionaries in China, all initially deliberate
mistranslations. The Jesuits translated *sanjiao*, "Three Doctrines," as "Three
Religions," so that they could carry on a missionary policy of converting those
who continued to practice normative Chinese religion. By ignoring Chinese
religion *per se*, they unsuccessfully attempted to avoid the criticism by Francis-
can and Dominican missionaries who knew better. The concept of Three Religions required the invention of "Confucianism," leading to endless debates as
to whether this fictitious religion is a religion. By extracting Sky from the compound Sky-Earth and calling it "Heaven" or translating Shangdi as "God,"
Christian missionaries determined that Chinese religion focused on a male
quasi-monotheistic deity, conveniently ignoring the female aspects of both
terms. These missionaries could then claim that ordinary Chinese perverted
Chinese religion by presenting offerings to their heathenish ancestral spirits,
again conveniently ignoring the fact that so did the emperor and empress and
everyone else.

These few missionary conventions were adopted by sinologists often but not
necessarily with a different understanding. How, then, could non-specialists not
utterly misconstrue Chinese religion? This process is hardly unique to the study
of Chinese religion. I could demonstrate almost exactly the same for Native
American traditions, particularly the religions of the Meso-American and
Andean civilizations, saving that the missionaries were not seeking to present
these traditions in a positive light. And, I am certain, this process is relevant to
the study of all non-Western religious traditions (feminist scholars have pointed
to similar problems in translating the Hebrew Bible[18]).

Chinese philosophy early developed a concept called *zhengming*, the "rectification of names." The concept assumes that we cannot know anything accurately unless we are precise about nomenclature. Perhaps we could apply this
concept to the comparative study of religion. If I have learned anything from
the realization of my own errors in these regards, it is to take seriously the feminist theological position of the "hermeneutics of suspicion." As scholars of religion, we no longer can take anything for granted, especially translations of
meaning-laden terms.

The Hermeneutics of Suspicion

Although I had carried out preliminary studies of many of the cultures covered in this work, I was continually surprised by what I found. For example, I was completely unaware, at least in my conscious thinking, of the crucial parallel roles of elite women in early and continuing Chinese rituals. Yet I had read these same texts many years before when I was a student. Again, I was unaware of the dual religio-political roles of male and female rulers in the African kingdoms. Those who read secondary and tertiary sources on the religions of other cultures have no means of knowing whether or not what they are reading has any connection to the actualities of the cultures examined. From the preceding, I trust it is clear that no statements concerning non-Western religion, particularly if they involve sex or gender, should be accepted without critical reflection. And I am not exempting my own writings.

There are a number of factors that lead to grossly misleading androcentric projections about the religions of other cultures. As outlined in the Introduction, one important cause is the history of religious studies in and of itself. By defining religion, whether explicitly or implicitly, as a male activity, the discipline has *ipso facto* doomed itself to significant distortions. Many of the early Western depictions of non-Western religions were written by missionaries, and this fact has imbued comparative religion with either Christian interpretations on non-Christian cultures from a positive perspective or manipulations to put traditions in the worst light for Westerners from a negative perspective. Historians of religions often rely on ethnology for their understanding of non-literate traditions without realizing that these reports can be of varying reliability. For example, when I carried out my research on the Native American "sacred pipe," part of my work involved going through museum archives. There I discovered from letters sent back from the "field" to the museums that some of the eminent early ethnologists often spent but a few weeks at most studying a culture, residing at the nearest comfortable hotel which could be hours away from the community they were researching. Informants were often Christian converts, because they could speak English, and almost always were male. These scholars then returned to their museums to write massive tomes on the "studied" culture, including its religion. A substantial portion of the material in the data banks much loved by some feminist social scientists is taken from these studies.

Not only can we not automatically accept established writings on the various religious traditions or the material placed in data banks by scholars from androcentric cultures, but we must exercise the same critical approach to the works of those writing from within, or claiming to be within, traditions. Most of the Africans who have written on African religions are Christian clergy. Until very recently, many Native Americans who wrote on Native traditions (with a few important exceptions) were the product of the Christian controlled boarding schools mentioned above. The most frequently read books on Native religions, *Black Elk Speaks* and *The Sacred Pipe,* are by a Lakota Holy Man, Black Elk. He was born prior to the domination of his tradition by Euroamerican culture but became a Catholic catechist, and, as he related to his nephew Fools Crow, deliberately sought to meld the two traditions together. Only in the last few years has it been acknowledged by specialists on Native American religions that Black Elk's two works are Roman Catholic reads on Lakota religion, although they are authentic and powerful representations of that synthesis. It is hardly remarkable that some of the most androcentric depictions of various traditions are based on these types of sources.

Aside from the problem of internal presentations of non-Western religious traditions written to varying degrees from Eurocentric perspectives, we have accepted ethnologists writing fiction that is taken by many to be ethnographic descriptions, perhaps the most notorious being Carlos Castaneda. There are also works by those implying that they are Natives who apparently are not; for example, Jamake Highwater. And then there are those making no such claims, but writing fiction that is accepted as actual Native experience, such as Lynne Andrews. Yet the reaction to these false depictions has been equally ludicrous. In North America, it is now "politically correct" to assume that cultural knowledge for Native Americans comes from DNA structure rather than upbringing. Some of the most bizarre works on Native American religions have been written by Natives who have had no experience with traditional Native religions or perhaps have but spent a weekend at an Elder's Conference held at a university.

Even contemporary works by recognized female scholars can virtually ignore women. An introduction to Chinese religion published in the mid-1990s by a well-known Christian, female, Chinese sinologist reserves a chapter for women totalling three pages! First, one could ask why female aspects of religion should be separated out so that they are perceived as minor or adjunct. Secondly, three pages out of an entire book presents the clear message that female spirituality in China is virtually non-existent and most unimportant. Accordingly, the author is stating, whether deliberately or not, that Chinese religion is a male activity. Of course, most religious-studies books written today still totally ignore the "second sex."

I trust that the variety and extent of traditions covered in this work are seen to be representative of human culture in general and that in all of these cultures—none was originally picked with the prior assumption that female spirituality was of particular importance given the received literature—female spirituality is pervasive and significant. Hence, religious studies has to start over again. The vast majority of studies of traditions other than Western, and even of the past of Western traditions, has by design excluded half the population, half the rituals, half the ritual roles, and (for the non-monotheistic cultures) often half the deities and spirits, and so patchwork remedies will not do. For comparative religion (history of religions) to be a credible science and to provide tenable results, virtually all traditions must be restudied with conscious attention to sex and gender and without privileging one sex over another.

Epilogue:
Through the Earth Darkly

I N THE LONG JOURNEY that was the creation of this book, I learned much, met many wonderful people, and gained a glimmer of what it means to be human. For in all the cultures studied and lands traveled, in spite of many differences, there was much commonality. What I came to understand is very simple.

Male or female, we begin our life's journey the same way, exiting through a long, dark passage into the light. But as the years pass, we differ. Females replicate the mother who gave them birth and can themselves give birth. Women are one with Earth: from clefts in their bodies, both bring forth life; with fluid from their bodies, both nurture life. And women are one with Moon, their bodies flowing in rhythm with her.

Men are but necessary for a moment; their life-giving power is fleeting, as a flash of lightning from Thunder, or potentially harsh, as Sun. Men can protect— or destroy. Their power is hard-earned; it is not innate as it is for women. And without women, their power has no meaning, for men participate in the miracle of life only by association. It is within woman's narrow, dark, warm, moist crevice that males encounter life's essence.

Women understand Earth from the very nature of their lives. Men must realize Earth indirectly: from the beat of the drum, Earth's heartbeat; from visions of Her manifestations; from the food and water She provides; and, most importantly, from women, their mothers, grandmothers, sisters, and wives.

By the bank of Bear Creek there is a cave, a dark hole in the Mother beside flowing water, Her outpouring blood. Entering the cave's quiet, still darkness, we intimately encounter Her essence.

266

AFTERWORD

by Catherine Keller

Through the Earth Darkly offers tantalizing glimpses into a dense and teeming underbrush covering much of the cultural surface of our planet, a life repeating within itself ancient memories of women's spiritual creativity, a life insistent in its present dignity. Much of it having been overgrown by the more aggressive species of androcentric religion, it has lain somewhat hidden to view, some of it already suffocated, some of it alive but stunted, some of it thriving but somehow imperceptible to the eyes of Western observers. Of course feminists interested in religion have already learned to perceive this layer of female spirituality, to clear away the obstacles from this or that patch; and we imagine what might have been when perception of what is proves too disappointing. But we are at the beginning of this work, and all that had constructed women's religious life as dangerous or inferior, invisible or trivial, still works within the tools feminists have available for the task.

So we may be grateful for the labor of Professor Jordan Paper on behalf of women's spirituality. He provides a resource rich in data, reflecting in its carefully sifted materials the teeming complexity he brings to light. Among the various texts and anthologies becoming available for comparative study of women's spiritualities, this one may be the broadest and most integrated to date. Professor Paper wisely does not attempt a feminist or gender analysis of the data, at least not in any developed sense. But he has let himself be guided by the desires and the needs of feminism, doing us the service of providing wonderfully useable narratives. Thus many gems emerge: I had not known that the Semitic *qadishtu*, "holy women," would rarely have signified religious prostitutes; that a Confucian such as Ban Zhao considered striking a wife grounds for her to get a divorce; that Mescalero women become divine.

Professor Paper wished for my comments as a feminist working in the context of the monotheistic traditions, indeed as a Christian theologian. Very well.

267

I acknowledge much validity in his polemical assessment of the monotheistic patriarchies and their secular Western heirs: these have indeed provided the most globally consistent elimination of female divine presence and of the kind of mirroring it might provide the life of women. I am not as convinced that in terms of social standing, family powers, and cultural creativity, the Jewish, Christian, and even Muslim traditions come off worse than any of the other great patriarchal traditions—like the Chinese religions in which he and Li Chuang Paper are expert. But I am persuaded that the indigenous spiritualities of North America and perhaps of Africa do recollect gendered arrangements of spirit and society so radically different from the "great world religions," that any facile equation of their constructions of gender complementarity with sexism may say more about our colonialism than our feminism. So I am not sure the important dividing line lies between monotheism and polytheism.

Certainly monotheism reduces the options of gender modelling to masculinity within male-dominant societies; but the presence of earth femininity, even when inseparable from sky-masculinity, for instance, seems only to have cultivated a more balanced and harmonious patriarchy. This is no more to dismiss the patriarchal polytheisms than their monotheistic Western analogues. The Western imperial projects have proven more successful in their aggressions, and they require the special deconstructive efforts of men and women who are their immediate heirs. But of course the work of feminists within the Western patriarchal traditions increasingly exposes a rich underbrush of vital, resistant female spirituality quite analogous to that of the present book. The prophetic monotheistic impulse toward social justice provides a driving force, however unacknowledged, in all work for women's freedom and dignity. Moreover, Christianity according even to such a neo-orthodox proponent as Jürgen Moltmann is not a monotheism: its trinity (the two guys and the bird) of three individual and distinct "persons" enabled its mission to flourish on polytheistic soil.

So I would want to tease out of Christian texts and practices not only the closeted and feathered femininity of the Spirit, but the femaleness of Hochma/Sophia and the Shekinah as well. Yet not because any or all of these would be "enough"—far from it. Yet if for the first time a critical mass of Christian thinkers began to take the trinitarian logic seriously, breaking it out of its literalist three-hood and applying its model of relational interdependence to all of reality, that very logic of pluralization, relation, and complexity would demand more honest encounters with the so-called polytheisms. The latter would no longer seem so dangerously or irrelevantly different: their difference can invite and mime our own internal differences, luring into awareness all that femininity and diversity which has been warped, ground under, tormented, and trivial-ized within our own traditions. Then we would not collude further in the translation of alternative into homogeneity: for instance, as Professor Paper has shown so definitively, in the reduction of colonized traditions into modes of monotheism (such as "Confucianism" or "Great Spirit") as a way of making them worthy of appropriation. Such condescending simplifications become unnecessary when we free ourselves of the illusory unities of our own monotheisms and monisms. Rather than merely rejecting these traditions in which we may find ourselves deeply rooted, we may then learn the spiritual disciplines of complexity (and perhaps the new sciences of chaos and complexity must lead the way against both cultural and naturalist reductionisms). Because I think we had best take responsibility for the transformation of whatever we can call our "own," I do not advocate mere—simple—delegitimation of Western traditions in favor of more exotic ones, which will in the long run not sustain our altogether Western fantasies of escape. Yet at the same time I am aware that much work of the sort Professor Paper has done so conscientiously, also gets dismissed far too conveniently (by feminists and other scholars) as "romanticizing" or as "expropriation of the other." I fear that his own idealization of femininity as maternity in his Epilogue, where he shifts from descriptive to normative discourse, may invite just such a response. To root ourselves as best we can in the shifting postmodern sands of our own places, communities, traditions, and ancestries does not mean just another excuse for Western hegemony. On the contrary, it means finding enough ground beneath our feet, enough earth between our toes, to engage in self-altering but not self-abdicating exchanges with that which appears first as alien, as minimal, or as merely and sheerly other. In the process, we practice, and are taught by Jordan Paper in our practice, what he takes from early Chinese philosophy, *zhengming,* "the rectification of names." To heal our Academic naming habits, habits of patronizing patronymics, of female anonymity, and even of feminist name-calling, we must listen deeply to such voices as name themselves in this text.

NOTES

Prologue: A Personal Journey

1. Jordan Paper, *The "Fu-tzu": A Post-Han Confucian Text*, T'oung Pao Monographie XIII (Leiden: E. J. Brill, 1987); "Fu Hsüan as Poet: A Man of His Season," in *Wen-lin*, Vol. 2, ed. Tse-Tsung Chow (Hong Kong: Chinese University of Hong Kong Press, 1989): 45–60—both actually written in the late 1960s.

2. E.g., Jordan Paper, "Religious Studies: Time to Move From A Eurocentric Bias?", in *Religious Studies: Issues, Prospects and Proposals*, ed. Klaus K. Klostermaier and Larry W. Hurtado (Atlanta: Scholars Press, 1991): 73–84; "Religious Transformations and Socio-Political Change: A Western Eurocentric Paradigm?" in *Religious Transformations and Socio-Political Change: Eastern Europe and Latin America*, ed. Luther H. Martin (Berlin: Walter de Gruyter, 1993): 61–72; and "Religions in Contact: The Effects of Domination from a Comparative Perspective," in *Religions in Contact*, ed. Iva Dolezalová, Bretislav Horyna, and Dalibor Papoušek (Brno: Czech Society for the Study of Religion, 1996): 39–56.

3. See Jordan Paper and Li Chuang Paper, "Matrifocal Rituals in Patrilineal Chinese Religion: The Variability of Patriarchality," *International Journal of Comparative Religion and Philosophy* 1/2 (1995): 27–39.

4. Jordan Paper, "The Post-contact Origin of An American Indian High God: The Suppression of Feminine Spirituality," *American Indian Quarterly* 7/4 (1983): 1–24; "The Persistence of Female Spirits in Patriarchal China," *Journal of Feminist Studies in Religion* 6 (1990): 25–40; "Through The Earth Darkly: The Female Deity in Native American Religions," in *Religion in Native North America*, ed. Christopher Vecsey (Moscow, Idaho: University of Idaho Press, 1990): 3–19; "Slighted Grandmothers: The Need for Increased Research on Female Spirits and Spirituality in Native American Religions," *Annual Review of Women in World Religions* III, ed. Arvind Sharma and Katherine K. Young (Albany: State University of New York Press): 88–106; "Comparative Cosmology and the Concepts of Good and Evil, Male and Female," *Explorations* 8 (1990): 17–28.

Chapter 1
Introduction

1. Rosemary Radford Ruether, *Sexism and God-talk: Toward a Feminist Theology* (Boston: Beacon Press, 1983): 18.

2. *Jesuit Relations* as cited in Eleanor Leacock, "Women's Status in Egalitarian Society: Implications for Social Evolution," *Current Anthropology* 19 (1978): 247–276/249. Paul B. Steinmetz, "The Sacred Pipe in American Indian Religions," *American Indian Culture and Research Journal* 8/3 (1984): 27–80/30; for the counter position, see Jordan Paper, *Offering Smoke: The Sacred Pipe and Native American Religion* (Moscow, Idaho: University of Idaho Press, 1988): 37–38.

3. In Jacques Gernet, *China and the Christian Impact*, trans. Janet Lloyd (Cambridge: Cambridge University Press, 1985): 25, 205, 199.

4. W. E. Soothill, *The Three Religions of China* (London: Hodder & Stoughton, 1913): 146 (emphasis added).

5. Theresa Kelleher, "Confucianism," in *Women in World Religions*, ed. Arvind Sharma (Albany: State University of New York Press, 1987).

6. E.g., Raffaele Pettazoni, *The All Knowing God* (London: Methuen & Co., 1956): 435. See the counter-position in Åke Hultkrantz, "North American Indian Religions in a Circumpolar Perspective," in *North American Indian Studies, European Contributions*, ed. P. Hovens (Göttingen: Edition Herodot, 1981).

7. Sam D. Gill, *Mother Earth* (Chicago: University of Chicago Press, 1987).

8. Gene Weltfish, *The Lost Universe, The Way of Life of the Pawnee* (New York: Basic Books, 1965).

9. Thomas Buckley, "Menstruation and the Power of Yurok Women: Methods in Cultural Reconstruction," *American Ethnologist* 9,1 (1982): 47–60.

10. Christine Hugh-Jones, *From the Milk River: Spiritual and Temporal Processes in Northern Amazonia* (Cambridge: Cambridge University Press, 1979); Stephen Hugh-Jones, *The Palm and the Pleiades: Initiation and Cosmology in Northern Amazonia* (Cambridge: Cambridge University Press, 1979).

11. Eleanor Leacock, *Myths of Male Dominance, Collected Articles on Women Cross-Culturally* (New York: Monthly Review Press, 1981).

12. Irene Silverblatt, *Moon, Sun, and Witches: Gender Ideologies and Class in Inca and Colonial Peru* (Princeton: Princeton University Press, 1987).

13. Marla Powers, *Oglala Women: Myth, Ritual and Reality* (Chicago: University of Chicago Press, 1986).

14. Émile Durkheim, *Les formes elementaires de la vie religieuse: le systeme totemique en Australia* (Paris: F. Alcan, 1912).

15. W. Lloyd Warner, *A Black Civilization: A Study of an Australian Tribe* (New York: Harper, 1937).

16. A. P. Elkin, *Aboriginal Men of High Degree* (St. Lucia: University of Queensland Press, 2nd ed. 1977 [1945]); Mircea Eliade, *Australian Religions: An Introduction* (Ithaca: Cornell University Press, 1973).

17. Rita M. Gross, "Menstruation and Childbirth as Ritual and Religious Experience among native Australians," in *Unspoken Worlds: Women's Religious Lives*, ed. Nancy A. Falk and Rita M. Gross (Belmont, Calif.: Wadsworth, 1989 [Harper & Row, 1980]): 257–266 [original longer version in *Journal of the American Academy of Religion* (Dec., 1977)]. See also Rita M. Gross, "Tribal Religions: Aboriginal Australia," in *Women in World Religions*, ed. Arvind Sharma and Katherine K. Young (Albany: State University of New York Press, 1987): 37–58; and Chris Knight, "Menstrual Synchrony and the Australian Rainbow Snake," in *Blood Magic: The Anthropology of Menstruation*, ed. Thomas Buckley and Alma Gottlieb (Berkeley: University of California Press, 1988): 232–255. Rita Gross is the first historian of religions to point to androcentrism in the comparative study of religion, her first publication appearing in 1974 and a major article in this regard in 1977: "Androcentrism and Androgyny in the Methodology of the History of Religions," in *Beyond Androcentrism: New Essays on Women and Religion*, ed. Rita M. Gross (Missoula, Mont., Scholars Press).

18. In Ronald M. Berndt, *Kunapipi: A Study of an Australian Aboriginal Religious Cult* (New York: International Universities Press, 1951): 55.

19. In Ronald M. Berndt, *Djanggawul: An Aboriginal Religious Cult of North-Eastern Arnhem Land* (London: Routledge & Kegan Paul, 1952): 41.

20. Warner, *A Black Civilization . . .* (see note no. 15): 268.

21. Catherine H. Berndt, "Interpretations and 'Facts' in Aboriginal Australia," in *Woman the Gatherer*, ed. Francis Dahlberg (New Haven: Yale University Press, 1981): 153–203.

22. Diane Bell, *Daughters of the Dreaming* (Melbourne: McPhee Gribble, 1983): 230.

23. For elaboration of the methodology, see Armin Geertz, Jeppe Sinding Jensen, and Jordan Paper, *Ethnohermeneutics* (forthcoming).

24. A corollary work from an anthropological perspective is Susan Starr Sered, *Priestess, Mother, Sacred Sister: Religions Dominated by Women* (New York: Oxford University Press, 1994). Although there is some overlap in the cultures covered in this study and Sered's, she discusses a number of other cultures not covered here. The difference in approach and focus between the two studies, although there is little in the way of major disagreements, will offer readers alternative interpretations with regard to female spirituality.

25. Cynthia Eller, *Living in the Lap of the Goddess: The Feminist Spirituality Movement in America* (Boston: Beacon Press, 1995).

Chapter 2
Saami Religion

1. The present revitalization involves an admixture of American New Age understandings as well as remnants of the indigenous traditions. The Christianization of Saami culture was relatively complete by the nineteenth century; no practicing Noides contin-

ued into the twentieth century. The renewed interest in shamanism is being influenced by workshops led by Michael Harner and his disciples, the basis being a form of shamanism distantly related to North and South American Native practices. See, for example, Michael Harner, "Helping Reawaken Shamanism Among Saami (Laplanders) of Northernmost Europe," *Newsletter, the Foundation for Shamanic Studies* 1/3 (1989); Bo Sommarström, "The Saami Shaman's Drum and the Star Horizons," in *The Saami Shaman Drum*, ed. Tore Ahlbäck and Jan Bergman (Stockholm: Almqvist & Wiksell, 1992): 136–168; legend for fig. 10b, p. 163.

2. A number of excellent articles on Saami religion will be found in two anthologies: Louise Bäckman and Åke Hultkrantz, ed., *Saami Pre-Christian Religion* (Stockholm: Almqvist & Wiksell, 1985); and Tore Ahlbäck, ed., *Saami Religion* (Stockholm: Almqvist & Wiksell, 1987). Much of the data in this study will be found in the articles of these two anthologies and in the following articles by Louise Bäckman: "Female—Divine and Human: A Study of the Position of Woman in Religion and Society in Northern Eurasia," in *The Hunters: Their Way of Life and Culture*, ed. Åke Hultkrantz and Ørnulf Vorren (Tromsø, Norway: Universitetsforlaget, 1982); "The Akkas: A Study of Four Goddesses in the Religion of the Saamis (Lapps)," in *Current Progress in the Methodology of the Science of Religions*, ed. Witold Tylock (Warsaw: Polish Scientific Publishers, 1984); and "The Master of the Animal: On Hunting Rites Among the Saami," *Proceedings of the 5th International Abashiri Symposium: Hunting Rituals of Northern Peoples* (Hokkaido: Association for Northern Cultural Promotion, 1991).

3. The drawings will be found in Ernst Manker, *Die lappische zaubertrommel* (Stockholm: Nordiska Musseet, *Acta Lapponica* I, 1938): p. 28, fig. 5 (1671); p. 35, fig. 12–14 (1689); p. 30, fig. 7, 2 drums (1673); p. 36, fig. 15 (1689); p. 37, fig. 16, (1689); see also p. 50, fig. 28 (1726–27). On two of these drums, the moon and sun are also found together.

Chapter 3
Israelite Religion and Its Precursors

1. Sources for this chapter include the following: Jerrold S. Cooper, "Sacred Marriage and Popular Cult in Early Mesopotamia," in *Official Cult and Popular Religion in the Ancient Near East: Papers of the First Colloquium on the Ancient Near East—The City and Its Life Held at the Middle Eastern Culture Center in Japan, March 20–22, 1992*, ed. E. Matushima, 1993: 81–96; Peggy L. Day, "Anat: Ugarit's 'Mistress of the Animals,'" *Journal of Near Eastern Studies* 51 (1992): 181–190; William G. Dever, "Asherah, Consort of Yahweh? New Evidence from Kuntillet 'Ajrud,'" *Bulletin of the American Schools of Oriental Research* 255 (1984): 21–37; Israel Finkelstein, *The Archaeology of the Israelite Settlement* (Jerusalem: Israel Exploration Society, 1988); Eugene J. Fisher, "Cultic Prostitution in the Ancient Near East? A Reassessment," *Biblical Theology Bulletin* 6 (1976): 225–236; Douglas Frayne, "Notes on the Sacred Marriage Rite," *Bibliotheca Orientalis* 42 (1985): 5–22; Tikva Frymer-Kensky, *In the Wake of the Goddesses:*

Women, Culture, and the Biblical Transformation of Pagan Myth (New York: Free Press, 1992); Rivkah Harris, *Ancient Sippar: A Demographic Study of an Old-Babylonian City (1894-1595 B.C.)* (Istanbul: Historisch-Archeologisch Institut, 1975); Richard A. Henshaw, *Female and Male, The Cultic Personnel: The Bible and the Rest of the Ancient Near East* (Allison Park, Pa.: Pickwick, 1994); Thorkild Jacobson, *The Treasures of Darkness: A History of Mesopotamian Religion* (New Haven: Yale University Press, 1976); Saul Olyan, *Asherah and the Cult of Yahweh in Israel* (Atlanta: Scholars Press, 1988); Raphael Patai, *The Hebrew Goddess* (Detroit: Wayne State University, 3rd ed., 1990); Susan Pollock, "Women in Men's World: Images of Sumerian Women," in *Engendering Archaeology: Women and Prehistory*, ed. Joan M. Gero and Margaret W. Conkey (Oxford: Blackwell, 1994); Mary K. Wakeman, "Ancient Sumer and the Woman's Movement: The Process of Reaching Behind, Encompassing and Going Beyond," *Journal of Feminist Studies in Religion* 1 (1985): 7–27; Diane Wolkstein and Samuel N. Kramer, *Inanna, Queen of Heaven and Earth: Her Stories and Hymns from Sumer* (New York: Harper Colophon, 1983).

2. Susan Ackerman, "'And the Women Knead Dough': The Worship of the Queen of Heaven in Sixth-Century Judah," in *Gender and Difference in Ancient Israel*, ed. Peggy L. Day (Minneapolis: Fortress Press, 1989): 109–124.

Chapter 4
Traditional China

1. For an expansion of the aspects of Chinese religion dealt with in this chapter, see Jordan Paper, *The Spirits are Drunk: Comparative Approaches to Chinese Religion* (Albany: State University of New York Press, 1995). Unless otherwise noted, all translations from the Chinese are by the author. A different perspective and some alternate interpretations for the same material will be found in Daniel L. Overmeyer, "Women in Chinese Religions: Submission, Struggle, Transcendence," in *From Benares to Beijing: Essays on Buddhism and Chinese Religion in Honour of Prof. Jan Yün-hua*, ed. Koichi Shinohara and Gregory Schopen (Oakville, Ontario: Mosaic Press, 1991): 91–120.

2. For more on Xiwangmu, see Michael Loewe, *Ways to Paradise: The Chinese Quest for Immortality* (London: George Allen & Unwin, 1979): Chap. 4; Suzanne Cahill, "Beside the Turquoise Pond: The Shrine of the Queen Mother of the West in Medieval Chinese Poetry and Religious Practice," *Journal of Chinese Religions* 12 (1984): 19–31; and "Performers and Female Taoist Adepts: Hsi Wang Mu as the Patron Deity of Women in Medieval China," *Journal of the American Oriental Society* 106 (1986): 155–168.

3. First 2/3rds of poem. Translation modified from Arthur Waley, *One Hundred and Seventy Chinese Poems* (London: Constable & Co., 1918): 65.

4. For her life and writings, see Nancy Lee Swann, *Pan Chao: Foremost Woman Scholar of China* (New York: American Historical Association, 1932). The quotation is from p. 84.

5. See Albert O'Hara, *The Position of Women in Early China, According to the Lieh Nü Chuan, "The Biographies of Chinese Women"* (Hong Kong: Orient Publishing, 1955).

6. See Kristofer Schipper, *The Taoist Body*, trans. Karen Duval (Berkeley: University of California Press, 1993): 58, 64, 150–51.

7. Huang Liu-hung, *Fu-hui ch'üan-shu, A Complete Book Concerning Happiness and Benevolence*, trans. Djang Chu (Tucson: University of Arizona Press, 1984): 609.

8. For translation, see CAO Xueqin, *The Story of the Stone*, 4 vols., trans. David Hawkes (Harmondsworth: Penguin Books, 1973–82).

9. For translation, see SHEN Fu, *Six Records of a Floating Life*, trans. Leonard Pratt and Chiang Su-hui (Harmondsworth, England: Penguin Books, 1983).

10. This material is summarized from Lee Rainey, "The Secret Writing of Chinese Women: Religious Practice and Beliefs," in *The Annual Review of Women in World Religions* IV, ed. Arvind Sharma and Katherine K. Young (Albany: State University of New York Press, 1996): 164–177. The interpretations, of course, are my own.

Chapter 5
Contemporary China

1. Wang Xiaoli contributed the material on childbirth practices in northern China, and Yang Lihui contributed the material on pilgrimages in central and western China. These studies are based on recent fieldwork.

2. Many of the topics covered in this chapter are discussed in detail, with complete references, in Jordan Paper, *The Spirits are Drunk: Comparative Approaches in the Chinese Religion* (Albany: State University of New York Press, 1995). For excellent, relevant studies of modern Chinese religion, see Emily Ahern, *The Cult of the Dead in a Chinese Village* (Stanford: Stanford University Press, 1973); and David K. Jordan, *Gods, Ghosts, and Ancestors: The Folk Religion of a Taiwanese Village* (Berkeley: University of California Press, 1972). We are indebted to Song Zhaolin of the National Historical Museum (Beijing) for his encouragement, for sharing his collection of folk-art prints of Chinese deities, and for his publications on Chinese fertility deities and rituals.

3. Jordan Paper and Li Chuang Paper, "Matrifocal Rituals in Patrilineal Chinese Religion: The Variability of Patriarchality," *International Journal of Comparative Religion and Philosophy* 1/2 (1995): 27–39.

4. For material in this subsection, we are indebted to Robert L. Chard, "Folktales on the God of the Stove," paper presented to the International Conference on Chinese Religion, Taibei: 1989.

5. For further discussion of material in this section, see Steven P. Sangren, "Female Gender in Chinese Religious Symbols: Kuan Yin, Ma Tsu, and the 'Eternal Mother,'" *Signs* 9 (1983): 4–25. For a slightly different interpretation with regard to the patriarchalization of Chinese female deities, see the synopsis by Lee Irwin, "Divinity and Salvation: The Great Goddesses of China," *Asian Folklore Studies* 49 (1990): 53–68.

6. A complete analysis of these myths will be found in Glen Dudbridge, *The Legend of Miao-shan* (London: Ithaca Press, 1978).

7. Anthony C. Yu, trans., *The Journey to the West*, 4 vols. (Chicago: University of Chicago Press, 1973–83).

8. Miriam Levering, "Women, the State and Religion Today in The People's Republic of China," in *Today's Woman in World Religions*, ed. Arvind Sharma and Katherine K. Young (Albany: State University of New York Press, 1994): 171–224/220.

9. For a fuller account of these myths, see James L. Watson, "Standardizing the Gods: the Promotion of T'ien Hou ('Empress of Heaven') Along the South China Coast, 960-1960," in *Popular Culture in Late Imperial China*, ed. David Johnson, Andrew J. Nathan, and Evelyn S. Rawski (Berkeley: University of California Press, 1985); and Judith Magee Boltz, "In Homage to T'ien-fei," *Journal of the American Oriental Society* 106 (1986): 211–32.

10. Lai Shu-fen, "Waiguo youren fang Qingcheng," *Lu-you Tian-fu* 2 (27 March 1985): 15–16, translated by Levering (see two notes previous): 208. For more information on the specifics of female alchemy, see Fabizio Pregadio, Review of *Immortelles de la Chine ancienne. Taoism et alchimie féminine* by Catherine Despeux, in *Taoist Resources* 3/1 (1991): 85–93; and Levering (2 notes previous): 210–211.

11. See Daniel L. Overmeyer, "Alternatives: Popular Religious Sects in Chinese Society," *Modern China* 7 (1981): 169–184; Susan Naquin, *Millenarian Rebellion in China: The Eight Trigrams Uprising of 1813* (New Haven: Yale University Press, 1976); David K. Jordan and Daniel L. Overmeyer, *The Flying Phoenix: Aspects of Chinese Sectarianism in Taiwan* (Princeton: Princeton University Press, 1986).

12. For a superb analysis of this issue, see Emily Ahern, "The Power and Pollution of Chinese Women," in *Women in Chinese Society*, ed. Margery Wolf and Roxanne Witke (Stanford: Stanford University Press, 1975).

13. Terry Wu's paper to date is unpublished. For a survey and analysis of the Indian texts, see Liz Wilson, *Charming Cadavers: Horrific Figurations of the Feminine in Indian Buddhist Hagiographic Literature* (Chicago: University of Chicago Press, 1996).

14. Anna Grimshaw, *Servants of the Buddha: Winter in a Himalayan Convent* (Cleveland: The Pilgrim Press, 1994): 47.

15. For translation, see SHEN Fu, *Six Records From a Floating Life*, Leonard Pratt and Chiang Su-hui, trans. (Harmondsworth: Penguin Books, 1983).

16. For examples, see the novel, *Hunglou meng* ("Dream of the Red Chamber," also to be found translated under the earlier title, "Story of a Stone").

Chapter 6
Effects of Chinese Religion on Neighboring Traditions

1. Selected relevant studies of female spirituality in Japan would include the following: Carmen Blacker, *The Catalpa Bow* (London: George Allen and Unwin, 1975); Rita Nakashima Brock, "On Mirrors, Mists, and Murmurs," in *Weaving the Visions: New*

Patterns in Feminist Spirituality, ed. Judith Plaskow and Carol P. Christ (New York: Harper and Row, 1989); Kyoko Nakamura, "No Women's Liberation: The Heritage of a Woman Prophet in Modern Japan," in *Unspoken Worlds: Women's Religious Lives in Non-Western Cultures*, ed. Nancy A. Falk and Rita M. Gross (San Francisco: Harper and Row, 1980), and "Revelatory Experience in the Female Life Cycle: A Bibliographical Study of Women Religionists in Modern Japan," *Japanese Journal of Religious Studies* 8 (1981): 187–205; Haruko Okane, *Die Stellung der Frau im Shinto* (Wiesbaden: Otto Harrassowitz, 1976); and Robert J. Smith and Ella Lury Wisell, *The Women of Suye Mura* (Chicago: University of Chicago Press, 1982).

2. Sources for this section include the following: Chong-Hong Park, "Historical Review of Korean Confucianism," in *Korean and Asian Religious Tradition*, ed. Chai-Shin Yu (Toronto: Korean and Related Studies Press, 1977): 173–188; Chu-Kuen Chang, "Korean Folk Belief: Shamanism and Shaman-song in Cheju Island," in Yu (see preceding): 136–150, also "An Introduction to Korean Shamanism, in *Shamanism: The Spirit World of Korea*, ed. Richard Guisso and Chai-shin Yu (Berkeley: Asian Humanities Press, 1988): 30–51 (the quotation is from p. 40); T'ae-gon Kim, "Regional Characteristics of Korean Shamanism," in Guisso and Yu (see preceding): 119–130; Jung Young Lee, *Korean Shamanistic Rituals* (The Hague: Mouton Publishers, 1981), also "The Communal Rituals of Korean Shamanism," *Journal of Asian and African Studies* 9 (1974), and "Concerning the Origin and Formation of Korean Shamanism," *Numen* 20 (1973): 135–59; and most importantly, Laurel Kendall, *Shamans, Housewives and Other Restless Spirits* (Honolulu: University of Hawaii Press, 1985) [the quotation is from pp. 164–66].

Chapter 7
Introduction: Four Vignettes

1. Christopher Columbus, *The Journal of Christopher Columbus*, trans. Cecil Jane (New York: Bonanza Books, 1989): 48, 54–55.

2. Material on the Tainos is from Irving Rouse, *The Tainos: Rise & Decline of the People Who Greeted Columbus* (New Haven: Yale University Press, 1992).

3. The Bulgarian, Sardinian and Siberian figures are illustrated in Marija Gimbutas, *The Language of the Goddess* (San Francisco: Harper & Row, 1989); see also her *The Goddesses and Gods of Old Europe, 6500–3500 BC: Myths and Cult Images* (Berkeley: University of California Press, 1982 [1974]: 152–63.

4. See Betty J. Meggers, *Ecuador* (New York: Frederick A. Praeger, 1966) for Valdivia material, and André Emmerick, *Sweat of the Sun and Tears of the Moon* (Seattle: University of Washington Press, 1965) for Incan material.

5. Father Bernabe Cobo, *Inca Religion and Customs*, trans. Roland Hamilton (Austin: University of Texas Press, 1990 [1653]); Irene Silverblatt, *Moon, Sun, and Witches: Gender Ideologies and Class in Inca and Colonial Peru* (Princeton: Princeton University Press, 1987).

6. From Pedro Sancho, *An Account of the Conquest of Peru* (1534), trans. P. A. Means, as cited in Sabine MacCormack, *Religion in the Andes: Vision and Imagination in Early Colonial Peru* (Princeton: Princeton University Press, 1991): 78. See also Juan Ruiz de Arce, *Relació de los servicios en Indias* (after 1542), as cited in MacCormack: 65.

7. Waldemar Bogoras, "Ideas of Space and Time in the Conceptions of Primitive Religion," *American Anthropologist* N.S. 27 (1925): 205–266/208.

8. Daniel Merkur, *Powers Which We Do Not Know: The Gods and Spirits of the Inuit* (Moscow, Idaho: University of Idaho Press, 1991). All of the data in this segment of the chapter derives from Merkur's masterful synthesis and analysis of Inuit ethnography, to which the reader is highly recommended. Since he and I discussed those issues dealt with in this segment as Merkur was writing his book, it is at times hard to separate our individual viewpoints from the conclusions that followed from his work. I take responsibility, however, for those at variance with Merkur's.

9. Irving Goldman, *The Cubeo: Indians of the Northwest Amazon* (Urbana: University of Illinois Press, 2nd. ed., 1979); Yolanda Murphy and Robert F. Murphy, *Women of the Forest* (New York: Columbia University Press, 2nd ed., 1985); Gerardo Reichel-Dolmatoff, *Amazonian Cosmos: The Sexual and Religious Symbolism of the Tukano Indians* (Chicago: University of Chicago Press, 1971); Michael F. Brown, *Tsewa's Gift: Magic and Meaning in Amazonian Society* (Washington, D.C.: Smithsonian Institution Press, 1985).

10. Sources for this segment are Irene Silverblatt, *Moon, Sun and Witches: Gender Ideologies and Class in Inca and Colonial Peru* (Princeton: Princeton University Press, 1987); Garcilaso de la Vega, *The Incas*, trans. Maria Jolas, ed. Alain Gheerbrant (New York: Orion Press, 1961 [1609]); Father Bernabe Cobo, *Inca Religion and Customs*, trans. Roland Hamilton (Austin: University of Texas Press, 1990 [1653]).

Chapter 8
Anishnabe Religion

1. For a general introduction to some of these rituals, see Jordan Paper, *Offering Smoke: The Sacred Pipe and Native American Religion* (Moscow, Idaho: University of Idaho Press, 1988); and "'Sweat Lodge': A Northern Native American Ritual for Communal Shamanic Trance," *Temenos* 26 (1990): 85–94.

2. Native American cultigens introduced to the rest of the world by Europeans also include most beans, hot peppers, tomatoes, chocolate, many types of squash, including pumpkins, and cotton.

3. See Jordan Paper, "'Sweat Lodge' . . . "; Joseph Bruchac, *The Native American Sweatlodge: History and Legends* (Freedom, Calif.: Crossing Press, 1993); Åke Hultkrantz, "Spirit Lodge, A North American Shamanic Séance," in *Studies in Shamanism*, ed. Carl Martin Edsman (Stockholm: Wiksell & Almqvist, 1967): 32–68; A. Irving Hallowell, "Bear Ceremonialism in the Northern Hemisphere," *American Anthropologist* N.S. 28 (1926): 1–175; and Jordan Paper, *Offering Smoke* . . . .

4. Material for this section comes from letters from and conversations with R. Clark Mallam, my own experience, and a two-volume report of archaeological investigations, edited by David G. Stanley, completed in March, 1993. In order to protect the described sites from unnecessary visitation and potential consequent damage, I prefer not to locate them precisely. For this reason, I cannot give the bibliographic details of the unpublished archaeological report, as this would give away the location. Special thanks to Lori A. Stanley of the archaeological team for making this report available to me and for her kind encouragement.

5. The sources for this section are Joan M. Vastokas and Romas K. Vastokas, *Sacred Art of the Algonkians: A Study of the Peterborough Petroglyphs* (Peterborough, Ontario: Mansard Press, 1973) and my own visits to the site.

6. The major sources for the following data are the experiences and understanding of Jacqui Lavalley who was brought up traditionally (e.g., menarche ritual) in central Ontario—she is a Midé initiate, teaches traditional culture at the First Nations School under the Toronto School Board, and leads Moon Ceremonies and other rituals; Marilyn Johnson, who is of mixed parentage and was brought up by her Anishnabe mother and grandmother, trained as a traditional healer (shaman) by a well-known shaman from northern Ontario, continues to function as a seer and healer, holds an M.A. in psychology and religion from York University, and is currently with the Ontario Ministry of Health; and my own sixteen years of participation in traditional Anishnabe rituals. Marilyn Johnson's words were recorded by my then graduate assistant, Cory Silverstein, in her unpublished paper, "Cycles of Power: An Ojibwa Shamaness' View of Menstrual Taboo" (1993). The primary literary sources are Ron Geyshick, *Te Bwe Win (Truth)* (Toronto: Summerhill Press, 1989)—the author is from an Anishnabe reserve where people still speak Ojibwe, on the Minnesota-Ontario border that can be accessed only by canoe or float/ski plane; and Sister M. Inez Hilger, *Chippewa Child Life and Its Cultural Background* (Washington, D.C.: Bureau of American Ethnology Bulletin 146, 1951), which is an account of field work from 1932–1940 on nine Ojibwe reservations in Minnesota, Wisconsin, and Michigan, with ninety-six male and female informants.

Reference is also made to the following texts: Maude Kegg, *Portage Lake: Memories of an Ojibwe Childhood*, ed. John D. Nichols (Edmonton: University of Alberta Press, 1991)—the author was born at the beginning of twentieth century; Ignatia Broker, *Night Flying Woman: An Ojibway Narrative* (St. Paul: Minnesota Historical Society Press, 1983)—the story of the author's great-great-grandmother; Diamond Jenness, *The Ojibwa Indians of Parry Island, Their Social and Religious Life* (Ottawa: National Museum of Canada Bulletin 78, 1935)—analysis of seven weeks' field work on Parry Island (Wasausink) in 1929; Francis Densmore, *Chippewa Customs* (Washington, D.C.: Bureau of American Ethnology Bulletin 86, 1929)—a report on 1917 field work at the White Earth Reservation in Minnesota; Ruth Landes, *The Ojibwa Woman* (New York: Columbia University Press, 1938)—a highly androcentric and Eurocentric analysis by a female anthropologist based on stories told her by an Ojibwa-Cree woman of the Manitou Reserve in Western Ontario in the early 1930s; and Ruth Landes, *Ojibwa Religion and the Midewiwin* (Madison: University of Wisconsin Press, 1968)—based on field work in the early 1930s with a man of the Cass Lake Reservation in Minnesota and the previously mentioned Ojibwa-Cree woman.

7. The term is used by A. Irving Hallowell in his "Ojibwa Ontology, Behavior, and World View," in *Culture in History*, ed. Stanley Diamond (New York: Columbia University Press, 1960).

8. For a discussion of the omnipresent "Great Spirit" concept, see Jordan Paper, "The Post-Contact Origin of an Amerindian High God: The Suppression of Feminine Spirituality," *American Indian Quarterly* 7/4 (1983): 1–24.

9. The age of the androcentric appellation of spirits is difficult to determine; certainly it was in place by the early twentieth century. Hallowell, basing his views on his field experience of the 1930s writes: "Collectively, persons of the other than human class are spoken of as 'our grandfathers' because the major figures are *all* of the male sex" (A. Irving Hallowell, *The Ojibwa of Berens River, Manitoba: Ehnography into History*, ed. Jennifer S. H. Brown [Fort Worth: Harcourt Brace Jovanovich, 1992]: 65 [emphasis added]). In the same compilation of Hallowell's articles and notes, one can find the typical assumption that puberty vision quests were a male activity, and that female dreams "had only personal significance" (88). Hallowell has contributed much to our understanding of early twentieth-century Anishnabe culture and religion and can hardly be blamed for being imbued with the extreme androcentrism of his culture.

10. Quotations are from Norval Morrisseau, *Legends of My People the Great Ojibway*, ed. Selwyn Dewdney (Toronto: Ryerson Press, 1965): 28; and Basil Johnston, *Ojibway Heritage: The Ceremonies, Rituals, Songs, Dances, Prayers and Legends of the Ojibway* (Toronto: McLelland and Stewart, 1976): 15.

11. Sources for this brief study include Hitakonanu'laxk, *The Grandfathers Speak: Native American Folk Tales of the Lenapé People* (New York: Interlink Books, 1994); and Herbert C. Kraft, ed., *A Delaware Indian Symposium* (Harrisburg: Pennsylvania Historical and Museum Commission Anthropological Series Number 4, 1974).

12. Eleanor Leacock, "The Montagnais 'Hunting Territory' and the Fur Trade," *American Anthropological Society*, Memoir 78 (1954) (Menasha, Wisconsin).

13. See Eleanor Leacock, "Women's Status in Egalitarian Societies: Implications for Social Evolution," *Current Anthropology* 19 (1978): 241–255; and Karen Anderson, *Chain Her by One Foot: the Subjugation of Native Women in Seventeenth-Century New France* (New York: Routledge, 1991).

14. For the early history, see John C. Ewers, *The Horse in Blackfoot Indian Culture* (Washington, D.C.: Bureau of American Ethnology Bulletin 159, 1955). The following analysis is based, in order of importance, on the following publications: Beverly Hungry Wolf, *The Ways of My Grandmothers* (New York: William Morrow, 1980); Walter McClintock, *The Old North Trail or Life, Legends and Religion of the Blackfoot Indians* (London: Macmillan, 1910)—McClintock was adopted by a Blackfoot elder and initiated into rituals during the last quarter of the nineteenth century for the express purpose of enlightening Euroamericans about Blackfoot religion; Ben Calf Robe, *Siksika': A Blackfoot Legacy* (Invermere, B.C.: Good Medicine Books, 1979); George Bird Grinnell, *Blackfoot Lodge Tales: The Story of a Prairie People* (New York: C. Scribner's Sons, 1892); the monographs of Clark Wissler, based on the formal ethnology of the early twentieth century, were not relied upon. Of importance is an 1897 manuscript by Robert Nathaniel Wilson, who spent most of his life on the Peigan and Blood Reserves,

"Ethnographical Notes on the Blackfoot 'Sun-dance'"; and tapes recorded in 1969 and 1974 by George First Rider of the Blood Reserve, who was born in 1904—both sources in the archives of the Glenbow-Alberta Museum.

15. The Anishnabe cultures do have sacred bundles, and they are of considerable importance among the Menomini, Sauk, and Mesquakie. However, they tend not to be as large as many of the Nitsitapi bundles nor to have as complex a ritual. This may be due to the ability of the horse travois to carry larger loads than people comfortably can when portaging canoes.

16. In the 1970s, Siksika elders allowed a film, "Okan," to be made to record the ritual, except for the esoteric parts; this film is in the keeping of the Glenbow-Alberta Museum and not for public distribution.

17. See E. Adamson Hoebel, *The Cheyennes: Indians of the Great Plains* (New York: Holt, Rinehart and Winston, 1960); George Bird Grinnell, *The Cheyenne Indians: Their History and Life Ways* (New Haven: Yale University Press, 1923); and Peter J. Powell, *Sweet Medicine: The Continuing Role of the Sacred Arrows, the Sun Dance, and the Sacred Buffalo Hat in Northern Cheyenne History* (Norman: University of Oklahoma Press, 1969). The fullest account (245 pages, including photographs) of the Oxheheom is in Powell, which unfortunately, being written by an "Anglo-Catholic" priest, plays down the role of the Sacred Woman. For contrary views, see Karl H. Schleiser, *The Wolves of Heaven: Cheyenne Shamanism, Ceremonies, and Prehistoric Origins* (Norman: University of Oklahoma Press, 1987).

Chapter 9
Hopi Religion

1. The author gratefully acknowledges the assistance of Alice Schlegel in the preparation of this chapter. Alice Schlegel, a professor of anthropology at the University of Arizona, has maintained contacts among the Hopi for over twenty years and has written extensively on gender aspects of Hopi society and religion as well as comparative studies of adolescence.

The sources for the data on sex/gender aspects of Hopi culture and religion are primarily the works of Alice Schlegel; the interpretations are predominantly due to her insights; and quotations not otherwise noted are from her writings: "The Adolescent Socialization of the Hopi Girl," *Ethnology* 12 (1973): 440–462; "Hopi Joking and Castration Threats," *Linguistics and Anthropology: In Honor of C.F. Voegelin*, ed. M. D. Kinkade, H. Hale, & O. Werner (Lisse, Netherlands: Peter de Ridder Press, 1975): 521–529; "Male and Female in Hopi Thought and Action," in *Sexual Stratification: A Cross-Cultural View*, ed. A. Schlegel (New York: Columbia University Press, 1977): 245–269; "Sexual Antagonism Among the Sexually Egalitarian Hopi," *Ethos* 7 (1979): 124–141; "Hopi Gender Ideology of Female Superiority," *Quarterly Journal of Ideology* 8/4 (1984): 44–52; "Fathers, Daughters, and Kachina Dolls," *European Review of Native American Studies* 3/1 (1989): 7–10; "Gender Meanings: General and Specific," in

Beyond the Second Sex: New Directions in the Anthropology of Gender, ed. P. R. Sanday & R. G. Goodenough (Philadelphia: University of Philadelphia Press, 1990): 23–41; and "The Two Aspects of Hopi Grandmotherhood" (manuscript).

The data for most other aspects of Hopi religion are from the writings of Armin Geertz, as well as extensive personal conversations with him, for which the author is most grateful. Of Geertz's many publications, the most relevant to this chapter are the following: "A Reed Pierced the Sky: Hopi Indian Cosmography on Third Mesa, Arizona," *Numen* 31 (1984): 216–241; *Hopi Indian Altar Iconography* (Leiden: E. J. Brill, 1987); with Michael Lomatuway'ma, *Children of Cottonwood: Piety and Ceremonialism in Hopi Indian Puppetry* (Lincoln: University of Nebraska Press, 1987) (*it is to be noted that the orthography for Hopi words are from this work*); "Hopi Hermeneutics: Ritual Person Among the Hopi Indians of Arizona," in *Concepts of Person in Religion and Thought* (Berlin: de Gruyter, 1990): 309–335; and "Structural Elements in Uto-Aztecan Mythology: The Hopi Example" (manuscript).

The material on ritual is in large part from Mischa Titiev, *Old Oraibi: A Study of the Hopi Indians of Third Mesa* (Cambridge: Peabody Museum, 1944). For Maasaw, Ekkehart Malotki and Michael Lomatuway'ma, *Maasaw: Profile of a Hopi God* (Lincoln: University of Nebraska Press, 1987) is important, as is Hamilton A. Tylor, *Pueblo Gods and Myths* (Norman: University of Oklahoma Press, 1964) for deities in general. Also referred to for this chapter are Leo W. Simmons, ed., *Sun Chief: The Autobiography of a Hopi Indian* (New Haven: Yale University Press, 1942) for a male perspective; and Tracy Pintchman, "Speculative Patterns in Hopi Cosmology," *Studies in Religion* 22 (1993): 351–364. The data on Papago religion is from Ruth M. Underhill, *Papago Woman* (New York: Holt, Rinehart and Winston, 1979). The analysis of Zuni culture is from John W. M. Whiting et al., "The Learning of Values," in *People of Rimrock: A Study of Values in Five Cultures*, ed. Evon Vogt and Ethel M. Albert (Cambridge: Harvard University Press, 1967): 83–125/107.

2. For the last two factors in particular, see Armin Geertz, *The Invention of Prophecy: Continuity and Meaning in Hopi Indian Religion* (Berkeley: University of California Press, 1994).

3. This understanding is far from general. Armin Geertz (personal communication) notes the following in this regard: "I am not convinced that Kookyangso'wuuti is a trickster. The myth that you summarize seems to be a deliberate smudge against the Spider Clan. Others also claim that Spider Woman was the first witch. She is by far a protective deity usually associated with her War Twins grandchildren."

Chapter 10
Diné Menarche Rituals

1. For a speculative analysis of this chronology, see Jordan Paper, "A Material Case for a Late Bering Straight Crossing Coincident with Potential Trans-Pacific Crossings," *Sino-Platonic Papers* 39 (1993): 1–17.

2. June Helm, *Prophecy and Power Among the Dogrib Indians* (Lincoln: University of Nebraska Press, 1994): 83.

3. For further background, see Guy H. Cooper, *Development and Stress in Navajo Religion* (Stockholm: Stockholm Studies in Comparative Religion 23, 1984); A. McFadyen Clark, "The Athapaskans: Strangers of the North," in *The Athapaskans: Strangers of the North* (Ottawa: National Museum of Man, 1974): 17–42; John W. Ives, *A Theory of Northern Athapaskan Prehistory* (Calgary: University of Calgary Press, 1990); Catharine McClellan, *Part of the Land, Part of the Water* (Vancouver: Douglas & McIntyre, 1987); Robin Riddington, "Stories of the Vision Quest Among Dunne-za Women," *Atlantis* 9/1 (Fall, 1983): 68–78.

4. Paul G. Zolbrod, *Diné Bahanè: The Navajo Creation Story* (Albuquerque, University of New Mexico Press, 1984): 273. The story summarized here will be found in full detail in this volume. Following quotations are from pages 275 and 55.

5. Leland C. Wyman, *Blessingway* (Tucson: University of Arizona Press, 1987): 32.

6. Morris Edward Opler, *Myths and Tales of the Jicarilla Apache Indians* (New York: American Folk-Lore Society, 1938): 26.

7. Inés Talamantez, "The Presence of Isanaklesh," in *Unspoken Worlds: Women's Religious Lives*, ed. Nancy Auer Falk and Rita M. Gross (Belmont, Calif.: Wadsworth, 1989): 246–56. For a list of the rituals preceding the menarche ceremony, see her "Images of the Feminine in Apache Religious Tradition," in *After Patriarchy: Feminist Transformations of the World Religions*, ed. P. M. Cooey, W. R. Eakin and J. B. McDaniel (Maryknoll, N.Y.: Orbis Books, 1991): 131–45.

8. Morris Edward Opler, *An Apache Life-Way: The Economic, Social, and Religious Institutions of the Chiricahua Indians* (New York: Cooper Square, 1965 [1941]) [unless otherwise noted, the quotations are from this work]: 82–134; Charlotte Johnson Frisbie, *Kinaaldá: A Study of the Navajo Girl's Puberty Ceremony* (Middletown, Conn.: Wesleyan University Press, 1967). All of the descriptive material is taken solely and entirely from these works, but references only to major quotations are provided to avoid repetition and tedium. However, interpretive statements are my own. For a brief, concise description of the similar Cibecue Apache menarch ritual, see Keith H. Basso, "The Gift of Changing Woman," *Bulletin of the Bureau of American Ethnology* 196 (1966—Anthopological Papers 76): 113–173.

9. The following three autobographical statements are from H. Henrietta Stockel, *Women of the Apache Nation: Voices of Truth* (Reno: University of Nevada Press, 1991): 75, 95, and 154–55.

Chapter 11
Glimpses of West Central African Religions

1. Rosalind J. Hackett, "Women in African Religions," in *Religion and Women*, ed. Arvind Sharma and Katherine K. Young (Albany: State University of New York Press, 1994): 61–92. I am indebted to Rosalind Hackett both for her many articles, which have

enormously assisted my understanding, and for her encouragement to continue with this work.

2. Most writings on sub-Saharan African religion are by Christian missionaries or Christian Africans. The former tend to work from a premise that monotheism is normative to humanity, polytheism being a perversion. The latter, adopting the Christian/Islamic valuing of a supreme deity, tend to assume that their culture, to which they relate positively, must have had a traditional understanding of a supreme deity. Other scholars, who do not work from Eurocentric values, have had their doubts. Perhaps the most thorough critique of the quasi-monotheistic assumption regarding African religious traditions is by Donatus Ibe Nwogo (from a culture neighboring to the Yoruba), *The Supreme God as Stranger in Igbo Religious Thought* (Ekreazu, Ahiazu Mbaise, Imo State, Nigeria: Hawk Press, 1984).

3. Olatunde B. Lawuyi, "The Reality and Meaning of Being a Woman in the Yoruba Cosmogonic Myths," *Ultimate Reality and Meaning* 11 (1988): 233–242/235.

4. See Jacob Kehinde Olupona, *Kingship, Religion, and Rituals in a Nigerian Community: A Phenomenological Study of Ondo Yoruba Festivals*, Stockholm Studies in Comparative Religion 28 (Stockholm: Almqvist & Wiksell, 1991): 23–43. Unless otherwise noted, all of this and the following material to the sub-section "Our Mothers" is based on and quotations are from this book.

5. Judith Gleason, *Oya: In Praise of the Goddess* (Boston: Shambhala, 1987): 3–4. All of the material on Oya is from Gleason's book.

6. This sub-section is based on Margaret Thompson Drewal, *Yoruba Ritual: Performers, Play, Agency* (Bloomington: Indiana University Press, 1992): particularly 177–78.

7. As a dancer reported to H. Ulli Beier, "Gelede Masks," *Odu* 6 (1958): 5–23/5, as cited in Henry John Drewal and Margaret Thompson Drewal, *Gelede: Art and Female Power Among the Yoruba* (Bloomington: Indiana University Press, 1990 [1983]): 105. All the following material, interpretations and quotations with regard Yoruba religion, unless otherwise noted in this sub-section are based on this work or the work by Drewel in the previous note.

8. Gleason: 84–86—her translation from Pierre Verger, "Grandeur et decadence du culte de Ìyámi Ôsòròngà," *Journal de la Société des Africanistes* 35 (1965): 201–219.

9. Unless otherwise noted, all data in this section have been provided by Paul and Elizabeth Adjin-Tettey as their own work. Nevertheless, I take full responsibility for all interpretations.

10. Recorded by Evelyn King, ca. 1960, in Noel Q. King, *African Cosmos: An Introduction to Religion in Africa* (Belmont, Calif.: Wadsworth, 1986): 21. All the quotations of Madam Yaa are from this work, as is the description of a mediumistic ritual by Noel King (pp. 63–65, the book includes photographs taken during the ritual).

11. See Olof Petterson, "Foreign Influences on the Idea of God in African Religions," in *Syncretism*, ed. Sven S. Hartman, (Stockholm: Instituti Donneriani Aboensis 3, 1969): 40–65; particularly 58–60.

12. Eva L. R. Meyerowitz, *The Akan of Ghana* (London: Faber and Faber, 1958): 131–33.

13. See, for example, Roy Sieber and Roslyn Adele Walker, *African Art in the Cycle of Life* (Washington, D.C.: Smithsonian Institution Press, 1987): plate 6.

14. See Jehanne H. Teilhet, "The Equivocal Role of Women Artists in Non-Literate Cultures," *Heresies* (Winter, 1978): 96–102.

Chapter 12
Candomblé: An African Religion in the Americas

1. A recent, excellent survey is Joseph M. Murphy, *Working the Spirit: Ceremonies of the African Diaspora* (Boston: Beacon Press, 1994). Concerning these traditions individually, readers of this book are especially recommended to Karen McCarthy Brown, *Madam Lola: A Vodou Priestess in Brooklyn* (Berkeley: University of California Press, 1991).

2. By Gregorio de Mattos cited in Roger Bastide, *The African Religions of Brazil: Towards a Sociology of the Interpenetration of Civilizations*, trans. Helen Sebba (Baltimore: Johns Hopkins University Press, 1978 [1960]): 134. Bastide provides the most important scholarly history of Candomblé; a wonderful history in novel form, written from an insider's perspective, is Jorge Amado, *Tent of Miracles*, trans. Barbara Shelby (New York: Alfred A. Knopf, 1971).

3. Ruth Landes, *The City of Women* (New York: Macmillan, 1947); Jim Wafer, *The Taste of Blood: Spirit Possession in Brazilian Candomblé* (Philadelphia: University of Pennsylvania Press, 1991); Serge Bramly, *Macumba: The Teachings of Maria-José, Mother of the Gods* (New York: St. Martin's Press, 1977—references are to the Avon 1979 ed.); Jorge Amado, *Shepherds of the Night*, trans. Harriet de Onís (New York: Alfred A. Knopf, 1966).

4. Transcribed by myself from the film *Candomblé: A Religion in Brazil with African Roots* (1989).

Chapter 13
Analysis and Conclusions

1. M. Kuusi, K. Bosley, and M. Branch, *Finnish Folk Poetry—Epic* (Helsinki: Finnish Literature Society, 1977): 88.

2. I am grateful to Savithri de Tourreil, a Nāyar herself, for sharing her unpublished scholarly papers with me. A fundamental starting point for the study of gender and Hinduism would be Nancy Auer Falk, *Women and Religion in India: An Annotated Bibliography of Sources in English 1975–92* (Kalamazoo: New Issues Press, 1994). Other new relevant studies include Rita M. Gross, *Buddhism After Patriarchy: A Feminist History, Analysis, and Reconstruction of Buddhism* (Albany: State University of New York Press, 1993); and Tracy Pintchman, *The Rise of the Goddess in the Hindu Tradition* (Albany: State University of New York Press, 1994).

3. G. N. Graceva, "Shaman Songs and Worldview," in *Shamanism in Eurasia*, ed. Mihaly Hoppal (Göttingen: Edition Herodot, 1984): 193–200/199.

4. For a superb depiction of life and religion as lived today in a matrifocal culture, see Barbara Tedlock, *The Beautiful and the Dangerous: Dialogues with the Zuni Indians* (New York: Penguin Books, 1992).

5. See David E. Armstrong, *Drinking With the Dead: Alcohol and Altered States in Ancestor Veneration Ritual of Zhou Dynasty China and Iron Age Palestine* (North York, Ontario: York University M.A. Thesis, 1993).

6. For counter-evidence see my *Offering Smoke: The Sacred Pipe and Native American Religion* (Moscow, Idaho: University of Idaho Press, 1988).

7. Jordan Paper, "The Post-contact Origin of an American Indian High God: The Suppression of Feminine Spirituality," *American Indian Quarterly* 7/4 (1983): 1–24/19. For an example of the quoting of this statement, see Åke Hultkrantz, "A Decade of Progress," in *Religion in Native North America*, ed. Christopher Vecsey (Moscow, Idaho: University of Idaho Press, 1990): 181.

8. Bruce Lincoln, *Emerging From the Chrysalis: Rituals of Women's Initiation* (New York: Oxford University Press, 1991 [1981]): 105. The following quotation is from Anne Keith, "The Navajo Girl's Puberty Ceremony," *El Palacio* 71 (1964): 27–36/30, to be found in Lincoln: 113.

9. W. Bogoros, "Primitive Ideas of Space and Time," *American Anthropologist* N.S. 27 (1925): 205–266/208.

10. In the last decade, there have been several studies arguing that "monotheism" is an inappropriate word to apply to Judaism until the last few centuries. For example, Peter Hayman ("Monotheism—A Misused Word In Jewish Studies?", *Journal of Jewish Studies* 42 [1991]: 1–15) argues that Judaism cannot be understood to be monotheistic until the "Middle Ages."

11. The roots of this understanding of earth go back to Sumeria and later Mesopotamian cultures. The realm of the dead below was perceived as a dreadful place by the Sumerians, and the Akkadians, and other later cultures, saw it as full of demons.

12. See Bernadette Brooten, *Women Leaders of the Ancient Synagogue* (Chico, Calif.: Scholars Press, 1982); Karen Jo Torjesen, *When Women Were Priests: Women's Leadership in the Eartly Church & the Scandal of their Subordination in the Rise of Christianity* (San Francisco: HarperSanFrancisco, 1993); and Leila Ahmed, *Women and Gender in Islam: Historical Roots of a Modern Debate* (New Haven: Yale University Press, 1992).

13. Thelma D. Sullivan, *A Scattering of Jades: Stories, Poems, and Prayers of the Aztecs* (New York: Simon & Schuster, 1994): 142–47.

14. For further analyses of these religions, see Jordan Paper, "The Divine Principle: The Bible From a Korean Perspective," *Studies in Religion* 15 (1986): 451–60; and "The Normative East Asian Understanding of Christian Scriptures," *Studies in Religion* 18 (1989): 451–65.

15. For example, Gerda Lerner's deservedly well-received *The Creation of Patriarchy* (New York: Oxford University Press, 1986). Lerner accepts as normative Sigmund Freud's theory of the origins of culture (see p. 53) which certainly does not fit non-Western cultures, assuming it does fit Western, a highly debatable notion (see Chapter 1).

16. For a study of celibacy in early Christianity, see Peter Brown, *The Body and*

Society: Men, Women, and Sexual Renunciation in Early Christianity (New York: Columbia University Press, 1988).

17. Robert Eno, "Was There a High God *Ti* in Shang Religion?" *Early China* 15 (1990): 1–26.

18. See, for example, Carol Meyer, *Discovering Eve: Ancient Israelite Women in Context* (New York: Oxford University Press, 1988): 78–86.

INDEX

[This index includes authors mentioned in main body of the text and terms, places, etc., found in two or more chapters.]